MW01253100

PSYCHOLOGY RESEARCH PROGRESS

BEYOND THE LAB: APPLICATIONS OF COGNITIVE RESEARCH IN MEMORY AND LEARNING

PSYCHOLOGY RESEARCH PROGRESS

Additional books in this series can be found on Nova's website
under the Series tab.

Additional E-books in this series can be found on Nova's website
under the E-book tab.

PERSPECTIVES ON COGNITIVE PSYCHOLOGY

Additional books in this series can be found on Nova's website
under the Series tab.

Additional E-books in this series can be found on Nova's website
under the E-book tab.

PSYCHOLOGY RESEARCH PROGRESS

BEYOND THE LAB: APPLICATIONS OF COGNITIVE RESEARCH IN MEMORY AND LEARNING

GLENDA ANDREWS
AND
DAVID NEUMANN
EDITORS

Nova Science Publishers, Inc.
New York

GUELPH HUMBER LIBRARY
205 Humber College Blvd
Toronto, ON   M9W 5L7

Copyright © 2012 by Nova Science Publishers, Inc.

All rights reserved. No part of this book may be reproduced, stored in a retrieval system or transmitted in any form or by any means: electronic, electrostatic, magnetic, tape, mechanical photocopying, recording or otherwise without the written permission of the Publisher.

For permission to use material from this book please contact us:
Telephone 631-231-7269; Fax 631-231-8175
Web Site: http://www.novapublishers.com

NOTICE TO THE READER

The Publisher has taken reasonable care in the preparation of this book, but makes no expressed or implied warranty of any kind and assumes no responsibility for any errors or omissions. No liability is assumed for incidental or consequential damages in connection with or arising out of information contained in this book. The Publisher shall not be liable for any special, consequential, or exemplary damages resulting, in whole or in part, from the readers' use of, or reliance upon, this material. Any parts of this book based on government reports are so indicated and copyright is claimed for those parts to the extent applicable to compilations of such works.

Independent verification should be sought for any data, advice or recommendations contained in this book. In addition, no responsibility is assumed by the publisher for any injury and/or damage to persons or property arising from any methods, products, instructions, ideas or otherwise contained in this publication.

This publication is designed to provide accurate and authoritative information with regard to the subject matter covered herein. It is sold with the clear understanding that the Publisher is not engaged in rendering legal or any other professional services. If legal or any other expert assistance is required, the services of a competent person should be sought. FROM A DECLARATION OF PARTICIPANTS JOINTLY ADOPTED BY A COMMITTEE OF THE AMERICAN BAR ASSOCIATION AND A COMMITTEE OF PUBLISHERS.

Additional color graphics may be available in the e-book version of this book.

Library of Congress Cataloging-in-Publication Data

Beyond the lab : applications of cognitive research in memory and learning / editors, Glenda Andrews and David Neumann.
    p. cm.
 Includes bibliographical references and index.
  ISBN 978-1-61324-845-4 (hbk. : alk. paper) 1. Memory. 2. Learning. 3. Cognition. I. Andrews, Glenda. II. Neumann, David (David Lester)
  BF371.B46 2011
  153.1--dc23
                    2011017291

Published by Nova Science Publishers, Inc. † New York

CONTENTS

PREFACE

Psychological research in perception, learning, memory, and cognition seeks to explain how these processes work and how they influence our behaviour. The findings are potentially relevant to human behaviour in a wide range of everyday situations. However, the links between fundamental research findings and their potential applications are often discussed only in general terms. A major aim of *Beyond the Lab* was to make these links more explicit. Thinking about how research in areas such as memory and learning can be applied to everyday situations has the potential to lead to new insights that could ultimately solve many practical issues that exist in society today.

In *Beyond the Lab,* three chapters provide up-to-date literature reviews of existing research on specific topics. The remaining eight chapters report new empirical research that was conducted in settings that ranged from research laboratories to more real world settings such as schools. Laboratory-based procedures allow precise control over extraneous factors. The variables of interest can be manipulated and the effects on other variables can be observed. The main strength of such procedures is that they permit inferences regarding the cause-effect relations between the manipulated and observed variables. A weakness is that the findings from laboratory-based research might not always generalize to natural settings. If so, their relevance to everyday functioning might be questioned. Research conducted in more natural settings will have higher ecological validity, if extraneous factors are controlled. However, such control is more difficult to achieve, and it is often not possible to make causal interpretations. A complete understanding of human behaviour requires research in both types of contexts.

The authors of the chapters in this volume used various means to explicate the links between the reported research and cognitive functioning in the real world. These included (i) pointing out the parallels between their laboratory-based procedures and situations encountered in everyday settings, (ii) seeking to minimise the effect of extraneous factors when research was conducted in real world settings, (iii) examining the links between performance on laboratory-based tasks and pre-existing differences in applied skills (e.g., reading, video game playing), visual perceptual functioning (visual discomfort), or affective states (depression, anxiety), and (iv) clearly describing the implications of the findings and their potential applications in real world settings. Our reviewing process confirmed that this emphasis on applications was achieved without compromising scientific rigour.

The chapters are grouped according to four general areas of application. These are memory performance; affective functioning; perceptual functioning; and children's literacy learning.

Memory Performance

Memory is a complex phenomenon that has a pervasive influence in many areas of everyday life. Three chapters report new empirical findings about potential ways to improve human memory.

The research reported by Murphy and colleagues in Chapter 1 examined short-term memory (STM) for visual and verbal information, and the potential links with video game playing. Given the increasing use of video games by children and adults, it is important to understand their effects on cognitive processes. In Experiment 1, expert and novice players of video games were compared on tests of visual and verbal STM at two points in time. Expert video game players made fewer errors and had faster response times than the novices on a visual STM test, but not on a test of verbal STM. This pattern of findings is consistent with the greater overlap in processing demands of video games and the visual STM task than of video games and the verbal STM task. In Experiment 2, the effect of 10 hours of video game training on visual and verbal STM was examined. Novice players of videogames completed tests of visual and verbal STM before and after they received training on either an action video game (Medal of Honour) or a non-action game (Tetris). Brief training on the action video game produced improvements in STM, but these were modest in size. More extensive training might produce greater improvements. The chapter discusses the potential role of video games in improving the efficiency of cognitive processes.

Andrews and colleagues report research that extends two classic findings in memory research. The research of Andrews, Todd and their colleagues in Chapter 2 examined the effects of organisation on free recall. It showed that material that is presented in an organised way is easier to recall than comparable material that is randomly arranged. It extended earlier work by demonstrating that presenting organised material first results in improved recall of subsequently presented, randomly arranged materials. Further analyses suggested that this improvement reflected increased use of relational processing over item-specific processing. The findings have implications for improving relational processing in individuals with Asperger's syndrome who have difficulty with relational processing.

The research of Andrews, Murphy and colleagues in Chapter 3 examined the self-reference effect in two episodic memory tasks. It showed that words that are encoded in relation to the self are easier to recognise than comparable words that are encoded in relation to another well known person. It extended earlier work by demonstrating that the self-reference effect is also observed on a recency discrimination task which assesses memory for the order in which the words were presented. The findings broaden the range of memory tasks to which the self-reference advantage applies. This makes it more likely that the facilitative effects of self-referent encoding observed in laboratory-based studies will generalise to memory performance in the real world.

Affective Functioning

Chapters 4, 5 and 6 have clinical relevance to the widely experienced affective states/disorders of anxiety and depression. Fear is a central feature of several anxiety disorders. Contemporary learning theory suggests that fears can be acquired and eliminated through Pavlovian conditioning mechanisms. The principles of Pavlovian conditioning provide the basis of behavioural approaches in the treatment of many anxiety disorders. The review by Bandarian Balooch and colleagues' in Chapter 4 focuses on the effects of context changes and associated variables on a phenomenon known as renewal. Renewal is one mechanism that can bring about a return of fear following acquisition and extinction in laboratory experiments. Two other mechanisms that can produce a return of fear are reinstatement and spontaneous recovery. In Chapter 5, D. Neumann and colleagues report empirical research in which these two mechanisms were studied in the laboratory. In the research reviewed by Bandarian Balooch and his colleagues and conducted by D. Neumnann and his colleagues, the procedures and experimental manipulations are designed to be directly analogous to real world situations in which fears are first acquired, then extinguished, and (under some conditions) reignited. These parallels enhance the relevance of the findings to relapse following therapeutic interventions for the treatment of anxiety. Moreover, as reviewed by Bandarian Balooch and colleagues, procedures that can attenuate the return of fear produced by renewal, have the potential to reduce relapse following treatment for anxiety disorders.

A common feature of depression is the tendency to interpret events in ways that are biased toward the negative. The review by Dati and colleagues in Chapter 6 investigates the proposal that such biases represent a failure in emotional regulation which is due to impaired top-down control of information in working memory. The authors distinguished two types of top-down inhibitory control, namely resistance to distractor interference and resistance to proactive interference. The chapter provides a comprehensive review of behavioural research and of the electrophysiological correlates as measured by event-related potentials (ERPs) of these inhibitory control processes in depression. They conclude that interventions that strengthen top-down cognitive control should help depressed individuals to disengage from negative cognitions and enhance their attendance to positive stimuli, which in turn should result in more effective emotional regulation and a reduced vulnerability to relapse. They also outline the potential usefulness of ERP techniques in clinical assessment, diagnosis, treatment prognosis, and treatment evaluation.

Perceptual Functioning

Exposure to some types of visual stimuli is known to produce unpleasant somatic and perceptual effects in susceptible individuals. These effects are known as visual discomfort. While visual discomfort is frequently observed in sufferers of migraine headache, this is not always the case and visual discomfort is also observed in individuals who do not experience migraine. In Chapter 7, Conlon and colleagues report five empirical studies examining (i) how experiences of migraine and visual discomfort are linked to subjective reports of unpleasant responses to striped repetitive patterns and to objective performance on lab-based tasks that assess sensitivity to temporal and spatial frequency, (ii) whether the negative impact of high levels of visual discomfort on reading efficiency can be reduced by variations in text presentation, and (iii) whether the negative impact of high levels of visual discomfort is also observed on a visual search task that involves visual clutter but not repetitive striped patterns. Some answers to these questions are provided by the research. They have implications for ameliorating the effects of visual discomfort in the workplace and study contexts that require sustained visual processing.

Colour influences our language, emotions, and social relationships with others. In Chapter 8, Hine and colleagues report empirical research in which psychophysical methodology was used to understand how we perceive and name different colours. Significantly, unlike much previous research conducted in the psychophysical laboratory, Hine and colleagues used higher levels of light; levels that are normally present in the natural environment. As a result, their research has direct relevance to colour vision in everyday situations. For example, Hine and colleagues use their findings to show that the colour red was the most stable colour across observers. In contrast, blue/yellow colours were less stable. As such, a red colour is recommended for situations in which signage needs to be detected quickly and consistently across people.

Children's literacy learning

The literature review of M. Neumann and colleagues in Chapter 9 examined the potential benefits of engaging multiple senses in children's literacy learning. They argued that while many lab-based tasks used in literacy research operate through a single sensory modality, acquisition of literacy skills in real word settings frequently involves multisensory learning. They describe how such techniques might be used by parents and teachers to scaffold children's early literacy learning (e.g., learning the names of alphabetic letter and their associated sounds). The authors note the paucity of well-controlled empirical research investigating the effectiveness of multisensory techniques and outline some criteria for methodologically sound research in this area.

In Chapter 10, Hood and colleagues examined literacy skills in preschool aged children and the cognitive and perceptual correlates that potentially contribute to their acquisition. The empirical research reported by Hood and colleagues examined the roles of auditory temporal processing and visual temporal processing in two emergent literacy skills, letter-word identification and phonological awareness, in 129 pre-school aged Australian children (mean age 5.36 years). Very little existing research has addressed this important issue. Temporal processing in auditory and visual modalities appears to be more strongly related to letter-word identification than to phonological processing. The contributions of visual and auditory temporal processing to letter-word knowledge were not attributable to age, nonverbal ability, attention, or memory. These findings, combined with the importance of letter-word identification in reading, raise that possibility that tests of visual and auditory temporal processing might be useful adjuncts to phonological processing in the early identification of children who are at risk of developing reading difficulties later on.

Chapter 11 is concerned with remediation of the reading difficulties encountered by some children during the primary school years. Wright and Conlon noted that despite the extensive research identifying the variables associated with effective reading interventions for children with word-level reading disability, it is not clear how effectively this research is being translated and employed at the school level. To address this issue, they examined the effectiveness of learning support services in eight Australian primary schools. Changes in word identification, phonological decoding, prose reading accuracy, and reading sub-skills were measured over one school year. Children with word-level reading disability at the outset made significant improvements in phonological awareness, but not in word identification, phonological decoding, prose reading accuracy, and pseudohomophone recognition. Following the intervention, just 4% of the children performed within the normal range for their age (standard score of ≥ 92) on word-level reading tests and 11% did so on the prose reading tests. These findings were contrasted with other findings from the literature, and with an earlier study that involved a more structured and intensive reading intervention program. The authors concluded that school-based interventions will be more effective if they incorporate an explicit, systematic phonics program with direct instruction. Providing teachers and para-professionals with explicit scripts to follow would be one way of ensuring that research findings are faithfully translated into practice.

Acknowledgements

We would like to thank the authors for their contributions to *Beyond the Lab* and for adhering to the timelines for initial submission and subsequent revision of their chapters. We also thank Mandy Mihelic for her work as editorial assistant and the Behavioural Basis of Health Research Program for financial support.

In closing, we acknowledge the contributions made by the reviewers in ensuring the high scientific quality of the work reported in *Beyond the Lab*. Reviewers were invited to conduct a rigorous peer-review of a chapter with the understanding that their contribution would be acknowledged or could remain anonymous. The reviewers who chose to have their role acknowledged are listed below in alphabetical order. Reviewers indicated by an asterisk were not authors of any chapters in *Beyond the Lab*. An additional 4 reviewers (3 who were not authors) chose to remain anonymous.

Glenda Andrews
*Damian Birney
Mark Boschen
*Michael D. Carey
*Raymond Chan
*Eugene Chekaluk
Tim Cutmore
*Matthew J. Gullo
Michelle Hood
*Nicole C. Huff
*Molly de Lemos
*Helena Purkis
*Anna Ma-Wyatt
Karen Murphy
David L. Neumann
*John O'Gorman
David Shum
Craig Wright

Glenda Andrews & David L. Neumann
Editors

Chapter 1

DOES VIDEO GAME PLAYING IMPACT ON SHORT-TERM MEMORY TASK PERFORMANCE?

Karen Murphy [1,2]*, Glenda Andrews [1,2] and Kirsty Williams [2]
[1] Applied Cognitive Neuroscience Research Unit,
Behavioural Basis of Health
Griffith Health Institute.
[2] School of Psychology, Gold Coast campus,
Griffith University, Australia.

ABSTRACT

Numerous studies have demonstrated a link between regular video game playing and improved performance on tasks that objectively assess attention skills. Some research has extended this work examining the impact of video game training on executive functions and short-term memory. This study will further contribute to this area by examining the links between video game playing and verbal and visual short-term memory performance. The current research compared expert video game players and non-video game players on measures of verbal and visual short-term memory (Experiment 1). Expert video game players had played video games for at least 4 hours per week for the previous 6 months, and non-video game players had played video games rarely or never. Experiment 2 examined the effects of 10 hours of video game training on non-video game players' verbal and visual short-term memory. In both experiments participants were tested on the verbal and visual short-term memory tasks on two occasions. Verbal short-term memory was assessed using a simple span task where participants recalled in serial order lists of auditorily presented words. In the visual short-term memory task participants were presented with two patterns on each trial and were required to indicate if the patterns were the same or different. Pattern complexity was also varied. The results for Experiment 1 showed that expert video game players made fewer errors and had shorter response times in the visual short-term memory task than non-video game players, particularly in the lower complexity conditions. There was no group difference for the verbal short-term memory span task. Experiment 2 showed that training on the action video game Medal of Honor improved verbal short-term memory performance relative to

*E-mail: k.murphy@griffith.edu.au

the group trained on the non-action game Tetris. There were no differences between the Medal of Honor and Tetris group in errors and response times in the low complexity visual short-term memory task. In the high complexity visual short-term memory task Tetris participants performed better than Medal of Honor participants in some conditions at time 1 and 2 testing occasions. Only the Medal of Honor group showed task improvements from time 1 to time 2 providing some limited evidence of the benefits of video game practice. The results suggest that extensive video game practice is required to improve visual short-term memory skills. These findings along with those currently reported in the literature have implications for rehabilitation and training programs.

INTRODUCTION

Video games have become an increasingly popular pastime in today's society. Modern video games require the rapid processing of simultaneously presented information in order to succeed at the game and there are often dire consequences for failing to process a target or allowing irrelevant information to interfere with this processing during game play. Whilst there are numerous reports of the negative consequences of chronic video game playing such as increased antisocial behaviour (e.g., Van Schie and Wiegman, 1997; Wiegman, O., and Van Schie, E.,1998), aggression (Anderson and Bushman, 2001; Anderson and Dill, 2000) and obesity (e.g., Blackwell, 2002; Robinson, 1999), there is mounting evidence of cognitive benefits from video game play. For example, expert video game players have been shown to have shorter response times (Castel, Pratt and Drummond, 2005), and better visuo-spatial skills (Gagnon, 1985; Greenfield, Brannon and Lohr, 1994; Okagaki and Frensch, 1994; Subrahmanyam and Greenfield, 1994) than non-video game players. They have also been shown to have better abilities to detect targets within crowded displays (Green and Bavelier, 2007), superior performance on divided attention tasks (Greenfield, DeWinstanley, Kilpatrick, and Kaye, 1994), and increased attentional capacity and abilities (Castel et al., 2005; Green and Bavelier, 2003, 2006a, 2006b). Recent evidence has shown that the superior performance of expert video game players compared to non-video game players is also evident in more complex tasks. Expert video game players have been found to be better than non-video game players at tracking multiple targets within a display (Trick, Jaspers-Fayer and Sethi, 2005), switching between tasks (Andrews and Murphy, 2006; Boot, Kramer, Simons, Fabiani, and Gratton, 2008; Colzato, van Leeuwen, van den Wildenberg, and Hommel, 2010; Karle, Watter, and Shedden, 2010), and expert video game players have been shown to have superior speed of processing abilities compared to non-video game players (Dye, Green, and Bavelier, 2009).

One limitation of some of the studies comparing expert video game players and non-video game players is the use of a correlation approach. Hence, it is possible that experts play video games because they have inherently superior cognitive skills allowing them to succeed at video games compared to non-video game players who may not enjoy something they are poor at. To this end numerous studies have utilized training groups to further investigate potential cause-effect relations between video game playing and cognitive skills.

One of the earliest studies to demonstrate a causal link between video game playing and enhanced visual attention was that of Greenfield et al. (1994). Expert video game players were found to have superior visual attention skills compared to non-video game players. In addition when non-video game players underwent video game training, they outperformed the control group, consistent with a causal link between video game playing and improved divided attention skills.

More recently, Green and Bavelier (2003) showed that expert video game players had greater visual attention capacity, better spatial distribution of attention and superior temporal attentional abilities compared to non-video game players. They also used an experimental design in which non-video game players were trained for ten hours on either an action game (i.e., one that involves simultaneously occurring events at different locations on the screen that the player must attend to), or a non-action game (i.e., one that requires focus on only one object at a time, but still challenges visuo-motor skills). Only those participants who were trained on the action video game improved on the attention tasks (Green and Bavelier, 2003). Since the publication of this work, numerous studies have demonstrated enhanced cognitive skills through video game training. For example, Green and Bavelier (2007) found that training on action video games improved participants' abilities to detect targets presented in crowded displays and Feng, Spence, and Pratt (2007) showed that action video game training increased the Useful Field of View in participants. Other training studies have shown that action video game experience leads to improved reaction times (Dye et al., 2009), enhanced abilities to count and direct temporal attention focus (Green and Bavelier, 2003; 2006a; 2006b), and to track multiple objects at any given time (Green and Bavelier, 2006b). In contrast, Boot et al. (2008) showed that training non-video game players on an action video game for 20 hours did not improve visual attention skills. Boot et al. suggested that task differences between studies may have been one reason for the lack of replication of Green and Bavelier's (2003) work. In addition they made the valid point that as most expert video game players have practiced since a young age it is unlikely that 20 hours of practice would equate to a lifetime of practice and thus it was not surprising that the training did not show an effect.

As most of the evidence indicates that regularly playing action video games results in some transfer of skills to standard cognitive tasks and that this improvement can be trained in non-video game players, it is evident that these attentional improvements are not simply due to superior visuo-motor coordination or test-retest improvements (Green and Bavelier, 2003). Moreover these results provide optimism for the future development of efficient rehabilitation programs (Green and Bavelier, 2008). This present study seeks to extend work in this area by examining the impact of playing an action video game on verbal and visual short-term memory (Experiment 1) and to examine the possible short-term memory benefits that might be gained from training non-video game players on an action video game (Experiment 2). This research is important for several reasons. Firstly, the majority of research in this area has examined the impact of video game play on visual attention skills and in comparison there is less work examining the impact of video game training on higher cognitive skills such as short-term memory. Secondly, if it can be shown that action video game training results in better visual and or verbal short-term memory skills this would be a clear indication of skill transfer to new and unlearned tasks which have important implications for rehabilitation program design and implementation. Finally, both visual and verbal short-term memory are used in the performance of everyday tasks such as remembering a list of items for shopping, completing simple maths calculations on the fly, and in the listening and understanding of conversations. Hence if it can be shown that video game training improves short-term memory then this could improve the performance of everyday tasks.

Green and Bavelier (2003, 2006b) showed that expert video game players had larger subitizing ranges than non-video game players. Subitizing is the process by which we quantify small sets of items. On average, adults quantify sets of 4 or 5 items as quickly as they quantify smaller sets (1 to 3 items), but as set size increases beyond 4 or 5, more time is required. Expert video game players were able to subitize more items than non-video game players. They also showed that action video game training resulted in larger subitizing scores compared to non-action video game training. While Green and Bavelier (2003, 2006b) interpreted these data as evidence of improved attentional skills, it is possible that action video game training improves visual short-term memory skills, as some researchers have indicated that subitizing uses short-term memory processes (e.g., Baddeley, 1986, 1990; Logie and Baddeley, 1987; Trick, 2005). Evidence to support this assumption of short-term memory improvements through video game playing is provided by Boot et al. (2008). They presented participants with different loads (2, 4 or 6 items) of various coloured lines at different orientations for 100 msec and after a 900 msec delay presented participants with a second array that was the same or had one element different to the original pattern. Participants decided if the two patterns were the same or different. Expert video game players were more accurate at this task than non-video game players especially for the larger set size condition. The groups trained on Medal of Honor (action video game), Tetris (non-action video game) or Rise of Nations (strategy game) did not show visual short-term memory benefits from video game training. While Boot et al. reported better visual short-term memory performance for expert video game players compared to non-video game players it is possible that their task may have enabled participants to use both verbal and visual short-term memory encoding. For example, the displays may have allowed the participants to verbally label the lines (e.g. red line horizontal top left corner) and thus the group differences may be driven by general memory capacity or processes or verbal short-term memory capacity or processes rather than visual short-term memory processes alone. The current study seeks to address this issue by using visual stimuli that cannot be verbally labelled and including a verbal short-term memory task to assess group differences on this measure. An overview of both visual and verbal short-term memory will follow.

Everyday actions require humans to process, store and act upon incoming visual information. One set of cognitive processes thought to play a vital role in these everyday functions is visual short-term memory. Most researchers agree that visual short-term memory capacity is limited to approximately four items (e.g., Luck and Vogel, 1997; Jiang, Olson and Chun, 2000; Phillips, 1974). In addition it is thought that representations within visual short-term memory are not detailed (e.g., O'Regan, Rensink, and Clark, 1999), as humans tend to use visual environmental information to assist and update visual memory (O'Regan et al.; Vogel, Woodman, and Luck, 2001).

To examine visual short-term memory, Phillips and Baddeley (1971) and Cermak (1971) presented participants with two successive novel visual stimuli that were either the same or differed by minimal amounts. Results of both studies showed that response times were shorter and accuracy was higher when the inter-stimulus interval between patterns was short (e.g., 0.2 s) compared to when it was 9 or 20 s. As these patterns could not easily be verbally labelled, Phillips and Baddeley and Cermak concluded that this type of task involved the use of visual short-term memory.

Phillips (1974) extended this work to differentiate between iconic memory and visual short-term memory, using varying levels of pattern complexity (matrix sizes of 4 × 4, 6 × 6 or

8×8 squares) and inter-stimulus intervals ranging from 0.2 to 9 s. At the 0.2 s inter-stimulus interval, participants showed over 90% accuracy for all pattern complexities. As the inter-stimulus interval increased response times were longer and accuracy was reduced with this effect more pronounced in the high compared to low complexity conditions. Phillips showed that visual short-term memory has limited capacity (cannot completely process 4×4 load) and that visual short-term memory functions well for inter-stimulus intervals of up to 600 msec (which may serve the function of integrating visual information across successive visual displays). There is also a continual loss of information that occurs over a 9 second period.

The effects of inter-stimulus interval between patterns (0.2, 1, 3 and 9 s) and of pattern complexity (4×4 and 8×8 square patterns) on response times and errors will be examined in this study. This will allow us to ensure replication of previous research in this area and will provide further clarification of the relationship between video game playing and visual short-term memory processes and capacity. For example, if expert video game players have better performance than non-video game players at each inter-stimulus interval then this would suggest greater memory capacity and less severe depletion rates of this information within visual short-term memory. The use of two different pattern complexity levels (4×4 and 8 x8 patterns) will further elucidate the relationship between video game playing and visual short-term memory capacity. Experiment 2 will examine the impact of video game training in non-video game players on these aspects of visual short-term memory.

Verbal short-term memory is a temporary store for visually or auditorily presented verbal information and is typically investigated using simple memory span tasks. Memory span is the capacity or longest list of words a person can repeat in serial order immediately after hearing them (e.g., Baddeley, 1986; Baddeley, Thomson, and Buchanan, 1975; Cowan, 2000; Roodenrys, Hulme, Lethbridge, Hinton, and Nimmo, 2002; Salame and Baddeley, 1982). Whilst earlier evidence suggested verbal memory span was equal to six or seven monosyllabic words (Miller, 1956), more recent research indicates that verbal memory span is approximately four items (Cowan, 2000). The limitation of verbal short-term memory is thought to be due to representation decay over time with a limited rehearsal mechanism (Baddeley, 1986) or through interference of items disrupting the memory trace of other words (Baddeley, 1990).

One study that has examined the impact of video game training on verbal short-term memory was conducted by Sayten (2003). Participants were tested on a verbal memory span task before and after video game training. There was no difference in verbal memory span between those trained for one or six hours suggesting video game playing has no effect on verbal short-term memory. However, the training did not use an action video game which has shown cognitive improvements in previous research (e.g., subitizing in Green and Bavelier, 2003, 2006b). This study will overcome this limitation by using an action and non-action video game training with novice game players in Experiment 2.

EXPERIMENT 1

Boot et al. (2008) demonstrated that expert video game players were better than non-video game players at detecting if two patterns were the same or different. While it is possible that this group difference was due to better visual short-term memory processes or larger capacity for expert video game players relative to non-video game players, it is possible that both verbal and visual short-term memory were recruited in the task used by Boot et al. Thus the aim of Experiment 1 was to compare performance of expert video game players and non-video game players on purer measures of visual and verbal short-term memory. If expert video game players are better than non-video game players at the visual short-term memory but not the verbal short-term memory task then playing action video games would appear to enhance visual short-term memory capacity or processes. If expert video game players outperform the non-video game players on both aspects of short-term memory then this could be taken as evidence that action video game playing contributes to general short-term memory improvements.

Method

Participants. There were 31 participants in this experiment. The 17 (4 female) expert video game players reported playing video games for at least one hour per day, 4 days per week, for the previous six months and during the course of the study played for an average of 10.92 hours per week (SD = 5.36) in their own time. Typically expert video game players reported playing first person shooter games (e.g., Far Cry, Halo, Counter Strike, Half Life, and Battlefield). In addition some players also reported playing car racing games (e.g. Need for Speed, Gran Turismo), strategy games (e.g., Command and Conquer, Warcraft III), or puzzle games (Tetris, Devil Dice). There were 14 (4 female) non-video game players in the control group. These participants had never or rarely (less than two hours in total) played video games during the six months prior to the study and did not play any video games during the study. Expert video game players were aged between 18 to 28 years of age (M = 20.59, SD = 2.58) and non-video game players were aged between 18 to 31 years of age (M = 22.21, SD = 3.66), t (29) -1.45, p = .158, d = 0.52. All participants reported normal or corrected normal vision. Course credit and/or a monetary incentive ($10 per hour) were paid for participation at the completion of the testing sessions and participants were free to choose the type of incentive or combination of incentives they received.

Apparatus. The DMDX program (Forster and Forster, 2003) was used to present the two tasks on a Pentium IV 2.66GHz PC computer with a Dell Ultra flat CRT monitor.

Procedure. All participants completed the two tasks twice and during the time between the two testing sessions were asked to keep playing video games with their usual frequency or refrain from playing any video games as per usual. Participants kept a log book of hours playing games during the two testing sessions. For all participants there was a maximum of 21 days between the two testing sessions.

Verbal Short-term Memory Task. Verbal memory span was assessed through verbal recall of lists of auditorily presented words. A subset of 75 words from Roodenrys et al. (2002) were pre-recorded onto the computer and were randomly sorted into lists ranging from two words to twelve words in length. Four lists were made for each list length. To ensure participants were familiar with the words they read through a printed list of all words prior to the span task. Participants were verbally given task instructions and read onscreen instructions prior to the task. Words were auditorily presented to participants via headphones at the rate of one item per second and each list concluded with an auditory cue (beep) to indicate participants should recall aloud the words in serial order. Participants completed two practice trials at each of the two and the three word list lengths. Experimental trials consisted of four trials at each list length starting at two words until participants could not get all four trials at a particular list length correct. Correct responses were scored by the experimenter and incorrect responses were recorded verbatim. Memory span was calculated as the longest list length at which each participant could recall all lists correctly plus .25 of a point for each subsequent list recalled correctly at list lengths beyond those where all four lists were recalled correctly (Hulme, Newton, Cowan, Stuart, and Brown, 1999).

Visual Short-term Memory Task. The stimuli used within this task were patterns of squares located within a 4 × 4 cell or 8 × 8 cell matrix. Each cell within the matrix was 4 mm × 4 mm and participants were seated approximately 60 cm away from the computer screen. For each trial 50% of the cells were filled white at any one time (the rest were black to blend with the background) and different patterns were used for each trial within the experiment. Only patterns that were not able to be given verbal labels were used as stimuli.

Participants were given verbal instructions with the aid of figures and read onscreen instructions prior to beginning the task. Presentation was blocked with 4 × 4 matrices and 8 × 8 matrices being presented separately, with separate instructions and practice trials. Pattern complexity was counterbalanced across participants. For both sets of trials, participants completed 20 randomly presented practice trials and one block of 80 randomly presented experimental trials, with 20 trials at each inter-stimulus interval (10 trials same patterns, 10 trials different patterns).

Each trial consisted of a white fixation cross "+" presented for 0.2 s, followed by a blank screen for 0.2 s, then the first pattern for 1 second. This was followed by presentation of the second pattern after a delay of 0.2, 1, 3, or 9 s and the second pattern remained onscreen until participants responded. The second pattern was either identical to the first pattern or had one square more or one square less filled. Participants were instructed to identify as soon as possible, whether the second pattern was the same or different to the first pattern. Responses were made by pressing one of the two shift keys on the keyboard. Participant accuracy and response time from onset of pattern two was recorded by DMDX program (Forster and Forster, 2003).

Design. For the verbal short-term memory task the independent variables were test time (a within subjects factor, time 1 or time 2) and group (a between subjects factor, expert video game players and non-video game players). The dependent variable memory span was calculated as indicated above. For the visual short-term memory task, the independent variables were group (a between subjects factor, expert video game players and non-video game players), test time (time 1 and time 2), inter-stimulus interval (0.2, 1, 3 and 9 s), trial type (two patterns same or different), and complexity (cells within the matrix either 4 × 4 or 8 × 8). These last four independent variables were all within subjects factors. The dependent variables were response time for correct trials and errors (%).

Results and Discussion

An α–level of .05 was used for the analyses for both the verbal and visual short-term memory tasks.

Verbal Short-term Memory Task. The data for the verbal short-term memory task were analysed using a 2 (group) × 2 (test time) mixed factorial ANOVA with memory span as the dependent variable. There was an improvement in memory span performance from time 1 to time 2, $F(1, 29) = 12.78$, $p = .001$, $\eta_p^2 = .31$, (Time 1 $M = 4.13$ words, $SE = .10$, Time 2 $M = 4.36$ words, $SE = .12$). The main effect of group, $F(1, 29) = 0.12$, $p = .74$, $\eta_p^2 = .004$, (Experts $M = 4.21$, $SE = 0.14$: Non-Video $M = 4.28$, $SE = 0.16$) and the interaction between group and test time were not significant, $F(1, 29) = 0.28$, $p = .601$, $\eta_p^2 = .01$. Although there was no difference between expert and non-video game players in memory span, their overall performance level was similar to that reported in previous research (e.g., Cowan, 2000).

The improvement in memory span performance from time 1 to time 2 indicates that task practice effects occurred equally for expert video game players and non-video game players. These results suggest that playing action video games does not result in beneficial effects for verbal short-term memory nor does it confer an advantage of greater benefit from task practice. This could be expected given that action video games emphasise the processing of visually presented information and therefore would be less likely to involve verbal than visual short-term memory processes. The lack of group differences on this task also indicates that any group differences on the visual short-term memory task cannot be due to action video game playing resulting in a general increase in short-term memory capacity or processes. Rather group differences could be attributed to action video game play specifically facilitating visual short-term memory capacity or processes.

Visual Short-term Memory Task. Data for the visual short-term memory task were analysed using a 2 (group) × 2 (test time) × 2 (trial type) × 4 (inter-stimulus interval) mixed factorial ANOVA. The dependent variables were response time (ms) and errors (%). Where appropriate the Huynh-Feldt correction for sphericity was applied to analyses involving inter-stimulus interval. The analyses were run separately for the two load conditions (4 × 4 and 8 × 8 conditions). The results for this task will be presented in two sections. The first section will evaluate the replication of standard effects for the response time and error data for the visual short-term memory task. The second section will examine the occurrence of any group differences between expert video-game players and non-video game players on this task.

Standard effects. For the error data for the 4 × 4 patterns there was an effect of inter-stimulus interval, $F(3, 82) = 50.48$, $p < .001$, $\eta_p^2 = .64$, and a significant interaction between inter-stimulus interval and trial type (same vs. different), $F(2.4, 70) = 4.44$, $p = .011$, $\eta_p^2 = .13$. The response time data also showed an effect of inter-stimulus interval, $F(3, 47) = 133.09$, $p < .001$, $\eta_p^2 = .82$, and a significant interaction between inter-stimulus interval and trial type, $F(3, 74) = 4.99$, $p = .005$, $\eta_p^2 = .15$. The 8 × 8 patterns also produced these results. For the error data there was an effect of inter-stimulus interval, $F(3, 87) = 11.93$, $p < .001$, $\eta_p^2 = .29$, and the interaction between inter-stimulus interval and trial type was significant, $F(3, 85) = 59.04$, $p < .001$, $\eta_p^2 = .67$. The response time data showed an effect of inter-stimulus interval, $F(3, 75) = 64.37$, $p < .001$, $\eta_p^2 = .69$, and the interaction between inter-stimulus interval and trial type was significant, $F(3, 77) = 3.99$, $p = .013$, $\eta_p^2 = .12$. For both levels of pattern complexity, errors and response times increased as inter-stimulus interval increased and these effects were more evident on trials in which the two patterns were different and in the higher level of pattern complexity. These results are consistent with those reported by Phillips (1974) and Phillips and Baddeley (1971), replicating the standard effects typically found for this task. In addition for the 8 × 8 condition there was a significant interaction between test time and inter-stimulus interval, $F(3, 87) = 3.11$, $p = .03$, $\eta_p^2 = .10$ for the error data. Comparisons revealed a reduction in errors from time 1 to time 2 for the inter-stimulus interval of 9 s ($p = .04$), providing some suggestion of task practice effects.

Video game group differences. The error data for the 4 × 4 patterns showed a marginally significant interaction between inter-stimulus interval, trial type and group, $F_{(2.4, 70)} = 2.54$, $p = .076$, $\eta_p^2 = .08$. The interaction between test time, inter-stimulus interval, trial type and group was significant, $F_{(3, 80)} = 2.83$, $p = .049$, $\eta_p^2 = .09$, and is shown in Figure 1. Pairwise comparisons examining group differences for each condition revealed that at time 1 for trials in which the two patterns were the same, expert video game players made fewer errors than non-video game players when the patterns were separated by 0.2 s (approached significance $p = .058$) and with an inter-stimulus interval of 3 s expert video game players showed a marginal trend towards fewer errors than non-video game players ($p = .087$). Also at time 1 when the two patterns shown were different and separated by a 9 s inter-stimulus interval, expert video game players made fewer errors than non-video game players (approached significance $p = .061$). There was also evidence of better task performance by expert video game players at the time 2 test phase. Expert video game players made fewer errors than non-video game players when the two patterns were the same and the inter-stimulus interval was 3 s ($p = .051$). Expert video game players also showed a marginal trend towards fewer errors than non-video game players when the two patterns were different and were separated by a 1 s inter-stimulus interval ($p = .082$). Hence expert video game players showed better performance than non-video game players in a number of conditions within the 4 × 4 pattern complexity of the visual short-term memory task.

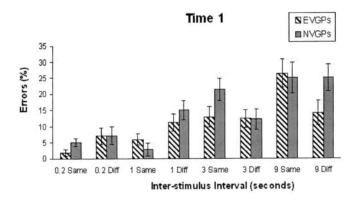

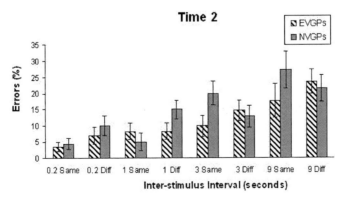

Figure 1. Experiment 1 mean errors at time 1 and time 2 for the 4 × 4 complexity visual short-term memory task for expert video game players and non-video game players. Error bars represent 1 SE.

To examine task practice effects, performance at time 1 and time 2 were compared for each group for each condition. Expert video game players made more errors at time 2 than time 1 on trials in which the two patterns were different and separated by 9 s (approached significance $p = .064$). No other comparisons examining task practice effects were significant.

For the response time data for the 4 × 4 pattern condition there was an effect of test time, $F(1, 29) = 16.35$, $p < .001$, $\eta_p^2 = .36$, and the interaction between test time and trial type (same vs. different) showed a trend towards significance, $F(1, 29) = 3.43$, $p = .074$, $\eta_p^2 = .11$. The interaction between test time, inter-stimulus interval, trial type, and group was significant, $F(2.4, 70) = 3.19$, $p = .028$, $\eta_p^2 = .10$, and is shown in Figure 2. Pairwise comparisons showed that at time 1 expert video game players had shorter response times than non-video game players for same (marginally significant $p = .074$) and different pattern trials ($p = .034$) at the 0.2 s inter-stimulus interval. No other group differences were evident for the response time data.

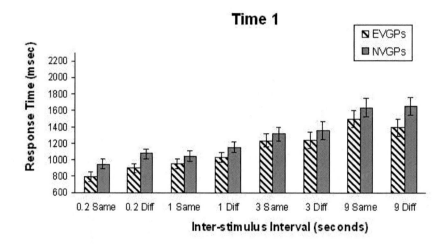

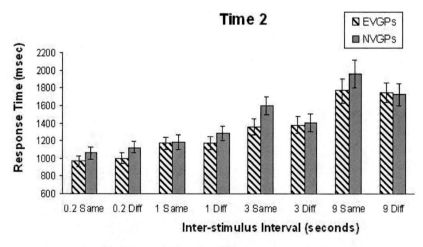

Figure 2. Experiment 1 mean response time at time 1 and time 2 for the 4 × 4 complexity visual short-term memory task for expert video game players and non-video game players. Error bars represent 1 SE.

In comparing response times for same and different patterns at time 1, expert video game players had shorter response times for same than different patterns at the inter-stimulus intervals of 0.2 s (p = .002) and 1 s (approached significance p = .061). Non-video game players showed this same pattern advantage for the 0.2 s and 1 s inter-stimulus intervals (ps < .05). At time 2, non-video game players had longer response times for same than different patterns trials at the 3 s and 9 s inter-stimulus intervals (ps < .05). Expert video game players did not show differences between same and different trials at time 2.

Comparisons investigating practice effects showed that expert video game players had longer response times for the same and different trials at time 2 than at time 1 for all inter-stimulus intervals except 3 s (all ps < .05). The non-video game players showed evidence of this slowing effect at the 0.2 s (marginal trend towards significance p = .075), 1, 3 and 9 s inter-stimulus intervals (all ps < .05) for same trials and for different trials at the 1 s inter-stimulus interval (approached significance p = .065). While it could be argued that these longer response times reflect a practice effect through a reduction in errors this is not the case. The only change in the error data across the two testing sessions was an increase in the number of errors made by the expert video game players at time 2 compared to time 1 when the two patterns were different and separated by 9 s. Thus these results do not detract from the superior performance of expert video game players compared to non-video game players in the 4 × 4 visual short term memory task as reported in the error data above. Further research is required to replicate the slowing effect and increased error effect from time 1 to time 2 in this visual short-term memory task.

In the low complexity condition expert video game players made fewer errors than non-video game players at a number of inter-stimulus intervals at both time 1 and 2, indicating superior task performance. These group differences were not due to speed-accuracy tradeoffs as expert video game players had shorter response times than non-video game players in the conditions in which they also had fewer errors or did not perform differently to the non-video game players. Thus both the error and response time data show evidence of better performance for expert video game players compared to non-video game players on the low complexity condition of the visual short-term memory task.

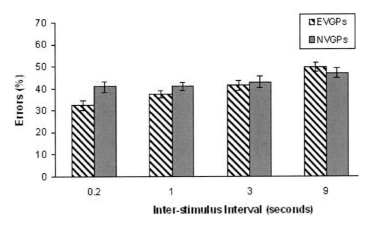

Figure 3. Experiment 1 mean errors for the 8 × 8 complexity visual short-term memory task for expert video game players and non-video game players across the inter-stimulus intervals. Error bars represent 1 SE.

The error data for the 8 × 8 patterns revealed a near significant interaction between group and inter-stimulus interval, $F(3, 87) = 2.68$, $p = .052$, $\eta_p^2 = .09$, as can be seen in Figure 3. There were fewer errors for expert video game players compared to non-video game players at the 0.2 s inter-stimulus interval ($p = .015$).

There was a main effect of trial type $F(1, 29) = 103.64$, $p < .001$, $\eta_p^2 = .78$ and test time and trial type interacted $F(1, 29) = 5.25$, $p = .029$, $\eta_p^2 = .15$. The 3-way interaction between test time, trial type and group approached significance, $F(1, 29) = 3.72$, $p = .064$, $\eta_p^2 = .11$, and is shown in Figure 4. At time 1 expert video game players outperformed non-video game players when the two patterns were different ($p = .009$). In comparing time 1 and time 2 performance to examine practice effects, only non-video game players showed an improvement from time 1 to time 2 for trials showing different patterns ($p = .012$). No effects involving group were significant for the response time data in the 8 × 8 condition.

Group differences were evident in the higher complexity condition only for the error data, thus there was no evidence of a speed-accuracy trade-off. Expert video game players made fewer errors than non-video game players at the 0.2 s inter-stimulus interval and during the time 1 test phase expert video game players made fewer errors than non-video game players on trials requiring different responses. Only non-video game players showed task practice effects for the error data.

Taken together, these results are consistent with Boot et al. (2008) who showed that expert video game players were more accurate than non-video game players at their visual short-term memory task. In particular in this study the group differences appeared to be more evident in the harder conditions (e.g., different trials), which is consistent with Boot et al's findings. The results also suggest that expert video game players have superior visual short-term memory capacity or processes compared to non-video game players as is evidenced by better performance at the 0.2 s inter-stimulus interval which reflects very little memory decay. An alternate explanation for these data will be examined in Experiment 2.

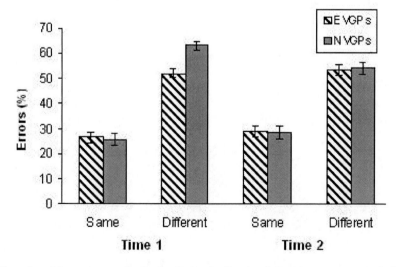

Figure 4. Experiment 1 mean errors for the 8 × 8 complexity visual short-term memory task for expert video game players and non-video game players at time 1 and 2 for same and different pattern trials. Error bars represent 1 SE.

EXPERIMENT 2

The results of Experiment 1 provided some evidence that expert video game players had better visual short-term memory skills than non-video game players. However, this evidence is based on correlation data and it may be explained by self-selection bias. That is, perhaps participants with inherently better visual short-term memory skills engage in video game playing as their natural cognitive skills allows them to succeed at playing action video games. In contrast, due to poorer visual short-term memory skills non-video game players never undertake this regular past-time. To examine this idea, Experiment 2 used a training regime between the time 1 and time 2 task testing sessions to examine the impact of action and non-action video game training on verbal and visual short-term memory task performance. If playing action video games modifies visual short-term memory skills or capacity then the group of non-video game players trained on the action game Medal of Honor (action video game) should outperform the group of non-video game players trained on Tetris (non-action video game).

Method

Participants. All participants in this experiment were non-video game players who had played games for less than 1 and half hours in the six months prior to the study. There were 13 participants (5 female) in the Medal of Honor group and 12 participants (5 female) in the Tetris group. Participants in the Medal of Honor group were aged between 18 to 26 years (M = 21.00, SD = 2.31) and participants within the Tetris group were aged between 17 to 29 years (M = 21.17, SD = 4.22), t (23) = -0.87, p = .395, d = .36. All participants reported normal or corrected normal vision. Course credit and/or a monetary incentive ($10 per hour) were paid for participation at the completion of the testing sessions and participants were free to choose the type of incentive or combination of incentives they received. Participants were randomly assigned to the two training groups.

Procedure. All participants completed the verbal and visual memory tasks twice as in Experiment 1. Testing session 1 was conducted prior to the video game training sessions and testing session 2 was conducted after participants had completed all 10 training sessions. Only information in addition to that given in Experiment 1 will be reported here. Between the two testing sessions, participants either played 10, one-hour sessions of the game Medal of Honour: Frontline or 10, one- hour sessions of the game Tetris Worlds (see game explanation provided below). These 10 training sessions were completed within a 19 day period and each video game session was supervised by a researcher. The training phase of the study was modelled on Green and Bavelier (2003). In training sessions one to eight, participants in both groups played one continuous game to see how far though the game they could progress in eight sessions. For training sessions nine and ten, participants returned to the beginning of the game and again played one continuous game to see how far they could progress in the final two sessions. This allowed the assessment of game learning across the eight practice sessions. All participants in both groups improved their level of game performance in sessions nine and ten compared to that achieved in sessions one and two.

Video Games. The action video game Medal of Honor: Frontline simulates combat scenarios from World War II. Participants played this game from the first person shooter perspective and completed missions throughout the game, such as killing enemy soldiers, destroying targets and gathering information and weapons. The non-action video game Tetris Worlds is a 2-D puzzle game where the player manipulates falling block pieces of various shapes to form horizontal rows which are cleared from the playing field and in doing so earn game points. Clearing more than one line at a time earns extra points (e.g., 4 lines are a Tetris). This game requires players to use spatial ability to rotate each block in two-dimensional space to its optimal position.

Design. For the verbal short-term memory task the independent variables were test time (a within subjects factor, time 1 or time 2) and group (a between subjects factor, Medal of Honor or Tetris). The dependent variable memory span was calculated as in Experiment 1. For the visual short-term memory task the independent variables were group (a between subjects factor, Medal of Honor or Tetris), test time (time 1 and time 2), inter-stimulus interval (0.2, 1, 3 and 9 s), trial type (two patterns same or different) and complexity (cells within the matrix either 4 × 4 or 8 × 8). These last four independent variables were all within subjects factors. The dependent variables were response time and errors (%) as in Experiment 1.

Results and Discussion

Verbal Short-term Memory. The data for the verbal short-term memory were analysed as for Experiment 1. There was no group difference in memory span, $F(1, 23) = .86$, $p = .364$, $\eta_p^2 = .04$ and memory span did not change from time 1 to time 2 during the study, $F(1,23) = 0.15$, $p = .70$, $\eta_p^2 = .01$. The interaction between group and test phase, $F(1, 23) = 5.90$, $p = .023$, $\eta_p^2 = .20$, revealed that even though the Tetris group had marginally better memory span performance than the Medal of Honour group at time 1 ($p = .089$), there was a significant improvement in memory span from time 1 to time 2 for the Medal of Honor group (time 1 $M = 3.87$ words , $SE = 0.16$: time 2 $M = 4.06$ words, $SE = 0.17$) ($p = .054$) but not the Tetris group (time 1 $M = 4.23$ words, $SE = 0.16$: time 2 $M = 4.06$ words, $SE = 0.18$) ($p = .172$). Thus Medal of Honor training for 10 hours appears to have benefited verbal memory span task performance. This result cannot be explained by task practice effects as the Tetris group did not show this same improvement across the two testing sessions. This result is also at odds with Sayten (2003), who did not find improvements in verbal short-term memory as a result of one or six hours of video game training. While it is possible that training on an action video game which Sayten did not use in her study, resulted in cognitive improvements, it is also possible that the Medal of Honor group had more room to show task improvement given their marginally lower time 1 scores compared to the Tetris group. Further research in this area is required to examine if this result is due to regression towards the mean for the Medal of Honor group or if action video game training results in improved verbal short-term memory.

Visual Short-term Memory. The data for the visual short-term memory were analysed the same as for Experiment 1. As for Experiment 1 standard findings are presented first followed by those results demonstrating group differences.

Standard findings. The error data for the 4 × 4 patterns showed a main effect of inter-stimulus interval, $F(3,69) = 43.49$, $p < .001$, $\eta_p^2 = .65$, and the interaction between inter-stimulus interval and trial type showed a trend towards significance, $F(3,69) = 2.75$, $p = .070$, $\eta_p^2 = .11$. The response time data revealed a main effect of inter-stimulus interval, $F(3,69) = 115.52$, $p < .001$, $\eta_p^2 = .83$, showing longer response times with increasing inter-stimulus interval. The interaction between inter-stimulus interval and trial type was not significant ($p > .05$).

In the 8 × 8 pattern condition for the error data there was a main effect of inter-stimulus interval, $F(3, 69) = 6.72$, $p < .001$, $\eta_p^2 = .23$ and trial type (same vs. different), $F(1, 23) = 49.03$, $p < .001$, $\eta_p^2 = .68$. The interaction between inter-stimulus interval and trial type (same vs. different) was also significant, $F(3, 46) = 14.84$, $p < .001$, $\eta_p^2 = .39$. Results revealed fewer errors for the same than different trials for all inter-stimulus intervals except the 9 s inter-stimulus interval (all $ps < .001$).

For the response time data there was a main effect of inter-stimulus interval, $F(3, 69) = 62.28$, $p < .001$, $\eta_p^2 = .73$ and of trial type (same vs. different), $F(1, 23) = 12.99$, $p = .001$, $\eta_p^2 = .36$. The interaction between inter-stimulus interval and trial type showed a marginal trend towards significance, $F(3, 69) = 2.39$, $p = .076$, $\eta_p^2 = .09$. Comparisons revealed shorter response times for same pattern trials than different pattern trials at all inter-stimulus intervals except the 9 s interval (all $ps < .05$). The interaction between test time and trial type, $F(3, 69) = 5.06$, $p = .034$, $\eta_p^2 = .18$, showed that same pattern trials had shorter response times than different pattern trials at time 1 ($p < .005$) but not time 2 ($p > .05$).

For both levels of patterns complexity the data are similar to the standard effects reported in Experiment1 for experts and non-video game players and also replicates the results reported by Phillips and Baddeley (1971) and Phillips (1974). Thus any group differences or lack of group differences found in this experiment cannot be attributed to the failure to find standard effects for this task.

Group differences. There were no group differences in errors for the 4 × 4 condition. For response times there was a main effect of test time, $F(1, 23) = 6.52$, $p = .018$, $\eta_p^2 = .22$. The interaction between test time, trial type (same vs. different) and group was significant, $F(1, 23) = 6.84$, $p = .015$, $\eta_p^2 = .23$, as was the interaction between test time, trial type, inter-stimulus interval and group, $F(3,69) = 6.96$, $p < .001$, $\eta_p^2 = .23$. This interaction is shown in Figure 5. Pairwise comparisons revealed that there was no difference between the groups for any conditions (all $ps > .05$). The Medal of Honor group had slower response times for time 2 compared to time 1 for same pattern trials at the 3 and 9 s inter-stimulus intervals ($ps < 05$). There was no change in response time across the testing occasions for other conditions. The Tetris group showed a slowing in response time from time 1 to time 2 for the same trials for the 0.2 s ($p = .018$) and 3 s ($p = .004$) inter-stimulus-intervals and for the different trials at the 9 s ($p = .001$) pattern interval.

When comparing same and different trials, the Medal of Honor group had shorter response times for same compared to different trials at the 3 s inter-stimulus interval at time 1 ($p = .017$). Participants in the Tetris group had shorter response time for same than different trials at inter-stimulus intervals of 0.2 s ($p = .047$), 3 s ($p = .067$ approached significance) and longer response times for same than different trials at the 9 s inter-stimulus interval ($p = .039$). At time 2 this group showed the same trial advantage for the 1 s inter-stimulus interval ($p = .021$). Thus the same pattern trial advantage appeared to be more evident for the Tetris than Medal of Honor group.

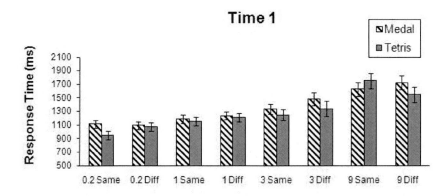

Inter-stimulus Interval (seconds)

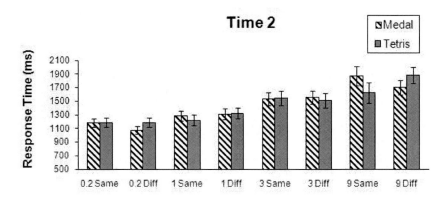

Inter-stimulus Interval (seconds)

Figure 5. Experiment 2 mean response times at time 1 and time 2 for the 4 × 4 complexity visual short-term memory task for Medal of Honor and Tetris groups. Error bars represent 1 SE.

There were no differences between the Medal of Honor and Tetris group in errors and response times in the 4 × 4 complexity visual short-term memory task. Both groups had slower response times on the second testing occasion although the inter-stimulus intervals showing these effects were different for the two groups. This slowing effect may be indicative of more measured performance at time 2 or perhaps reflect reduced participant motivation for the task after engaging in 10 hours of exciting video game play. The Medal of Honour group only showed a response time advantage for same compared to different pattern trials at the 3 s interval at time 1. This advantage was more evident for the Tetris group who had shorter response times for same than different patterns at the 0.2, and 3 s intervals at time 1 and at time 2 the 1 s interval. These same trial advantage effects were not due to speed accuracy trade-offs as there was no group differences in the error data for this condition and an overall same pattern advantage was only evident in the 1 s inter-stimulus interval.

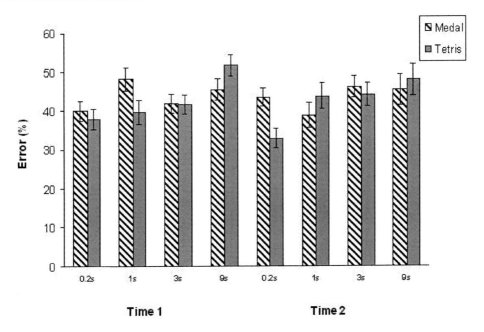

Figure 6. Experiment 2 mean errors at time 1 and time 2 for the 8 × 8 complexity visual short-term memory task for Medal of Honor and Tetris groups across the inter-stimulus intervals. Error bars represent 1 SE.

The error data for the 8 × 8 condition showed that the interaction between inter-stimulus interval and group $F(3, 69) = 2.37$, $p = .078$, $\eta_p^2 = .09$, showed a marginal trend towards significance. The interaction between test time, inter-stimulus interval and group was significant, $F(3, 69) = 2.37$, $p = .025$, $\eta_p^2 = .13$, and is shown in Figure 6. At time 1 the Tetris group made fewer errors than the Medal of Honor group for the 1 s inter-stimulus interval (approached significance $p = .065$) and at time 2, this difference favouring the Tetris group appeared at the 0.2 s inter-stimulus interval ($p = .007$). Participants in the Medal of Honor group significantly reduced their number of errors from the time 1 to time 2 at the inter-stimulus interval of 1 s (approached significance $p = .061$). No practice effects were evident for the Tetris group. There were no group differences apparent in the response time data for the 8 × 8 condition.

Although participants in the Medal of Honor group significantly reduced their number of errors from the time 1 to time 2 at the inter-stimulus interval of 1 s, they also made more errors at time 1 than the Tetris group in this condition. Hence while this could be taken as evidence of a training effect in the Medal of Honor group it is at best very modest and undermined by this groups' poorer performance at time 1 allowing greater room for improvement at time 2. Moreover, given the similarity between the block patterns used in this visual short-term memory task and those used within the Tetris game it is surprising that practice effects were not evident for this group. These data suggest that 10 hours of action video game training might not be enough to produce improvement in visual short-term memory. This result is consistent with the training results of Boot et al. (2008) who found that 20 hours of action video game training did not enhance visual short-term memory skills. However, given that the Medal of Honor group showed practice improvements in both tasks it is possible that action video game training lead to general memory or strategy improvement rather than just visual short-term memory improvements. Further research with a battery of short-term memory tasks and various training durations is required to provide a clearer picture of the utility of action video game training for enhancing short-term memory.

GENERAL DISCUSSION

In both experiments the data for the verbal and visual short-term memory tasks replicated previous effects reported in the literature hence the tasks were testing the desired cognitive functions. Experiment 1 showed that expert video game players had better visual short-term memory skills than non-video game players, although these differences were significant only at some inter-stimulus intervals. This performance advantage for experts compared to non-video game players is consistent with the results reported by Boot et al. (2008).

Experiment 2 employed a training design to assess the impact of action video game training non-video game players' short-term memory performance. There was some evidence to indicate that Medal of Honor training lead to improvements in the form of task practice effects in verbal and visual short-term memory relative to the group of non-video game players who were trained on Tetris. Although the Medal of Honor did show task practice effects (that the Tetris group did not) in both short-term memory tasks, these effects were not as large or as consistently apparent in the data as the group difference reported in Experiment 1 for the visual short-term memory task. The use of only 10 hours of video game training in Experiment 2 may be one possible reason for the modest effects of action video game training. However this amount of training is the same as employed by Green and Bavelier (2003) who demonstrated large training effects on visual attention tasks with similar sample sizes to Experiment 2 reported here. [1] Moreover, Boot et al. (2008) found that even 20 hours of action video game training was not enough to produce group differences in non-video game players trained on action and non-action video games. Hence it is possible that video game practice over a longer time period is required before short-term memory skills are enhanced.

Further it is also possible that the use of video games other than action games may have produced better training effects in Experiment 2. That is, if games with an emphasis on short-term memory requirements had been utilised perhaps the results would have shown positive transfer effects to the measures of short-term memory used within this study. Moreover, only limited aspects of short-term memory were tested in this study and thus further research testing multiple components such as iconic memory, visual short-term and long–term memory is required to fully understand the benefits of regular video game training for improved cognitive skills.

---

[1] The sample sizes for Experiment 1 and 2 are larger than those used by Green and Bavelier (2003) who had between 8 and 11 participants per group in all of their experiments. In addition Experiment 1 had more participants in the expert video game player and non-video game player groups than Boot et al. (2008) who had 10 and 11 participants in each of these groups respectively and although Boot et al. had 20 participants per group in their training study they too failed to find evidence of video game training enhancing visual short-term memory performance. While increasing the sample size for each group may have resolved a number of marginally significant results, given that the largest overall effects sizes were between .20 and .23 this would require extremely large sample sizes to ensure adequate power to detect group differences within this study. Thus it would appear that video game training in the short-term has little impact on visual short-term memory performance.

APPLICATIONS

The findings that expert video game players had better visual short-term memory skills than non-video game players and that those trained on Medal of Honours showed some minimal improvement across time in both verbal and visual short-term memory provides another example of the transfer of trained cognitive processes to other tasks. Findings of this nature have practical implications for a range of populations including the elderly, young children, persons suffering from brain trauma and in terms of improving professional skills training.

One of the earliest studies to demonstrate that video game play enhanced functioning in elderly participants was Drew and Waters (1986). They showed that elderly participants (aged 61 to 78 years) who were trained on the game Crystal Castles for 1 hour per week for 2 months, improved relative to the their pre-test scores on the WAIS-R (general IQ although this may have been a speed of processing effect rather than IQ improvement), Purdue Pegboard (manual dexterity), and Rotary Pursuit tasks (eye-hand coordination). The control group who did not complete any video game training did not show such improvements. Importantly participants who were in the video game training group reported being more careful with daily activities. This shows that video game playing can enhance a range of cognitive functions in elderly participants as well as their ability to feel better about everyday tasks thus improving their quality of life.

Clark, Lanphear, and Riddick (1987) investigated the impact of video game play in elderly participants (57 to 83 years) on a response time task. Half the participants trained on video games for 7 weeks (at least 2 hours per week) and the remainder (control group) did not play games. The training group had shorter response times at post-test than the controls and also showed a smaller stimulus incompatibility effect indicating that video game training enhanced response selection and the ability to ignore distracting information. These improvements in response time would be important for elderly drivers by allowing them to have better braking times and better abilities to focus on relevant visual information, both of which would result in reduced accident rates.

Improvements in cognitive function for elderly participants have also been found for executive functions which suffer age related decline. Basak, Boot, Voss, and Kramer (2008) trained elderly participants on a strategy video game and found that this resulted in significant improvements in the tasks measuring executive control functions (task switching, working memory and reasoning) in comparison to the control participants. Improvements were not shown for the visuo-spatial tasks (e.g., attentional blink, functional field of view, mental rotation and enumeration tasks) which were consistent with the researchers' predictions that a strategy game would result in broad transfer of learning to the skills and cognitive processes exercised in the video game, specifically executive control and memory processes.

In addition to showing improvements on laboratory based measures of cognitive function, Wills et al (2006) showed that training on reasoning strategies transferred to other tasks as reported in activities of daily living. Thus elderly participants reported better reasoning skills in their everyday lives which would have assisted with carrying out regular activities and in turn improved participant's quality of life.

Research in this area has also shown improvements in cognitive skills of children through video game training. Subrahmanyam and Greenfield (1994) examined the effect of video game practice on spatial skills in 5th grade males and females. Participants were assessed on their spatial skills prior to and after video game training. The control group played a word computer game and the experimental group were trained on the game Marble Madness for three 45 mins sessions within one week. Marble Madness participants showed greater improvement on the spatial skills test than participants who had been trained on the word game and this effect was most evident in participants with poorer spatial skills. This finding is also consistent with the results of Feng et al. (2007) who found that 10 hours of action video game training was sufficient time to improve participants' attentional field of view and mental rotation skills, particularly in persons who had poorer attentional skills at the outset.

Dunbar, Hill and Lewis (2001) found a relationship between children's ability to switch attention rapidly within a computer game and their care in crossing the road. In particular children with poor concentration were found to have higher levels of impulsive behaviour and crossed roads in an uncontrolled manner. Given this relationship and the evidence that training on action video games leads to improved attention skills and task switching abilities it is clear that video game training may result in improved road crossing behaviour which, in turn, would assist children avoid accidents.

Research is also examining the use of video games for treatment of Amblyopia, a developmental visual disorder with problems in spatial vision including increased crowding effects and reduced contrast sensitivity (Achtman, Green, and Bavelier, 2008). Eastgate et al (2006) used cartoon displays and video game training presented in a virtual reality environment to improve interest in training sessions and training adherence in amblyopic children. The majority of children (87%) showed some improvement in their condition within three to four training sessions. The immediate improvements were evident to parents and children and almost all the children indicated a desire to use the training system (only 2/39 children refused the training system). Given these promising results, this has implications for the currently used approach of a long duration of training program to remediate this disorder. For example, it would appear that a virtual reality environment and video game package might, through effective short-term results, ensure better adherence rates to training programs by increasing patient motivation and interest levels. In the longer term this should result in significant improvements in this visual disorder.

Video games are also being used with stroke patients in order to reduce the impact of the visual deficits caused by strokes (Achtman et al, 2008). This training involves practice at making certain types of eye movements with a view to assist with everyday tasks such as reading. Given that the video game literature indicates a transfer of perceptual learning to other tasks it is possible that this is another area where video game practice may be useful in rehabilitation.

Evidence of the beneficial effects of video game training in various professions has also been reported in the literature. For example, laparoscopic surgery skills have been shown to positively correlate with video game playing experience (Rosser et al. 2007). This performance relationship was evident in fewer errors and faster surgery completion times for video game players. Although this study used correlation data it does suggest that the use of video games, particularly those related to surgery based tasks, may result in improved surgery outcomes.

A report by McKinley, McIntire and Funke (2009) showed that while trained pilots outperformed action video game players on a number of tasks that were specific to flying aircrafts, gamers and pilots performed equally well on the aircraft landing task. Video gamers performed better than pilots who performed better than control participants on tasks assessing the acquisition of visual information, and in tracking and identifying targets. These findings indicate that skills learned during video game play transfer to other tasks and hence video game training in addition to flight simulator training may be a viable option to assist in the training of skilled pilots.

CONCLUSION

The finding that expert video game players had better visual short-term memory skills than non-video game players adds to be body of knowledge investigating the impact of video game playing and training on cognitive functions. The results of the training study showed that while action video game training was linked to task practice effects, these results may have been due to poorer task performance at time 1 compared to time 2, allowing greater room for improvement across time. Action video game training also resulted in improved verbal short-term memory performance from time 1 to time 2. Further research is required to determine the relevant training parameters such as game type, and training duration to allow thorough investigation in this area. In addition various components of visual and verbal short-term memory and long-term memory should also be examined to fully understand the outcomes of video game training. By clearly understanding the impact of regular video game playing on cognitive functions this will allow further development of cognitive training and rehabilitation programs assisting with the development of professional skills, recovery from disorders, and the development of children.

AUTHOR NOTES

This research was supported by a Griffith University Research Grant and a Griffith University Business School grant awarded to Drs Murphy and Andrews.

REFERENCES

Achtman, R. L., Green, C. S., and Bavelier, D. (2008). Video games as a tool to train visual skills. *Restorative Neurology and Neuroscience, 26,* 435-446.
Anderson, C., and Bushman, B. (2001). Effects of violent video games on aggressive behaviour, aggressive cognition. *Psychological Science, 12,* 353-359
Anderson, C. A., and Dill, K. E. (2000). Video games and aggressive thoughts, feelings, and behaviour in the laboratory and in life. *Journal of Personality and Social Psychology, 78,* 772-790.
Andrews, G., and Murphy, K. (2006). Does video-game playing improve executive function? In M. A. Vanchevsky (Ed.) *Frontiers in Cognitive Sciences* (pp. 145-161). New York: Nova Science Publishers Inc.
Baddeley, A. (1986). *Working Memory*. Oxford: Oxford University Press.

Baddeley, A. (1990). *Human Memory: Theory and Practice*. East Sussex, UK: Lawrence Erlbaum Associates Ltd.

Baddeley, A., Thomson, N., and Buchanan, M. (1975). Word length and the structure of short-term memory. *Journal of Verbal Learning and Verbal Behaviour, 14*, 575-589.

Basak, C., Boot, W., Voss, M., and Kramer, A. (2008). Can training in a real-time strategy video game attenuate cognitive decline in older adults? *Psychology and Aging, 23*, 765-777.

Blackwell, G. (2002). Playing with fire? Computer gaming has been blamed for everything from obesity to school shootings. *Today's Parent, 19*, 72-75.

Boot, W. R., Kramer, A. F., Simons, D. J., Fabiani, M., and Gratton, G. (2008). The effects of video game playing on attention, memory, and executive control. *Acta Psychologica, 129*, 387-398.

Castel, A. D., Pratt, J., and Drummond, E. (2005). The effects of action video game experience on the time course of inhibition of return and the efficiency of visual search. *Acta Psychologica, 119*, 217-230.

Cermak, G. W. (1971). Short-term recognition for complex free-form figures, *Psychonomic science, 25*, 209-211.

Clark, J. E., Lanphear, A. K., and Riddick, C. C. (1987). The effects of videogame playing on the response selection processing of elderly adults. *Journal of Gerontology, 42*, 82-85.

Colzato, L. S., van Leeuwen, P. J. A., van den Wildenberg, W. P. M., and Hommel, B. (2010). DOOM'd to switch: Superior cognitive flexibility in players of first person shooter games. *Frontiers in Psychology, 1*, 1-18.

Cowan, N. (2000). The magical number 4 in short-term memory: A reconsideration of mental storage capacity. *Behavioral and Brain Sciences, 24*, 87-185.

Drew, D., and Waters, J. (1986). Video games: Utilization of a novel strategy to improve perceptual motor skills and cognitive functioning in the non-institutionalized elderly. *Cognitive Rehabilitation, 4*, 26–31.

Dunbar, G., Hill, R., and Lewis, V. (2001). Children's attentional skills and road behavior, *Journal of Experimental Psychology: Applied, 7*, 227–234.

Dye, M., Green, C., and Bavelier, D. (2009). Increasing speed of processing with action video games. *Current Directions in Psychological Science, 18*, 321.

Eastgate, R. M., Griffiths, G. D., Waddingham, P. E., Moody, A. D., Butler, T. K. H., Cobb, S. V et al. (2006) Modified virtual reality technology for treatment of amblyopia. *Eye, 20*, 370–374.

Feng, J., Spence, I., and Pratt, J. (2007). Playing an action video game reduces gender differences in spatial cognition. *Psychological Science, 18*, 850-855.

Forster, K. I., and Forster, J. C. (2003). DMDX: A windows display program with millisecond accuracy. *Behaviour Research Methods, Instruments, and Computers, 35*, 116-124.

Gagnon, G. (1985). Videogames and spatial skills: An exploratory study. *Educational Communication and Technology Journal, 33*, 263-275.

Green, C. S., and Bavelier, D. (2003). Action video game modifies visual selective attention. *Nature, 423*, 534-537.

Green, C., and Bavelier, D. (2006a). Effect of action video games on the spatial distribution of visuospatial attention. *Journal of experimental psychology: Human perception and performance, 32*, 1465-1478.

Green, C., and Bavelier, D. (2006b). Enumeration versus multiple object tracking: The case of action video game players. *Cognition, 101*, 217-245.

Green, C., and Bavelier, D. (2007). Action-video-game experience alters the spatial resolution of vision. *Psychological Science, 18*, 88.

Green, C. S., and Bavelier, D. (2008). Exercising your brain: A review of human brain plasticity and training-induced learning. *Psychology and Aging, 23*, 692-701.

Greenfield, P. M., Brannon, C., and Lohr, D. (1994). Two-dimensional representation of movement through three-dimensional space: The role of video game expertise. *Journal of Applied Developmental Psychology, 15*, 87-103.

Greenfield, P. M., DeWinstanley, P., Kilpatrick, H., and Kaye, D. (1994). Action video games and informal education: Effects on strategies for dividing visual attention. *Journal of Applied Developmental Psychology, 15*, 105-123.

Hulme, C., Newton, P., Cowan, N., Stuart, G., and Brown, G. (1999). Think before you speak: Pauses, memory search and trace redintegration processes in verbal memory span. *Journal of Experimental Psychology: Learning, Memory and Cognition, 25*, 447-463.

Jiang, Y., Olson, I., and Chun, M. (2000). Organization of visual short-term memory. *Learning, Memory, 26*, 683-702.

Karle, J. W., Watter, S., and Shedden, J. M. (2010). Task switching in video game players: Benefits of selective attention but not resistance to proactive interference. *Acta Psychologica, 134*, 70-78.

Logie, R. H., and Baddeley, A. D. (1987). Cognitive processes in counting. *Journal of Experimental Psychology: Learning, Memory and Cognition 13*, 310-326.

Luck, S., and Vogel, E. (1997). The capacity of visual working memory for features and conjunctions. *Nature, 390*(6657), 279-280.

McKinley, R., McIntire, L., and Funke, M. (2009). Operator selection for unmanned aerial vehicle operators: A comparison of video game players and manned aircraft pilots. Unpublished Report.

Miller, G. A. (1956). The magical number seven, plus or minus two: Some limits on our capacity for processing information. *Psychological Review, 63*, 81-97.

Okagaki, L., and Frensch, P. A. (1994). Effects of video game playing on measures of spatial performance: Gender effects in late adolescence. *Journal of Applied Developmental Psychology, 15*, 33-58.

Phillips, W. A. (1974). On the distinction between sensory storage and short-term visual memory. *Perception and Psychophysics, 16*, 283-290.

Phillips, W. A., and Baddeley, A. (1971). Reaction time and short-term visual memory. *Psychonomic Science, 22*, 73-74.

Robinson, T. N. (1999). Reducing children's television viewing to prevent obesity: A randomized controlled trial. *Journal of the American Medical Association, 282*, 1561-1567.

Roodenrys, S., Hulme, C., Lethbridge, A., Hinton, M., and Nimmo, L. M. (2002). Word-frequency and phonological-neighbourhood effects on verbal short-term memory. *Journal of Experimental Psychology: Learning, Memory and Cognition, 28*, 1019-1034.

Rosser, J. C., Lynch, P. J., Cuddihy, L., Gentile, D. A. Kolnsky, J. and Merrell, R. (2007). The impact of video game on training surgeons in the 21st century. *Archives of Surgery, 142*, 181-186

Salame, P., and Baddeley, A. (1982). Disruption of short-term memory by unattended speech: Implications for the structure of working memory. *Journal of Verbal Learning and Verbal Behaviour, 21*, 150-164.

Sayten, L (2003). *Improving skills of divided attention.* Poster presented at the International Conference on Cognitive Science, University of New South Wales, Sydney Australia.

Subrahmanyam, K., and Greenfield, P. M. (1994). Effect of video game practice on spatial skills in girls and boys. *Journal of Applied Developmental Psychology, 15,* 13-32.

Trick, L. M., Jaspers-Fayer, F., and Sethi, N. (2005). Multiple-object tracking in children: The "Catch the Spies" task. *Cognitive Development, 20,* 373-387.

Trick, L. M. (2005). The role of working memory in spatial enumeration: Patterns of selective interference in subitizing and counting. *Psychonomic Bulletin and Review, 12,* 675-681

Van Schie, E. G., and Wiegman, O. (1997). Children and video games: Leisure activities, aggression, social interaction, and school performance. *Journal of Applied Social Psychology, 27,* 1175-1194.

Vogel, E., Woodman, G., and Luck, S. (2001). Storage of features, conjunctions, and objects in visual working memory. *Journal of Experimental Psychology, 27,* 92-114.

O'Regan, J., Rensink, R., and Clark, J. (1999). Change-blindness as a result of 'mudsplashes'. *Nature, 398*(6722), 34.

Wiegman, O., and Van Schie, E. (1998). Video game playing and its relations with aggressive and prosocial behaviour. *The British Journal of Social Psychology, 37,* 367-378.

Willis, S. L., Tennstedt, S. L., Marsiske, M., Ball, K., Elias, J., Koepke, K. M. et al. (2006). Long-term effects of cognitive training on everyday functional outcomes in older adults. *The Journal of the American Medical Association, 296,* 2805–2814.

Chapter 2

PRIOR EXPOSURE TO WORDS IN MEANINGFUL CONCEPTUAL HIERARCHIES IMPROVES RECALL OF RANDOMLY ARRANGED WORDS

Glenda Andrews[1]*, Joanne M. Todd, Jade Maurer, Kaya Beinke, Robert Teese and Magnus Reiestad
Behavioural Basis of Health Program, Griffith Health Institute &
School of Psychology, Griffith University, Gold Coast Campus
4222 Australia.

ABSTRACT

The research investigated the effects of meaningful organisation and presentation order on undergraduates' free recall of words. All participants studied words that were presented in meaningful conceptual hierarchies and words that were presented in randomly arranged displays. The same spatial layout was used in both types of display. The classic finding of superior recall for conceptually organised words was replicated. We extended previous research by also examining the effects of presentation order. Fifty percent of students received the conceptually organised words before the randomly arranged words and the remainder received the reverse order. Prior exposure to conceptually organised words facilitated recall of subsequently presented randomly arranged words. Indices of relational processing and item-specific processing suggested that the observed enhancement in recall reflects increased relational processing of the randomly arranged words for the participants who received the conceptually organised words first. The findings are discussed in terms of their implications for improving study skills and for encouraging relational processing in individuals with Asperger's syndrome who tend to rely more on item-specific processing in free recall tasks.

---

[1] E-mail: g.andrews@griffith.edu.au

INTRODUCTION

Research in human memory has demonstrated that study materials that are arranged in a meaningful manner are easier to remember than similar materials that are randomly arranged (Bower, Clark, Lesgold, and Winzenz, 1969). The research reported in this chapter builds on this classic finding by examining whether prior encoding and recall of organised words affects subsequent encoding and recall of randomly arranged words. This research has practical implications for programs designed to enhance students' study skills, to remediate problems following brain injury, and to improve memory performance in general. We start by providing a brief review of research findings relevant to the effects of organisation on recall. We then describe our research and interpret our empirical findings. Finally, we will consider some practical applications of our findings.

Researchers of human memory have investigated the effects of organisation using a range of methods. One such method involves recall of categorised words. Recall is better if the study list consists of multiple instances of a small number of taxonomic categories (e.g., animals, vegetables, professions) than if the list consists of conceptually unrelated words. Recall is further improved if the words in the categorised lists are grouped according to category, for example, if all animal words are presented in sequence followed by all vegetable words and so on. Grouping during the study phase also increases clustering in recall. Clustering occurs when several instances of the same category are reported in succession. For example, several animal words might be recalled one after another, followed by a group of profession or vegetable words (Cofer, Bruce, and Reicher, 1966). The presence of clustering is usually interpreted as evidence that participants detected the conceptual relations among the study items and used this relational information to facilitate retrieval.

Despite these positive findings, Bower et al. (1969) noted that the size of the observed effects were usually quite small. They proposed a more potent manipulation of organisation which differed in three ways from earlier research. The first modification was that the words to be recalled included category labels (e.g., fruit) as well as instances of the categories (e.g., apple, banana). The second modification was that each set of words corresponded to a 4-level conceptual hierarchy of nested categories, such that words at higher and lower levels formed class inclusion relationships. For example, the conceptual hierarchy for occupations is shown in Figure 1. The general category occupations (Level 1) can be organised according to their primary funding sources into two subcategories, public and private (Level 2), each of which includes further subcategories, namely government and education within public occupations and construction, business, and professional within private occupations (Level 3). Each of these level 3 subcategories contains multiple instances (Level 4). The third modification was that Bower et al. presented complete sets of words for simultaneous study, whereas previous research had presented words one at a time. These changes were intended to make it easier for participants to discover the conceptual relations among the study words. This in turn was expected to enhance encoding and retrieval of the words.

The impact of these modifications was evident in Bower et al.'s (1969) findings. In Experiment 1, free recall was 3.5 times better when words were presented in meaningful conceptual hierarchies than when the same words were intermixed and presented in a random arrangement, but using the same spatial layout. This finding was replicated in Experiment 2, which tested recognition as well as free recall. As with free recall, recognition was higher for words presented in conceptual hierarchies. However, the difference between conceptually organised displays and randomly arranged displays was smaller for recognition than for free recall. This difference was interpreted as showing that the effect is (in part) a retrieval phenomenon. Retrieval demands are lower in recognition tests than in free recall tests therefore independent variables that impact on retrieval have weaker effects on recognition than on recall. Subsequent studies (Atwood and Shavelson, 1976; Wittrock and Carter, 1975) using modified versions of Bower et al.'s (1969) procedure replicated the finding that meaningful organisation enhances free recall, although the effect sizes were not always as large as those observed by Bower et al.

While the effect of semantic organisation on recall continues to be of interest to researchers (e.g., Guerin and Miller, 2008), Bower et al.'s (1969) method appears to have fallen into disuse. Our literature search revealed just one recent study using Bower et al.'s method. This was Bowler, Gaigg, and Gardiner's (2009) research examining free recall in adults with and without a diagnosis of Asperger's Syndrome. Earlier research had yielded mixed evidence regarding the extent to which individuals with autism spectrum disorders such as Asperger's Syndrome make use of the semantic relations of learned material to aid their recall. Bowler et al. found that although the comparison group's free recall was marginally higher than the Asperger's group, both groups showed significant effects of organisation. Free recall was superior for words presented in meaningful conceptual hierarchies than for randomly arranged words. In Bowler et al.'s research, all participants received both conceptually organised and randomly arranged words, whereas earlier studies had employed between-groups designs in which different groups of participants received different display types. The findings demonstrated the facilitative effects of organisation in a within-subjects design. Bowler et al. interpreted their findings in terms of the distinction between item-specific processing and relational processing, which built on a distinction proposed by Hunt and Einstein (1981).

According to Hunt and Einstein (1981), relational processing involves encoding the similarities among a class of events. It results in a representation that is highly integrated and organised around the commonalities within the study materials. By contrast, individual-item processing involves encoding item-specific information that emphasises the distinctiveness of individual items. Hunt and Einstein argued that relational and individual-item processing produce qualitatively different memory traces and that both types of information are useful for optimal memory. Their empirical research supported these claims, and showed that orienting instructions in the study phase and characteristics of the study material influence the extent to which participants engage in individual-item processing and relational processing.

Gaigg, Gardiner, and Bowler (2008) claimed that item-specific processing allows individuals to make use of the links between each item and their existing knowledge base, which includes the categories to which the items belong (e.g., apple-fruit; horse-animal). Thus their interpretation of item-specific processing appears broader than Hunt and Einstein's (1981) view that individual-item processing emphasises item distinctiveness and the differences between items.

According to Gaigg et al. (2008) individuals with Asperger's Syndrome have a tendency to engage more in item-specific processing than in relational processing of the study items. They are less inclined to engage in relational processing which would be required to make use of the more complex relationships among the items in multi-level conceptual hierarchies of the type used by Bower et al. (1969). These complex hierarchical relations require a higher level of awareness than the inter-item associations (Gaigg et al., 2008). The claim that hierarchical relations are more complex than class membership is consistent with relational complexity theory (Halford, Wilson, and Phillips, 1998). It is also consistent with empirical findings in cognitive development research showing that inferences based on classification hierarchies emerge later in development than inferences based on category membership (Andrews and Halford, 2002; Halford, Andrews, and Jensen, 2002).

Consistent with this, Bowler et al. (2009) found that their comparison group's higher recall performance reflected their greater use of relational processing. This was inferred from their higher category-access scores. Category-access scores reflected the proportion of Level-3 categories from which at least one word was recalled. The Asperger's group had significantly lower category-access scores than the comparison group. The Asperger's and comparison groups did not differ in item-specific processing, as inferred from the items per category scores. Items-per-category scores reflect the average proportion of Level-4 words recalled from the Level 3 categories. Thus, the Asperger's group retrieved as many Level 4 words as the comparison group but the words were drawn from fewer of the Level 3 categories. Participants in the comparison group were better able to represent the hierarchical relations and this facilitated access to and sampling from the Level 3 categories. The distinction between item-specific and relational processing provides a useful way to understand the memory-related difficulties experienced by individuals with Asperger's syndrome (Gaigg et al., 2008).

As noted already, in Bowler et al.'s (2009) study all participants received both conceptually organised and randomly arranged words. This appears to be the only published study that has used a within-subjects design to examine the effects of conceptual organisation on free recall. However, Bowler et al. included only a single order of presentation. All participants received the randomly arranged words before the conceptually organised words. The order was fixed to avoid alerting participants to the conceptual relations in the words sets. The authors reasoned that if the conceptually organised words had been presented first, recall of the randomly arranged words (presented second) would have been facilitated, thereby reducing the difference between conceptually organised and random conditions. Thus, while Bowler et al.'s work provides no evidence relevant to the effect of presentation order, their justification for using a constant order of presentation implies that prior exposure to conceptually organised words would facilitate recall of randomly arranged words, at least for unimpaired participants.

Our search of the literature failed to find any studies in which presentation order of conceptually organised and randomly arranged words was manipulated. However, Bower et al. (Experiment 4, 1969) employed a within-subjects design to examine the effects of organisation and presentation order, using associatively-related rather than conceptually-related words. One of the associatively-related word sets consisted of words associated with cheese. This and other word sets were generated by starting with an initial Level 1 word, in this case, cheese. Three different words (bread, mouse, and yellow) that were all strong verbal associates of cheese were then chosen as Level 2 words. Two strong verbal associates for each of the Level 2 words were then selected as Level 3 words. The Level 3 words were milk and wheat (associated with bread), cat and trap (associated with mouse) and sun and butterfly (associated with yellow). Finally two verbal associates for each of the six Level 3 words were then selected as Level 4 words, using the same process. As Bower et al. noted, while the associative links between successive word pairs were intuitively sensible, the connections among more distant words were sensible only by virtue of their intervening pairwise associations between adjacent words. Furthermore, there was no sense in which the any of the Level 2, 3, or 4 words could be interpreted as labels for members of the superordinate class, cheese.

Participants received the organised words on day 1 and randomly arranged words on day 2, or the reverse order. The spatial layout of the words was the same as in their earlier experiments. Free recall was higher for associatively organised than randomly arranged words, although recall of associative hierarchies was poorer than for the conceptual hierarchies used in earlier experiments. This suggests that conceptual relations provide stronger retrieval cues than associative relations. There was no significant effect of presentation order on recall of associatively-organised or randomly arranged words. Experiencing the organised lists first did not facilitate recall of the random lists. However, given that Bower et al.'s (1969) null finding was obtained using associatively-related words, and with a long interval between the two conditions, it remains possible that prior presentation of conceptually-related words will facilitate recall of subsequently presented randomly arranged words when the words are presented in the same session.

The present research addressed this question using a within-subjects design with presentation order counterbalanced. All participants received two displays in which words were conceptually organised and two displays in which the words were randomly arranged. Participants were assigned to one of two presentation orders: conceptually organised displays first or randomly arranged displays first. There was a free recall test following each display type. Three dependent variables were derived from the free recall responses. These were free recall accuracy, category-access scores and items-per-category scores. The frequency of repetition and intrusion errors was also checked.

We expected to replicate the effect of display type observed in previous studies (Atwood and Shavelson, 1976; Bower et al., 1969; Bowler et al., 2009; Wittrock and Carter, 1975). Participants were expected to recall more words from conceptually organised displays than from randomly arranged displays. To the extent that conceptual organisation facilitates relational processing and item-specific processing, higher category-access and items-per-category scores were expected for conceptually organised displays than for randomly arranged displays. This would replicate Bowler et al.'s (2009) findings.

Use of a within-subjects design in which all participants serve in both conditions, and in which presentation order of the conditions was counterbalanced, allowed us to examine the effect of presentation order. More specifically, we examined whether prior presentation of words in conceptually organised displays facilitates recall of subsequently presented words that are randomly arranged. If so, then a further question is whether this occurs through enhanced relational processing or through enhanced item-specific processing or through enhancements in both types of processing. If relational processing can be facilitated, this would have implications for interventions aimed at improving relational processing in persons with Asperger's syndrome and in other populations where relational processing deficits are present.

METHOD

Participants

The participants were 48 undergraduate students (11 males, 37 females) enrolled in an introductory psychology course at Griffith University, Australia. Their mean age was 22.67 years (*SD* = 7.08). Twelve participants received each of the four versions of the task which are described below.

Materials

The stimuli were 104 words, 26 words from each of four semantic categories; organisms, foods, occupations, and minerals. The four word lists, which are shown in Table 1, were drawn from Bower et al. (1969) and St James, Schneider, and Rogers (1994).

Table 1. Word Lists Used to Construct the Conceptually Organised and Randomly Arranged Displays

List			
1	2	3	4
accountant	bear	alloys	animal
business	carnation	aluminium	apple
carpenter	cedar	brass	banana
clerk	collie	bronze	beans
construction	cow	common	butter
dentist	dogs	copper	cheese
education	domestic	diamond	corn
engineer	elephant	emerald	cream
governor	flowers	gold	dairy
government	horse	granite	fish
lawyer	huskie	iron	foods
manager	lion	lead	fruit
mason	mammals	limestone	hamburger
mayor	maple	marble	milk
occupation	oak	masonry	meat
physician	organisms	metals	peach
plumber	ox	minerals	pear
principal	pine	platinum	peas
private	plants	precious	pork
professional	poodle	rare	salmon
professor	rose	ruby	sausage
public	sheep	sapphire	steak
senator	tiger	silver	trout
salesman	trees	slate	tuna
teacher	tulip	steel	vegetables
welder	wild	stones	vegetarian

Four versions of the experiment were created to avoid confounding word list with display type and presentation order. The same words were used in all versions, but no participants encountered the same words in both the conceptually organised and the randomlyarranged conditions.

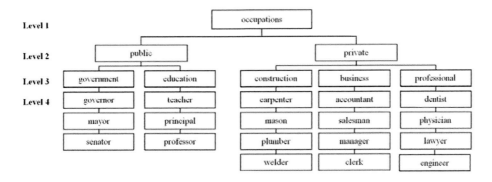

Figure 1. An example of a conceptually organised word display. Levels 1, 2, 3 and 4 are indicated here only to facilitate description. They did not appear in the displays used in the research.

In versions A and C, the words from the occupations and minerals categories were arranged into two separate meaningful conceptual hierarchies. The occupations hierarchy is as shown in Figure 1. The 26 words from List 1 in Table 1 were distributed over four levels of the hierarchy. At the topmost level, Level 1, there was one word which was the label for the superordinate category, *occupations*. At Level 2, there were two words which were labels for two subclasses of the superordinate category (*public* and *private*). At Level 3, there were five words which were the labels for two or three subordinate classes of each of the Level 2 subclasses. That is, *government* and *education* were the labels of subordinate classes of public occupations, and *construction*, *business* and *professional* were the labels of the subordinate classes of private occupations. At Level 4, the eighteen words were instances of the five Level 3 subordinate classes. The words from the minerals category (List 3 in Table 1) were likewise arranged into a separate meaningful conceptual hierarchy. The words from the organisms and foods hierarchies (Lists 2 and 4 in Table 1) were intermixed. They were presented in random order on two slides using the same spatial layout as the conceptually organised word sets. Figure 2 shows an example of a randomly arranged display. Note that the arrangement is random and not meaningful. The words at Levels 1, 2, 3 and 4 do not form a conceptual hierarchy. In versions B and D, the words from the organisms and foods categories were arranged into separate meaningful conceptual hierarchies. The words from the occupations and minerals hierarchies were intermixed and presented in random order on two slides using the same spatial layout as the conceptually organised word sets.

In versions A and D, the conceptually organised hierarchies were presented before the randomly arranged hierarchies, whereas in versions B and C the randomly arranged hierarchies were presented before the conceptually organised hierarchies. Thus, versions A and D constitute one presentation order, conceptually organised first. Versions B and C constitute the other presentation order, randomly arranged first.

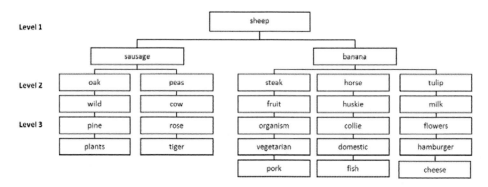

Figure 2. An example of a randomly arranged display. Levels 1, 2, 3 and 4 are indicated here only to facilitate description. They did not appear in the displays used in the research.

Procedure

All participants received two study-test sequences. The same procedures were used for the conceptually organised and randomly arranged displays. The words were presented using PowerPoint software running on a laptop computer. Screen images were projected onto a large white screen that was easily visible to all participants. Instructions were displayed on the screen and were also read aloud by the experimenter. In each study phase, two sets of words were displayed, one set at a time for 1 minute per set. Participants studied the words while they are displayed. A written free recall test was administered after the second word set of each study phase. Participants were allowed 3 minutes to recall as many of the study words as possible and to write them on the recall sheet provided. The words could be recalled in any order.

Design

The within-subjects independent variable was display type. It had two levels, conceptually organised and randomly arranged. The between-subjects independent variable was presentation order. It had two levels, conceptually organised first and randomly arranged first. The dependent variable was the total number of words recalled. Two additional dependent variables were computed. Category-access scores reflected the proportion of Level 3 categories from which at least one Level 4 word was recalled. Items-per-category scores corresponded to the average proportion of words recalled from each of the Level 3 categories.

RESULTS

Preliminary analyses showed that there were no significant differences in free recall, items-per-category scores or category-access scores, and intrusions between versions A and D in which the conceptually organised displays were presented before the randomly arranged displays. Similarly, were there no significant differences between versions B and C in which the randomly arranged displays were presented before the conceptually organised displays. Therefore the data were collapsed across this distinction.

The mean age of the participants in the two presentation orders did not differ, $t(46) = 0.90$, $p = .38$, and there was no significant association between presentation order and gender balance, $\chi^2 (N = 48, 1) = 0.12$, $p = .731$.

Free Recall

Mean recall scores for the conceptually organised and randomly arranged displays in the two presentation orders are shown in Table 2. A mixed 2 (display type) × 2 (presentation order) ANOVA revealed a significant main effect of display type, $F(1, 46) = 94.21$, $p < .001$, $\eta_p^2 = .672$. Free recall was higher for conceptually organised displays ($M = 26.98$; $SE = 1.13$) than for randomly arranged displays ($M = 16.65$; $SE = 0.66$). The main effect of presentation order, $F(1, 46) = 0.19$, $p = .66$, $\eta_p^2 = .004$, was not significant. However, there was a significant Display type × Presentation order interaction, $F(1, 46) = 9.08$, $p = .004$, $\eta_p^2 = .165$. Our hypotheses related to the effects of both presentation order and display type, therefore the interaction was partitioned by each variable in turn. This interaction was first investigated by examining the effect of display type within each presentation order. Paired sample t-tests showed that mean free recall scores were significantly higher for the conceptually organised displays than for the randomly arranged displays when the randomly arranged displays were presented first, $t(23) = 8.24$, $p < .001$, and also when the conceptually organised displays were presented first, $t(23) = 5.26$, $p < .001$.

Table 2. Mean (SE) Number of Words Recalled from the Conceptually Organised and Randomly Arranged Displays in each Presentation Order Condition. $N = 48$

Presentation Order	Display type	
	Conceptually organised	Randomly arranged
Randomly arranged first	28.25	14.71
	(1.60)	(0.94)
Conceptually organised first	25.71	18.58
	(1.60)	(0.94)

Sign tests confirmed that these effects of display type were not due to a small number of individuals. In the randomly arranged displays first condition, 96% of participants had higher recall for the conceptually organised than for the randomly arranged displays, $p < .001$. In the conceptually organised displays first condition, 87.5% of participants had higher recall for the conceptually organised than for the randomly arranged displays, $p < .001$. The interaction was further investigated by examining the effects of presentation order on free recall for each display type. Independent samples t-tests showed that the group that received the conceptually organised displays first recalled significantly more words from the randomly arranged displays than did the group that received the randomly arranged displays first, $t(46) = 2.93$, $p = .005$. However, there was no significant effect of presentation order on recall of words from the conceptually organised displays, $t(46) = 1.22$, $p = .27$. Thus, prior exposure to the conceptually organised displays appears to have increased recall of randomly arranged words to a level that is higher than that observed for the participants who received the randomly arranged words first. Recall of conceptually organised words was not affected by presentation order.

Item-Per-Category Scores

Table 3 shows the mean items-per-category scores for the conceptually organised and randomly arranged displays in the two presentation orders. A mixed 2 (display type) × 2 (presentation order) ANOVA revealed a significant main effect of display type, $F(1,46) = 57.85$, $p < .001$, $\eta_p^2 = .557$. Mean items-per-category scores were higher for words from conceptually organised displays ($M = .505$; $SE = .024$) than for words from randomly arranged displays ($M = .335$; $SE = .013$). The main effect of presentation order, $F(1, 46) = 0.61$ $p = .44$, $\eta_p^2 = .013$, was not significant. However, there was a significant Display type × Presentation order interaction, $F(1, 46) = 5.30$, $p = .026$, $\eta_p^2 = .103$.

Paired sample t-tests showed that mean items-per-category scores were significantly higher for words from the conceptually organised displays than the randomly arranged displays when the randomly arranged words were presented first, $t(23) = 6.15$, $p < .001$, and also when the conceptually organised displays were presented first, $t(23) = 4.47$, $p < .001$.

Sign tests confirmed that these effects of display type were not due to a small number of individuals. In the randomly arranged displays first condition, 92% of participants had higher items-per-category scores for the conceptually organised than for the randomly arranged displays, $p < .001$. In the conceptually organised displays first condition, 79% of participants had higher items-per-category scores for the conceptually organised than for the randomly arranged displays, $p = .007$.

Independent samples t-tests showed that the group that received the conceptually organised words first had significantly higher items-per-category scores for words from the randomly arranged displays than did the group that received the randomly arranged displays first, $t(46) = 2.86$, $p = .006$. However, there was no significant effect of presentation order on items-per-category scores for the conceptually organised displays, $t(46) = 0.58$, $p = .567$. The pattern of findings for the items-per-category scores parallels the pattern for free recall.

Table 3. Mean (SE) Items-per-Category (IPC) scores for the Conceptually Organised and Randomly Arranged Displays in each Presentation Order Condition. $N = 48$

Presentation Order	Display type	
	Conceptually organised	Randomly arranged
Randomly arranged first	0.519 (0.033)	0.297 (0.019)
Conceptually organised first	0.492 (0.033)	0.373 (0.019)

Category-Access Scores

Table 4 shows the mean category-access scores for words from the conceptually organised and randomly arranged displays in the two presentation orders. A mixed 2 (display type) × 2 (presentation order) ANOVA revealed a significant main effect of display type, $F(1,46) = 8.72$, $p = .005$, $\eta_p^2 = .159$. Mean category-access scores were higher for conceptually organised displays ($M = .781$; $SE = .02$) than for randomly arranged displays ($M = .715$; $SE = .022$). The main effect of presentation order, $F(1, 46) = 0.51$, $p = .48$, $\eta_p^2 = .011$, was not significant. However, there was a significant Display type × Presentation order interaction, $F(1, 46) = 5.75$, $p = .021$, $\eta_p^2 = .111$.

Table 4. Mean (SE) Category-Access scores for the Conceptually Organised and Randomly Arranged Displays in each Presentation Order. $N = 48$

Presentation Order	Display type	
	Conceptually organised	Randomly arranged
Randomly arranged first	0.796 (0.028)	0.675 (0.031)
Conceptually organised first	0.767 (0.031)	0.754 (0.031)

Paired sample t-tests showed that mean category-access scores were significantly higher for the conceptually organised displays than for the randomly arranged displays when the randomly arranged displays were presented first, $t(23) = 3.22$, $p = .004$, but not when the conceptually organised displays were presented first, $t(23) = 0.50$, $p = .622$.

Sign tests revealed a similar pattern. In the randomly arranged displays first condition, 67% of participants had higher category-access scores for the conceptually organised than for the randomly arranged displays, $p = .004$. In the conceptually organised displays first condition, 33.3% of participants had higher category-access scores for the conceptually organised than for the randomly arranged displays, $p = 1.00$ (ns).

T-tests for independent samples showed that the group that received the conceptually organised displays first had higher category-access scores for the randomly arranged displays than did the group that received the randomly arranged displays first, $t(46) = 1.80$, $p = .039$ (one-tailed). However, there was no significant effect of presentation order on category-access scores for the conceptually organised displays, $t(46) = 0.74$, $p = .464$.

Thus, prior exposure to the conceptually organised words appears to have increased relational processing of randomly arranged words to a level that is comparable to that observed on conceptually organised words and higher than that of the group who received the randomly arranged words first.

Correlations

To the extent that processing of conceptually organised words influenced subsequent processing of the randomly arranged words, we would expect significant correlations across the two display types, but only when the conceptually organised words were presented first. The correlations among free recall, items-per-category scores, and category-access scores for each display type were computed separately for the two presentation order conditions. They are shown in Table 5.

Table 5. Zero-Order Correlations Among Item-per-Category (IPC) scores and Category-Access (CA) scores for Randomly Arranged and for Conceptually Organised Displays in the Randomly Arranged Displays First (above the diagonal) and the Conceptually Organised Displays First (below diagonal) Conditions

	Recall random	Recall organised	IPC random	IPC organised	CA random	CA organised
Recall random		.36	.96***	.33	.76**	.25
Recall organised	.46*		.30	.98***	.29	.80***
IPC random	.94***	.49*		.27	.76***	.15
IPC organised	.51*	.94***	.50*		.26	.80***
CA random	.60**	.79***	.64**	.81***		.09
CA organised	.57**	.66***	.57**	.72***	.69***	

$^*p < .05; ** p < .01; *** p < .001$.

For the randomly arranged displays first condition (shown above the diagonal in Table 5), the correlations within each display type were all significant and positive. That is, free recall, items-per-category, and category-access scores for the randomly arranged displays were significantly inter-correlated. Similarly, free recall, items-per-category, and category-access scores for the conceptually organised displays were significantly inter-correlated. However, none of the correlations involving both display types reached significance. For example, the correlation between category-access scores for randomly arranged words and category-access scores for conceptually organised words was not significant.

For the conceptually organised displays first condition (shown below the diagonal in Table 5) the correlations within each display type were all significant and positive. In addition, all the correlations involving different display types reached significance. Of particular interest is the significant positive correlation between category-access scores for randomly arranged words and category-access scores for conceptually organised words. This association remained significant when recall from the randomly arranged displays was controlled, r (21) = .52, p = .01, which was not the case for the items-per-category scores, r (21) = -.17, p = .43. This pattern of results is consistent with a carry-over of relational processing from the conceptually organised displays to the subsequently presented randomly arranged displays.

Repetitions and Intrusions

Further analyses were conducted to examine the extent to which repetition errors and intrusion errors were made. The overall number of repetitions was very low (M = .052; SE = .022). A mixed 2 (display type) × 2 (presentation order) ANOVA revealed no significant main effects and no significant interaction.

Intrusion errors occur when category instances that were not actually presented during study are reported. For example, although *doctor* is an instance of the superordinate category *occupations,* it was not presented during the study phase, therefore reporting *doctor* constitutes an intrusion error. The overall number of intrusions across the four displays was very low ($M = 1.50$; $SE = .20$). The means for each condition are shown in Table 6. A mixed 2 (display type) × 2 (presentation order) ANOVA revealed a marginally significant main effect of display type, $F(1,46) = 3.30$, $p = .07$, $\eta_p^2 = .067$, reflecting a trend toward more intrusions for the conceptually organised displays ($M = .917$; $SE = .152$) than for randomly arranged displays ($M = .583$; $SE = .116$). The main effect of presentation order, $F(1, 46) = 0.71$, $p = .41$, $\eta_p^2 = .015$, was not significant. However, there was a significant Display type × Presentation order interaction, $F(1, 46) = 10.11$, $p = .003$, $\eta_p^2 = .18$. Paired sample *t*-tests showed that the mean number of intrusions was significantly higher for the conceptually organised displays than for the randomly arranged displays when the randomly arranged words were presented first, $t(23) = 3.25$, $p = .004$, but not when the conceptually organised words were presented first, $t(23) = 1.06$, $p = .30$. *T*-tests for independent samples showed that the group that received the randomly arranged displays first made more intrusion errors on the conceptually organised displays than did the group that received the conceptually organised displays first, $t(46) = 2.47$, $p = .017$. The group that received the conceptually organised displays first tended to make more intrusion errors on the randomly arranged displays, $t(46) = -1.80$, $p = .039$ (one-tailed), than did the group that received the randomly arranged displays first.

Table 6. Mean (SE) Number of Intrusion Errors for the Conceptually Organised and Randomly Arranged Displays in each Presentation Order. $N = 48$

Presentation Order	Display type	
	Conceptually organised	Randomly arranged
Randomly arranged first	1.292 (0.215)	0.375 (0.164)
Conceptually organised first	0.542 (0.215)	0.792 (0.164)

The forgoing analyses showed that the pattern of intrusion errors differed as a function of presentation order. To ensure that these differences do not compromise interpretation of the findings, a further set of analyses was conducted in which the dependent variable was corrected recall scores. Corrected recall scores were computed by reducing the free recall scores (Table 2) by the number of intrusion errors (Table 6). This was done for each participant and for each display type. A mixed 2 (display type) × 2 (presentation order) ANOVA with follow-up tests yielded the same pattern of significance as was reported earlier for free recall.

DISCUSSION

The classic finding that organised material is easier to recall than randomly arranged material was replicated in the present study. More words were recalled from conceptually organised displays than from randomly arranged displays. This is consistent with Bowler et al. (2009) who also used a within-subjects manipulation of organisation, and also with earlier studies (e.g., Atwood and Shavelson, 1976; Bower et al., 1969; Wittrock and Carter, 1975) in which between-groups designs were employed. However, the findings for the two presentation orders differed in some respects, so each condition will be described in turn, then the differences will be highlighted.

For the group that received the randomly arranged displays first, the present findings for free recall, items-per-category and category-access scores parallel those of Bowler et al. (2009), who used this presentation order exclusively. In that study and in the present one, free recall, items-per-category and category-access scores were higher for the conceptually organised words than the randomly arranged words. This suggests that the enhanced recall of conceptually organised words reflects both item-specific and relational processing. The links between instances of the same category and the relations between categories at different levels of the hierarchies were readily apparent in the conceptually organised displays, and would have been available to serve as effective retrieval cues. These links were also present in the randomly arranged displays but they would have been far less obvious because the words from two lists were intermixed and distributed over two displays. Consequently, the links were less likely to be encoded and less likely to be available as retrieval cues. The pattern of intrusion errors is also consistent with this explanation. This group had very few intrusions for the randomly arranged words, presumably because the conceptual relations were not obvious in the random displays. By contrast, this group had significantly more intrusions for the conceptually organised words, where the conceptual relationships were more obvious.

For the group that received the conceptually organised displays first, free recall and items-per-category scores were higher for the conceptually organised words than the randomly arranged words. However, the category-access scores for the randomly arranged and conceptually organised displays did not differ significantly. Inspection of the means in Table 4 suggests that this is due to increased relational processing of the randomly arranged words, rather than reduced relational processing of the conceptually organised words. Experiencing the organised displays first appears to have alerted participants to the possibility that subsequently encountered words were also conceptually linked (Bowler et al., 2009). This might have prompted them to search for the categories and to impose their own organisation on the randomly arranged displays. Examination of differences between the two presentation orders and the Display type × Presentation order interactions provides further clarification. While there was no evidence that memory for the conceptually arranged words was sensitive to presentation order, this was not the case for randomly arranged words. Prior exposure to the conceptually organised displays facilitated free recall of the randomly arranged words. This appears to be a new finding, which reflects increased relational processing in the group that received the conceptually organised displays first. For this group, category-access scores for the randomly arranged words increased to a level that was not significantly different from the conceptually organised words, while the corresponding items-per-category scores remained significantly below the level observed for conceptually organised words. A carry-over of relational processing might also explain the trend for this group to make more intrusion errors on randomly arranged words compared to the group who received the randomly arranged words first. The correlational findings also supported the interpretation of a carry-over in relational processing from the conceptually organised displays to the randomly arranged displays.

A possible alternative interpretation of our findings is that the higher free recall, items-per-category scores, and category-access scores for the randomly arranged words in the group that received the conceptually organised displays first relative to the group that received the randomly arranged displays first reflects increased familiarity with the study-test procedure by the second study-test phase. Considered in isolation, this seems plausible. However, if this explanation were correct, we might expect a group difference in the opposite direction for the conceptually organised displays, that is, higher free recall, items-per-category scores, and category-access scores for the conceptually organised words in the group that received the randomly arranged display first. The means in Tables 2, 3, and 4 show numerical differences in this direction, but none of these differences reached significance. Furthermore, it is unclear how increased familiarity with procedures would account for the correlational evidence, and for the pattern of intrusion errors. Therefore, familiarity with the procedures does not seem to provide an adequate explanation.

Nevertheless, the robustness of our findings could be further tested using an expanded experimental design, which includes two conditions in addition to the conceptually organised first and randomly arranged first conditions used here. Participants in the new conditions would also receive two study-test phases, however, these would not differ in terms of display type. In the randomly arranged only condition, words in both study phases would be presented using randomly arranged displays. In the conceptually organised only condition, words in both study phases would be presented using conceptually organised displays. To the extent that familiarity with the study-test procedure explains the current findings, performance improvements should be observed from the first to the second test phase in these new conditions. Furthermore, performance in the second test phases of these new conditions should be comparable in magnitude to those observed in the conceptually organised first and randomly arranged first conditions reported here. Replication using this expanded design and with a larger sample size would also allow us to apply statistical tests to determine whether the patterns of correlations in the presentation order conditions are significantly different. We turn next to a discussion of some potential applications of the findings.

Applications

Applications of the classic finding that organised material is easier to recall than randomly arranged material are already evident. The facilitative effect of meaning-based systems of organisation on memory is recognised (at least implicitly) by the writers of textbooks and other study materials. Chapter outlines and hierarchical systems of headings and subheadings have obvious parallels to the conceptual hierarchies used in the present research, in that they organise the material and highlight the relations among the concepts being studied. To the extent that students notice and encode this structural information their retrieval of the material will be enhanced.

Authors of textbooks also include diagrams to complement the textual information and to make the organisational structure of the material more explicit. Diagrams can illustrate many kinds of relations. One example is the use of hierarchies to illustrate taxonomic categories in biology. Another example is the use of time lines to convey the temporal relationships among important historical events. Flow charts and box and arrow diagrams also provide useful depictions of the sequence of events in information processing models of human cognition. One implication of the current finding that prior exposure to conceptual hierarchies increased relational processing on randomly arranged displays is that repeated exposure to well-organised textual information and diagrams might prompt students to incorporate more organisation into their study methods.

Increased organisation might be evident in their written summaries, or in their increased use of mind maps, diagrams, flow charts, and time lines to supplement textual materials. Research by Lahtinen, Lonka, and Lindblom-Ylanne (1997) showed that medical students who made use of mind maps and written summaries of their lecture notes during their revision sessions were more successful in their exams than those who did not.

Perhaps the main implication of our findings relates to possible ways to improve memory in individuals with diagnoses of Asperger's Syndrome and other autism spectrum disorders. According to Gaigg et al. (2008) memory impairments in this population can be characterised as an over-reliance on item-specific processing and an under-reliance on relational processing. If future research establishes that prior exposure to the conceptually organised displays increases relational processing on randomly arranged displays in individuals with Asperger's Syndrome, then this would suggest a way to improve their memory. Techniques that alert these individuals to the relational structure of the material should be effective in improving their memory. According to Smith, Gardiner, and Bowler (2007), explicit methods such as verbal instructions about the categorised nature of the study materials and how to rehearse items from categorised lists have proved ineffective in improving recall in this population. However, less explicit methods that provide prior experience with well-structured material might be more effective. For example, orienting tasks that involve sorting word cards into hierarchically arranged categories could be employed.

CONCLUSION

The research reported in this chapter investigated the effects of meaningful organisation on free recall by contrasting words presented in conceptually organised displays with words presented in randomly arranged displays using a within-subjects design. The classic finding of superior recall of words from the organised displays was replicated. The research extended previous findings by also examining the effects of presentation order of the two display types. Prior exposure to conceptually organised displays facilitated recall of words from subsequently presented randomly arranged displays. The observed enhancement in recall appears to reflect increased relational processing of the randomly arranged words for the participants who received the conceptually organised displays first. The findings have implications for the design of techniques to improve study skills by enhancing relational memory and for encouraging relational processing in individuals with Asperger's syndrome who tend to rely more on item-specific processing.

REFERENCES

Andrews, G., and Halford, G. S. (2002). A cognitive complexity metric applied to cognitive development. *Cognitive Psychology, 45*, 153-219.

Atwood, N. K., and Shavelson, R. J. (1976). An empirical test of predictions based on a semantic processing and a generative processing model of encoding. *The Journal of Educational Research, 70*, 106-111.

Bower, G. H., Clark, M. C., Lesgold, A. M., and Winzenz, D. (1969). Hierarchical retrieval schemes in recall of categorized word lists. *Journal of Verbal Learning and Verbal Behavior, 8*, 323-343.

Bowler, D. M., Gaigg, S. B., and Gardiner, J. M. (2009). Free recall learning of hierarchically organised lists by adults with Asperger's syndrome: Additional evidence for diminished relational processing. *Journal of Autism and Developmental Disorders, 39*, 589-595.

Cofer, C. N., Bruce, D. R., and Reicher, G. M. (1966). Clustering in free recall as a function of certain methodological variations. *Journal of Experimental Psychology, 71*, 858-866.

Gaigg, S. B., Gardiner, J. M., and Bowler, D. M. (2008). Free recall in autism spectrum disorder: The role of relational and item-specific encoding. *Neuropsychologia, 46*, 983-992.

Guerin, S. A., and Miller, M. B. (2008). Semantic organization of study materials has opposite effects on recall and recognition. *Psychonomic Bulletin and Review, 15*, 302-308.

Halford, G. S., Andrews, G., and Jensen, I. (2002). Integration of category induction and hierarchical classification: One paradigm at two levels of complexity. *Journal of Cognition and Development, 3*, 143-177.

Halford, G. S., Wilson, W. H., and Phillips, S. (1998). Processing capacity defined by relational complexity: Implications for comparative, developmental, and cognitive psychology. *Behavioural Brain Sciences, 21*, 803-831.

Hunt, R. R., and Einstein, G. O. (1981). Relational and item-specific information in memory. *Journal of Verbal Learning and Verbal Behavior, 20*, 497-514.

Lahtinen, V., Lonka, K., and Lindblom-Ylanne, K. (1997). Spontaneous study strategies and the quality of knowledge construction. *British Journal of Educational Psychology, 67*, 13-24.

Smith, B. J., Gardiner, J. M., and Bowler, D. M. (2007). Deficits in free recall persist in Asperger's syndrome despite training in list-appropriate learning strategies. *Journal of Autism and Developmental Disorders, 37*, 445-454.

St. James, J., Schneider, W. and Rogers, K. A. (1994). *MEL LAB: Experiments in Perception, Cognition, Social Psychology and Human Factors.* Pittsburgh PA.: Psychology Software Tools Inc.

Wittrock, M. C., and Carter, J. F. (1975). Generative processing of hierarchically organised words. *The American Journal of Psychology, 88*, 489-501.

Chapter 3

SELF-REFERENT ENCODING FACILITATES RECENCY DISCRIMINATION AND RECOGNITION IN EPISODIC MEMORY

Glenda Andrews[1], Karen Murphy, Michele Dunbar
and Jillian Boyce*

Behavioural Basis of Health Program, Griffith Health Institute &
School of Psychology, Griffith University, Gold Coast Campus,
4222 Australia.

ABSTRACT

Information encoded in relation to the self produces superior memory than does encoding in relation to another person. This is known as the self-reference effect. While there have been many demonstrations of self-reference effects on recognition and recall tests of item memory, no previous research has examined self-reference effects on recency discrimination tasks, which assess memory for the temporal order in which items were presented. We examined self-reference effects in recognition memory and recency discrimination tasks. In the encoding phase, participants judged the extent to which trait adjectives described either themselves (self-referent condition) or Kevin Rudd, the Prime Minister of Australia at the time of the study (other-referent condition). In the test phase, participants completed either a new-old recognition test or a recency discrimination test. There were four main findings. First, self-referent encoding produced better recognition memory of the adjectives than other-referent encoding did. Second, item recognition was easier than recency discrimination. Third, there was a significant distance effect on recency discrimination. Discrimination was easier if the words being compared had occurred farther apart (far pairs) during the study phase than if the words had occurred in closer proximity (near pairs). These three findings replicated previous research. Fourth, self-referent encoding improved recency discrimination of far pairs and near pairs. These are new findings. The findings have implications for facilitating learning and retention of ideas in education, and for improving recency discrimination in older adults and

---

[1] E-mail: g.andrews@griffith.edu.au

individuals with damage to the prefrontal regions of the brain, for whom recency discrimination is especially difficult.

INTRODUCTION

The self construct has long been recognised as an influential factor in human behaviour and thinking (James, 1890). Its role in memorial processes has interested researchers in cognitive and social psychology since at least the early 1970s (Symons and Johnson, 1997). Information encoded in relation to the self produces superior performance on memory tests than does encoding in relation to another person or semantic encoding. This is known as the self-reference effect in memory. The experiment reported in this chapter extended previous research on this topic by examining whether self-referent encoding also facilitates participants' performance on a recency discrimination task. Recency discrimination tasks assess memory for the temporal order in which items were presented. If self-referent encoding facilitates memory for temporal order, this would broaden the range of memory phenomena to which the self-reference effect applies. This in turn, would have implications for intervention programs because the positive effects of training in self-referent encoding would extend to more of the memory tasks encountered in educational settings and in everyday life.

Self-reference effects in memory are usually investigated using an incidental learning procedure, which consists of an encoding phase and a test phase. In the encoding phase, a study list of words is presented and participants make a judgment about each item. The type of judgment is manipulated. In the self-referent condition, words are judged in relation to the self. For example, participants might be asked to rate the extent to which trait adjectives (e.g., *patient, selfish*) describe themselves. In the other-referent condition, participants would be asked to make similar judgments with respect to a well-known person such as a celebrity (e.g., *Angelina Jolie*) or a politician (e.g., the current Prime Minister or President). Additional or alternative encoding conditions are sometimes included. In semantic encoding conditions, participants might be asked to generate a synonym or evaluate the general meaningfulness, likeability, or pleasantness of the words. In an acoustic encoding condition, they might be asked to indicate whether the words contain a specific phoneme. The test phase follows the encoding phase. Memory for the study items is assessed using recognition or recall tests, but consistent with the incidental nature of the procedure, participants are not told beforehand that memory will be assessed. A distracter task, interpolated between the encoding and test phases ensures that even if participants suspect that their memory might be tested, there is little or no opportunity for them to rehearse the words.

There have been many demonstrations of the self-reference effect. Symons and Johnson (1997) reported a meta-analysis of studies conducted in the two decades up to 1994. They concluded that significant self-reference effects are observed when self-referent encoding is contrasted with either other-referent or semantic encoding. The self-reference effect size was significantly larger when the comparison task involved semantic encoding ($d = 0.65$; 95% confidence interval (CI) = $0.58 - 0.71$) than when it involved other-referent encoding ($d = 0.35$; 95% CI = 0.29 to 0.42). Effect sizes for self-other comparisons varied according to various task parameters and presentation conditions. For example, effects sizes were significant when the stimuli were trait adjectives ($d = 0.53$; 95% CI = $0.45 - 0.60$) but not nouns, and were significantly larger on recognition ($d = 0.50$; 95% CI = $0.39 - 0.61$) than free recall ($d = 0.28$; 95% CI = $0.21 - 0.36$) tests of memory. Symons and Johnson concluded that the facilitative effect of self-referent encoding occurs because it produces more elaborative and more organised processing.

The self-reference effect in memory continues to interest researchers. Turk, Cunningham, and Macrae (2008) investigated whether the self-reference effect would also be observed in the absence of explicit evaluative processing of the adjectives. In the encoding phase of the standard methodology participants evaluate the self- or other-descriptiveness of trait adjectives. For example, *Does this word describe you?* (self-referent condition) *Does this word describe Angelina Jolie?* (other-referent condition). Turk et al. contrasted this standard evaluative encoding condition with two non-evaluative (face, name) encoding conditions. In the face condition, an image of the participant's own face (self) or Angelina Jolie's face (other) was presented in the centre of the screen just prior to the appearance of a trait adjective at one of several screen locations. Participants made judgments about the spatial relations between the face images and the trait adjectives. They judged whether or not the trait adjective was presented above the face. The name condition was similar except that printed names of the participants and Angelina Jolie were used instead of face images. Significant self-reference effects on recognition of trait adjectives emerged in the non-evaluative and evaluative encoding conditions. The significant self-reference effect in the non-evaluative conditions was interpreted as showing that evaluative encoding was not necessary for the self-reference effect to occur. However, recognition was more accurate and the self-reference effect was stronger in the standard evaluative encoding condition than in the non-evaluative encoding conditions.

Symons and Johnson's (1997) conclusion that self-referent encoding produces more elaborative and more organised processing concurs with Klein and Loftus' study (1988). Klein and Loftus claimed that elaborating a word entails forming associations between the word and other material already in memory. For example, the study word *dance* might be associated with memories of *ballet lessons, dance partners,* or *going to a ball.* Embellishing and elaborating the encoded item in this way produces better recall because multiple routes to retrieval are created. Organised processing involves encoding the items in the study list in relation to one another. Relational information can include item-to-item associations, and associations that emerge when list items share a common category. For example, *dance* and *music* can be organised as direct associates of one another (e.g., *dance* occurred before *music* in the study list) and also under the category label, *things connected to parties.* Organising a list of study items facilitates recall by establishing inter-item associative paths in memory that can be used during retrieval.

According to Klein and Loftus (1988), study words in self-reference experiments can be represented in memory by both item-specific and relational information, depending on the type of processing they receive. Because self-referent encoding produces both elaborative and organisational processing, the resulting memorial representation should incorporate both item and relational information. However past research has focussed almost exclusively on memory for the study items, as indicated by the number of words recalled or recognised. One exception is the index of clustering reported by Klein and Loftus. They found that self-referent encoding produced more clustering of study list nouns around ad hoc categories than semantic encoding did. This finding is consistent with their claim that self-referent encoding enhances organisation.

The recognition and recall tasks used in self-reference research are tests of episodic memory. Episodic memory is made up of temporally dated recollections of personal experiences. Episodic memory can be contrasted with semantic memory, which contains general knowledge that is not temporally dated. Research by Conway and Dewhurst (1995) suggests that episodic memory is involved to a greater extent in self-referent than in other-referent and semantic encoding conditions. In Experiment 3, they used an incidental learning procedure. Trait adjectives were presented in self-referent, other-referent and semantic encoding conditions. In the test phase participants were shown a list of adjectives and they indicated which words had been presented on the study list (new-old recognition test). For words recognised as having occurred earlier, participants also indicated whether they "remembered" these items or simply "knew" that they were on the study list. According to Tulving (1989), feelings of remembering and knowing can be used to distinguish between the involvement of episodic memory and semantic memory in memory performance. Feelings of remembering typically involve conscious recollective experiences, whereby participants can recall sensory aspects of the original events, or thoughts and feelings that occurred during the events. Recollective experience necessarily entails a remembrer (the self) and might also entail information that goes beyond specific item information to include aspects of the study context (i.e., relational and contextual information). Feelings of knowing are not accompanied by recollective experience. Rather they involve familiarity with the items (i.e., semantic memory).

Conway and Dewhurst (Exp. 3, 1995) found that self-referent encoding produced higher recognition than other-referent encoding, and recognition was comparable in self-referent and semantic encoding conditions. However, consistent with the greater involvement of episodic memory in self-referent encoding, participants in the self-referent condition reported more feelings of remembering and fewer feelings of knowing than those in the other-referent and semantic conditions.

The purpose of the current research was twofold. The first was to replicate previous findings of a self-reference effect on recognition of the study list items. Based on earlier (e.g., Symons and Johnson, 1997) and more recent (Turk et al., 2008) research, we predicted that recognition accuracy of study items would be higher in the self-referent than in the other-referent encoding condition.

The second purpose was to further investigate the self-reference effect by determining whether it is observed on a different test of episodic memory, namely a recency discrimination task in which pairs of study items are presented and participants identify the word in each pair that occurred later (more recently) in the study list. Recency discrimination tasks explicitly assess memory for the temporal order of the study items, which is a type of relational or contextual information that is characteristic of episodic memory. If self-referent encoding facilitates memory for context, which is a defining characteristic of episodic memory, then the self-reference effect should also be observed on the recency discrimination task. That is, recency discrimination accuracy should be higher in the self-referent than in the other-referent encoding condition.

Most studies show that recency discrimination is more difficult than item recognition (e.g., Cabeza, Anderson, Houle, Mangels, and Nyberg, 2000; Milner, Corsi, and Leonard, 1991). Recency discrimination is also more sensitive than recognition to age-related decline in later adulthood. Older adults' recency discrimination accuracy was close to chance level in some studies (e.g., Cabeza et al., 2000; Czernochowski, Fabiani, and Friedman, 2008; Fabiani and Friedman, 1997). Lesion studies (e.g., Milner, 1995; Milner et al., 1991) and imaging studies (Cabeza., et al. 2000; Konishi et al., 2002; Marshuetz, Smith, Jonides, DeGutis, and Chenevert, 2000) suggest that recency discrimination involves the prefrontal regions of the brain, therefore the degenerative effects of normal aging on these brain regions might underpin poor recency discrimination in older adults.

One factor that affects the difficulty of recency discrimination is the relative positions in the study list of the items. Recency discrimination is easier if the two items being compared occurred farther apart in the study sequence. Conversely, recency discrimination is more difficult if the two items being compared occurred closer together in the study sequence. Such findings are known as distance effects. Distance effects are observed under a number of stimulus and procedural variations, as discussed next.

Fabiani and Friedman (1997) assessed new-old recognition and recency discrimination using a procedure in which study trials and test trials for recognition and recency were interleaved. Long lists of word stimuli and pictorial stimuli were presented. Significant distance effects were observed on accuracy and response times for words, but not for pictures. The latter finding was contrary to an earlier study by Milner et al. (1991) who used a similar procedure but found significant distance effects for both words and representational drawings. Larger distances were associated with more accurate recency discrimination for both types of stimuli.

Distance effects have also been observed with shorter study lists. In their fMRI study, Konishi et al. (2002) presented multiple study lists of 10 words. Each study list was followed by a recency discrimination test, which consisted of pairs of words that had been separated by either three positions or eight positions in the previous study list. Recency discrimination was faster and more accurate when distance was greater (eight). Marshuetz et al. (2000) compared item recall and judgments of temporal order in a short-term memory task involving short lists of five alphabetic stimuli. A significant distance effect was observed on order judgments.

Distance effects are sometimes interpreted as evidence for magnitude coding (Marshuetz et al., 2000) which is used for encoding many psychophysical dimensions (e.g., physical size). Distance effects are observed on size discrimination of objects that are not currently present but must be remembered. When participants compare pairs of objects for size, response times are faster for more disparate items. For example, judgments about the relative sizes of *elephant* and *flea* are made more quickly than similar comparisons involving *mouse* and *flea* which are closer in size. Distance effects are also observed on tasks based on the mental number line. For example, when participants are asked to judge which of two numbers is greater, responses are faster and more accurate if the difference between the two numbers is larger (12, 98) than if the difference is smaller (53, 98).

Dehaene, Piazza, Pinel, and Cohen (2003) claimed that there is a distinct neural circuitry for this analog-magnitude system, namely the horizontal segment of the intraparietal sulcus bilaterally. They proposed that this site is involved in nonverbal representation of numerical quantity, possibly a mental number line, which supports an intuitive understanding of what a given quantity means and the proximity relations between quantities. This region is also activated during tasks involving other categories that have a strong spatial or serial component (e.g., alphabet, days of the week) and distance effects have been observed with many types of stimuli and dimensions.

Marshuetz et al. (2000) reported a significant distance effect in their behavioural results (as noted above). Their fMRI data showed that the brain areas that were significantly more activated in the order discrimination task included the parietal and prefrontal cortices. Parietal activations overlapped with those areas involved in number processing, suggesting that the underlying representations of order and number involve magnitude coding.

Based on the research reviewed above we expected a significant distance effect on the recency discrimination task. Specifically, recency discrimination accuracy should be lower for test pairs in which the words occurred closer together in the study list (near pairs) than for test pairs in which the words occurred farther apart in the study list (far pairs). We will also examine whether self-referent encoding facilitates recency discrimination and whether this occurs for both near pairs and far pairs.

METHOD

Participants

The participants were 228 undergraduate students (63 males, 165 females) enrolled in an introductory psychology course at Griffith University, Australia. Their mean age was 20.98 years ($SE = 0.38$ years). English was the first language of all participants. Fifty-seven students were assigned to each of four conditions which corresponded to the combinations of the two encoding conditions (self-referent, other-referent) and the two test types (recognition, recency discrimination). There were no significant differences in age or gender balance across the four conditions.

Stimuli and Materials

Ninety-six trait adjectives were selected from Anderson (1968). There were equal numbers of positive (mean likeability rating = 4.93, range = 4.28 to 5.73) and negative (mean likeability rating = 0.30, range = 0.01 to 1.21) words. The study list consisted of 64 of these adjectives (32 positive, 32 negative). The remaining 32 adjectives (16 positive, 16 negative) were used as new adjectives in the new-old item recognition test. The recognition test consisted of 32 pairs of words. Each pair consisted of one adjective from the study list and a new adjective. There were 16 pairs of positive adjectives and 16 pairs of negative adjectives. For the recency discrimination test, the 64 study list adjectives were arranged into 16 pairs of positive adjectives and 16 pairs of negative adjectives. The distance between the pair members in the study list varied from 2 to 55 positions with a mean of 21.25 positions. There were no significant differences in likeability (Anderson, 1968) or word frequency (Kucera and Francis, 1967) between the correct and incorrect response options in the recognition or recency discrimination tests. An additional 40 word-pairs were used for the rhyme judgment distracter task. The words in 20 pairs rhymed (e.g., *kite, plight*) whereas the words in the remaining 20 pairs did not rhyme (e.g., *vent, boot*).

Procedure

Students participated in groups of between 10 and 25 individuals.

Encoding phase. Initial instructions to participants indicated that the study would investigate the meaning of words that describe personality characteristics. PowerPoint software was used to present the study list adjectives in the encoding phase. Background colour was dark blue and text colour was yellow. Each word was presented on a separate slide and was visible for 7 seconds. The transitions between slides were automatically timed and marked by a gunshot sound. Participants in both encoding conditions were instructed to read each word as it was displayed on the screen and to make a judgment about each word. Participants in the other-referent condition judged the extent to which the trait word described Kevin Rudd, who was Prime Minister of Australia at the time. Those in the self-referent condition judged the extent to which the trait word described themselves. They judged each trait adjective as being never (0), rarely (1), sometimes (2) or almost always (3) descriptive of the referent.

Filler task. A rhyme judgment task was presented immediately after the encoding task. PowerPoint software was used to present 40 word pairs, one pair per slide for 5 seconds per slide. The background colour was light green and the text colour was black. Slide transitions were automatically timed and were marked by a typewriter sound. Participants read the two words in each pair and judged whether or not they rhymed. They recorded their Yes/No responses on the sheets provided.

Test phase. In the test phase, participants completed either a new-old recognition test or a recency discrimination test. The response forms for both tests listed 32 pairs of adjectives. For the new-old recognition task, one word in each pair had appeared on the study list, whereas the other word had not. Participants circled the word in each pair that had been presented in the study phase. For the recency discrimination task, both words had appeared on the study list. Participants circled the adjective in each pair that had occurred later (more recently) in the study list. Participants in both conditions were allowed 5 minutes to complete the 32 items.

Design

There were two independent variables. Encoding condition had two levels (self-referent, other-referent) and was manipulated between groups. Type of test had two levels (new-old recognition, recency discrimination) and was also manipulated between groups. The dependent variable was accuracy, the number of correct responses in the test phase. There was an additional independent variable (distance) within the recency discrimination task. Distance was a within subjects variable with two levels (near, far) as described further below.

RESULTS

Table 1 shows the mean number of correct responses (out of 32) on the recognition and recency discrimination tests for participants in the other-referent and self-referent encoding conditions. A 2 (encoding condition) × 2 (test type) between groups ANOVA yielded significant main effects of encoding condition, $F(1, 224) = 25.08$, $p < .001$, $\eta_p^2 = .101$, and of test type, $F(1, 224) = 652.62$, $p < .001$, $\eta_p^2 = .744$. Accuracy was higher in the self-referent encoding condition ($M = 24.89$; $SE = 0.29$) than in the other-referent encoding condition ($M = 22.82$; $SE = 0.29$), and higher for recognition ($M = 29.13$; $SE = 0.29$) than for recency discrimination ($M = 18.57$; $SE = 0.29$). Although the Encoding condition × Test type interaction was not significant, further analyses were conducted to determine whether the self-reference effect was observed on both tasks. The effect of encoding context was significant for recognition, $F(1, 112) = 10.92$, $p = .001$, $\eta_p^2 = .089$, and for recency discrimination $F(1, 112) = 14.39$, $p < .001$, $\eta_p^2 = .114$. In both tasks, accuracy was higher in the self-referent condition than in the other-referent condition.

Table 1. Mean Number of Correct Responses (Standard Errors)
by Encoding Condition and Test Type

	Encoding condition	
Test type	Self-referent	Other-referent
	M (SE)	M (SE)
Recognition	30.12 (0.41)	28.14 – (0.41)
Recency Discrimination	19.65 (0.41)	17.49 – (0.41)

The recency discrimination task was examined more closely. First, a recency discrimination accuracy score was computed for each of the 32 word pairs by collapsing over the responses of the 114 participants who completed this test. The correlation between recency discrimination accuracy and the degree of separation between the members of the word pairs in the study list was examined. These item-based correlations revealed a significant positive correlation, $r = .53$, $p = .002$. That is, accuracy was higher for word pairs in which the members had occurred further apart in the study list. This provides evidence of a distance effect in recency discrimination. Second, in order to determine whether the effect of encoding condition differed as a function of distance, the word pairs were classified as either near pairs or far pairs based on a median split of the distance values. Recency discrimination accuracy was subjected to a mixed 2 (distance) × 2 (encoding condition) factorial ANOVA in which distance (near, far) was a within-subjects variable and encoding condition (self-referent, other-referent) was the between groups variable. Table 2 shows the relevant means and standard errors. As reported previously, there was a significant main effect of encoding condition, $F(1, 112) = 14.38$, $p < .001$, $\eta_p^2 = .114$. There was also a significant effect of distance, $F(1, 112) = 44.66$, $p < .001$, $\eta_p^2 = .285$, indicating that recency discrimination was more accurate for far pairs ($M = 10.19$; $SE = 0.22$) than for near pairs ($M = 8.39$; $SE = 0.16$).

Although the Distance × Encoding condition interaction was not significant, further analyses were conducted to examine the self-reference effect for near and far pairs. The effect of encoding context was significant for near pairs, $F(1, 112) = 9.74$, $p = .002$, $\eta_p^2 = .080$, and for far pairs, $F(1, 112) = 6.33$, $p = .013$, $\eta_p^2 = .053$. For both near pairs and far pairs, accuracy was higher in the self-referent condition than in the other-referent condition.

**Table 2. Recency Discrimination Accuracy of Near and
Far Pairs as a Function of Encoding Condition**

	Encoding Condition	
Distance	Self-referent	Other referent
	M (SE)	M (SE)
Near pairs	8.90* (0.23)	7.88 (0.23)
Far pairs	10.75* (0.32)	9.63* (0.32)

*significantly above chance level (8 out of 16).

Distance effects in each encoding condition were also examined separately. The distance effect was significant in the self-referent condition, $F(1, 56) = 25.04, p < .001, \eta_p^2 = .309$, and also in the other-referent condition, $F(1, 56) = 19.95, p < .001, \eta_p^2 = .263$. In both encoding conditions, recency discrimination accuracy was higher for far pairs than for near pairs. Sign tests showed that these distance effects were not due to a minority of individuals. Specifically, of the 57 participants in the self-referent encoding condition, 38 (67%) had higher accuracy for far pairs than for near pairs, 10 showed the reverse pattern, $Z = 3.90, p < .001$. Of the 57 participants in the other-referent encoding condition, 38 (67%) had higher accuracy for far pairs than for near pairs, 12 showed the reverse pattern, $Z = 3.54, p < .001$.

Inspection of the means in Table 2 suggests that recency discrimination was very difficult for the near pairs, especially in the other-referent encoding condition. Single sample t-tests confirmed this. The means for the far pairs exceeded chance level (8 correct out of 16) in the self-referent condition, $t(56) = 9.04, p < .001$, and in the other-referent condition $t(56) = 5.01$, $p < .001$. The mean for the near pairs was significantly higher than chance in the self-referent condition, $t(56) = 4.28, p < .001$, but not in the other-referent condition, $t(56) = -0.49, p = .626$.

DISCUSSION

The differential effects of self-referent and other-referent encoding were examined in two tasks, new-old recognition of items and recency discrimination of the items in the study list. The findings for each task will be discussed, before we consider the practical implications of our findings.

Results for the new-old recognition test showed that self-referent encoding produced more accurate recognition of adjectives than did other-referent encoding. The effect size ($d = .61$) in the current study is at the upper end of the confidence intervals reported for recognition tasks in Symons and Johnson's (1997) meta-analysis. Symons and Johnson concluded that the self-reference effect occurs because self-referent encoding promotes elaboration and organisation in memory. Elaboration entails creating associative links between the study words and other material in semantic memory. Organisation entails creating relational links between the study words. In both cases, retrieval is enhanced because multiple routes are created.

The self-reference effect on recognition is consistent with more recent findings of Turk et al. (2008), who also used the standard methodology in which trait adjectives were evaluated in relation to the self or other at encoding. Turk et al. also observed significant (though smaller) self-reference effects in their face and name conditions. In the latter, the spatial location of the trait adjectives in relation to face images or names of the self and other were judged at encoding.

Earlier findings (Keenan, Golding, and Brown, 1992) had shown that evaluative questions at encoding produced self-reference effects, but factual questions did not. Evaluative questions were thought to produce a self-reference effect because they exploit the imbalance between the large amount of information stored in self-schema compared to the smaller amount of information stored in schema for other people. The consequence is that self-referenced events produce more elaborate encodings than other-referenced events. Factual questions did not produce a self-reference effect because they tap comparable amounts of information about the self and others. With factual questions, self-referent and other-referent encoding produced equivalent amounts of elaboration.

Turk et al. (2008) interpreted their findings as showing that pairing of self images or names with the target stimuli is sufficient to enhance memory and that elaborative processing might not be necessary to produce a self-reference effect. However, this interpretation holds only if it assumed that no evaluative processing occurred in their face and name conditions, and that self-referent and other-referent encoding resulted in equivalently elaborated memory traces. Further research is required to check the validity of these assumptions.

The greater difficulty of recency discrimination compared to recognition is consistent with previous findings (Cabeza et al., 2000; Fabiani and Friedman, 1997; Milner et al., 1991) and also with lesion (Milner, 1995; Milner et al, 1991), and neuroimaging studies (Konishi et al., 2002; Marshuetz et al., 2000), demonstrating the involvement of the prefrontal brain regions in recency discrimination. Prefrontal brain regions are also involved in many difficult tasks including those that tap the other contextual aspects of memory such as source memory (Janowsky, Shimamura, and Squire, 1995; Van Petten, Senkfor, and Newberg, 2000).

Recency discrimination was more difficult for near pairs than for far pairs. This replicates previous findings of distance effects in recency discrimination tasks with long lists (Fabiani and Friedman, 1997; Milner et al., 1991) and shorter lists (e.g., Konishi et al., 2002; Marshuetz et al., 2000). Such distance effects are usually interpreted as evidence for magnitude coding. Greater distance between the words at encoding makes their positions in the study list more distinctive and therefore easier to discriminate. This finding supports the view that distance effects are not restricted to numerical tasks.

The results for the recency discrimination test indicate that the facilitative effect of self-referent encoding is not restricted to item memory. The self-reference effect size for the recency discrimination task ($d = 0.71$) was comparable to the recognition test. In comparison to other-referent encoding, self-referent encoding enhanced retrieval of information about the temporal order of the study words. This was the case for far pairs and also for near pairs. Recency discrimination of the more difficult near pairs increased from chance level in the other-referent condition to significantly above chance level in the self-referent condition. These are new findings which extend the boundaries of the self-reference effect to include a contextual aspect of episodic retrieval, namely temporal order. One interpretation of this finding is that self-referent encoding resulted in stronger relational links between the study words, and that this relational information included information about the temporal order of the adjectives. This would concur with the view that self-referent encoding promotes organisation in memory (Burns, 2006; Klein and Loftus, 1988; Symons and Johnson, 1997).

The recency discrimination task used in the current study was limited to its specific parameters. That is, encoding condition was a between-subjects variable, the stimuli were trait adjectives, the memory test was unexpected, a distracter task was interpolated between encoding and test phases and the participants were undergraduate students. Future research could examine the robustness of the self-reference effect on recency discrimination to variations in these parameters, some of which have previously been shown to affect the significance or size of the self-reference effect in recognition and recall tasks (Symons and Johnson, 1997). For example, nouns or picture stimuli could be used in place of trait adjectives. Inclusion of older adults and children would help to establish whether self-referent encoding facilitates recency discrimination at different stages of the lifespan. The length of the delay between study and test could be varied to determine how long-lasting the self-reference effect is. The effect of self-referent encoding on other contextual aspects of memory could also be examined.

Applications

We turn now to the implications of our findings for improving memory performance in educational and remediation settings. The facilitative effects of self-referent encoding on item memory have long been recognised and the current findings suggest that this facilitation also extends to memory for contextual and relational material.

In educational settings, the importance of accurate retrieval of item and contextual information to performance on exams is self-evident. For example, students of history need to remember not only what events occurred but also their historical sequence. Our results suggest that self-referent encoding would facilitate retrieval of both types of information. Therefore students would be well advised to relate the material to themselves or their own experience during their study sessions. If teachers and instructors are aware of the facilitative effects of self-referent encoding on memory, they will be better placed to assist their students' learning by designing exercises that encourage self-referent encoding. For example, students of history might be encouraged to imagine themselves living through an historical event (e.g., an invasion of their homeland) and to write about their imagined experiences from a first-person perspective. Instructors can also model self-referent encoding by providing examples from their own experience. For example, *When the topic of Parkinson's Disease arises, I always think about my aunt, who had this condition in her later years. I observed the progression of her symptoms over a period of about three years. On my first visit after her diagnosis, I noticed .... . On my second visit a few months later, I noticed ...* Of course, the facilitative effects of self-referent encoding do not negate the importance of other aspects of educational and instructional design in promoting acquisition of complex knowledge and understanding. However, training in self-referent encoding could be a useful and inexpensive addition to these other techniques.

As noted previously, recency discrimination appears to involve the prefrontal cortex of the brain (Cabeza et al., 2000; Konishi et al., 2002; Marshuetz et al., 2000; Milner, 1995; Milner et al., 1991). This brain region is more sensitive than other regions to the degeneration as a function of normal aging. For example, a morphometric study reported a 1% reduction in brain volume in the temporal, parietal, and occipital cortices, but a 10% reduction in the frontal cortex in older (75 to 85 years) relative to younger (20 to 40 years; Haug and Eggers,

1991) brains. The poorer recency discrimination observed in older adults (Fabiani and Friedman, 1997) might be a functional manifestation of this loss. However, evidence that such age-related decline in performance is not always observed. Czernochowski et al. (2008) suggest that it might be preventable. If future research shows that self-referent encoding facilitates recency discrimination in older adults as it did in the younger adults in the research reported in the current chapter, this would suggest that the age-related decline in recency discrimination accuracy might be slowed if older adults engaged in more self-referent encoding. Self-referent encoding could also be incorporated into memory training programs for individuals with frontal lobe injury due to stroke or other trauma. Given the effect of distance on recency discrimination, it would be advisable to start with the easier, far pairs before proceeding to the more difficult, near pairs.

CONCLUSION

Self-reference effects in recognition memory and recency discrimination tasks were examined using a two-phase procedure. In the encoding phase, participants judged the extent to which trait adjectives described either themselves (self-referent condition) or Kevin Rudd (other-referent condition). In the test phase, participants completed either a new-old recognition test or a recency discrimination test of the adjectives.

There were four main findings. First, self-referent encoding produced more accurate recognition memory of the adjectives than other-referent encoding did. This replicates the self-reference effects observed in many previous studies. Second, as in previous research, recency discrimination of the items was more difficult than recognition of the items. Third, recency discrimination was easier if the two words being compared had occurred farther apart in the study list (far pairs) than if the words had occurred closer in the study sequence (near pairs). This replicated previous findings of distance effects in recency discrimination. Fourth, a significant self-reference effect in recency discrimination was observed. This is a new finding. Self-referent encoding improved recency discrimination for both far pairs and near pairs. Self-referent encoding might promote organisation in memory by facilitating encoding and/or retrieval of the temporal order relations between the adjectives. The findings of the study have implications for facilitating learning and retention of ideas in education, and for the design of interventions to improve recency discrimination, especially in older adults and individuals with damage to the prefrontal regions of the brain.

REFERENCES

Anderson, N. (1968). Likableness ratings for 555 personality trait words. *Journal of Personality and Social Psychology, 9*, 272-279.

Burns, D. J. (2006). Assessing distinctiveness: Measures of item-specific and relational processing. In R. R. Hunt and J. B. Worthen (Eds.), *Distinctiveness and memory* (pp. 109-130). New York: Oxford University Press.

Cabeza, R., Anderson, N. D., Houle, S., Mangels, J. A., and Nyberg, L. (2000). Age-related differences in neural activity during item and temporal-order memory retrieval: A positron emission tomography study. *Journal of Cognitive Neuroscience, 12,* 197-206.

Conway, M. A., and Dewhurst, S. A., (1995). The self and recollective experience. *Applied Cognitive Psychology, 9,* 1-19.

Czernochowski, D., Fabiani, M., and Friedman, D. (2008). Use it or lose it? SES mitigates age-related decline in a recency/recognition task. *Neurobiology of Aging, 29,* 945-958.

Dehaene, S., Piazza, M., Pinel, P., and Cohen, L. (2003). Three parietal circuits for number processing. *Cognitive Neuropsychology, 20,* 487-506.

Fabiani, M., and Friedman, D. (1997). Dissociations between memory for temporal order and recognition memory in aging. *Neuropsychologia, 35,* 129-141.

Haug, H., and Eggers, R. (1991). Morphometry of the human cortex cerebri and corpus striatum during aging. *Neurobiology of Aging, 12,* 336-338.

James, W. (1890). *The principles of psychology.* New York: Holt

Janowsky, J. S., Shimamura, A. P., and Squire, L. R. (1995). Source memory impairment in patients with frontal lobe lesions. *Neuropsychologia, 27,* 1043-1056.

Keenan, J. M., Golding, J. M., and Brown, P. (1992). Factors controlling the advantage of self-reference over other-reference. *Social Cognition, 10,* 79-94.

Klein, S. B., and Loftus, J. (1988). The nature of self-referent encoding: The contributions of elaborative and organizational processes. *Journal of Personality and Social Psychology, 55,* 5-11.

Konishi, S., Uchida, I., Okuaki, T., Machida, T., Shirouzu, I., and Miyashita, Y. (2002). Neural correlates of recency judgment. *The Journal of Neuroscience, 22,* 9549-9555.

Kucera, J., and Francis, W. N. (1967). *Computational analysis of present day American English.* Providence, RI: Brown University Press.

Marshuetz, C., Smith, E. E., Jonides, J., DeGutis, J., and Chenevert, T. L. (2000). Order information in working memory: fMRI evidence for parietal and prefrontal mechanisms. *Journal of Cognitive Neuroscience, 12,* 130-144.

Milner, B. (1995). Aspects of frontal lobe function. *Advances in Neurology, 66,* 67-84.

Milner, B., Corsi, P., and Leonard, G. (1991). Frontal-lobe contribution to recency judgements. *Neuropsychologia, 29,* 601-618.

Symons, C. S., and Johnson, B. T. (1997). The self-reference effect in memory: A meta-analysis. *Psychological Bulletin, 121,* 371-394.

Tulving, E. (1989). Remembering and knowing the past. *American Scientist, 77,* 361-367.

Turk, D. J., Cunningham, S. J., and Macrae, C. N. (2008). Self-memory biases in explicit and incidental encoding of trait adjectives. *Consciousness and Cognition, 17,* 1040-1045.

Van Petten, C., Senkfor, A. J., and Newberg, W. M. (2000). Memory for drawings in locations: Spatial source memory and event-related potentials. *Psychophysiology, 37,* 551-564.

Chapter 4

CONTEXT EFFECTS ON MEMORY RETRIEVAL FOLLOWING THE PAVLOVIAN EXTINCTION PROCESS IN HUMANS AND ITS APPLICATION IN THE REDUCTION OF RETURN OF FEAR

Siavash Bandarian Balooch[1], David L. Neumann[1,2,]
and Mark J. Boschen[1,2]*

[1] School of Psychology, Griffith University.
[2] Behavioural Basis of Health Program,
Griffith Health Institute, Griffith University.

ABSTRACT

Despite the apparent efficacy of exposure based treatments for anxiety disorders, many of those treated can experience relapse of anxiety symptoms, also known as return of fear. The occurrence of a return of fear suggests that the mechanism that underlies the original fear is not removed during exposure treatment. The present chapter reviews the mechanism of renewal to show how a return of fear may be modulated by contextual cues present during initial learning, new learning, and retrieval of learning from memory. Laboratory-based research investigating fear renewal in humans is reviewed to show how it can be produced and what variables influence the strength of fear renewal. The review identifies seven methods of attenuating renewal, including conducting exposure sessions in multiple treatment contexts and the use of portable physical cues that are associated with the exposure sessions. It is concluded that the findings from laboratory-based research can be readily applied to enhance the efficacy of the standard exposure therapy protocol and reduce the return of fear post treatment.

---

*E-mail: d.neumann@griffith.edu.au

INTRODUCTION

Fear is an emotional response to threats that are percieved as immediate and are present in the environment (Marks, 1987), such as the threat of being attacked by a dangerous animal. Anxiety, in contrast, is regarded as a combination of unpleasant emotions including worry and panic (Messenger and Shean, 1998) that are responses to less immediate threats (Marks, 1987). Anxiety can, for example, be an emotional response to the anticipation of negative events that may (or may not) occur at one's workplace. Both anxiety and fear are natural cross-species emotions that promote survival. For instance, being able to learn to fear or worry about encountering objects that are likely to harm us increases our likelihood of survival by increasing our propensity towards avoiding these objects. However, individuals can sometimes develop excessive and maladaptive fears of objects or situations, termed a *phobia*. The phobias are regarded as a type of anxiety disorder where excessive fear is a central component (American Psychiatric Association, 2000). The specific phobias, for instance, are the most commonly occurring group of psychiatric disorders (Chapman, 1997) and are characterized by marked and persistent fear of an object or situation (e.g., spider or flying) that significantly interferes with a person's normal routine (American Psychiatric Association, 2000). The situations that may give rise to phobic responses are either endured with intense fear or distress, or are avoided altogether (American Psychiatric Association, 2000).

Exposure-based treatments have been found effective in the treatment of specific phobias (Craske, 1999; Emmelkamp, Bouman, and Scholing, 1992; Olatunji, Cisler, and Deacon, 2010). Exposure treatment mainly involves repeated and prolonged presentation of the feared object to the person experiencing phobia until the fear is significantly reduced (Barlow, Craske, Cerny, and Klosko, 1989; Craske, 1999; Öst, 1989). There are slight variations among the specific applications of exposure treatment in the clinic. For instance, exposure treatment that is based on systematic desensitization usually encourages the person to encounter the feared object in scenarios that are increasingly fear provoking until the most fear provoking scenario is reached. A flooding method is used when the first exposure to the feared object is in one of the most fear provoking scenarios. However, despite the efficacy of exposure therapy, approximately 30-50 % of individuals who are treated for their phobia using exposure therapy alone or in combination with other treatments experience relapse of anxiety symptoms post treatment (Craske and Rachman, 1987; Rachman, 1966; Rose and McGlynn, 1997; Wolpe, 1958). This suggests that exposure therapy does not remove the fear of the object, but that fear remains latent and can reappear at a later time if the right circumstances exist.

The relapse of anxiety symptoms post clinical treatment is often referred to as return of fear (for review see, Boschen, Neumann, and Waters, 2009; Rachman, 1989). The Pavlovian conditioning process largely provides the theoretical basis of exposure therapy (Davey, 1992) and has provided an experimental analogue to study the return of fear in laboratory-based research in non-clinical human samples (e.g., Neumann, Lipp, and Cory, 2007). The phenomenon known as renewal is of interest in this chapter, as are the experimental manipulations that lead to the prevention of renewal in laboratory settings. Such manipulations are likely to be applicable to the prevention of a return of fear following exposure therapy. The present chapter will draw on this literature to identify possible reasons for the return of fear following exposure therapy and how it can be reduced. The fundamental concepts and theories that underlie the conditioning process will initially be outlined. Subsequently, research will be reviewed to show that the extinction process does not remove fear of the object. The mechanism of renewal as a pathway to the return of fear will be the main focus in this discussion. Methods to reduce renewal-based return of fear will be reviewed to show how the knowledge gained from the experimental literature can be applied to the exposure therapy process.

PAVLOVIAN CONDITIONING AND EXTINCTION OF FEAR

Pavlovian conditioning (Pavlov, 1927) is a learning process that has long been thought to be involved in the etiology and maintenance of anxiety disorders, particularly anxiety disorders characterised by fear of objects and situations (e.g., simple phobia and social phobia; Bouton, Mineka, and Barlow, 2001; Mineka and Zinbarg, 2006). Pavlovian conditioning is used not only to explain how people may develop fears (Field, 2006), but also to provide a framework with which to study fear acquisition and extinction in the laboratory. The hypothesised underlying mechanism of Pavlovian conditioning in fear learning allows laboratory-based research to be used to understand more about how anxiety disorders develop. Moreover, it opens the door for laboratory-based research to test ways to make the extinction of fear more effective in the long term when treatment is given in the clinic.

In Pavlovian conditioning, a conditional stimulus (CS) and unconditional stimulus (US) are used. The CS is typically neutral prior to conditioning (e.g., a simple tone). In contrast, the US is typically a biologically salient event (e.g., a mild electric shock that causes pain). In the acquisition of Pavlovian conditioned responses, the CS is presented contingently with the US. In human conditioning procedures, this is most commonly done by presenting the CS for a set time (e.g., 8 s) and then presenting the US immediately following CS offset. Over repeated pairings of the CS and US, the CS acquires the property in which its mere presentation will elicit a conditioned response (CR). Following this procedure, the subject typically displays both fear and anxiety responses (Grillion, 2002). The fear responses are displayed in the presence of the CS (termed cued fear conditioning) and typically dissipate shortly after its offset. The anxiety responses however, are a result of contextual conditioning and are displayed as a response to being in the context in which the CS has been paired with an aversive US (Grillion, 2002). Following cued fear conditioning, the subject typically displays fear responses in the presence of the CS. For example, following pairings of a geometric shape CS and mild shock US, presentations of the CS alone will elicit fear responses such as skin conductance responding, heart rate deceleration, startle blink potentiation, and an increased expectancy that the US will follow (Neumann and Waters, 2006). Following the acquisition of Pavlovian CRs, an extinction procedure can be used. In this procedure, the CS is repeatedly presented on its own, in the absence of any US. Over the repeated presentations, the CRs will diminish.

Pavlovian conditioning provides a model for the acquisition and extinction of fears and anxiety when the US is an aversive stimulus. Watson and Rayner (1920) were among the first to demonstrate this. The investigators observed a fear response (CR) in a child following a presentation of a white rat alone (CS) after having paired the rat with a loud noise (US).

Watson and Rayner suggested that fear is developed towards any object that is present while experiencing a traumatic event (Field, 2006). Despite the elegance and predictive power of this early fear conditioning model, it encountered several criticisms (Öhman and Mineka, 2001; Rachman, 1977). For instance, individuals who experience traumatic events do not always develop phobias (Aitken, Lister, and Main, 1981; Lautch, 1971; Liddell and Lyons, 1978) and fears of some objects are much more prevalent than others (e.g., a fear of spiders is much more common than a fear of flowers).

Recent fear conditioning conceptualisations have elaborated on the basic fear conditioning process and countered many of the criticisms made of earlier models (Field, 2006; Öhman and Mineka, 2001). For instance, the propensity to fear, and thus avoid, potentially dangerous objects (e.g., fear-relevant stimuli such as spiders), but not others (e.g., fear-irrelevant stimuli such as flowers) may have been linked to our ancestors likelihood of survival (Davey, 2002). Due to our past evolutionary history, it became adaptive to develop fear more rapidly towards fear-relevant stimuli that threatened our survival than fear-irrelevant stimuli that are not dangerous (Öhman and Mineka, 2001). In this way, fear conditioning models can explain why not all traumatic events result in the development of phobia and why some objects elicit fear responses more readily than others. Thus, contemporary fear conditioning models are more multifaceted and better equipped than earlier models to deal with the complex processes involved in the development of phobia. Furthermore, contemporary fear conditioning models are also more complex in how they explain the extinction of conditioned fear responses.

THEORETICAL CONCEPTUALISATIONS OF THE ACQUISITION AND EXTINCTION OF PAVLOVIAN CONDITIONED RESPONSES

The acquisition of Pavlovian conditioned responses is regarded to be due to the learning of an association between the CS and US (i.e., stimulus-stimulus learning). To explain the extinction of CRs, early ideas proposed that there was a destruction of this previously learnt CS-US association. As noted by Bouton (2002), this idea is common among several influential models of conditioning (e.g., Rescorla and Wagner, 1972; McClelland and Rumelhart, 1985). It may also lead to the belief that extinction-based therapy for phobia is effective because it destroys the maladaptive learning that caused the phobia. However, for several decades now, evidence has been mounting to suggest that extinction does not destroy the CS-US association (e.g., Bouton, 2002; 2004; Bouton, Westbrook, Corcoran, and Maren, 2006; Neumann, Boschen, and Waters, 2008).

The idea that extinction does not destroy the original CS-US association was present in the writings of Pavlov (1927). Similar ideas were suggested by researchers that followed Pavlov (e.g., Konorski, 1948; Pearce and Hall, 1980). Extinction has been explained in various ways, including the learning that the rate of reinforcement for the CS is lower in extinction, a decrement in generalisation from acquisition to extinction, learning to inhibit the CR during extinction, violation of reinforcer expectation, and learning of a CS-noUS association (see Bouton, 2004 for a discussion). In the human conditioning research reviewed in this chapter, the concept of generalisation decrement and the learning of a CS-noUS association have been most commonly used to interpret the results.

The notion of a generalisation decrement suggests that a configural CS-context stimulus is formed during acquisition. For example, a geometric shape CS and dark laboratory room is processed as a configural whole, rather than as separate elements, that enter into an association with the US during acquisition. The CS-context configural stimulus does not generalise well when extinction is conducted in a new context (see Neumann et al., 2008). The generalisation decrement is due to the new CS-context configural stimulus that is encountered in extinction (e.g., geometric shape CS and light laboratory room configural whole). The generalisation decrement from acquisition to extinction suggests that no destruction of the CS-US association occurs during extinction, nor does any new learning occur. In contrast, the notion that a CS-noUS association is learnt during the extinction procedure suggests that new learning occurs.

Bouton (1993, 1994; Bouton and Nelson, 1998) described a model of acquisition and extinction in which contextual cues modulate what learnt association is expressed in behaviour. As previously discussed, during the Pavlovian conditioning procedure a CS-US association is learnt during acquisition and a CS-noUS association is learnt during extinction. The CS-noUS association does not destroy the previously learnt CS-US association, rather they are both stored in memory. After extinction learning the CS becomes ambiguous because it has two associations with the US (i.e., CS-US and CS-noUS associations). Contextual cues are used to retrieve one of these associations and the result of this memory retrieval influences behaviour (Bouton and Bolles, 1979). Context refers to the cues present in the external environment (e.g., sights, sounds, smells) and interoceptive environment (e.g., drug state, affective state). For example, if the context matches that which was present during extinction, the CS-noUS association is retrieved and no CRs result. However, if the context does not match the extinction context then the CS-US association is likely to be retrieved due to the relative context independent nature of the first thing that is learnt (the original CS-US association learnt during acquisition when compared to the CS-noUS association learnt during extinction).

An important aspect of Bouton's (1993, 1994; Bouton and Nelson, 1998) model of acquisition and extinction is that the original acquisition learning is relatively context free. This notion is able to explain why the original CS-US association should be retrieved and expressed in behaviour in not just the original acquisition context, but in any novel context that is encountered. There is ample evidence to support the claim that acquisition learning is relatively context free when compared to extinction learning (e.g., Bouton and King, 1983; Bouton and Swartzentruber, 1986; Hall and Honey, 1989; Lovibond, Preston, and Mackintosh, 1984). For instance, Kaye, Preston, Szabo, Druiff, and Mackintosh (1987) conducted several experiments using rats to show that acquisition learning remained relatively robust even after changing the physical context in which subsequent testing occurred. Other research has revealed that acquisition learning remains stable even when tested weeks after learning first occurred (e.g., Bouton and Peck, 1989). This is not to say that acquisition learning is completely context free, there is for instance evidence that acquisition learning can diminish following a change in context (e.g., Hall and Honey, 1990). However, acquisition learning is much less influenced by context changes when compared to extinction learning which seems to be highly context specific. Researchers have found, for instance, that extinction learning is completely lost when there is a 25 day interval between extinction and subsequent testing (Thomas, 1979). Others have found that extinction learning does not transfer well when there is a change in context between extinction and subsequent testing (e.g., Bouton and Brooks, 1993; Bouton and Nelson, 1993; Nelson, 2002). Thus, contextual cues have a stronger impact on modulating the retrieval of the CS-noUS association than the CS-US association. As a consequence, if the CS is encountered in a novel context, it is more likely that the CS-US association will be retrieved and CRs will result.

Current ideas about the mental processes that underlie acquisition and extinction have important implications for conditioning models of anxiety disorders. The notion that extinction does not result in unlearning suggests that the original fear learning that resulted in the disorder will always be present. It is not destroyed following extinction-based treatments like exposure therapy. As a result, relapse remains an ever-present danger depending on what contextual cues might be present in a given situation (Boschen et al., 2009; Bouton, 2000). However, it also suggests that further research on the factors that modulate acquisition and extinction learning can be used to design more effective exposure-based treatment programs for anxiety disorders like phobia. For this reason, an increasing amount of research has examined fear learning, extinction, and the return of extinguished conditioned responses following context changes in human laboratory research.

CONTEXTUALLY MODULATED MECHANISMS OF RETURN OF FEAR

Most of the existing literature on examining context effects on aversive conditioning consists of laboratory studies (for a review see Bouton, 2002; Neumann et al., 2008). This may, for some, raise doubts as to the applicability of these findings to the return of fear in real world clinical settings. Nevertheless, these laboratory experiments are important because they provide a means for rigorous experimental control of the contexts in which the initial CS-US association is learnt. This allows researchers to test the effects of extinction treatment using a multitude of different research designs. It is also important because it allows researchers to test some of the underlying conditioning concepts on which exposure therapy is based (Vansteenwegen et al., 2005). Furthermore, clinical-analogue research that has examined context effects on the return of fear in highly fearful participants through exposure treatment has revealed comparable results to laboratory based studies (e.g., Mineka, Mystkowski, Hladek, and Rodriguez, 1999; Mystkowski, Craske, and Echiverri, 2002; Mystkowski, Craske, Echiverri, and Labus, 2006; Mystkowski, Mineka, Vernon, and Zinbarg, 2003; Rodriguez, Craske, Mineka, and Hladek, 1999). Such findings confirm that the laboratory-based research is relevant for the real world application of exposure therapy.

Bouton (2002) used the phenomena of spontaneous recovery, reinstatement, reacquisition, and renewal to explain how context influences the memory retrieval of extinguished Pavlovian conditioned responses. In spontaneous recovery, for instance, time acts as an ever changing context (i.e., temporal context) that promotes the retrieval of the CS-US association rather than the CS-noUS association due to the context independence of the former. It is beyond the scope of the current review to discuss all of these phenomena (for review see, Neumann et al., 2008; see also Neumann, Lipp, and McHugh in this volume for a discussion of reinstatement and spontaneous recovery in humans). Renewal effects have been found to be robust using a variety of different conditioning procedures in both animals (for reviews, see Bouton, 2002; 2004; Bouton and Swartzentruber, 1991) and humans (for a review, see Neumann et al., 2008). It has also been extensively studied in human laboratory-based research. For these reasons, the present review will focus on renewal.

There are typically three phases involved in the renewal procedure: an acquisition, extinction, and test phase. These phases are conducted in a particular context (e.g., sights and sounds). During the acquisition phase, a CS (e.g., light) is repeatedly paired with a US (e.g., shock) in context A. Subsequently, during the extinction phase, the CS is repeatedly presented alone in context B that is different to the acquisition context. The procedure is concluded in the test phase where the CS is presented alone again in a different context to that experienced in extinction. Most typically, this is the initial acquisition context A (as in ABA renewal) or it can be in a completely novel context C (as in ABC renewal).[1]

The experiment by Milad et al. (2005) provides an example of the ABA renewal procedure in human research. They showed photographs of a conference room and office on a computer screen as contextual manipulations. Each photograph contained a lamp that when lit provided either a blue or red coloured light which constituted the CSs. They administered electric shocks to the participants' fingers as the US. Fear of receiving a shock was measured using skin conductance responses. During the acquisition phase using, for instance, the office photograph as context, participants received pairings of the light CS and shock US. During the extinction phase in the conference room, the light CS was repeatedly presented in the absence of the shock US. A renewal of fear responses was observed following CS presentations again in the test phase where the light CS was presented in the office context.

A return of fear via a renewal effect has also been found in clinical-analogue studies. In this research, individuals who have high fear of an object (e.g., fear of spiders) participate in a procedure that lacks an explicit acquisition phase (because fear has already been acquired), but includes extinction and test phases. As such, these studies use a "BC" renewal design wherein exposure treatment is conducted in one context (e.g., clinician's office) and the follow up session is conducted in a novel context (e.g., outdoor patio). Nevertheless, for the sake of consistency the term ABC renewal will continue to be used to describe these effects. For instance, Rodriguez et al. (1999) provided exposure treatment to individuals who were fearful of spiders. They used the presence and absence of the therapist, geographical location of the room and the interior design of each room as contextual manipulations. During exposure treatment participants were required to approach the spider and perform increasingly fear provoking tasks until a significant reduction was observed in their self reported fear. During follow-up, a return of fear via an ABC renewal effect was observed as indicated by an increase in heart rate for the participants who received follow up in a context that was different to the exposure therapy context.

The mechanisms that underlie a return of fear via an ABC renewal effect in, for instance, a person who is experiencing phobia of spiders can be explained using Bouton's model (1993, 1994; Bouton and Nelson, 1998). Bouton's model (1993, 1994; Bouton and Nelson, 1998) shows how subsequent to having an aversive encounter with a spider (e.g., being bitten) in the garage, the person may develop fear of spiders because they have learnt an association between the spider (CS) and pain (US; i.e., CS-US association is learnt). The person may be treated for their fear of spiders in the therapist's clinic using exposure therapy. The person

---

[1] Another form of renewal is based on an AAB design where acquisition occurs in context A, extinction in context A, and test in context B. However, there is less evidence for AAB renewal in animal research (e.g., Bouton and Ricker, 1994, Tamai and Nakajima, 2000) and the current review did not find any evidence for it having been tested in humans. Therefore, it will not be discussed further.

learns that the spider (CS) is not associated with pain (US; i.e., CS-noUS association is learnt) in that context. According to Bouton's model, this leaves two meanings regarding the nature of the association between the spider and pain. This ambiguity regarding the threat of spiders is resolved by the context that the spider is encountered in. As previously mentioned, the initial CS-US association that is learnt is relatively context free, suggesting that the person will more likely fear spiders in any context, except for the exposure therapy context (i.e., the therapists clinic). In this way, the model can explain why a return of fear via renewal occurs following a re-encounter of the spider in both the original acquisition context and a novel context (e.g., Mystkowski et al., 2006; Rodriguez et al., 1999). Furthermore, the model provides insight into how laboratory-based renewal research can be applied to the clinic to explain the return of fear post exposure treatment.

RESEARCH ON RENEWAL IN HUMANS

A literature review was conducted by searching the PsycINFO and ScienceDirect (psychology related fields only) databases combining the key terms "renewal" and "conditioning" or "renewal" and "return of fear", and resulted in 699 articles. Google Scholar databases were searched using a combination of the key terms "renewal" and "return of fear" and "conditioning" which resulted in 199 hits. The resulting hits were screened to exclude non-psychology related articles (e.g., energy policy), non-peer reviewed articles, non-empirical reports such as reviews, animal research, and non-aversive/fear conditioning renewal research. The resulting articles identified through the literature search (22 articles) were used as the basis of the review. Concentrating on these studies may shed light on the bigger and much more diverse picture that is involved in full relapse following exposure therapy and how relapse may be reduced.

LABORATORY FINDINGS ON RETURN OF FEAR VIA RENEWAL AND ITS ECOLOGICAL VALIDITY

The generality of renewal across different stimuli and contexts. One of the strengths of the theory of renewal of conditioned fear responses is that it has been found in a wide range of studies using different CSs, USs, and contexts. The generality of the renewal effect is important because life is diverse and humans are presented with a limitless number of stimuli and contextual cues in the environment. It is therefore important that laboratory studies on renewal can reflect this diversity so that it can remain relevant to clinical applications. The reviewed literature shows that this is the case for renewal research.

Vansteenwegen et al. (2005) used neutral face line drawings as CSs and an unpleasant noise as a US and different lighting levels (dark or light) as contexts. US expectancy was measured using retrospective self reports and fear was measured using skin conductance responses. During acquisition in context A, one of the faces was paired with the aversive noise resulting in increased responses following that CS presentation. During extinction in context B, the CSs were presented in the absence of the US, resulting in reduced expectancy and fear of receiving the US. During the test phase conducted in context A, the participants' expectancy and fear of the loud noise was renewed. When interpreted within Bouton's (1993, 1994; Bouton and Nelson, 1998) model of renewal, the re-encounter of the CS in the acquisition context seems to have promoted return of fear via an ABA renewal effect through increased likelihood of retrieval of the CS-US association from memory compared to the CS-noUS association.

Of additional interest, Vansteenwegen et al. (2005) counterbalanced the nature of the contexts used as context A and B. Some participants received acquisition and test in the dark and extinction in the light, whereas other participants received the opposite configuration. Comparisons between these two groups of participants showed no differences in the magnitude of renewal between them. These findings were replicated in a recent experiment by Bandarian Balooch and Neumann (2011) using a self-report measure of learning. Based on these findings it would seem that renewal does not depend on the type of lighting (i.e., dark context versus light context) in which extinction was learnt. Rather, it seems to depend more on a mere change in lighting.

Similar to the Vansteenwegen et al. (2005) study, further research has found ABA renewal within fear conditioning paradigms following changes in lighting (e.g., dark versus light or green versus red) as contextual manipulations (Bandarian Balooch and Neumann, 2011; Dibbets, Havermans, and Arntz, 2008; Effting and Kindt, 2007; Finlay and Forsyth, 2009; Neumann et al., 2007; Vansteenwegen et al., 2005; Vansteenwegen et al., 2006; Vervliet, Vansteenwegen, and Hermans, 2010). Other studies found ABA renewal by using photographs of real life environments (e.g., office) as the contextual manipulation (Milad et al., 2006; Milad et al., 2005; Neumann and Kitlertsirivatana, 2010; Neumann and Longbottom, 2008). Using more ecologically valid contextual manipulations, such as photographs, is important because they provide a greater range of contextual cues and information that otherwise might not have been detected by, for instance, changing the lighting level of the room.

Neumann and Longbottom (2008) found ABA renewal effects in a sample of university students. They paired fear-relevant stimuli CSs (spiders and snakes) or fear-irrelevant stimuli CSs (mushrooms and flowers) with electrotactile shocks as USs using photographs of real life environments as contextual manipulations. Figure 1 shows samples of the photographs used as context alone, and context plus fear-relevant and fear-irrelevant stimuli used by Neumann and Longbottom. They found that following acquisition in one context and extinction in another, participants' expectancies of receiving a shock and skin conductance responses were renewed when again exposed to the CS in the original acquisition context. The renewal of fear may have occurred due to the retrieval of the CS-US association from memory being promoted by the contextual cues that were present during the test phase.

Furthermore, Neumann and Longbottom (2008) found an interaction between the type of stimuli used (fear-relevant versus fear-irrelevant) and the context in which they were presented. Renewal was stronger for fear-irrelevant stimuli when acquisition and test were conducted in the bush context and extinction in the office context. For the fear-relevant stimuli, however, stronger renewal was found when acquisition and test were conducted in an office context and extinction in a bush context. The authors tentatively explained these results as due to a violation of expectations that may have occurred during extinction. A snake encounter in a bush context represents a congruent context in which it is more likely to expect to see a snake and be harmed by one. Because participants did not receive the US in this context (as it was an extinction phase) it increased surprise and resulted in added attention to

Figure 1. Example stimuli used by Neumann and Longbottom (2008). The photographs depict either a context alone or a context and CS in combination. The examples show an office context alone (top left panel), bush context alone (top right panel), fear-irrelevant flower CS in office context (middle left panel), fear-irrelevant mushroom CS in bush context (middle right panel), fear-relevant snake CS in office context (bottom left panel), and fear-relevant spider CS in bush context (bottom right panel).

the relationship between the CS and US and the contextual cues. As a result of this increased attention, extinction learning became much more context-specific than when the extinction phase occurred in an incongruent context (i.e., not receiving the US following fear-relevant stimuli in an office environment was less surprising than for a bush context). The greater degree of context-specificity of extinction learning resulted in an enhanced renewal effect during the test phase. Neumann and Longbottom did not offer an explanation for why renewal for fear-irrelevant stimuli was influenced by the nature of the context. However, it may be speculated that for the fear-irrelevant stimuli, the omission of the US during extinction may have elicited greater surprise in the office context. This may have resulted in relatively more attention being paid to the contextual cues during extinction, resulting in a stronger renewal during test. These findings are important because they provide added information regarding the intricate interactions between various CSs and contexts and how these may affect the renewal of fear.

Human perception of an environment is not fixed as in a single photograph. Additional research has taken this into account in various ways. Huff, Hernandez, Blanding, and Labar (2009) used changes in physical location (i.e., different laboratory rooms) to manipulate context. Research by Neumann and Longbottom (2008) and Neumann and Kitlertsirivatana (2010) used photographs of the CS and context taken at different angles and locations in the same general context (e.g., spider on desk in office and spider on floor in office) to create an impression of a global context. A more dynamic approach was used by Alvarez, Johnson, and Grillion, 2007 (see also Grillion, Alvarez, Johnson, and Chavis, 2002) in which the context was manipulated using virtual reality environments in an airport, subway, and city streets. In a virtual reality environment, there are a multitude of contextual cues available that can be used during the retrieval of previously learnt associations from memory, immensely increasing the ecological validity of such a procedure. Alvarez et al. (2007) found that extinction was indeed context dependent. A renewal of fear occurred when they shifted from the extinction context to the acquisition context during test and this was not affected by contextual conditioning.

Finlay and Forsyth (2009) noted that previous research has used USs such as shocks and loud tones and that these USs, although aversive, may not fully generalise to the experience of anxiety symptoms. To increase the generality of renewal to clinical symptoms of anxiety they used inhalation of carbon dioxide enriched air as a US during the acquisition phase. Inhalation of carbon dioxide enriched air results in partial oxygen deprivation and a variety of both psychological and autonomic physiological responses that are similar to the fear responses observed in the clinic and symptoms of panic attacks (Forsyth, Eifert, and Canna, 2000; Forsyth, Lejuez, and Finlay, 2000). Participants were not required to breathe the carbon dioxide enriched air during the extinction phase. The switch from the extinction context to the original acquisition context during the test phase resulted in increased fear of receiving the US. The return of fear via an ABA renewal effect using oxygen deprivation observed in this study provides evidence that renewal is not restricted to laboratory-based USs such as loud noises and shocks.

The research reviewed so far has used physical context manipulations to examine renewal. Physical context manipulations are easily translated to a clinical context where, for instance, changes in location from the therapist's office, the client's home, or the client's workplace function as the changing contexts. However, Bouton (2002) suggested that previously learnt associations may not only be modulated by external contexts (e.g., physical location), but also by internal contexts or states (e.g., drug state, affective state). This phenomenon is more widely recognised as state-dependent learning and is not unfamiliar to exposure therapy researchers (for a review, see Craske, 1999). The ability of changes in internal states to function as a change of context that promotes renewal has been examined in clinical-analogue research. Mystkowski et al. (2003) used a sample of high spider fearful individuals to examine whether a return of fear would occur when there is a change in internal context manipulated through caffeine administration. They found a return of fear for those who received exposure treatment in one context (i.e., caffeine administered) and follow up testing in another context (i.e., placebo administered). This suggests that a return of fear may occur via a renewal effect even when the change in context is internal. When interpreted in the context of Bouton's (1993, 1994; Bouton and Nelson, 1998) model, the ambiguity regarding the meaning of the previously feared object may be resolved not only by external contextual cues, but also by internal cues.

THE GENERALITY OF THE RETURN OF FEAR TO AN ABC RENEWAL DESIGN

The ABA renewal effect is limited to laboratory investigations where the context in the acquisition, extinction and test phases can be manipulated. It cannot be investigated in clinical-analogue studies because the acquisition context is presumed to be different to the experimentally manipulated test context. The control over the acquisition context in laboratory-based research is important to our understanding of how the context interacts with our learning experiences to modulate the return of fear. However, the return of fear via an ABA renewal effect is limited because it involves a re-encounter of the previously feared stimulus in the original acquisition context after treatment. There may be instances when the client is not aware of the exact location of initial fear acquisition. It may then be more applicable to the clinic to consider return of fear via an ABC renewal effect where a re-encounter of the feared object occurs in any novel context that is not the acquisition or the extinction context (Bouton, 2002; 2004).

Effting and Kindt (2007) aimed to produce a return of fear via an ABC renewal effect in a sample of University students using line drawings of faces as CSs, shocks as the US, and pink and yellow lights as contextual manipulations. Although they did observe an increased expectancy of receiving a US when test was conducted in a novel context, an increase in expectancy was also observed in a control stimulus that had never been paired with the US. As such, their results did not provide clear evidence of ABC renewal, but suggested that exposure to any CS in a novel context will increase expectancy of the US.

Neumann and Kitlertsirivatana (2010) suggested that Effting and Kindt (2007) did not reproduce the ABC renewal effect in humans due to the low strength of the contextual manipulations used (i.e., changes in lighting of a room). They used an aversive conditioning procedure in which shocks were administered as a US. By strengthening the contextual manipulations by using photographs of tools (i.e., screwdrivers) as CSs in real contextual environments (i.e., office), they successfully reproduced ABC renewal in humans. These findings are important because they provide the appropriate methodology to replicate the ABC renewal effect in humans. In addition, the findings from clinical analogue studies in which test trials are conducted in a novel context (Mineka et al., 1999; Mystkowski et al., 2002; 2003; 2006; Rodriguez et al., 1999; Vansteenwegen, Vervliet, Iberico, et al., 2007) converge with the Neumann and Kitlertsirivatana (2010) study. They also lend support to the notion that return of fear can occur via an ABC renewal effect.

In a clinical analogue study, Mineka et al. (1999) used a high spider fearful sample to investigate whether there would be a return of fear when the context was different from exposure treatment to subsequent follow up. They used self reports, behavioural avoidance tests and heart rate to measure fear. During exposure treatment conducted in the clinician's office (context B) the participants learnt to gradually approach the spider and perform increasingly bold tasks, such as holding the spider in their bare hands. When the participants were able to hold the spider in their hand while reporting low levels of fear they were considered as having successfully completed the treatment.

During follow up, participants were again asked to hold the spider in their hands either in the same context as during exposure treatment or in a novel context. Mineka et al. (1999) found an increase in participants' subjective fear ratings relative to post-extinction when follow up was conducted in a novel treatment room (context C). The shift of context from exposure treatment to follow up seems to have resulted in a return of fear due to retrieval of the CS-US association. However, similar to a previous study that had found a return of fear via an ABC renewal effect (e.g., Rodriguez et al., 1999) the size of the return of fear was relatively modest.

Mystkowski et al. (2002) aimed to produce a larger return of fear and provide greater real world application of contextual manipulations by using a therapy room and an outdoor patio as contextual manipulations. They found a significant decrease in self reported fear ratings from pre exposure to post exposure treatment. But this decrease did not generalise to novel contexts as a moderate increase in fear ratings was observed when there was a switch between the contexts used from exposure treatment to follow up.

The findings from Mystkowski et al. suggest that although there was a clinically meaningful decrease in the participants' fear level from pre to post exposure, they were still vulnerable to return of fear. Subsequent to exposure treatment, both acquisition and extinction learning may have been stored in memory. Upon re-encounter of the spider in the novel context these associations may have led to competing responses. Due to the more or less context free nature of acquisition learning when compared to extinction learning, the former was more likely to be expressed, resulting in return of fear.

Summary of the Generality of Return of Fear to an ABC Renewal Design

A great deal of the early laboratory research on renewal in humans successfully validated the application of renewal to the etiology and treatment of various disorders (for discussion see, Mineka and Zinbarg, 2006). Human fear conditioning studies have shown that renewal is general across a range of CSs, from geometric figures to faces. Renewal is also general across a range of different context manipulations, from background colours, lighting changes, photograph backgrounds, to virtual reality. Renewal may also be produced by both external and internal context changes in humans. Finally, research has demonstrated both ABA and ABC renewal. However, much of this work has been focused on demonstrating the renewal effect using various methods with human samples. Neumann et al. (2008) noted that these studies tend to focus on the procedural details of how to produce large and reliable renewal effects in humans. It is, however, equally important to examine which factors affect renewal as this knowledge may suggest ways to reduce relapse by enhancing the exposure therapy process.

EFFECTS OF EXPERIMENTAL MANIPULATIONS ON RENEWAL

A series of researchers who have investigated the return of fear via a renewal effect in humans have found factors that may act to reduce it rather than enhance it (Bandarian Balooch and Neumann, 2011; Huff et al., 2009; Mystkowski et al., 2006; Neumann et al., 2007; Vervliet et al., 2010; Vansteenwegen et al., 2006; Vansteenwegen, Vervliet, Hermans, et al., 2007; Vansteenwegen, Vervliet, Iberico, et al., 2007). Table 1 provides a summary of the findings from research that has aimed to test procedures that may reduce the return of fear via a renewal effect. As can be seen, this research has used various types of experiments and types of participant samples. Mystkowski et al. (2006) attempted to reduce the return of fear via an ABC renewal effect in a sample of spider fearful individuals. Participants received exposure treatment in one context and follow up in a different context. During follow up, participants were asked either to attempt to mentally retrieve the memories of the treatment context or memories of non-treatment related events. They found smaller renewal effects for participants who were asked to retrieve memories of the extinction context. The authors suggested that the reduced renewal may have been due to participants having mentally reinstated memories of cues that were present during extinction treatment and that this resulted in the attenuation of renewal. Using a non fearful sample, Vansteenwegen et al. (2006) obtained comparable results to Mystkowski et al. (2006) in a laboratory experiment using an ABA renewal design. However, instead of mentally reinstated cues, Vansteenwegen et al. used an actual cue (projection of a small black cross). The cue had either been presented earlier during acquisition or during extinction. Renewal was smaller in the group that was presented with the cue during extinction when compared to when the cue was presented during acquisition. The authors did, however, note that the lack of a control group creates uncertainties regarding whether the results reflected enhanced renewal in the acquisition cue group or reduced renewal in the extinction cue group. Similar findings to Vansteenwegen et al. (2006) were produced by Dibbets et al. (2008) using geometric figures as CSs, loud noises as a US, and orange and blue coloured lighting as contextual manipulations. They found that renewal was reduced for those who received an extinction cue during test when conducted in the original acquisition context when compared to those that did not receive an extinction cue. One important note to be made is that both Vansteenwegen et al. and Dibbets et al. reduced ABA renewal but did not completely remove it (i.e., the CRs to the CS in the experimental condition was still higher than in the control condition). Both ABA renewal and spontaneous recovery were removed by Huff et al. (2009) by providing extinction treatment 24 hours post acquisition rather than immediately post acquisition. They used photographs of snakes and spiders as CSs, and shocks to the wrist as a US and changes in actual locations (laboratory room vs domestic room). Their results showed both spontaneous recovery and ABA renewal of fear in participants who received acquisition and extinction on the same day but test on the next day. These effects were not apparent for the group that received 24 hours between each of the acquisition, extinction and test phases. Interestingly, it was observed that delaying extinction treatment and test removes renewal completely.

Table 1. A Short Summary of Various Methods of Reducing Return of Fear via a Renewal Effect

Authors	Methodology					Stimuli type		Attenuation of renewal	
	Sample type	N	Procedure	Attenuation method	Design	CS	US	ABA	ABC
Mystkowski et al. (2006)	High fearful	48	Clinical-analogue	Mental Cue	ABC	Real Spider	N/A	N/A	Yes
Vansteenwegen et al. (2006)	Non fearful	32	Fear-conditioning	Visual Cue	ABA	Face line drawings	Noise	Yes	N/A
Dibbets et al. (2008)	Non fearful	75	Fear-conditioning	Visual Cue	ABA	Shapes	Noise	Yes	N/A
Huff et al. (2009)	Non fearful	66	Fear-conditioning	Delayed extinction	ABA	Spider and Snake photographs	Shock	Yes	N/A
Vervliet et al. (2010)	Non fearful	32	Fear-conditioning	Unpaired US presentations	ABA	Face line drawings	Shock	Yes	N/A
Neumann et al. (2007).	Non fearful	27[1]	Fear-conditioning	MEC	ABA	Shapes	Shock	No	N/A
Bandarian Balooch and Neumann, (2011)	Non fearful	99	Fear-conditioning	MEC + context similarity	ABA	Shapes	Shock	Yes	N/A
Vansteenwegen, Vervliet, Hermans, et al. (2007)	Phobic	32	Clinical-analogue	MEC	ABC	Real Spider	N/A	N/A	Yes
Vansteenwegen Vervliet, Iberico, et al. (2007)	High fearful	54	Clinical-analogue	MEC	ABC	Spider videos	N/A	N/A	Yes

Note: [1] N was derived by averaging across two experiments. MEC = Multiple extinction contexts. N/A = not applicable. ABA = acquisition in context A, extinction in a novel context B and test again in context A. ABC = acquisition in context A, extinction in a novel context B and test in a novel context C.

The authors suggested that the added delay after acquisition promoted consolidation of extinction learning in memory, thus increasing the likelihood of extinction memory recall during test and removing renewal.

Milad et al. (2006) also found that internal state influences recall of extinction learning during test. They compared healthy adult females who were either in their early menstrual cycle or late menstrual cycle to males using an ABA renewal design. Interestingly they found that males exhibited larger renewal than females overall. Moreover, females in their late menstrual cycle showed less extinction memory recall than females in their early menstrual cycle. This was measured by examining the participants' responses towards the CS in the same context as during extinction but one day later. However, this difference was not pronounced on the renewal test where there was no difference between the two groups of females. The authors made the intriguing suggestion that the mixed results may be due to the increased estrogen production during the females' menstrual cycle. They argued that estrogen has both anxiety increasing and decreasing properties that may have affected various phases of the experiment accordingly. The most interesting outcome of this research may be that it raises awareness that extinction learning and fear renewal may be affected not just by external contextual change but also by the internal state (e.g., stress or mood) of the individual.

One of the most researched ways of attenuating the renewal of fear is the use of extinction treatment conducted in multiple extinction contexts (Bandarian Balooch and Neumann, 2011; Neumann et al., 2007; Vansteenwegen, Vervliet, Hermans, et al., 2007; Vansteenwegen, Vervliet, Iberico, et al., 2007). The context specific nature of extinction learning may lead to the renewal of previously conditioned behaviour when the CS is encountered in the acquisition context or a novel context. Providing extinction in multiple contexts may increase the shared cues between the extinction and subsequent test contexts which may promote retrieval of the CS-noUS association when the CS is re-encountered in either the acquisition or a novel context during test.

Vasteenwegen, Vervliet, Hermans, et al. (2007) failed to find the renewal effect in a sample of participants with spider phobia when test was conducted three months post exposure treatment. They found no differences between those tested after three months in the same room and building as during exposure treatment and those tested in a different room and building for any of their measures (behavioural, self report and physiological measures). However, at one year follow up the participants who had been previously tested in the same room and building (context A) reported a significantly larger return of fear. The authors suggested that the difference in return of fear observed was a product of the group with significantly more return of fear only having been tested in one context prior to 1 year follow up whereas the other group was tested in multiple contexts prior to 1 year follow up.

The effects of conducting multiple extinction contexts on return of fear via an ABC renewal effect was explicitly tested by Vansteenwegen, Vervliet, Iberico, et al. (2007) in a clinical analogue experiment. They presented a sample of spider-anxious students with repeated confrontations of videotaped spiders in either a single context or in multiple contexts. Four different rooms in a house (kitchen, basement, living room and bathroom) with and without the presence of a spider were videotaped and used as contexts. They found evidence of ABC renewal for the single extinction context groups but not for the multiple extinction context group and the control group (no context switch between extinction and follow up). The most important implication that can be drawn from these results is that the use of multiple extinction contexts may potentially attenuate return of fear via an ABC renewal effect even when the circumstances surrounding the acquisition of fear learning are not known.

A criticism of the use of multiple extinction contexts was made by Bouton et al. (2006). They emphasised that although multiple extinction contexts may enhance generalisation of extinction learning these effects are negated when acquisition learning also occurs in multiple contexts. Arguably, in real life, the acquisition of fear of, for instance, spiders does not prohibit future aversive encounters. Phobias may develop through a variety of aversive encounters with the feared object in multiple contexts. The finding by Vansteenwegen, Vervliet, Iberico et al. (2007) shows that for humans, this may not be much of an issue as their sample had naturally acquired their fear of spiders, and yet, renewal was attenuated using multiple extinction contexts. Whether multiple extinction contexts can attenuate renewal following acquisition in multiple contexts may be readily tested using laboratory based experiments wherein the acquisition phase can be manipulated.

Neumann et al. (2007) aimed to test whether renewal via an ABA design can be attenuated by conducting extinction in multiple contexts in a fear conditioning paradigm in humans. They conducted two experiments using geometric shapes as the CS and a shock as the US. Context was manipulated using different lights and sounds. The results showed no attenuation of renewal following extinction in multiple contexts in either experiment. No significant differences were found in expectancy of being shocked at test between the single context extinction group and when extinction was conducted in three or five contexts. The results suggested that using multiple extinction contexts does not necessarily enhance generalisation of extinction learning, at least not enough to attenuate renewal via an ABA design.

ABA renewal effects have been found to be stronger than ABC renewal effects (Neumann and Kitlertsirivatana, 2010). For ABA renewal, the external contextual cues between acquisition and test are identical. Therefore, the added shared cues between the multiple extinction contexts and test context may still be too few for the CS-noUS association to be retrieved during test. Alternatively, ABA renewal at test might be promoted due to the same context used during acquisition via a context-US association and that this is sufficiently strong to outweigh the benefits of multiple extinction contexts. Using additional methods to increase the likelihood that the CS-noUS association is retrieved (e.g., increased number of extinction trials) may therefore be necessary to attenuate ABA renewal.

Bandarian Balooch and Neumann (2011) highlighted the notion that a combination of methods may be required to attenuate ABA renewal. They used line drawings of triangles and squares as CSs, shocks as a US, and a combination of different light levels ranging from dark to light as contextual manipulations. To attenuate renewal they used a combination of multiple extinction contexts and extinction treatment conducted in contexts that were similar between acquisition, extinction, and test. Using this method they found when multiple extinction contexts were combined with similar contexts between acquisition, extinction, and test, renewal was completely abolished. However, when either multiple extinction contexts or a single similar extinction context was used, renewal was only attenuated and not abolished. The results suggested that using multiple extinction contexts that are similar to the acquisition and test context enhances the generalisability of extinction learning through an increased number of shared cues between the acquisition, extinction, and test context. It must be noted, however, that it may be sufficient to use multiple extinction contexts alone to attenuate renewal in an ABC design because the contexts are all equally different to one another. As such, using multiple extinction contexts alone may be enough to provide more shared contextual cues between extinction and test than acquisition and test, thus resulting in the CS-noUS association being retrieved during test, ultimately abolishing renewal via an ABC design.

Summary of the Effects of Experimental Manipulations on Renewal

Taken together, the above research provides a variety of variables that may act to reduce return of fear via a renewal effect. Researchers have reduced the return of fear via a renewal effect by using mental or visual cues of the extinction process, delaying the extinction trials, administering unpaired US presentations during extinction and manipulating the context of exposure. The replication of the research presented here and further research that tests other novel ways to attenuate return of fear via a renewal effect is important. Further research may provide the means for clinicians to enhance their understanding of the underlying theoretical mechanisms that govern the exposure therapy process. Most importantly, this line of research creates an avenue for researchers to test various exposure treatment protocols with the aim of improving exposure treatment, such that less return of fear is observed post treatment.

APPLICATIONS

Increasing recognition and understanding of the phenomenon of renewal can assist in explaining the high rates of relapse observed when anxiety disorders are treated in the clinical setting. Understanding these processes, in turn, provides insight into some potential methods by which relapse risk can be reduced. Previous research suggests that there are seven mechanisms which can reduce the level of return of fear, and thereby reduce the risk of relapse due to renewal effects. These mechanisms are the use of appropriate contexts, the use of a range of treatment contexts, the use of homework tasks involving exposure sessions in multiple contexts, the use of exposure with a range of interoceptive cues, the use of mental reinstatement when encountering the phobic stimulus, the use of portable contextual cues, and allowing the appropriate amount of time between treatment and follow-up sessions. This section briefly reviews each of these, with examples from clinical practice.

1. Similarity between the Extinction Context and Future Contexts

The first method generated through an understanding of renewal of fear that can assist in reducing relapse after successful treatment is to conduct exposure sessions repeatedly in a context similar to that where the phobic stimulus is likely to be encountered in the future (Bandarian Balooch and Neumann, 2011). Most of the experiments conducted on return of fear via an ABC renewal effect have reported a generalization of extinction learning when therapy and follow up are conducted in the same context (Mineka et al., 1999; Mystkowski et al., 2002; Mystkowski et al., 2006; Rodriguez et al., 1999; Vansteenwegen, Vervliet, Iberico, et al., 2007). While it may not always be possible (e.g., where the client expects to encounter spiders while trekking in South-American rain forests, but is treated for their fear of spiders by their local clinician in Australia), the use of exposure in contexts where the feared stimulus may be encountered in the future, can be incorporated in treatments where these appropriate contexts are accessible and feasibly used. Such methods ensure that the contextual cues in the environment where the person is likely to encounter their feared stimulus are also present during the treatment. If the feared stimulus is encountered after treatment in this context, the cues available in the environment may assist with retrieval of the CS-noUS association and thereby prevent a fear conditioned response. A clinical example of this is where a child who is afraid of dogs undergoes exposure treatment in the local park where her family regularly visits, and where she is most likely to come into contact with dogs in the future.

2. Extinction Treatment in a Range of Different Contexts

The second method by which renewal of fear due to changes in context may be attenuated is to conduct exposure treatments in a range of different environmental contexts. By using a range of different treatment contexts, the clinician aims to ensure that the CS-noUS association is experienced in the presence of a wide range of environmental cues. Future encounters with the phobic stimulus are thereby more likely to occur in the presence of some of these environmental cues. The final aim of this is to enhance the likelihood that the CS-noUS association is retrieved. Previous research has demonstrated that exposure in multiple contexts can attenuate renewal (Bandarian Balooch and Neumann, 2011; Gunther, Denniston, and Miller, 1998; Vansteenwegen, Vervliet, Iberico, et al., 2007; cf. Neumann et al., 2007). In clinical practice, for example, a clinician may provide exposure therapy to a client with spider phobia in multiple Australian forest scenarios that shares cues similar to the South-American forests that a client expects to visit in a future holiday. Doing this may increase the number of shared cues between the context in which exposure therapy occurs and those in which spiders might be re-encountered following therapy.

3. Homework Exposure Tasks

The use of homework exposure tasks is a third mechanism by which renewal may be reduced. Similar to the first two mechanisms outlined above, the use of homework tasks can allow the client to encounter their feared stimulus in the presence of a range of different contextual cues. Where the phobic stimulus is encountered in future, the presence of these cues may facilitate retrieval of the CS-noUS association, thereby reducing the anxiety response. For example, a client that is afraid of elevators may work with their therapist to develop homework tasks that involve exposure to a wide variety of different elevators.

4. Recognition of Internal Cues as Contexts

The fourth method to reduce return of fear through renewal is to recognise the importance of internal cues as contexts which may affect return of fear through renewal (Bouton, 2002). Huff et al. (2009) and Milad et al. (2006) both showed that internal state factors do affect the return of fear via a renewal effect. When paired together with the findings by Mystkowski et al. (2003) that a shift in internal context alone may be enough to renew fear of an object it becomes evident that these factors must be considered in the clinic. For example, clinicians could be aware that the lack of return of fear following exposure therapy treatment may in some instances reflect temporary anxiety reducing hormonal states. In fact, the possibility exists of renewed fear following such a period due to shifts in internal state alone as seen in Mystkowski et al. It is not only hormonal changes that occur depending on the day or month but also changes in, for instance, sleep pattern (e.g., weekend) and diet (e.g., Christmas holidays). To control for such effects, clinicians could conduct exposure therapy and subsequent follow up tests in multiple locations and during different days of the month and hours of the day. This may ensure that no systematic internal state shift such as menstrual cycle, irregularities of diet (e.g., more coffee in the day than in the night), use of medications or other drugs (e.g., nicotine) limit the effectiveness of exposure.

5. Mental Reinstatement of the Treatment Context

The fifth method by which renewal-based return of fear may be attenuated is the use of mental reinstatement of the treatment context by the client, when they encounter the phobic stimulus in future. A return of fear via a renewal effect has been attenuated when participants were encouraged to use mental cues that reminded them of the exposure treatment context (Mystkowski et al., 2006).

Given the wide array of internal cues available, clinicians could provide a range of different mental cues to their clients to "carry with them" as a reminder of the exposure treatment. For example, exposure therapy to a fear of snakes may be conducted while playing a specific piece of music in the background. The client may then mentally "play back" the piece of music as they walk through long grass on a bushwalk in the future.

6. Use of Portable Physical Extinction Cues

The sixth method of reducing renewal of the anxiety response is to make use of portable physical cues that have been associated with the treatment context. When a client encounters, or expects to encounter, their phobic situation or object, they can use these portable cues to remind them of the treatment context, and facilitate retrieval of the CS-noUS association. Return of fear has been reduced in previous research, where participants were encouraged to use cues (Dibbets et al., 2006; Vansteenwegen et al., 2006) that reminded them of the exposure treatment context.

Many clinicians would see the eventual aim as relinquishing what may become problematic safety objects, but the use of these portable cues may still be considered in treatment planning. For example, a client who is afraid of heights has exposure conducted while holding a watch given to him by the therapist. When the client is required to approach a window in a tall building, he can carry the same watch as a way of reducing the renewal of their anxiety through cues shared with the treatment context.

7. Permitting Time to Lapse between Phases of Learning and Testing

A final way to battle return of fear via renewal may be to allow for sufficient time to lapse between the moment of fear acquisition and extinction treatment and subsequent follow up (Huff et al., 2009). Clinicians may for example increase the time between each exposure therapy session. Doing this may allow clients to fully consolidate the memory of prior exposure therapy sessions potentially enhancing clients' ability to process new learning. Clinicians may also allow for longer time to lapse between the final exposure therapy session and the subsequent follow up sessions. Early follow up sessions may show elevated levels of fear that may reflect the lack of exposure therapy memory consolidation rather than a long lasting return of fear. Providing added time between each exposure therapy session and the subsequent follow up sessions may promote consolidation of exposure therapy memory resulting in a reduced return of fear via a renewal effect. However, further lab based studies may be required before the optimal amount of time needed between each phase can be reliably determined.

Summary of applications

Fear-conditioning research on factors that affect renewal suggests that there is a multitude of ways that this literature can be applied to the clinic to enhance exposure therapy. The suggestions made above are tentative and require further research. Furthermore, they may not be the only ways that this literature can be adapted to the clinic. Researchers are encouraged to explore new and novel ways to both attenuate renewal in laboratory findings as well as finding applications in the clinic. These findings could be further tested in both clinical-analogue and fully clinical studies to ensure their efficacy both when combined with other common treatment components and when conducted on clinical samples.

CONCLUSION

Modern day conditioning models of anxiety disorders are much more complex than they were more than eight decades ago (for a discussion, see Field, 2006; Mineka and Zinbarg, 2006). Today they provide explanations such as why some people acquire fears and some do not and they show how a person can acquire a fear simply by being exposed to other people's fear (i.e., vicarious learning of fear associations). As seen in the current chapter, modern conditioning models can explain how contextual changes modulate the return of fear post treatment. This is important because these models explain why anxiety disorders develop and provide hints as to how they can be treated. Cognitive behavioural treatments of anxiety disorders involve more than exposure therapy alone (Craske, 1999). A combination of methods is used to, for instance, battle the cognitive distortions, coping inabilities, and avoidance behaviours that are associated with anxiety disorders to mention a few. Even in these more complex treatments the exposure therapy process has been implicated as one of the key components (Emmelkamp, 2004). The relatively high occurrence of relapse following treatment suggests that there is a need for clinicians to not only introduce new treatment methods that can be combined with current exposure therapy norms. But there is also a need to develop and improve upon the methods of the exposure process itself. Laboratory-based research remains as an important component in this future work. It allows researchers to have control over the initial acquisition of fear learning and control other extraneous variables that may obscure the underlying learning process. Discoveries made in the laboratory can be extended to semi-clinical studies with highly fearful individuals, and ultimately, to the clinical context with individuals that suffer from anxiety disorders.

Fear is an important component in all of the anxiety disorders. The relative ease with which fears are reduced during exposure therapy treatment such as that seen in Öst's (1998) one session treatment for specific phobias should not be an indication to clinicians that their clients are "cured". The initial fear learning is not removed during treatment, thus presenting a much more complex opponent than originally thought. Modern day exposure therapy treatments need to be enhanced to competently battle these complexities. To assist in this process, researchers could use methodology that is increasingly generalisable to the clinic and provide easy to follow explanations to clinicians about how their research findings could be applied and tested in the clinic. The current chapter heeded this advice and provided some methods that clinicians can add to their current exposure therapy treatment plans to reduce the return of fear via a renewal effect following successful treatment.

REFERENCES

Alvarez, R. P., Johnson, L., and Grillion, C. (2007). Contextual-specificity of short delay extinction in humans: Renewal of fear-potentiated startle in a virtual environment. *Learning and Memory*, 14, 247-253.

Aitken, R. C. B., Lister, J. A., and Main, C. J. (1981). Identification of features associated with flying phobia in aircrew. *British Journal of Psychiatry*, 139, 38−42.

American Psychiatric Association (2000). *Diagnostic and Statistical Manual of Mental Disorders* (Revised 4th ed.). Washington, DC: Author.

Barlow, D. H., Craske, M. G., Cerny, J. A., and Klosko, J. S. (1989). Behavioral treatment of panic disorder. *Behavior Therapy*, 20, 261-282.

Bandarian Balooch, S., and Neumann, D. L. (2011). Effects of Multiple Contexts and Context Similarity on the Renewal of Extinguished Conditioned Behavior in an ABA Design with Humans. *Learning and Motivation*, 42, 53-63.

Boschen, M. J., Neumann, D. L., and Waters, A. M. (2009). Relapse of successfully treated anxiety and fear: Theoretical issues and recommendations for clinical practice. *Australian and New Zealand Journal of Psychi*atry, 43, 89-100.

Bouton, M. E. (1993). Context, time, and memory retrieval in the interference paradigms of Pavlovian learning. *Psychological Bulletin*, 114, 80-99.

Bouton, M. E. (1994). Conditioning remembering and forgetting. *Journal of Experimental Psychology: Animal Behaviour Processes*, 20, 219-231.

Bouton, M. E. (2002). Context, ambiguity, and unlearning: Sources of relapse after behavioral extinction. *Biological Psychiatry*, 52, 976-986.

Bouton, M. E. (2004). Context and behavioural processes in extinction. *Learning and Memory*, 11, 485-494.

Bouton, M. E., and Bolles, R. C. (1979). Contextual control of the extinction of conditioned fear. *Learning and Motivation*, 10, 445-466.

Bouton, M. E., and Brooks, D. C. (1993). Time and context effects on performance in a Pavlovian discrimination reversal. *Journal of Experimental Psychology: Animal Behaviour Processes*, 19, 165-179.

Bouton, M. E. and King, D. A. (1983). Contextual control of the extinction of conditioned fear: Tests for the associative value of the context. *Journal of Experimental Psychology: Animal Behavior Processes*, 9, 248-265.

Bouton, M. E., Mineka, S., and Barlow, D. H. (2001). A modern learning theory on the etiology of panic disorder. *Psychological Review*, 108, 4-32.

Bouton, M. E., and Nelson, J. B. (1993). Context-specificity of target vs. feature inhibition in a feature negative discrimination. *Journal of Experimental Psychology: Animal Behavior Processes,* 20, 51-65.

Bouton, M. E., and Nelson, J. B. (1998). Mechanisms of feature-positive and feature-negative discrimination learning in an appetitive conditioning paradigm. In N. Schmajuk and P.C. Holland (Eds.), *Occasion setting: Associative learning and cognition in animals* (pp. 69-112). Washington, DC: American Psychological Association.

Bouton, M. E., and Ricker, S. T. (1994). Renewal of extinguished responding in a second context. *Animal Learning and Behavior*, 22, 317-324.

Bouton, M. E., and Swartzentruber, D. (1986). Analysis of the associative and occasion-setting properties of contexts participating in a Pavlovian discrimination. *Journal of Experimental Psychology: Animal Behavior Processes*, 12, 333-350.

Bouton, M. E., and Swartzentruber, D. (1991). Sources of relapse after extinction in Pavlovian and instrumental learning. *Clinical Psychology Review*, 11, 123-140.

Bouton, M. E., Westbrook, K. A., Corcoran, K. A., and Maren, S. (2006). Contextual and temporal modulation of extinction: Behavioral and biological mechanisms. *Biological Psychiatry*, 60, 352-360.

Craske, M. G. (1999). *Anxiety disorders: Psychological approaches to theory and treatment.* Bolder, CO: Westview Press.

Craske, M. G., and Rachman, S. J. (1987). Return of fear: Perceived skill and heart rate responsivity. *British Journal of Clinical Psychology*, 26, 187-200.

Davey, G.C.L. (1992). Characteristics of individuals with fear of spiders. *Anxiety Research*, 4, 299-314.

Davey, G. C. L. (2002). 'Non-specific' rather than 'non-associative' pathways to phobias: A commentary on Poulton and Menzies. *Behaviour Research and Therapy*, 40, 151-158.

Dibbets, P., Havermans, R., and Arntz, A. (2008). All we need is a cue to remember: The effect of an extinction cue on renewal. *Behaviour Research and Therapy*, 46, 1070-1077.

Effting, M., and Kindt, M. (2007). Contextual control of human fear associations in a renewal paradigm. *Behaviour Research and Therapy*, 45, 2002-2018.

Emmelkamp, P. M. G. (2004). Behaviour therapy with adults. In A. E. Bergin and S. L. Garfield (Eds). *Handbook of psychotherapy and behaviour change*, (5th ed, pp. 393-446). New York: Wiley.

Emmelkamp, P. M. G., Bouman, T. K., and Scholing, A. (1992). Anxiety disorders: A practitioner's guide. Chichester, England: Wiley.

Field, A. P. (2006). I don't like it because it eats sprouts: Conditioning preferences in children, *Behaviour Research and Therapy*, 44, 439-455.

Finlay, C. G., and Forsyth, P. J. (2009). Context and renewal of conditioned fear: An experimental evaluation using 20% carbon dioxide-enriched air as an unconditioned stimulus. *Journal of Anxiety Disorders*, 23, 737-745.

Forsyth, J. P., Eifert, G. H., and Canna, M. A. (2000). Evoking analogue subtypes of panic attacks in a nonclinical population using carbon dioxide-enriched air. *Behaviour Research and Therapy*, 38, 559-572.

Forsyth, J. P., Lejuez, C. W., and Finlay, C. G. (2000). Anxiogenic effects of repeated administrations of 20% CO2-enriched air: Stability within sessions and habituation across time. *Journal of Behavior Therapy and Experimental Psychiatry*, 31, 103-121.

Grillion, C. (2002). Startle reactivity and anxiety disorders: Aversive conditioning, context, and neurobiology. *Biological Psychiatry*, 52, 958-975.

Grillion, C., Alvarez, P. R., Johnson, L., and Chavis, C. (2002). Contextual specificity of extinction of delay but not trace eyeblink conditioning in humans. *Learning and Memory*, 15, 387-389.

Gunther, L. M., Denniston, J. C., and Miller, R. R. (1998). Conducting exposure techniques in multiple settings can prevent relapse. *Behaviour Research and Therapy*, 36, 75-91.

Hall, G., and Honey, R. C. (1989). Contextual effects in conditioning, latent inhibition, and habituation: Associative and retrieval functions of contextual cues. *Journal of Experimental Psychology: Animal Behavior Processes*, 15, 232-241.

Hall, G. and Honey, R.C. (1990). Context-specific conditioning in the conditioned-emotional-response procedure. *Journal of Experimental Psychology: Animal Behavior Processes*, 16, 271-278.

Huff. C. N., Hernandez, A. J., Blanding, Q. N., and Labar, S. K. (2009). Delayed extinction attenuates conditioned fear renewal and spontaneous recovery in humans. *Behavioral Neuroscience,* 123, 834-843.

Kaye, H., Preston, G. C., Szabo, L., Druiff, H., and Mackintosh, N. J. (1987). Context specificity of conditioning and latent inhibition: Evidence for a dissociation of latent inhibition and associative interference. *Quarterly Journal of Experimental Psychology*, 39,127-145.

Konorski, J. (1948). Conditioned Reflexes and Neuron Organization. Cambridge, UK: Cambridge University Press.

Lautch, H. (1971). Dental phobia. *British Journal of Psychiatry*, 119, 151-157.

Liddell, A., and Lyons, M. (1978). Thunderstorm phobias. *Behaviour Research and Therapy*, 16, 306-308.

Lovibond, P. F., Preston, G. C., and Mackintosh, N. J. (1984). Context specificity of conditioning, extinction, and latent inhibition. *Journal of Experimental Psychology: Animal Behavior Processes*, 10, 360-375.

Marks, I. M. (1987). *Fears, Phobias, and Rituals*. New York: Academic Press.

Messenger, C., and Shean, G. (1998). The effects of anxiety sensitivity and history of panic on reactions to stressors in a non clinical sample. *Journal of Behavior Therapy and Experimental Psychiatry*, 29, 279-288.

McClelland, J. L., and Rumelhart, D. E. (1985). Distributed memory and the representation of general and specific information. *Journal of Experimental Psychology General*, 114, 159-188.

Milad, M. R., Goldstein, M. J., Orr, P. S., Wedig, M. M., Klibanski, A., and Pitman, K. R, et al. (2006). Fear conditioning and extinction: Influence of sex and menstrual cycle in healthy humans. *Behavioral Neuroscience*, 120, 1196-1203.

Milad, M. R., Quinn, T. B., Pitman, K. R., Orr, P. S., Fischl, B., and Raush, L. S. (2005). Thickness of ventromedial prefrontal cortex in humans is correlated with extinction memory. *Proc. Natl. Acad. Sci. USA*, 102, 10706-10711.

Mineka, S., Mystkowski, J. L., Hladek, D., and Rodriguez, B. I. (1999). The effects of changing contexts on return of fear following exposure treatment for spider fear. *Journal of Consulting and Clinical Psychology*, 67, 599-604.

Mineka, S., and Zinbarg, R. A. (2006). Contemporary learning theory perspective on the etiology of anxiety disorders: It's not what you thought it was. *American Psychologist*, 61, 10-26.

Mystkowski, J. L., Craske, M. G., and Echiverri, A. M. (2002). Treatment context and return of fear in spider phobia. *Behavior Therapy*, 33, 399-416.

Mystkowski, J. L., Craske, M. G., Echiverri, A. M., and Labus, J. S. (2006). Mental reinstatement of context and return of fear in spider fearful participants. *Behavior Therapy*, 37, 49-60.

Mystkowski, J. L., Mineka, S., Vernon, L. L., and Zinbarg, R. E. (2003). Changes in caffeine states enhance return of fear in spider phobia. *Journal of Consulting and Clinical Psychology*, 71, 243-250.

Nelson, J. B. (2002). Context specificity of excitation and inhibition in ambiguous stimuli. *Learning and Motivation*, 33, 284-310.

Neumann, D. L., Boschen, M. J., and Waters, A. M. (2008). The return of extinguished conditioned behaviour in humans: New research and future directions. In L. N. Piccard (Ed.). *Biological Psychology: New Research* (pp. 1-42). New York: Nova Science Publishers.

Neumann, D. L., and Kitlertsirivatana, E. (2010). Exposure to a novel context after extinction causes a renewal of extinguished conditioned responses: Implications for the treatment of fear. *Behaviour Research and Therapy*, 48, 565-570.

Neumann, D. L., Lipp, O. V., and Cory, S. E. (2007). Conducting extinction in multiple contexts does not necessarily attenuate the renewal of shock expectancy in a fear conditioning procedure with human. *Behaviour Research and Therapy*, 45, 385-394.

Neumann, D. L., and Longbottom, P. L. (2008). The renewal of extinguished conditioned fear with fear-relevant and fear-irrelevant stimuli by a context change after extinction. *Behaviour Research and Therapy*, 46, 188-206.

Neumann, D. L., and Waters, A. M. (2006). The use of an unpleasant sound as an unconditional stimulus in a human aversive Pavlovian conditioning procedure. *Biological Psychology*, 73, 175-185.

Öhman, A., and Mineka, S. (2001). Fears, phobias and preparedness: Toward an evolved module of fear and fear learning. *Psychological Review*, 108, 483-522.

Olatunji, B. O., Cisler, J. M., and Deacon, B. J. (2010). Efficacy of cognitive behavioral therapy for anxiety disorders: A review of meta-analytic findings. *Psychiatric Clinics of North America*, 33, 557-577.

Öst, L. G. (1989). One-session treatment for specific phobias. *Behaviour Research and Therapy*, 27, 1-7.

Pavlov, I. P. (1927). *Conditioned reflexes*. London: Oxford University Press.

Pearce, J. M., and Hall, G. (1980). A model for Pavlovian conditioning: Variations in the effectiveness of conditioned but not unconditioned stimuli. *Psychological Review*, 87, 332-352.

Rachman, S. (1966). Studies in desensitization-III. Speed of generalization. *Behaviour Research and Therapy*, 4, 7-16.

Rachman, S. (1977). The conditioning theory of fear acquisition: A critical examination. *Behaviour Research and Therapy*, 15, 375-387.

Rachman, S. (1989). The return of fear: Review and prospect. *Clinical Psychology Review*, 9, 147-168.

Rescorla, R. A., and Wagner, A. R. (1972). A theory of Pavlovian conditioning: Variations in the effectiveness of reinforcement and nonreinforcement. In A. H. Black and W. K. Prokasy (Eds.), *Classical conditioning II: Current research and theory* (pp. 64-99). New York: Appleton-Century-Crofts.

Rodriguez, B. I., Craske, M. G., Mineka, S., and Hladek, D. (1999). Context-specificity of relapse: Effects of therapist and environmental context on return of fear. *Behaviour Research and Therapy*, 37, 845-862.

Rose, M. P., and McGlynn, F. D. (1997). Toward a standard experiment for studying post-treatment return of fear. *Journal of Anxiety Disorders*, 11, 263-277.

Tamai, N., and Nakajima, S. (2000). Renewal of formerly conditioned fear in rats after extensive extinction training. *International Journal of Comparative Psychology*, 13, 137-147.

Thomas, D. A. (1979). Retention of conditioned inhibition in a bar-press suppression paradigm. *Learning and Motivation*, 10, 161-177.

Vansteenwegen, D., Hermans, D., Vervliet, B., Francken, G., Beckers, T., and Baeyens, F., et al. (2005). Return of fear in a human differential conditioning paradigm caused by a return to the original acquisition context. *Behaviour Research and Therapy*, 43, 323-336.

Vansteenwegen, D., Vervliet, B., Hermans, D., Beckers, T., Baeyens, F., and Eelen, P. (2006). Stronger renewal in human fear conditioning when tested with an acquisition retrieval cue than with an extinction retrieval cue. *Behaviour Research and Therapy*, 44, 1717-1725.

Vansteenwegen, D., Vervliet, B., Hermans, D., Thewissen, R. and Eelen, P. (2007). Verbal, behavioural and physiological assessment of the generalization of exposure-based fear reduction in a spider-anxious population. *Behaviour Research and Therapy*, 4, 1717-1725.

Vansteenwegen, D., Vervliet, B., Iberico, C., Baeyens, F., Van den Bergh, O., and Hermans, D. (2007). The repeated confrontation with videotapes of spiders in multiple contexts attenuates renewal of fear in spider-anxious students. *Behaviour Research and Therapy*, 45, 1169-1179.

Vervliet, B., Vansteenwegen, D., and Hermans, D. (2010). Unpaired shocks during extinction weaken the contextual renewal of a conditioned discrimination. *Learning and Motivation*, 41, 22-31.

Watson, J. B., and Rayner, R. (1920). Conditioned emotional reactions. *Journal of Experimental Psychology*, 3, 1-14.

Wolpe, J. (1958). *Psychotherapy by reciprocal inhibition*. Stanford, CA: Stanford University Press.

Chapter 5

THE RELATIONSHIP BETWEEN DIFFERENT MEASURES OF FEAR LEARNING FOLLOWING TESTS FOR REINSTATEMENT AND SPONTANEOUS RECOVERY OF EXTINGUISHED CONDITIONED FEAR

David L. Neumann[1,2,*], Ottmar V. Lipp[3] and Meredith J. McHugh[4]

[1] School of Psychology, Griffith University, Australia.

[2] Behavioural Basis of Health Program, Griffith Health Institute, University, Australia.

[3] School of Psychology, The University of Queensland, Australia.

[4] The National Institute on Drug Abuse, The United States of America.

ABSTRACT

Exposure therapy, which is based on extinction in Pavlovian conditioning, is effective in the treatment of anxiety disorders. However, a return of fear (relapse) can occur after treatment. Reinstatement and spontaneous recovery provide two explanations for return of fear. These mechanisms can be difficult to investigate in real-world clinical contexts for practical or ethical reasons. The present research used a laboratory-based fear learning task to examine reinstatement and spontaneous recovery using different measures of fear learning.

A differential fear conditioning procedure was used. In acquisition, one conditional stimulus (CS+) was paired with a shock unconditional stimulus (US) and a CS- was presented alone. Both CS+ and CS- were presented alone during extinction. Presentations of the US (reinstatement) or a time delay (spontaneous recovery) were given prior to test trials. During test, shock expectancy was greater for CS+ than CS- for reinstatement and was non-differential, although higher than at the end of extinction, for spontaneous recovery. The CS+ was rated as more unpleasant, more arousing, and more dominating than the CS- for both procedures. Skin conductance responses did not differ between the CS+ and CS-. The results show dissociations between the measures that may reflect differential sensitivity to the learning processes that underlie the return of fear. The

---

[*] E-mail: d.neumann@griffith.edu.au

application of the results for understanding the possible mechanisms for relapse following exposure therapy for anxiety disorders is discussed.

Keywords: Exposure therapy, Pavlovian conditioning, reinstatement, spontaneous recovery.

INTRODUCTION

Anxiety disorders are a prevalent form of mental illness affecting 14.4% of the Australian population over a one year period and have a lifetime prevalence of 26.3% (Slade, Johnston, Oakley Browne, Andrews, and Whiteford, 2009). Similar 12 month prevalence rates are reported in other countries like New Zealand (14.8%; Wells et al., 2006) and the United States of America (18.1%; Kessler and Wang, 2008). Anxiety disorders are characterized by pathological fear and anxiety that may be episodic by being elicited by discrete stimuli or situations or may be continuous by occurring across several stimuli and situations. Anxiety disorders produce significant impairments in functioning (Kroenke, Spitzer, Williams, Monahan, and Lowe, 2007) and reduce the quality of life in the sufferer (Olatunji, Cisler, and Tolin, 2007). The high prevalence and significant impairments associated with anxiety disorders emphasizes the need for laboratory-based and clinical research to better understand them. Moreover, it is important to develop treatment approaches that are efficacious in both the short and long term.

Meta-analyses and reviews have established that exposure therapy is an efficacious treatment method for many anxiety disorders, including panic disorder, post-traumatic stress disorder, social phobia, specific phobia, and obsessive-compulsive disorder (Chambless and Ollendick, 2001; Deacon and Abramowitz, 2004). Although exposure therapy produces beneficial short-term change, relapse can occur in the long-term. Relapse of anxiety symptoms, also termed the return of fear (Rachman, 1989), can be investigated through clinical studies that examine symptomatology following treatment or in laboratory-based studies that adopt experimental models of anxiety.

The present research adopted an experimental model of anxiety acquisition, extinction, and relapse by studying the spontaneous recovery and reinstatement of a return of fear. Experimental models are particularly useful because they allow variables to be manipulated to promote the return of fear in a non-clinical sample of individuals. An experimental approach can be difficult to adopt in clinical research due to the practical requirements of the research and the ethical issues that it raises.

PAVLOVIAN CONDITIONING MODELS OF ANXIETY

Pavlovian conditioning has provided an influential model of the acquisition of fears and anxieties (Field, 2006). Pavlovian conditioning is a form of associative learning in which a relationship is learnt between two previously unrelated stimuli. The form of conditioning most relevant to anxiety disorders is fear conditioning (sometimes referred to as aversive conditioning).

In a fear conditioning procedure, a neutral conditional stimulus (CS) is presented contingently with an aversive unconditional stimulus (US). Prior to the contingent presentations, the CS will elicit little fear. However, following the pairing of the CS and US, the presentation of the CS on its own will elicit fear behaviour. In a human fear conditioning experiment, learning may be shown by subjective fear ratings, increased expectancy of the US, or increased physiological responses (e.g., skin conductance) reflecting increased attention and arousal.

Pavlovian fear conditioning plays a central role in contemporary learning models of anxiety (Field, 2006; Mineka and Zinbarg, 2006). For example, a previously neutral stimulus (e.g., elevator) may be paired with an aversive outcome (e.g., panic attack) to produce a phobic fear response when the stimulus is encountered on future occasions (i.e., fear of riding in an elevator).

Contemporary learning models are grounded in experimental psychology and are able to explain how additional factors can inhibit or promote the development of fears. For example, fear may be acquired without direct experience of the pairing of a neutral stimulus and an aversive outcome due to vicarious learning or through verbal transmission of knowledge (Field, 2006). Fears may also be more prevalent to some stimuli (e.g., snakes, spiders) than to other stimuli (e.g., cars, electrical outlets) because the former are examples of prepared stimuli that are more likely to enter into feared associations due to our prior evolutionary history (Mineka and Öhman, 2002). The contemporary learning approach does not negate the influence of genetics, personality, contextual variables, and post-event variables in explaining how and why fears develop. Rather, these variables are incorporated to explain how differences can emerge in the acquisition and subsequent extinction of conditioned fear.

The extinction of fear can be produced in a Pavlovian conditioning procedure by merely presenting the feared CS on its own after acquisition. Extinction is observed as the reduction in fear across the repeated presentations of the CS. The clinical application of extinction is commonly referred to as exposure therapy. Exposure therapy can take a number of forms, although in vivo exposure in which a person is exposed to the object of fear (rather than merely imagining it) is generally considered to be the most effective (e.g., Emmelkamp and Wessels, 1975). Cognitive-behaviour therapies routinely employ the techniques of exposure, and are often the treatment of choice for many anxiety disorders (Barlow, 2002; Barlow, Raffa and Cohen, 2002; Hermans et al, 2005). As noted earlier, exposure therapy is an efficacious treatment method for many anxiety disorders (Chambless and Ollendick, 2001; Deacon and Abramowitz, 2004).

However, relapse of anxiety symptoms (i.e., a return of extinguished fear) can occur in the long-term. Relapse can happen in approximately 30-50% of individuals who are treated for fear using exposure therapy alone or in combination with other treatments (Craske and Rachman, 1987; Rachman, 1966; Rose and McGlynn, 1997; Wolpe, 1958).

RETURN OF FEAR FOLLOWING FEAR EXTINCTION

Experimental manipulations that have been shown to produce a return of extinguished fear behavior following extinction, the experimental equivalent to relapse, have the potential to explain what conditions promote relapse following exposure therapy (see Bouton, 2000, 2002). Four procedures that produce a return of extinguished fear are reinstatement, renewal, spontaneous recovery, and rapid reacquisition (see Boschen, Neumann, and Waters, 2009;

Bouton, Westbrook, Corcoran, and Maren, 2006; Hermans, Craske, Mineka, and Lovibond, 2006; Neumann, Boschen and Waters, 2008, for reviews). Most of the laboratory-based experimental research in humans has investigated renewal with the least directed at rapid reacquisition (Neumann et al., 2008).

Renewal is observed as a return of fear when the CS is presented in a different context to that in which the extinction CS-only presentations were made (see Bandarian Balooch, Neumann, and Boschen, this volume). The renewal of fear has been found in skin conductance responses, expectancy ratings, and fear ratings (e.g., Bandarain Balooch and Neumann, 2011; Neumann and Kitlertsirivatana, 2010; Neumann, Lipp, and Cory, 2007; Neumann and Longbottom, 2008; Vansteenwegen et al., 2007). The present research examined the procedures of spontaneous recovery and reinstatement.

SPONTANEOUS RECOVERY

Spontaneous recovery was the first known process to result in the return of extinguished conditioned responses and was observed by Pavlov (1927). Spontaneous recovery is observed as the return of conditioned responses to the CS when it is presented after an extended time delay following extinction. The conditioned responses to the test trials of the CS can be as large as those observed at the end of conditioning (e.g., Brooks and Bouton, 1993). Spontaneous recovery has been observed in a wide variety of animal conditioning experiments (see Rescorla, 2004 for a review). However, research on spontaneous recovery in human participants has been surprisingly limited. Nevertheless, spontaneous recovery may provide a mechanism for relapse due to the mere passage of time after exposure therapy has been completed.

As noted by Neumann et al. (2008), an apparently clear demonstration of the spontaneous recovery of fear was reported by Ellson (1939; see also Hovland, 1937). Spontaneous recovery was examined after intervals of 5, 20, 60, and 180 min following extinction. Conditioned responses, as reflected in the galvanic skin response, showed a curvilinear trend across the time intervals. The trend showed that the relative increase in the size of the spontaneous recovery effect became increasingly smaller as the time interval was increased (e.g., the increase from 5 min to 20 min was larger than the increase from 20 min to 60 min). A similar pattern has been found in animal studies of spontaneous recovery (e.g., Ellson, 1939). Spontaneous recovery in humans has been investigated in other fear conditioning procedures (Guastella, Lovibond, Dadds, Mitchell, and Richardson, 2007; Huff, Hernandez, Blanding, and Labar, 2009; Norrholm et al., 2008) as well as eyelid conditioning (Beeman and Grant, 1961; Franks, 1963) and causal learning tasks (Vila and Rosas, 2001; Vila, Romero, and Rosas, 2002).

The more recent investigations of spontaneous recovery of fear in humans have tended to use very long time intervals following extinction. Guastella et al. (2007) used a fear conditioning procedure that was conducted over three separate sessions of acquisition, extinction, and test. A 2 to 3 hour or one day delay occurred between acquisition and extinction, and the test session occurred on a day that followed extinction. Three CSs were used: A was paired with the shock in all phases, B was never paired with the shock in any phase, and C was paired with the shock only during acquisition. Evidence for spontaneous recovery in stimulus C was found in that expectancy of the shock US and skin conductance responses were larger during this stimulus than during stimulus B. However, responses to C were not as large as that to stimulus A, suggesting that spontaneous recovery was partial. In addition, similar results were observed regardless of whether the CSs were neutral coloured blocks or were images of fear-relevant snakes and fear-irrelevant flowers.

Two additional studies focused on varying the time interval between acquisition and extinction and its effect on spontaneous recovery. Huff et al. (2009) used a differential fear conditioning procedure[1] in which fear learning was measured by skin conductance responses. Extinction was carried out either immediately or after 24 hours in different groups of participants. All participants received spontaneous recovery test trials 24 hours after extinction. The authors reported that spontaneous recovery of fear (i.e., larger responses to the CS+ than the CS-) was observed in participants who received immediate extinction, but no spontaneous recovery of fear was observed when extinction was delayed by 24 hours. The spontaneous recovery in the immediate extinction group was most strongly evident when change scores were calculated based on the individual level of responding during acquisition and extinction. The amount of spontaneous recovery seemed to be much more limited when the raw skin conductance means observed during the test trials were compared between the CS+ and CS-.

A longer delay between acquisition and extinction was used by Norrholm et al. (2008). The investigators also examined spontaneous recovery using a single cue (one CS) and differential conditioning procedure. Participants received extinction either 10 minutes (immediate) or 72 hours (delayed) after acquisition and a test for spontaneous recovery 96 hours after extinction. Spontaneous recovery in fear potentiated startle was observed in US expectancy ratings regardless of whether extinction was immediate or delayed and whether a single cue or differential conditioning procedure was used. However, expectancy tended to increase for both the CS+ and CS- for participants who received the differential conditioning procedure.

The results obtained with a measure of fear potentiated startle were more complex. For participants who received a single cue conditioning procedure, initial analyses suggested that spontaneous recovery of startle was present when participants received delayed extinction, but was absent when extinction was immediate. However, this appeared to reflect a difference in overall startle magnitude between the groups. Startle responses were increased from the end of extinction to the start of spontaneous recovery test in the immediate extinction group, but not in the delayed group. For participants who received a differential conditioning procedure, startle responses increased on test for both immediate and delayed extinction, but were only significantly larger during the CS+ than the CS- in the delayed extinction group.

Taken together, the results from prior research in humans suggest that spontaneous recovery can be observed after a delay of as little as 5 min between extinction and test (Ellson, 1939). Spontaneous recovery may not always be complete (i.e., reaching the same level of conditioned responding as a non-extinguished CS; Guastella et al., 2007). However, contradictory results have been found as to whether spontaneous recovery is larger if extinction is immediate versus delayed (Huff et al., 2009; Norrholm et al., 2008). In addition,

---

[1] A differential conditioning procedure most commonly uses two CSs. During acquisition, a CS+ is paired with the US and a CS- is presented alone. During extinction (and test), the CS+ and CS- are both presented alone. The CS- thus serves as within-subjects control to measure conditioned responses. For example, conditioned responding is inferred as larger skin conductance responses to the CS+ than the CS-.

spontaneous recovery may be more clearly seen when individual variability is taken into account. For example, Huff et al. (2009) assessed return of fear by using difference scores calculated from values observed at late acquisition, late extinction, and test. This approach was said to account for individual differences in responding that could otherwise obscure the observation of a return of fear. Research has also suggested that an increase in conditioned responding may be observed for a control stimulus (CS-) and this may result in non-differential responding between a CS+ and CS- in a differential conditioning procedure (Huff et al., 2009; Norrholm et al., 2008).

REINSTATEMENT

The reinstatement procedure involves the re-presentation of the US after extinction has been completed. Conditioned responses will emerge when the CS is presented following the US alone presentations. Reinstatement has been extensively studied in laboratory studies using animals (e.g., Bouton and Bolles, 1979; Bouton and King, 1983; Rescorla and Heth, 1975; Westbrook, Iordanova, McNally, Richardson, and Harris, 2002). This research has shown that the extinction context is an important factor that determines the presence or size of the reinstatement effect (Westbrook et al., 2002).

A similar result emerged in research with humans in a fear conditioning experiment. LaBar and Phelps (2005) observed the reinstatement of extinguished skin conductance responses when the US alone presentations given after extinction were made in the same room as the subsequent test presentations of the CS. However, no reinstatement of skin conductance responses was observed when the US alone presentations were made in a different room to the subsequent CS test presentations.

A different finding has emerged in research that used a conditioned suppression task. Neumann (2008) reported that a reinstatement of extinguished conditioned suppression was observed regardless of whether the US alone presentations given after extinction were made in the same or different context to the subsequent test CS presentations. The nature of context manipulations used in each experiment may explain the contradictory results. For example, LaBar and Phelps used different rooms in the laboratory to change the context between experimental phases. In contrast, Neumann conducted the whole experiment in the same room. Context was manipulated by changing the colour of the lights in the room and the background sound and this may have produced a smaller context shift than that used by LaBar and Phelps.

Research on reinstatement conducted by Hermans, Dirikx and colleagues (Dirikx, Hermans, Vansteenwegen, Baeyens, and Eelen, 2004; Hermans et al., 2005; Van Damme, Crombez, Hermans, Koster, and Eccleston, 2006) has employed a differential conditioning paradigm. The most recent of these experiments, by Van Damme et al. (2006), measured conditioned behavior by adopting Posner's (1980) spatial cueing paradigm. Participants were asked to detect a visual target that appeared either to the left or right side of a fixation point. The target was preceded by a cue at the same spatial location (valid cue trials) or in the opposite spatial location (invalid cue trials). Reaction times are typically faster for valid cue trials than for invalid cue trials due to the engagement of attention to the cued location on valid cue trials and the costs involved in disengaging attention away from the cued location on invalid cue trials. Van Damme et al. (2006) used CSs as the cues. The resulting reaction times in this form of the cueing paradigm were suggested to indicate attentional biases that can accompany conditioned fear. Consistent with this interpretation, an attentional bias towards CS+ cues developed during acquisition and largely disappeared during extinction. Moreover, a reinstatement effect was observed when the cueing task was administered after the US-only presentations. For these reinstatement test trials, attentional biases were greater when the cueing task involved CS+ presentations than when it involved CS- presentations.

The two earlier experiments on reinstatement in humans by Hermans, Dirikx, and colleagues (Dirikx et al., 2004; Hermans et al., 2005), measured conditioned responses with US expectancy ratings, subjective fear ratings, and secondary task reaction time to auditory probes presented during the visual CSs. The most consistent evidence for reinstatement was observed for fear ratings. Fear ratings of the CS+ increased from extinction to the reinstatement test trial when unwarned presentations of the US were given after extinction. In addition, rated fear during test was higher for the CS+ than for the CS-. Ratings of US expectancy showed a similar pattern as the fear ratings during test trials (i.e., higher expectancy of US for CS+ than CS-) in one experiment (Hermans et al., 2005), but not in the other experiment (Dirikx et al., 2004). Likewise, evidence of reinstatement in secondary task reaction time (i.e., slower reaction time during CS+ than during CS- during test trials) was found in one experiment (Dirikx et al., 2004), but not in the other experiment (Hermans et al., 2005).

A subsequent investigation of reinstatement by Norrholm et al. (2006) measured fear-potentiated startle and trial-by-trial ratings of US expectancy. In this study, the US was an aversive blast of air. Participants who received unsignaled US presentations after the last extinction trial showed an increase in fear-potentiated startle and US expectancy to the subsequent presentations of an extinguished CS+. Moreover, this increase was not observed in a CS- control stimulus. Although the results for fear-potentiated startle and US expectancy ratings were consistent, some dissociations between the measures were observed during extinction. For example, the US expectancy measure appeared to show greater extinction than did startle.

The results obtained in prior research on reinstatement in humans suggest that reinstatement is a replicable phenomenon, although it may not be observed consistently across all measures within one experiment. Skin conductance responses have been used (LaBar and Phelps, 2005), although the results have been mixed and suggest that this measure might not be as reliable as self-report measures in effectively demonstrating reinstatement (Milad, Orr, Pitman, and Rauch, 2005). However, even with US expectancy reinstatement was obtained in two experiments (Hermans et al., 2005; Norrholm et al., 2006), but not in another (Dirikx et al., 2004). The failure to find reinstatement was due to an increase in expectancy for both the CS+ and CS- during test, which seems to be a result common with spontaneous recovery (Huff et al., 2009; Norrholm et al., 2008). Following the US alone presentations, participants may be uncertain about what will happen and consider all CS presentations as potentially dangerous (Dirikx et al., 2004).

THEORETICAL EXPLANATIONS FOR SPONTANEOUS RECOVERY AND REINSTATEMENT

The observations of spontaneous recovery and reinstatement suggest that extinction does not "destroy" the original CS-US association that is learnt in acquisition. Rather, the CS-US association remains intact and can reappear if there is a significant time delay or presentations of the US after extinction.

Extinction has been explained in various ways, including learning that the rate of reinforcement for the CS is lower in extinction, a decrement in generalisation from acquisition to extinction, learning to inhibit the CR during extinction, violation of reinforcer expectation, and learning of a CS-noUS association (see Bouton, 2004 for a discussion). The latter mechanism – that there is new learning of a CS-noUS association – is commonly invoked to explain spontaneous recovery and reinstatement in the human conditioning literature.

Bouton (1993, 2004; Bouton and Nelson, 1998) described a model of acquisition and extinction in which the CS is rendered ambiguous following extinction. In this model, a CS-US association is learned in acquisition and a CS-noUS association is learnt in extinction. Future presentations of the CS will thus cause ambiguity regarding the meaning of the CS. To resolve this ambiguity, Bouton (1993, 2004; Bouton and Nelson, 1998) suggests that contextual cues are used. If the CS is encountered in a context that is different to that experienced during extinction, the CS-US association is more likely to be retrieved and conditioned responses will result.

While context is most commonly used to refer to the external sights, sounds, and smells in the environment, it can also refer to internal cues. As such, the passage of time represents a temporal context that leads to spontaneous recovery. Reinstatement also appears to be dependent on context in that it is observed when the unsignalled US presentations are made in the same context as the subsequent test CS presentations (LaBar and Phelps, 2005).

AIMS AND HYPOTHESES

The present experiment aimed to provide a test for spontaneous recovery and reinstatement in a laboratory-based fear conditioning procedure with healthy adults. Different measures of conditioned responding were taken and the relationships between the measures in the observed spontaneous recovery and reinstatement effects were examined.

The design of the present experiment was based on a differential conditioning procedure that used a shock US as has been employed in previous research (e.g., Dirikx et al., 2004; Hermans et al., 2005; Van Damme et al., 2006). This procedure provides a within-subjects control for conditioning (the CS-) and allows reinstatement to be tested in two ways (a) a comparison between the responses to the CS+ and CS- in the test phase, and (b) a comparison between responses to each CS at the end of extinction and on test trials.

Following acquisition and extinction trials, a delay of approximately 3.5 minutes was given and during this time a reinstatement group received unwarned presentations of the shock US. A second group that did not receive the shock US presentations was also used. However, as this group also received an extended time delay between the extinction and test phases, the results seen during the test phase in this group were taken to reflect spontaneous recovery effects. Trial-by-trial measures of US expectancy and skin conductance were taken as indices of conditioning.

Based on prior reports showing that trial-by-trial US expectancy and skin conductance responses are sensitive to the stimulus contingencies in acquisition and extinction (e.g., Lipp, Neumann, and Mason, 2001; Mitchell and Lovibond, 2002; Neumann, Lipp, and Siddle, 1997) and are sensitive to a range of conditioning phenomena in humans, such as inhibitory conditioning (Neumann et al., 1997) and blocking (Mitchell and Lovibond, 2002), it was hypothesized that these measures would show evidence of reinstatement and spontaneous recovery.

In addition, subjective ratings of the CSs were taken on the dimensions of valence, arousal, dominance, and interest to test for reinstatement and to examine the relationship between evaluative judgments and the other measures of conditioned behavior.

METHOD

Participants

Thirty-six undergraduate students (17 male and 19 female) participated. The students had a mean age of 23.3 years (range 17 to 45 years) and received partial course credit for participation. Participants were randomly allocated to either the Reinstatement group or the Spontaneous Recovery group such that there were a similar number of males and females in each group.

Due to equipment malfunction, one participant in the Reinstatement group did not have any skin conductance data for the test phase and one participant in the Reinstatement group did not have shock US expectancy data for any phase of the experiment. Prior to participation, all participants provided informed written consent to a protocol approved by the institutional human research ethics committee.

Apparatus

A Grass Model 7D Polygraph running with a paper speed of 2.5mm/s recorded skin conductance, respiration, and shock expectancy. The participant operated a custom-built dial and pointer with the preferred hand to indicate his or her expectation of the shock. The pointer could be rotated about 180°. The labels *certain the shock is NOT about to occur* and *certain the shock is about to occur* were placed on the left and right extremes, respectively. The central position was labeled *uncertain*. Grass 7P1 DC pre-amplifiers were used to amplify the skin conductance and respiration signals. Skin conductance activity was recorded by attaching 5 mm diameter Ag/AgCl electrodes to the distal phalanges of the first and second fingers of the non-preferred hand. The electrodes were filled with 0.05 M NaCl electrolyte and a constant 0.5 V current was applied. Respiration was measured with a Phipps and Bird chest strain gauge.

The electric shock was applied to the volar surface of the participant's preferred forearm via a concentric electrode. The shocks were pulsed at a frequency of 50 Hz and duration of 500 ms via a custom built apparatus. Geometric shapes were used as the CSs and as the control stimuli. The CSs were the two shapes that were presented during the acquisition, extinction, and test phases. Two filler shapes were also used and these were presented only during the rating phases at the start and end of the experiment.

The geometric shapes were outlines of a circle, square, diamond, and triangle and were back projected onto a projection area using a Leitz Pradovit 153 projector equipped with a Gerbrand Model G1166CS tachistoscopic shutter. The projection area subtended $6.13° \times 8.17°$ visual angle and was positioned at eye level, 1.5 m in front of the participant. The duration of each CS was 8 s.

Procedure

The participant sat in one room and the experiment was monitored via a closed circuit video system from an adjoining room. The mean temperature and humidity in the participant room was 19°C and 55%, respectively. The experiment began with the attachment of the electrodes and transducers for the physiological recordings.

Next, the intensity of the shock US was set. The 500 ms shock stimulus was presented at 0 V and increased by 5 V increments until the participant reported the level to be "uncomfortable, but not painful". This intensity level was used for the remainder of the experiment. The mean shock intensity level was 69.3 V. A 3-min acclimatization period followed the shock work-up procedure in which the participant was instructed to rest quietly with his or her eyes open.

Next, the participant was instructed that he or she would be presented with various shapes during the experiment and that they would initially be shown the shapes so that they would become familiar with them. The four geometric shapes were then shown to the participant in a predetermined order. The first shape presented was always a control stimulus, the next two shapes were CSs, and the final shape was the second control stimulus.

The nature of which shape served as the CSs/control stimuli and the presentation order of the CS+ and CS- were counterbalanced. The intertrial interval was randomly varied between 25, 28, and 33 s, shape offset to shape onset, for this and all subsequent phases of the experiment. Following pre-exposure to the shapes, the participants were instructed that the shapes would be presented again.

The participant was asked to make subjective ratings according to how each shape made him or her feel or think. The shapes were presented again, in the same order as the pre-exposure phase. After the presentation of a shape, the participant made four ratings on 7-point linear scales. The participant answered the question of "How does this shape make you feel?" on three rating scales that had the anchors for the numbers 1 and 7 respectively of *pleasant* and *unpleasant*, *excited* and *calm*, and *in control* and *controlled*. In order, these scales represented the dimensions of valence, arousal, and dominance. The fourth rating scale was preceded by the question "What do you think about this shape?". The rating scale ranged from *interesting* and *dull* for the numbers 1 and 7, respectively, to represent the dimension of interest.

After the participant completed the ratings for a shape, the experimenter presented the next shape in the sequence. Following the initial rating phase, the participant was given instructions on how to use the shock expectancy dial. Participants were instructed that they would be presented with the shapes and the shock stimulus and that they should indicate their expectation of the shock by using the dial-and-pointer.

The experiment proper began, consisting of the acquisition, extinction, and test phases. Each phase followed on from the previous one without any further intervention or instructions. This was done in order to avoid interrupting the experiment, and thus potentially producing dishabituation of skin conductance responses that could cloud the observed reinstatement and spontaneous recovery effects.

The acquisition phase consisted of 32 trials such that each CS was presented for 16 trials. One stimulus, the CS+, was followed by the shock stimulus. Shock onset coincided with CS offset. The second stimulus, the CS-, was presented alone. The nature of the first stimulus presented (CS+ or CS-) was counterbalanced between participants. Subsequent stimulus presentations followed a random sequence with the restriction that no more than two consecutive trials were the same, and that the first two trials were a CS+ and CS- trial.

At the conclusion of the acquisition phase, the extinction phase began. The extinction phase consisted of 16 trials, such that there were 8 each of the CS+ and CS-. The development of the sequence of extinction trials followed the methods used in acquisition, but no shock was presented.

Following extinction, there was a delay that varied at random between 190 and 205 seconds before the test phase began. This delay was thus approximately six times longer than that experienced between successive CS presentations during the acquisition and extinction phases. For the participants in the Spontaneous Recovery group, no stimuli were presented during the delay. For the participants in the Reinstatement group, six presentations of the shock US were made, each separated by an intertrial interval randomly varied from 23 to 33 seconds. The test phase was next conducted. Test consisted of 8 presentations of the CSs, 4 each of the CS+ and CS-. The sequence of stimuli followed the development of the acquisition and extinction phases. As in the extinction phase, no shocks were presented.

At the conclusion of the test phase, the participants completed subjective ratings for each of the four geometric shapes. The procedure was identical to that used in the first rating phase. However, during these ratings it was stressed that the participant should make their rating based on their initial reactions to the stimuli at the present time and that their ratings may have changed across the course of the experiment.

Participants also completed a post-experimental questionnaire to determine if they had learnt the contingency between the geometric shapes and the electrical stimulus. The questionnaire indicated that all participants could verbalize the contingencies learnt in the acquisition phase.

SCORING, RESPONSE DEFINITION AND STATISTICAL ANALYSES

Shock US expectancy ratings were scored by measuring the maximum pen deflection from the *uncertain* baseline level that occurred during the CS presentation. Expectancy ratings were converted into a percentage change from the uncertain baseline level. The percentage change scores ranged from +100 (certain of shock) through zero (uncertain) to -100 (certain of no shock).

Non-specific skin conductance responses during the 3-min baseline period were quantified by counting the number of responses that were larger than or equal to 0.05 μS. Groups did not differ in the frequency of non-specific responses, t (34) = 1.07, $p > .05$. Respiration-induced artifacts in skin conductance responses were detected from the polygraph records. Skin conductance responses were not scored if they coincided with sighs, deep breaths or sneezing.

The skin conductance response was quantified by scoring the magnitude of the response that began within a latency window of 1 – 4 s after CS onset. A square root transformation was applied to normalize the distributions. Prior to statistical analyses, subjective ratings on the scales of pleasantness (valence), arousal, and interest were reversed and ratings for the dominance scale was left unchanged so that higher scores indicate higher levels of pleasantness, arousal, dominance, and interest.

Statistical analyses were conducted by mixed-model ANOVAs with Greenhouse-Geisser adjusted degrees of freedom to correct for violations of the sphericity assumption. The F ratios are reported with the unadjusted degrees of freedom and the Greenhouse Geisser ε used in the correction where relevant. Post-hoc comparisons were made with t tests that were adjusted for the accumulation of Type I error by using Šidák's multiplicative inequality (Games, 1977). The α-level was set at .05 for all analyses.

RESULTS

US Expectancy Judgments

Expectancy of the shock US during each trial in the acquisition, extinction, and test phases for the Spontaneous Recovery and Reinstatements groups is shown in Figure 1. Shock expectancy was examined with a $2 \times 2 \times 16$ (Group × CS × Trial) ANOVA for the acquisition phase.

As can be seen in Figure 1, expectation of shock developed during the CS+ and expectation of no shock developed during the CS-. This pattern was confirmed by a highly significant main effect for CS, F (1, 33) = 131.18, $p < .0005$ and CS × Trial interaction, F (15, 495) = 42.29, ε = .31, $p < .0005$. No other main effects or interactions were significant, all other Fs < 2.16.

In the extinction phase, the expectation of the shock during the CS+ was lost such that on the last trial of extinction, participants did not expect the shock during either the CS+ or CS-. A $2 \times 2 \times 8$ (Group × CS × Trial) ANOVA showed a main effect for CS, F (1, 33) = 44.66, p <.0005, main effect for Trial, F (7, 231) = 31.21, ε = .44, $p < .0005$, and a CS × Trial interaction, F (7, 231) = 21.59, ε = .54, $p < .0005$. A CS × Trial × Group interaction, F (7, 231) = 2.74, ε = .54, $p < .05$, was also found.

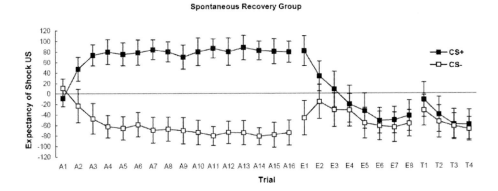

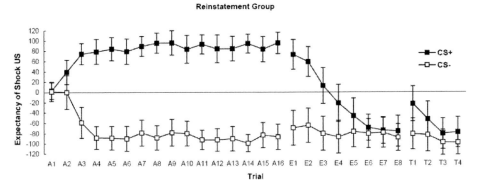

Figure 1. Percent expectancy of the shock unconditional stimulus (US) in the Spontaneous Recovery group (top panel) and Reinstatement group (bottom panel) for the acquisition, extinction, and test phases in Experiment 1. Trials A1 to A16 indicate the 16 trials in the acquisition phase, trials E1 to E8 indicate the 8 trials in the extinction phase, and trials T1 to T4 indicate the 4 trials in the test phase. Error bars depict the 95% confidence interval of the mean.

Post hoc comparisons showed that the interaction between Group, CS, and Trial was due to a slightly faster rate of extinction in the Spontaneous Recovery group than in the Reinstatement group. In the Spontaneous Recovery group, expectation of the shock was higher during the CS+ than during the CS- on extinction trials 1 and 2, both $ts < 2.63$, $p < .05$. In the Reinstatement group, expectation of the shock differed between the CS+ and CS- for extinction trials 1 to 3, all $ts < 5.01$. Importantly, there were no differences between the CS+ and CS- on the last extinction trial for both groups, both $ts < 1$. All other main effects and interactions were not significant, all $Fs < 2.82$.

The return of shock expectancy during the test trials was tested in two ways. The first was to conduct similar analyses as made in the acquisition and extinction phases, by using a 2 × 2 × 4 (Group × CS × Trial) ANOVA during the test phase trials. This analysis resulted in a main effect for CS, $F (1, 33) = 25.85$, $p < .0005$, a main effect for Trial, $F (3, 99) = 17.21$, $\varepsilon = .59$, $p < .0005$, and a near significant CS × Trial interaction, $F (3, 99) = 3.24$, $\varepsilon = .52$, $p = .06$. However, groups differed in the pattern of shock expectancies, as reflected in a CS × Group interaction, $F (1, 33) = 5.71$, $p < .05$. Post hoc comparisons between the CSs separately for each group indicated that expectancy of the shock did not significantly differ between the CS+ and CS- in the Spontaneous Recovery group, $t = 1.92$, $p > .05$. In the Reinstatement group, expectancy of the shock was higher during the CS+ than during the CS-, $t = 5.36$, $p <$ .01, consistent with a reinstatement effect. No other main effects or interactions were significant in the ANOVA, all other $Fs < 2.27$.

The second analyses compared between the last extinction trial and first test trial for each CS with a $2 \times 2 \times 2$ (Group $\times$ CS $\times$ Trial) ANOVA. This analysis yielded a main effect for CS, $F(1, 33) = 20.26$, $p < .0005$, main effect for Trial, $F(1, 33) = 21.15$, $p < .0005$, CS $\times$ Trial interaction, $F(1, 33) = 5.85$, $p < .05$, and a CS $\times$ Trial $\times$ Group interaction that approached significance, $F(1, 33) = 3.76$, $p = .06$. Post hoc comparisons were conducted to compare between the last trial of extinction and first test trial separately for each CS in each group. For the Spontaneous Recovery group, expectancy of the shock US was higher on the test trial than on the last extinction trial for the CS+ $t = 2.80$, $p < .05$, whereas the difference for the CS- approached significance, $t = 2.33$, $p = .10$. For the Reinstatement group, expectancy of the shock US was higher on test than at the end of extinction for the CS+, $t = 4.93$, $p < .05$, but not for the CS-, $t < 1$.

In sum, there was evidence of a return of expectancy of the US during the test trials in the Reinstatement group, and this effect was strongly specific to the CS+. There was also evidence of a return of conditioned behavior in the Spontaneous Recovery group, although this effect appeared to be more general in nature in that the increase in expectancy was not significantly different between the CS+ and CS-.

Skin Conductance Responses

Prior to statistical analyses, skin conductance responses were averaged into blocks of two trials. This was done to ensure that there were no missing cells in the ANOVA due to responses rejected due to the presence of respiratory or movement artifacts.

As a result of the blocking of trials, skin conductance responses were examined with separate $2 \times 2 \times 8$ (Group $\times$ CS $\times$ Block) ANOVAs for the acquisition phase and a $2 \times 2 \times 4$ (Group $\times$ CS $\times$ Block) ANOVA for the extinction phase. Mean skin conductance responses for both groups in the acquisition phase were larger during the CS+ ($M = .23$ μS, $SD = .20$) than during the CS- ($M = .14$ μS, $SD = .16$), as confirmed by a main effect for CS, $F(1, 34) = 23.82$, $p < .0005$. This confirms the establishment of conditioned responses during acquisition. Responses also declined across trials, main effect for Block, $F(7, 238) = 11.89$, $\varepsilon = .63$, $p < .0005$. No other main effects were significant, all $Fs < 2.13$.

The differential responding that was established during acquisition was lost during the extinction phase with no effect involving the CS factor reaching significance. Responses continued to decline across trials, main effect for Block, $F(3, 102) = 4.54$, $\varepsilon = .87$, $p < .01$. In addition, responses were overall larger in the Reinstatement group ($M = .19$ μS, $SD = .22$) than in the Spontaneous Recovery group ($M = .058$ μS, $SD = .22$), main effect for Group, $F(1, 34) = 6.19$, $p < .05$. No other effects reached significance, all other $Fs < 1.48$.

The skin conductance responses during the test trials were examined with a $2 \times 2 \times 2$ (Group $\times$ CS $\times$ Block) ANOVA. In the test phase, responses declined across trials, main effect for Block, $F(1, 33) = 8.39$, $p < .01$. Like the extinction phase, skin conductance responses were larger in the Reinstatement group ($M = .16$ μS, $SD = .16$) than in the Spontaneous Recovery group ($M = .08$ μS, $SD = .07$), main effect for Group $F(1, 33) = 4.05$, $p = .05$. This between group difference may simply reflect a carry on effect from the extinction phase, in which skin conductance responses were also larger in the Reinstatement group, rather than enhanced responding due to the unwarned shock presentations that were made after extinction. To examine this possibility, an analysis of covariance was conducted by using a $2 \times 2 \times 2$ (Group $\times$ CS $\times$ Block) design and the mean skin conductance responses across all extinction trials as the covariate. No main effect or interaction involving the group factor was significant with this analysis, all $Fs < 1$, suggesting that the between group difference in the test phase was due to the difference that developed during the extinction phase. A $2 \times 2 \times 2$ (Group $\times$ CS $\times$ Trial) ANOVA that compared the last block of extinction trials and the first block of test trials confirmed this impression with no effects reaching statistical significance, all $Fs < 3.77, p > .05$.

In sum, although acquisition and extinction of skin conductance responses were established, there was no evidence of reinstatement or spontaneous recovery during the test phase with this measure[2].

Subjective Ratings

The subjective ratings for the three dimensions of valence (pleasantness), arousal, and dominance for the CS+ and CS- during the baseline rating trials at the start of the experiment and after the test trials at the conclusion of the experiment are shown in Table 1. As can be seen, the ratings showed a similar pattern in both the Spontaneous Recovery and Reinstatement groups.

Subjective ratings were examined by comparing the mean ratings for each CS and experimental phase with separate $2 \times 4 \times 2$ (Group $\times$ CS $\times$ Phase) ANOVAs. The pleasantness ratings differed as a function of the CS and phase, as supported by a main effect for CS, $F (1, 34) = 22.92, p < .0005$, main effect for Phase, $F (1, 34) = 14.58, p < .001$ and a CS $\times$ Phase interaction, $F (1, 34) = 27.36, p < .0005$. All other main effects and interactions were not significant, all $Fs < 1.79$. The CS $\times$ Phase interaction was examined by comparing ratings between the phases, separately for each CS. These comparisons showed that the CS+ was rated as less pleasant in the post-experimental rating phase than in the pre-experimental rating phase, $t = 4.61, p < .01$, whereas there was no significant difference for the CS-, $t = 2.10, p > .05$.

Arousal ratings showed a main effect for CS, $F (1, 34) = 8.34, p < .01$, main effect for Phase, $F (1, 34) = 5.24, p < .05$ and a CS $\times$ Phase interaction, $F (1, 34) = 12.84, p < .01$. No other main effects or interactions were significant, all other $Fs < 1$. The CS $\times$ Phase interaction reflected that arousal ratings were significantly higher in the post-experimental rating phase than in the pre-experimental rating phase for the CS+, $t (102) = 4.23, p < .01$, but not for the CS-, $t = 0.11, p > .05$.

The dominance ratings differed between the CS and phase, main effect for CS, $F (1, 34) = 12.59, p < .001$, main effect for Phase, $F (1, 34) = 7.89, p < .01$, and the CS $\times$ Phase interaction was marginally significant, $F (1, 34) = 3.69, p = .06$. No other main effects and interactions were significant, all other $Fs < 1.47$. The interaction reflected that dominance ratings were higher for the CS+ in the post-experimental rating phase than in the pre-

---

[2] Additional analyses were carried out, taking into account individual variability in skin conductance responses (e.g., the use of range corrected scores). None of these analyses had any impact on the results.

experimental rating phase, $t = 3.08$, $p < .05$, whereas there was no difference for the CS-, $t = 0.38$, $p > .05$. Statistical analyses for the interest ratings yielded no significant effects, all Fs < 3.15, $p > .05$.

Table 1. Mean ratings for the CS+ and CS- for baseline (prior to acquisition trials) and for test (after test trials) in the Spontaneous Recovery and Reinstatement groups for the dimensions of valence, arousal, dominance, and interest. Standard deviations are in parentheses

Rating	Baseline		Test	
	CS+	CS-	CS+	CS-
Valence				
Spontaneous Recovery	3.61 (1.33)	3.83 (1.42)	2.11 (1.18)	4.00 (1.28)
Reinstatement	3.67 (1.24)	3.72 (1.23)	1.89 (1.18)	4.00 (1.14)
Arousal				
Spontaneous Recovery	2.67 (1.64)	2.33 (1.57)	4.00 (1.24)	2.44 (1.50)
Reinstatement	2.83 (1.25)	2.72 (1.27)	3.83 (1.15)	2.56 (1.54)
Dominance				
Spontaneous Recovery	3.44 (1.50)	3.22 (1.44)	4.50 (1.82)	3.67 (1.78)
Reinstatement	3.83 (1.47)	3.61 (1.29)	5.11 (1.23)	3.44 (1.65)
Interest				
Spontaneous Recovery	3.72 (1.96)	3.44 (1.69)	2.72 (1.36)	3.75 (1.67)
Reinstatement	3.72 (1.41)	3.67 (1.53)	3.11 (1.23)	3.17 (1.05)

Notes: All ratings were made on a seven point linear scale for valence (unpleasant – pleasant), arousal (calm – exciting), dominance (in control – controlled), and interest (interesting – dull). Higher ratings indicate higher levels of pleasantness, arousal, dominance, and interest.

CORRELATIONS

Bivariate correlations were also conducted to examine the relationship between the evaluative ratings in the test phase and the amount of spontaneous recovery or reinstatement observed in US expectancy ratings and skin conductance responses. Following Dirikx et al. (2004), the difference between the CS+ and CS- was calculated for each dependent measure.

The calculations for the US expectancy and skin conductance responses were calculated based on the data obtained in the first two trials of test. The pattern of correlations was the same for the Spontaneous Recovery and Reinstatement groups. Significant correlations between the difference in valence ratings and both the difference in arousal ratings ($r = -.53$, $p < .001$) and dominance ratings ($r = .40$, $p < .05$) were found, indicating that the decrease in valence (pleasantness) ratings found for the CS+ relative to the CS- was associated with an increase in arousal ratings and a decrease in dominance ratings. No correlations between the change in US expectancy or change in skin conductance responses and the valence, arousal, and dominance ratings were statistically significant.

DISCUSSION

The present experiment examined spontaneous recovery and reinstatement following extinction in several measures of conditioned behavior. Reinstatement was observed in a trial-by-trial measure of US expectancy as an increase in expectancy during the CS+ relative to the CS- on the test trials and relative to the CS+ on the last extinction trial. Spontaneous recovery of US expectancy was also found as evidenced by higher expectation on the first test trial relative to the last extinction trial. However, the expectancy was not different between the CS+ and CS- on the test trial. No evidence for reinstatement or spontaneous recovery of skin conductance conditioned responses was found despite the fact that this measure supported significant acquisition and extinction in the earlier phases of the experiment. Subjective ratings obtained during the test phase indicated that the CS+ was evaluated as less pleasant, more arousing, and more dominant than at the start of the experiment, whereas there was no change in the evaluation for the CS-. Although the evaluative ratings were correlated among themselves, they were not correlated with the US expectancy or skin conductance responses obtained during the test phase.

The pattern of results obtained with the US expectancy measure extends the prior investigations of reinstatement by Dirikx et al. (2004), Hermans et al. (2005), and Norrholm et al. (2008). Dirikx et al. did not find reinstatement in US expectancy and it was suggested that participants can be uncertain about what will happen after the reinstating USs and consider all CS presentations as potentially dangerous. An alternative reason could be that the expectancy ratings were obtained at the conclusion of the each experimental phase (i.e., acquisition, extinction, and test) rather than for each presentation of the CS. Collins and Shanks (2002) showed that when participants make judgments about the CS-US association frequently, they tend to base their judgments on the most recently experienced trials. In contrast, when judgments about the CS-US association are made at the end of the experiment, participants base their judgment on the aggregate contingency experienced across the entire experiment. Participants may have thus considered a larger aggregate of trials when making contingency judgments at the end of each phase and that this may have weakened the size of the reinstatement effects. Requiring participants to make expectancy judgments more frequently might be more sensitive to changes in the CS-US associations that occur throughout the experiment and be a more reliable method for detecting reinstatement effects.

The present results show that reinstatement of expectancy can be found when a trial-by-trial measure of US expectancy is employed. Moreover, this trial-by-trial measure shows that the reinstatement effect is relatively short-lived in that the increased expectancy present for the CS+ on the first test trial quickly diminishes across subsequent test presentations. Such a pattern is likely to reflect that the test phase consisted of unreinforced presentations of the CS+ and CS- and as such is equivalent to a second extinction phase. Neumann et al. (2007) employed a trial-by-trial measure of US expectancy to investigate the return of fear that can result when test trials are conducted in a different environmental context to the extinction treatment (i.e., a renewal effect; Bouton et al., 2006). Consistent with the present results, a renewal effect was observed with the US expectancy measure. The measurement of US expectancy on a trial-by-trial basis thus appears to be highly sensitive to return of fear phenomena produced by reinstatement or renewal procedures.

However, a limitation of the present results obtained with the US expectancy measure in the Reinstatement group was that the mean level of expectancy shown on the first test trial for the CS+ was below zero. Thus, although participants had a higher expectation of the US during the CS+ than the CS-, the participants did not give a strong expectation of actually receiving the shock. Inspection of the 95% confidence intervals in Figure 1 shows that the error bars overlapped with the middle "uncertain" region. As such, participants may be more appropriately described as having changed their expectation from not receiving the US at the end of extinction to being uncertain about receiving the shock on the test trials. Previous research on reinstatement in humans has also found that the level of US expectancy observed on test was less than that observed at the end of acquisition (Dirikx et al., 2004; Hermans et al., 2005). It may be necessary to use a stronger manipulation of the unwarned US presentations after extinction (e.g., more intense US, more US presentations) or some other type of change to the experimental design to increase the magnitude of reinstatement so that participants have a positive expectation of receiving the US during the test phase.

The pattern in US expectancy that was obtained during the test trials in the Spontaneous Recovery group is particularly noteworthy. Although an increase in expectancy was found during test, the expectancy judgments were not statistically different between the CS+ and CS-. The spontaneous recovery manipulation involved the same time delay between the last extinction trial and first test trial as that used for the reinstatement manipulation. The only difference between the two manipulations was the presentation of the shock US during the time delay for the reinstatement group. It would thus appear that the US presentations had the effect of increasing expectancy more specifically to the CS+, whereas an extended time delay on its own following extinction had the effect of increasing overall expectancy to any CS. The overall increase in US expectancy in the Spontaneous Recovery group may have reflected that the extended time delay after extinction lead to a confusion on the part of the participants or the belief that some aspect of the experiment had changed. This may have led participants to believe that the contingencies that occurred in the earlier phases of the experiment were no longer in operation. This could have produced the expectation that the CS- was now as potentially dangerous and predictive of the shock US as the CS+.

In a differential conditioning procedure, a common finding has been that responses increase to the CS- during test. While in some cases, a larger increase is found for the CS+, in other cases the increase in responses to the CS+ and CS- have been similar (e.g., Neumann, 2006; Effting and Kindt, 2007). The exact mechanism for why conditioned responses increase to the CS- remains to be determined (see discussion by Neumann, 2006). In a spontaneous recovery procedure, the length of the time interval may be one such factor. Although an early experiment observed spontaneous recovery after a delay of as little as 5 min (Ellson, 2939), more recent research has employed longer delays of 24 hours (Guastella et al., 2007; Huff et al., 2009) and 96 hours (Norrholm et al., 2008). Most notably, the experiment by Guastella et al. (2007) observed spontaneous recovery in US expectancy and skin conductance responses and replicated this effect across different samples of participants. Future research could more systematically manipulate the amount of delay from very short (< 5 mins) to very long (> 24 hours) to determine whether a longer delay causes a more specific increase in expectancy for the CS+ relative to the CS-.

Contrary to expectations, no evidence of reinstatement or spontaneous recovery was observed in skin conductance responses. The lack of reinstatement or spontaneous recovery effects is unlikely to reflect that this measure is not sensitive to the contingency between the CS and US because statistically significant acquisition and extinction of skin conductance responses was found in the earlier phases of the experiment. The fact that reinstatement effects were observed in US expectancy suggests that an increase in expectancy of the US is not a sufficient condition to produce reinstatement in skin conductance responses. It may be that a more powerful manipulation is required to observe the return of extinguished behavior in skin conductance responses. For instance, García-Gutiérrez and Rosas (2003) found that a combination of a reinstatement and renewal procedure produced the largest return of extinguished judgments in a causal learning task. Nevertheless, it would appear that dissociations between different measures of conditioned responses are a common result from experiments that examine reinstatement in humans. For example, Dirikx et al. (2004) found reinstatement in fear ratings and secondary task reaction time, but not in US expectancy judgments. Hermans et al. (2005) found reinstatement in fear ratings and US expectancy judgements, but not in secondary task reaction time. The different outcomes across the different experiments may reflect that the different measures have varying levels of sensitivity to the psychological processes that accompany the reinstatement of conditioned behavior. Verbal subjective measures, such as fear ratings and US expectancy, appear to be the most sensitive to reinstatement, particularly if expectancy judgments are required on a trial-by-trial basis. In contrast, non-verbal measures, such as secondary task reaction time or skin conductance responses, are less sensitive to reinstatement effects. If reinstatement in humans is mediated by cognitive processes that involve language and reasoning processes, it would explain why measures most sensitive to these processes would be more reliable in detecting reinstatement effects.

Dirikx et al. (2004) suggested that stimulus valence was an important factor in whether reinstatement was observed. This suggestion was based on significant correlations between evaluative valence ratings obtained at the end of extinction and the amount of reinstatement observed in the secondary task reaction time measure. No significant correlation was found between the evaluative ratings and US expectancy (see also Hermans et al., 2005). In the present experiment we obtained evaluative ratings after the test trials. No correlations between the evaluative ratings and the difference between the CS+ and CS- in US expectancy or skin conductance responses were found. The lack of any association between the measures obtained following the reinstatement or spontaneous recovery manipulation further points to the independence of the different measures of conditioned behavior. The independence of changes in stimulus valence and changes in US expectancy might be expected based on the notion that the former is more sensitive to the evaluative meaning of the CS, whereas the latter is sensitive to the predictive meaning of the CS. This explanation is supported by research which argues that the amygdala and the hippocampus play different roles in fear (e.g.

Mineka and Öhman, 2002; Öhman and Mineka, 2001). While the hippocampus operates at a cognitive level, processing through the amygdala is automatic, encapsulated, and not amenable to conscious control. The observed dissociation between US expectancy and evaluative ratings is to be expected if these measures assessed learning in different pathways.

The Reinstatement and Spontaneous Recovery groups showed a similar pattern of results in the subjective ratings for the dimensions of valence, arousal, and dominance. In both groups, participants rated the CS+ as less pleasant, more arousing, and more dominant at the end of test than at the start of the experiment, prior to any acquisition trials. The high correlations between these measures also indicate that they are influenced in a similar way by the experimental manipulation given after extinction. This is to be expected based on the theory of emotion proposed by Lang (1995) in which unpleasant stimuli also tend to be highly arousing. Although the difference between the CS+ and CS- in the evaluative ratings obtained at the end of the experiment are consistent with reinstatement and spontaneous recovery effects, more definitive conclusions would require that evaluative judgments are made throughout the entire experiment. Hermans et al. (2005) found that evaluative ratings of stimulus valence were higher for the CS+ than for the CS- when collected both after the extinction phase and after the test phase. Given that global evaluative judgments may reflect an averaged evaluation across several trials or phases of the experiment (Lipp and Purkis, 2006), it would seem necessary that future research measure evaluative judgments with greater resolution. Adapting the trial-by-trial measure of US expectancy used in the present experiment by requiring participants to make ratings on each trial using a scale that has the anchors of *pleasant* and *unpleasant* would be one way to achieve this aim.

APPLICATIONS

Return of conditioned behavior phenomena, such as spontaneous recovery and reinstatement, have practical implications for the use of exposure therapy for anxiety disorders such as simple phobia, social phobia, and obsessive-compulsive disorder. The aversive conditioning procedure has been used as an experimental analogue for the development of fears and anxieties in the laboratory (Field, 2006). The outcomes of the present experiment provide convergent evidence with prior animal research (see Bouton, 2000, 2002) to suggest that reinstatement may provide a mechanism for relapse following exposure therapy. For example, in the case of simple phobia, a reinstatement mechanism might result in relapse following exposure therapy if the client suffers undue stress or has a panic attack independent of the phobic stimulus. Clinical observations seem to support this scenario as a potential mechanism for relapse (Jacobs and Nadel, 1985; Steketee, 1993; Wade, Monroe, and Michelson, 1993).

The present data, in combination with the results reported by others (Dirikx et al., 2004; Hermans et al., 2005; Norrholm et al., 2006), suggest that a verbal measure of expectancy or emotion associated with the CS will be the most sensitive to reinstatement effects. These measures are also advantageous in applications in the clinic because they are easily obtained and interpreted. Clients are able to verbally report their level of anxiety or expectations in a given situation and such reports are a routine part of the exposure therapy process.

Although the magnitude of the reinstatement in conditional behavior did not reach the same level as at the end of acquisition, at least as measured by US expectancy, such a mechanism can still account for relapse since a full-blown relapse may be the result of successive lapses that progressively increase in intensity (Allsop, Saunders, Phillips, and Carr, 1997). From a clinical perspective, the development of techniques that can reduce the likelihood of a lapse or relapse is of particular interest. While the problem of relapse has been considered by many researchers and we have seen the emergence of comprehensive relapse-prevention models (e.g., Quigley and Marlatt, 1999) it is attractive to think that simple strategies could be introduced to substantially reduce the potential for relapse associated with reinstatement effects. The examination of reinstatement in humans opens the door for the exploration of not only behavioral interventions, but also cognitive mechanisms, such as instructed revaluation of the reinstating aversive events or the use of explicit memory cues.

The present results obtained with spontaneous recovery suggest that it too provides a mechanism for relapse following therapy. However, a return of fear may generalise to other CSs that are encountered. In the present experiment, this included the safety signal (CS-). As such, spontaneous recovery may be a less specific relapse mechanism than reinstatement. However, this conclusion is limited by the methods used in the present experiment. The delay between extinction and test was very short, although it was longer than that experienced between the CS presentations during extinction. In clinical applications it would be unlikely that such a short delay would be found. However, additional research that has used delays of 24 hours or more between extinction and test has shown reliable spontaneous recovery effects in humans (Guastella et al., 2007; Huff et al., 2009; Norrholm et al., 2008).

Boschen et al. (2009) discussed several procedures that may result in a return of fear. Based on existing laboratory and clinical research, they provided a list of recommendations for clinical practice that might serve to thwart a return of fear following exposure therapy. Many of these recommendations would apply to reducing relapse that is caused by reinstatement and spontaneous recovery. These include variables related to the exposure session, namely extending the duration of exposure sessions, increasing the number of exposure sessions, using massed exposure sessions. In addition, asking patients to relinquish distraction techniques, varying the nature of the feared stimulus, not placing excessive demands on the client, using homework tasks, and cognitive restructuring were also suggested. The authors noted that many of these recommendations were tentative and in need of further research to establish their effectiveness. Clearly, such work can be done through laboratory-based research that uses the procedures of reinstatement and spontaneous recovery. Based on the present findings, such research should employ a range of measures of conditioned fear as some may be more sensitive than others. It should also be guided by the methodology used in prior research to ensure that reliable reinstatement and spontaneous recovery effects are observed. This might include, for example, using a long delay between extinction and test for investigations of reducing return of fear due to spontaneous recovery.

CONCLUSION

Spontaneous recovery and reinstatement are two phenomena which demonstrate that there can be a return of extinguished conditioned responses. When translated into the context of extinction-based therapy for anxiety disorders, they provide two mechanisms by which a return of fear can be observed. Laboratory-based research on spontaneous recovery and reinstatement in humans can contribute significantly to our knowledge of the basic mental processes that underlie the return of extinguished conditioned responses. Part of this research process is to gain a greater understanding of what measures may be most sensitive to cognitive and affective learning processes that underlie each. The present experiment has suggested that US expectancy is the most sensitive of these measures, although subjective ratings of states may also be useful. Skin conductance responses, while having the objectivity that physiological responses bring to research, do not appear to be as sensitive as the self-report measures. Future research may be needed to examine the extent to which these differences between the measures is a function of real psychological processes or are merely methodological challenges for researchers in the field. Further research can also be conducted to examine procedures by which a return of fear by reinstatement and spontaneous recovery can be avoided.

AUTHOR NOTE

The data collection for the research reported in this chapter was completed at The University of Queensland. Data scoring and analysis and manuscript preparation were completed at Griffith University. We acknowledge the assistance of Mandy Mihelic for assistance with the preparation of this manuscript.

REFERENCES

Allsop, S., Saunders, B., Phillips, M., and Carr, A. (1997). A trial of relapse prevention with severely dependent male problem drinkers. *Addiction, 92*, 61-74.

Bandarian Balooch, S., and Neumann, D. L. (2011). Effects of multiple contexts and context similarity on the renewal of extinguished conditioned behavior in an ABA design with humans. *Learning and Motivation, 42,* 53-63.

Barlow, D. H. (2002). *Anxiety and its disorders: The nature and treatment of anxiety and panic* (2nd ed.). New York: The Guilford Press.

Barlow, D. H., Raffa, S. D., and Cohen, E. M. (2002). Psychosocial treatments for panic disorders, phobias, and generalized anxiety disorder. In P. E. Nathan and J. M. Gorman (Eds.), *A guide to treatments that work* (2nd ed., pp. 301-335). New York: Oxford University Press.

Beeman, E. Y. and Grant, D. A. (1961). Delayed extinction and spontaneous recovery following spaced and massed acquisition of the eyelid CR. *The Journal of General Psychology, 65,* 293-300.

Boschen, M. J., Neumann, D. L., and Waters, A. M. (2009). Relapse of successfully treated anxiety and fear: Theoretical issues and recommendations for clinical practice. *Australian and New Zealand Journal of Psychiatry, 43,* 89-100.

Bouton, M. E. (1993). Context, time, and memory retrieval in the interference paradigms of Pavlovian learning. *Psychological Bulletin, 114*, 80- 99

Bouton, M. E. (2000). A learning theory perspective on lapse, relapse, and the maintenance of behavior change. *Health Psychology, 19,* 57-63.

Bouton, M. E. (2002). Context, ambiguity, and unlearning: Sources of relapse after behavioral extinction. *Biological Psychiatry, 52,* 976-986.

Bouton, M. E. (2004). Context and behavioral processes in extinction. *Learning and Memory, 11,* 485-494.

Bouton, M. E., and Bolles, R. C. (1979). Role of conditioned contextual stimuli in reinstatement of extinguished fear. *Journal of Experimental Psychology: Animal Behavior Processes, 5,* 368-378.

Bouton, M. E., and King, D. A. (1983). Contextual control of the extinction of conditioned fear: Tests for the associative value of the context. *Journal of Experimental Psychology: Animal Behavior Processes, 9,* 248-265.

Bouton, M. E., and Nelson, J. B. (1998). Mechanisms of feature-positive and feature-negative discrimination learning in an appetitive conditioning paradigm. In N. Schmajuk and P. C. Holland (Eds.), *Occasion setting: Associative learning and cognition in animals* (pp. 69-112). Washington, DC: American Psychological Association.

Bouton, M. E., Westbrook, R. F., Corcoran, K. A., and Maren, S. (2006). Contextual and temporal modulation of extinction: Behavioral and biological mechanisms. *Biological Psychiatry, 60,* 352-360.

Brooks, D. C., and Bouton, M. E. (1993). A retrieval cue for extinction attenuates spontaneous recovery. *Journal of Experimental Psychology: Animal Behavior Processes, 20,* 366-379.

Chambless, D. L., and Ollendick, T. H. (2001). Empirically supported psychological interventions: Controversies and evidence. *Annual Review of Psychology, 52,* 685-716.

Collins, D. J., and Shanks, D. R. (2002). Momentary and integrative response strategies in casual judgment. *Memory and Cognition, 30,* 1138-1147.

Craske, M. G., and Rachman, S. J. (1987). Return of fear: Perceived skill and heart rate responsivity. *British Journal of Clinical Psychology, 26,* 187-200.

Deacon, B. J., and Abramowitz, J. S. (2004). Cognitive and behavioral treatments for anxiety disorders: A review of meta-analytic findings. *Journal of Clinical Psychology, 60,* 429-441.

Dirikx, T., Hermans, D., Vansteenwegen, D., Baeyens, F., and Eelen, P. (2004). Reinstatement of extinguished conditioned responses and negative stimulus valence as a pathway to return of fear in humans. *Learning and Memory, 11,* 549-554.

Effting, M. and Kindt, M. (2007). Contextual control of human fear associations in a renewal paradigm. *Behaviour Research and Therapy, 45,* 2002-2018.

Ellson, D. G. (1939). Spontaneous recovery of the galvanic skin response as a function of the recovery interval. *Journal of Experimental Psychology, 25,* 586-600.

Emmelkamp, P. M. G., and Wessels, H. (1975). Flooding in imagination vs. flooding in vivo: A comparison with agoraphobics. *Behaviour Research and Therapy, 13,* 7-15.

Field, A. P. (2006). Is conditioning a useful framework for understanding the development and treatment of phobias? *Clinical Psychology Review, 26,* 857-875.

Franks, C. M. (1963). Ease of conditioning and spontaneous recovery from experimental extinction. *British Journal of Psychology, 54,* 351-357.

Games, P. A. (1977). An improved *t* table for simultaneous control on *g* contrasts. *Journal of the American Statistical Association, 72,* 531-534.

García-Gutiérrez, A., and Rosas, J. M. (2003). Empirical and theoretical implications of additivity between reinstatement and renewal after interference in causal learning. *Behavioural Processes, 63*, 21-31.

Guastella, A. J., Lovibond, P. F., Dadds, M. R., Mitchell, P., and Richardson, R. (2007). A randomized controlled trial of the effect of D-cycloserine on extinction and fear conditioning in humans. *Behaviour Research and Therapy, 45*, 663-672.

Hermans, D., Craske, M. G., Mineka, S., and Lovibond, P. F. (2006). Extinction in human fear conditioning. *Biological Psychiatry, 60*, 361-368.

Hermans, D., Dirikx, T., Vansteenwegen, D., Baeyens, F., Van den Bergh, O., and Eelen, P. (2005). Reinstatement of fear responses in human aversive conditioning. *Behaviour Research and Therapy, 43*, 533-551.

Hovland, C. I. (1937). The generalization of conditioned responses: III. Extinction, spontaneous recovery, and disinhibition of conditioned and generalized responses. *Journal of Experimental Psychology, 21*, 47-62.

Huff, N. C., Hernandez, J. A., Blanding, N. Q., and LaBar, K. S. (2009). Delayed extinction attenuates conditioned fear renewal and spontaneous recovery in humans. *Behavioral Neuroscience, 123*, 834-843.

Jacobs, W. J., and Nadel, L. (1985). Stress-induced recovery of fears and phobias. *Psychological Review, 92*, 512-531.

Kessler, R. C., and Wang, P. S. (2008). The descriptive epidemiology of commonly occurring mental disorders in the United States. *Annual Review of Public Health, 29*, 115-129.

Kroenke, K., Spitzer, R. L., Williams, J. B., Monahan, P. O., and Lowe, B. (2007). Anxiety disorders in primary care: Prevalence, impairment, comorbidity, and detection. *Annals of Internal Medicine, 146*, 317-325.

LaBar, K. S., and Phelps, E. A. (2005). Reinstatement of conditioned fear in humans is context dependent and impaired by amnesia. *Behavioral Neuroscience, 119*, 677-686.

Lang, P. J. (1995). The emotion probe: Studies of motivation and attention. *American Psychologist, 50*, 372-385.

Lipp, O. V., Neumann, D. L., and Mason, V. (2001). Stimulus competition in affective and relational learning. *Learning and Motivation, 32*, 306-331.

Lipp, O. V., and Purkis, H. M. (2006). The effects of assessment type on verbal ratings of conditional stimulus valence and contingency judgments: Implications for the extinction of evaluative learning. *Journal of Experimental Psychology: Animal Behavior Processes, 32*, 431-440.

Milad, M. R., Orr, S. P., Pitman, R. K., and Rauch, S. L. (2005). Context modulation of memory for fear extinction in humans. *Psychophysiology, 42*, 456- 464.

Mineka, S., and Öhman, A. (2002). Phobias and preparedness: The selective, automatic, and encapsulated nature of fear. *Biological Psychiatry, 52*, 927-937.

Mineka, S., and Zinbarg, R. (2006). A contemporary learning theory perspective on the etiology of anxiety disorders: It's not what you thought it was. *American Psychologist, 61*, 10-26.

Mitchell, C. J., and Lovibond, P. F. (2002). Backward and forward blocking in human electrodermal conditioning: Blocking requires an assumption of outcome additivity. *Quarterly Journal of Experimental Psychology: Comparative and Physiological Psychology, 55B*, 311-329.

Neumann, D. L. (2006). The effects of physical context changes and multiple extinction contexts on two forms of renewal in a conditioned suppression task with humans. *Learning and Motivation, 37,* 149-175.

Neumann, D. L. (2008). The effects of context changes on the reinstatement of extinguished conditioned behavior in a conditioned suppression task with humans. *Learning and Motivation, 39,* 114-135.

Neumann, D. L., Boschen, M. J., and Waters, A. M. (2008). The return of extinguished conditioned behaviour in humans: New research and future directions. In L. N Piccard (Ed.). *Biological Psychology: New Research* (pp. 1-42). Hauppauge NY: Nova Science Publishers.

Neumann, D. L., and Kitlertsirivatana, E. (2010). Exposure to a novel context after extinction causes a renewal of extinguished conditioned responses: Implications for the treatment of fear. *Behaviour Research and Therapy, 48,* 565-570.

Neumann, D. L., Lipp, O. V., and Cory, S. E. (2007). Conducting extinction in multiple contexts does not necessarily attenuate the renewal of shock expectancy in a fear conditioning procedure with humans. *Behaviour Research and Therapy, 45,* 385-394.

Neumann, D. L., Lipp, O. V., Siddle, D. A. T. (1997). Conditioned inhibition of autonomic Pavlovian conditioning in humans. *Biological Psychology, 46,* 223-233.

Neumann, D. L., and Longbottom, P. L. (2008). The renewal of extinguished conditioned fear with fear-relevant and fear-irrelevant stimuli by a context change after extinction. *Behaviour Research and Therapy, 46,* 188-206.

Norrholm, S. D., Jovanovic, T., Vervliet, B., Myers, K. M., Davis, M., and Rothbaum, B. O., et al. (2006). Conditioned fear extinction and reinstatement in a human fear-potentiated startle paradigm. *Learning and Memory, 13,* 681-685.

Norrholm, S. D., Vervliet, B., Jovanovic, T., Boshoven, W., Myers, K. M., and Davis, M., et al. (2008). Timing of extinction relative to acquisition: A parametric analysis of fear extinction in humans. *Behavioral Neuroscience, 122,* 1016-1030.

Öhman, A., and Mineka, S. (2001). Fears, phobias, and preparedness: Toward an evolved module of fear and fear learning. *Psychological Review, 108,* 483-522.

Olatunji, B. O., Cisler, J. M., and Tonlin, D. F. (2007). Quality of life in the anxiety disorders: A meta-analytic review. *Clinical Psychology Review, 27,* 572-581.

Pavlov, I. (1927). *Conditioned Reflexes.* New York: Oxford University Press.

Posner, M. I. (1980). Orienting of attention. *Quarterly Journal of Experimental Psychology, 32,* 3-25.

Quigley, L. A. and Marlatt, G. A. (1999). Relapse prevention: Maintenance of change after initial treatment. In B. S. McCrady and E. E. Epstein (Eds.), *Addictions: A comprehensive guidebook* (pp. 370-384). New York, NY: Oxford.

Rachman, S. J. (1966). Studies in desensitization – III: Speed of generalization. *Behaviour Research and Therapy, 4,* 7-15.

Rachman, S. J. (1989). The return of fear: Review and prospect. *Clinical Psychology Review, 9,* 147-168.

Rescorla, R. A. (2004). Spontaneous Recovery. *Learning and Memory, 11,* 501-509.

Rescorla, R. A., and Heth, C. D. (1975). Reinstatement of fear to an extinguished conditioned stimulus. *Journal of Experimental Psychology: Animal Behavior Processes, 1,* 88-96.

Rose, M. P., and McGlynn, F. D. (1997). Toward a standard experiment for studying post-treatment return of fear. *Journal of Anxiety Disorders, 11,* 263-277.

Slade, T., Johnston, A., Oakley Brown, M. A., Andrews, G., and Whiteford, H. (2009). 2007 National Survey of Mental Health and Wellbeing: methods and key findings. *Australian and New Zealand Journal of Psychiatry, 43,* 594-605.

Steketee, G. (1993). Social support and treatment outcome of obsessive compulsive disorder at 9-month follow-up. *Behavioural Psychotherapy, 21,* 81-95.

Van Damme, S., Crombez, G., Hermans, D., Koster, E. H. W., and Eccleston, C. (2006). The role of extinction and reinstatement in attentional bias to threat: A conditioning approach. *Behaviour Research and Therapy, 44,* 1555-1563.

Vansteenwegen, D., Vervliet, B., Iberico, C., Baeyens, F., Van den Bergh, O., and Hermans, D. (2007). The repeated confrontation with videotapes of spiders in multiple contexts attenuates renewal of fear in spider-anxious students. *Behaviour Research and Therapy, 45,* 1169-1179.

Vila, N. J., and Rosas, J. M. (2001). Reinstatement of acquisition performance by presentation of the outcome after extinction in causality judgments. *Behavioural Processes, 56,* 147-154.

Vila, N. J., Romero, M. A., and Rosas, J. M. (2002). Retroactive interference after discrimination reversal decreases following temporal and physical context changes in human subjects. *Behavioural Processes, 59,* 47-54.

Wade, S. L., Monroe, S. M., and Michelson, L. K. (1993). Chronic life stress and treatment outcome in agoraphobia. *American Journal of Psychiatry, 150,* 1491-1495.

Wells, J. E., Oakley Browne, M. A., Scott, K. M., McGee, M. A., Baxter, J., and Kokaua, J. (2006). Prevalence, interference with life and severity of 12 month DSM-IV disorders in Te Rau Hinengaro: The New Zealand Mental Health Survey. *Australian and New Zealand Journal of Psychiatry, 40,* 845-854.

Westbrook, R.F., Iordanova, M., McNally, G., Richardson, R., and Harris, J.A. (2002). Reinstatement of fear to an extinguished conditioned stimulus: Two roles for context. *Journal of Experimental Psychology: Animal Behavior Processes, 28,* 97-110.

Wolpe, J. (1958). Psychotherapy by reciprocal inhibition. Stanford, CA: Stanford University Press.

Chapter 6

EVENT-RELATED POTENTIAL (ERP) INDICES OF EMOTIONAL BIASES IN DEPRESSION: THE ROLE OF WORKING MEMORY INHIBITORY CONTROL DEFICITS

Rachel A. Dati[1,2]*, Tim R. H. Cutmore[1,2] and David H. K. Shum[1,2]
[1] School of Psychology and Behavioural Basis of Health, Griffith Health Institute.
[2] Griffith University, Brisbane, Queensland Australia.

ABSTRACT

The high recurrence rate in depression suggests that there are specific factors that increase an individual's risk for developing repeated episodes of this disorder. One factor implicated in the literature is biases in processing negative information, such as sustained attention and elaboration of negative material versus positive material and biased autobiographical memory for negative versus positive events. Recent empirical evidence and theories suggest that these negative cognitive biases appear to be mediated by the impaired ability to exert inhibitory control over the access (resistance to distractor interference) and removal (resistance to proactive interference) of irrelevant negative information in working memory. The aim of this chapter is to review event related potential (ERP) data on emotion information processing in depression and integrate it with that derived from behavioural and neuroimaging investigations. We specially focus on attention and memory biases, deficits in working memory control and emotional regulation. Based on this review, we suggest that interventions that strengthen top-down cognitive control may help depressed patients to (a) disengage from negative cognitions and (b) enhance attendance to positive stimuli. Together, this may serve to regulate their depressed mood and reduce vulnerability to relapse. We also argue that incorporating ERP into clinical interventions with depressed patients may aid clinical assessment, diagnosis, and treatment prognosis and evaluation.

* E-mail: r.dati@griffith.edu.au

INTRODUCTION

Emotion generation and regulation involve the interaction between two modes of information processing: (1) automatic, reflexive, *bottom-up processing*, and (2) slow, controlled and strategic *top-down processing* (Clark and Beck, 2010; Ochsner and Gross, 2005). Research finds little difference between non-depressed and depressed individuals in their initial, bottom-up response to negative events (Rottenberg, 2007). However, depressed individuals show greater problems in disengaging from processing negative material when required. This deficit in effective top-down processing is dependent on inhibitory control of working memory by prefrontal neural systems (Nieuwenhuis and Yeung, 2003). Behavioural research has identified the presence of emotional information processing differences between non-depressed and depressed samples, and neuroimaging methods have allowed the identification of the precise locations of neural mechanisms that underlie these processes. Nevertheless, these two techniques are relatively insensitive to temporal fluctuations associated with automatic cognitions involved in information processing. We aim to make a convincing case that because of its high temporal resolution—in the millisecond range—electroencephalograph (EEG) and event-related potentials (ERPs) can provide key indicators for the specific stage of processing that may lead to this disturbance of emotional information processing in depression. Unlike proxy measures of cognitive processing such as behavioural reaction times or neuroimaging blood level deoxygenation (BOLD), ERPs *directly* reflect cognitive processes, with neural activity recorded almost simultaneously.

The intent of this chapter is to collate, review, and integrate data on emotional information processing biases in depression derived from electrophysiological investigations, together with that derived from behavioural and neuroimaging investigations. Use of the term 'bias' here is not intended to imply either accuracy or inaccuracy, but simply a tendency to process information so as to favour certain types of emotional salience or meaning (Matthews and MacLeod, 2005). This amalgamation may contribute to a better understanding of specific cognitive mechanisms that are involved in depressive disorders. To help interpret these findings, the following sections will provide a brief review of methodological issues in depression research and a brief summary of the relevant ERP literature. Following this, we outline historical and modern cognitive models of depression, which demonstrate a progression towards greater focus on defective top-down cognitive control over the traditionally emphasized, bottom-up cognitions. We will then review the evidence based on the predictions of these modern models, specifically on emotional attention, memory, inhibition, and emotional regulation in depression. The chapter will conclude with a discussion of the clinical implications of these findings and suggest avenues for future research.

METHODOLOGICAL ISSUES

Major depressive disorder is a diagnosis made by appropriately qualified professionals according to validated diagnostic systems, such as the Diagnostic and Statistical Manual of Mental Disorders–Fourth Edition (DSM-IV-TR) or International Classification of Disease-10th edition (ICD-10). However, time and funding limitations often necessitate researchers to define depression in terms of specific cut-off scores on self-report measures (e.g., Beck Depression Inventory-Second Edition [BDI-II]). This approach is justified as it is based on empirical support for the dimensional qualities of the disorder (Ruscio, Brown, and Ruscio, 2009; Ruscio and Ruscio, 2000). For instance, a recent meta-analysis of 89 studies (pooled sample size = 7032), of implicit cognition in depression found that effect sizes in studies that used clinical ($r = .17$), undergraduate (dysphoric; $r = .23$), and community samples ($r = .25$) did not differ significantly (Phillips, Hine, and Thorsteinsson, 2010). Further, negative biases in attention, memory, interpretation, and self-esteem all significantly predicted depression across all samples. However, research on the dimensional nature of depression is not conclusive, with data suggesting qualitative and quantitative differences between subclinical and clinical depression and between different subtypes of depression (e.g., with melancholic, atypical, psychotic features; see Ingram and Siegle, 2009).

UTILITY OF THE ERP IN COGNITIVE RESEARCH

It is widely accepted that cognition intimately depends on the functioning of the cerebral cortex. Understanding the neural basis of cognition, therefore, offers the potential to increase our understanding of cognitive processes, particularly in relation to subtle cognitive activities. Scalp EEG measures generally reflect the summed activity of post-synaptic dendrites of millions of pyramidal neurons in the neocortex or in sub-cortical structures such as the thalamus (Yamashita, Galka, Ozaki, Discay, and Valdes-Sosa, 2004). An ERP is a consistent electrical response to an event, such as a stimulus word, that is repeatedly presented. It includes positive or negative voltage fluctuations in the EEG that result from sensory, motor, or cognitive events that are repeated and averaged to resolve them from the flux of background EEG (Luck, 2005). A 2000 ms signal-averaged trace of EEG may contain several 'components', each relating to different perceptual and cognitive processes. These components are typically named by their voltage—P for positive and N for negative—and by their order of appearance (*i.e., P1, N1, P2, N2, P3;* see Figure 1) or time of manifestation (*i.e., P100, N100, P200, N200, P300*).

There are three measurable aspects of the ERP waveform: amplitude, latency, and scalp topography. Amplitude provides an index of the magnitude of neural activation, possibly reflecting the raw number of co-activated neurons. Latency reveals the temporal processing of stimuli with early components (less than 100ms) being sensitive to exogenous properties of the stimulus and later components (greater than 100ms) to various endogenous cognitive factors such as attention, recognition, and evaluation. Scalp distribution provides information on possible cortical neural network activity necessary for the cognitive process (Friedman, Cycowicz, and Gaeta, 2001). Comparisons of these three properties of the ERP elicited by different stimuli, tasks, or in different populations allow one to infer whether they engender different patterns of neural activity and, hence, reflect different functional processes (Luck, 2005). Table 1 summarizes the characteristics of key ERPs evoked by pertinent experimental methods used in research on information processing in depression.

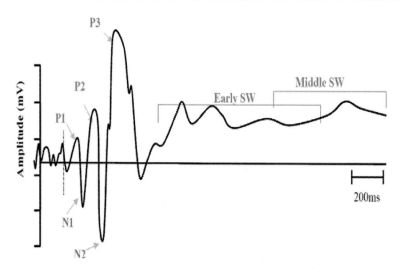

Figure 1. ERP components from an averaged waveform. The dotted line represents stimulus onset. SW refers to slow wave.

Table 1. Key ERP Components and Methods

ERP Component	Cognitive Process	Latency and Topography	Suggested Neural Generators	Reference
Error Related Negativity (ERN) or Ne	Response Monitoring or Conflict Detection	50-150ms Frontal and central sites	Anterior cingulate cortex (ACC)	(Alexopoulos et al., 2007; Chiu and Deldin, 2007; Ruchsow et al., 2008)
P2	Hypervigilance	150-270ms Frontal and central sites	Medial frontal source	(Rossignol, Philippot, Crommelinck, and Campanella, 2008; Shestyuk and Deldin, 2010)
N2a	Automatic detection of deviant stimuli	150-250ms Frontal sites	Supratemporal auditory cortex. Right frontal lobe.	(Folstein and van Petten, 2008; Lim et al., 1999)
N2b	Orienting response	150-350ms Central maximum	Auditory and visual cortex.	(Folstein and van Petten, 2008; Lim et al., 1999)
N400	Semantic Incongruence	300-500ms Left frontal and temporal Maximum	Left posterior temporal cortex., left superior temporal gyrus, and left inferior frontal cortex	(Khateb, Pegna, Landis, Mouthon, and Annoni, 2010; Kutas and Hillyard, 1980, 1982; Lau, Phillips, and Poeppel, 2008)
N450/Medial Frontal Negativity (MFN)	enhanced inhibition in Stoop Task	450 – 600ms Frontal-central maximum	Inferior frontal cortex and ACC	(McNeely, Christensen, West, and Alain, 2003; McNeely, Lau, Christensen, and Alain, 2008; Tays, Dywan, Mathewson, and Segalowitz, 2008; Vanderhasselt and De Raedt, 2009)

ERP Component	Cognitive Process	Latency and Topography	Suggested Neural Generators	Reference
Novelty or P3a	Automatic Shifting or Orientating Attention	220-350ms Frontal-central maximum	Relatively unknown; suspected ACC, and hippocampual	(Friedman et al., 2001; Polich, 2003, 2007)
Classical or P3b	Selective Attention/ Context Updating	300-700ms Temporal Parietal	Parietal-temporal junction, Hippocampal sources, and the cingulated cortex.	(Friedman et al., 2001; Polich, 2003, 2007)
Late Positive Potential (LPP)	Sustained processing/ Emotional Regulation	300ms – 4000ms Parietal and Occipital	Visual cortical structures such as lateral occipital, inferotemporal, and parietal visual areas	(Hajcak, MacNamara, and Olvet, 2010; Sabatinelli, Lang, Keli, and Bradley, 2007)
Slow Wave (SW)	Elaborative Encoding/ working memory rehearsal	600-5000ms Prefrontal and parietal sites	Left and parietal regions' however a distributed network of cortical regions has been identified.	(Deldin, Deveney, Kim, Casas, and Best, 2001; Deveney and Deldin, 2004; Hansell et al., 2001; Shestyuk, Deldin, Brand, and Deveney, 2005)
Mid Frontal Old/New effect	Explicit Episodic Memory, (familiarity)	200-500ms Frontal sites	Left posterior cingulated, medial temporal cortex, and the precuneous	(Curran and Friedman, 2004; Dietrich et al., 2000; Kayser et al., 2010; Rugg and Curran, 2007)
Left Parietal Old/New effect	Explicit Episodic Memory, (recollection)	400-800ms Left Parietal sites	Left posterior cingulated, medial temporal cortex, and the precuneous	(Curran and Friedman, 2004; Dietrich et al., 2000; Kayser et al., 2010; Rugg and Curran, 2007)
Nogo-N2	Interference Inhibitory Control (pre-motor control)	220-380ms Frontal sites	Rostral ACC; Nigrostrial dopamine-system	(Beste, Willemssen, Saft, and Falkenstein, 2010; Chiu, Holmes, and Pizzagalli, 2008; Smith, Smith, Provost, and Heathcote, 2010)
Nogo-P3	Interference Inhibitory Control (post-motor control)	310-410ms Frontal – central maximum	Rostral ACC; Mesocortico-limbic dopamine system	(Beste et al., 2010; Chiu et al., 2008; Smith et al., 2010)

We, like others (e.g., Deldin, Shestyuk, and Chiu, 2003; Williams, Watts, MacLeod, and Mathews, 1997), argue that incorporating emotion-evoking, affectively salient stimuli into ERP investigations will provide insights into emotional information processing biases and deficits in depression. To critically appraise this research, however, we first need to have some understanding of the known impact of depression on ERPs in non-emotional paradigms. Although it is beyond the scope of this chapter to outline this literature in detail—interested readers should refer to Bruder, Kayser, and Tenke (in press) for a recent review—it is important to note that majority of this research reports reduced component amplitudes in depressed samples. Reduced ERP amplitude is observed in both early (*i.e., P1, N1, N2a, N2b, P2, P3a:* Bruder et al., 1998; Burkhart and Thomas, 1993; Ogura et al., 1993; Pause et al., 2003; Pierson et al., 1996) and late latency components (*P3b, mean Cohen's d = 0.85:* Anderer, Saletu, Semlitsch, and Pascual-Marqui, 2002; Kawasaki, Tanaka, Wang, Hokama, and Hiramatsu, 2004; Roschke and Wanger, 2003; Urretavizcaya et al., 2003). Given that ERP amplitude is regarded as a marker of neural activation of mental effort, these findings suggest depression is marked by deficits in mental exertion in cognitive tasks. This might explain the attention, concentration, and memory impairments associated with the disorder. However, results are not always consistent with this simple view with some studies finding enhanced ERP amplitudes (*P1, N1:* Blackwood et al., 1987; Bruder et al., 1995; Ogura et al., 1993; *P3a:* Pierson et al., 1996; Sara et al., 1994). Bruder et al. (in press) argue that differences in the characteristics of patient samples, such as clinical subtype (e.g., bipolar, melancholic, psychotic or atypical depression), age, medication status, or the presence of unaccounted comorbid diagnoses can explain a substantial degree of error variance among ERP investigations with depressed individuals. We will now briefly turn our attention to discussion of the key cognitive models that initiated this research.

COGNITIVE MODELS OF DEPRESSION

We will first discuss the traditional models proposed up to 50 years ago, and then focus on the more recent models based on existing empirical findings. The main models that initiated research on emotional information processing biases in depression were Beck's (1967) *schema theory*, Bower's (1981) *associative network theory*, and Nolen-Hoeksema's (1991) *ruminative response style theory*.

Traditional Cognitive Models of Depression

Beck's (1967) schema theory of depression implicates the activation of existing negative memory representations (schemas)—characterized by themes of loss, rejection, worthlessness, and failure. These schemas skew a person's information processing system by leading to bottom-up preferential encoding and retrieval of internal and external information that is consistent with these negative themes. The product of this aberrant information processing bias is the development of a *vicious cycle* of escalating negative automatic rumination about the self, world, and future (*negative cognitive triad:* Beck, Rush, Shaw, and Emery, 1976). This is predicted to result in the manifestation and perpetuation of the person's depressive symptoms. With repeated activation, core negative schemas become hypersensitive and acquire a more rigid, coherent, and elaborated organisation (*morph into depressive modes:* Beck, 1996; Clark and Beck, 1999). This negative cognitive cycle, therefore, becomes more readily accessible and entrenched, decreasing the person's ability to cognitively reappraise their situation and increasing their vulnerability to repeated depressive episodes.

Bower's (1981) *associative network theory* is based on the assumption that human memory encompasses a number of reciprocal associative networks, comprised of multiple distinct *nodes*. Nodes are idiosyncratic configurations of related life experiences, cognitions, and behavioural expressions that become activated by unique situational triggers. Bower argued that each emotion–such as joy, anxiety, or depression—has a specific innate node in memory. When an appropriate evoking cue triggers an emotion node, it primes activation of its uniquely associated memory structures. This produces bottom-up activation of cognitive, affective, and behavioural patterns assigned to that emotion (*mood-congruent processing:* Bower, Monteiro, and Gilligan, 1978). Each emotion node also reciprocally inhibits the activation of an emotion node of opposing quality, such that a depressive node will inhibit the joy node and its associated pleasurable memories and behaviours. Bower's theory is a general model of the relationship between mood and memory, rather than one that concerns with cognitive aspects of emotional psychopathology. However, it has the potential to explain how the reinforcing cycle between sustained negative affect, negative processing biases, and emotional regulation deficits in depression might be mediated (Ingram, 1984; Teasdale, 1983, 1988).

Both Beck's (1967) and Bower's (1981) models specify that depression should bias all aspects of emotional information processing—including attention, interpretation, memory, and reasoning. Although the activation of negative thoughts has been found to play a role in the vulnerability for depression (Alloy et al., 2000), the research does not specify the cognitive mechanisms that might be responsible for the recycling of negative cognitions and affect. Interested in this problem, Nolen-Hoeksema (1991) argued that a propensity to a ruminative response style might exacerbate depressed mood by increasing the reprocessing of negative cognitions.

Rumination is a relatively stable process and is defined as the difficulty in disengaging from recurring thoughts about the causes and consequences of one's situation (Johnson, Nolen-Hoeksema, Mitchell, and Levin, 2009; Nolen-Hoeksema, 1991). Rumination in the context of depressed affect appears to enhance accessibility to negative memories, possibly by increasing activation and attention to core negative self-schemas (Ciesla and Roberts, 2007; Joormann, 2004, 2005; Joormann, Eugene, and Gotlib, 2008; Joormann, Yoon, and Zetsche, 2007; Robinson and Alloy, 2003). It is found to significantly increase the development, perpetuation, and reoccurrence of depression in at-risk samples (Joormann et al., 2008; Nolen-Hoeksema, Wisco, and Lyubomirsky, 2008; Thompson et al., 2010). Recent research and theory into why people ruminate implicate deficits in working memory inhibitory control (see Joormann, 2009). Before reviewing this research, however, we will briefly discuss the constructs of working memory and cognitive inhibitory control.

CONCEPTUALISATION OF WORKING MEMORY AND COGNITIVE INHIBITION

Working memory is involved in all of our consciousness manipulations (see Figure 2). The original model of working memory proposed by Baddeley and Hitch (1974) outlined three main components; the *central executive,* which acts as a supervisory system and controls the flow of information from and to its *slave systems*: the *phonological loop* and *visuospatial sketchpad*. These slave systems are short-term storage systems dedicated to a content domain (verbal and visuospatial, respectively).

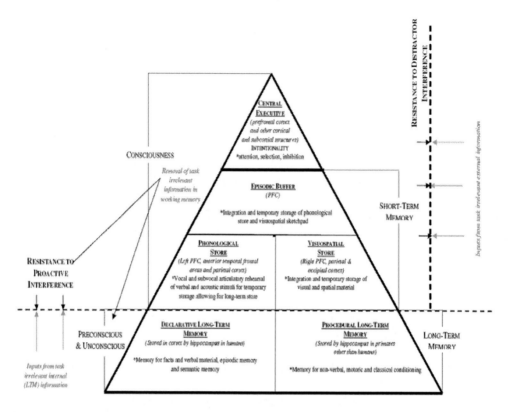

Figure 2. A Modification of Baddeley's Working Memory Model. Vertical dotted line and black horizontal arrows demonstrates resistance to distractor inhibitory control from irrelevant external information. Horizontal dotted line and black vertical arrows denote resistance to proactive interference inhibitory control from irrelevant internal information. Image adapted and reprinted by permission of Coolidge and Wynn (2009). All rights reserved.

The central executive is similar to the construct of a supervisory attentional system regulating thought and goal setting (Norman and Shallice, 1986) and to the construct of attentional control (Engle and Kane, 2004). In 2000, Baddeley added a third slave system to his model, the *episodic buffer*, which is said to hold representations that integrate phonological, visual, and spatial information. An important characteristic of working memory, and one that differentiates it from long-term memory, is its capacity-limited focus. Successful task performance requires that the contents of working memory be effectively monitored and updated to reflect task needs. This is hypothesised to entail efficient functioning of cognitive inhibitory control (Hasher and Zacks, 1988; Hasher, Zacks, and May, 1999). In a recent meta-analysis of studies of inhibitory processing, Friedman and Miyake (2004) found evidence for three latent inhibition factors. The first, *Prepotent Response Inhibition*, refers to the non-controversial form of motor inhibition that requires the suppression of unwanted reflexive behavioural actions. The second, *Resistance to Distractor Interference*, denotes a form of cognitive inhibitory control that resists or resolves interference from information in the external environment that is irrelevant to the current task (represented as the horizontal dotted barrier in Figure 2). The third, *Resistance to Proactive Interference*, is also a form of cognitive inhibition, which involves the ability to resist or remove working memory intrusions that were once, but are no longer, relevant (represented as the vertical dotted barrier in Figure 2).

Modern Cognitive Models of Depression

Joormann (2010) outlined a model of depression that argued that impaired ability to exert top-down inhibitory control over the contents of working memory results in lack of control over the bottom-up negative memory and attention biases and ruminative response styles related to this disorder. She implicates deficits in both resistance to distractor interference and resistance to proactive interference in this model. Joormann suggests that poor working memory inhibitory control results in sustained activation of irrelevant negative stimuli in consciousness, leading to rehearsal or rumination (Hertel, 1997; Joormann, 2004, 2005; Joormann et al., 2008; Linville, 1996; Nolen-Hoeksema et al., 2008). The depressed individual's cognitive resources are thereby depleted, limiting their ability to reappraise or recall mood-incongruent information to regulate their mood. Furthermore, this can lead to facilitation of long-term memory for negative events, which serves to reinforce the cycle of negative cognitions, sustaining and exacerbating the depressed mood.

Beck (2008) recently updated his cognitive model of depression to implicate diminished top-down inhibitory control over negative schemas at the core of depressive cognition and maintenance. He was particularly interested in outlining the neurobiological correlates of these processes and proposes that amygdala hyperactivity in individuals with genetic predisposition to depression (i.e., polymorphisms of the short allele serotonin transporter gene 5-HTTLPR) is associated with heightened reactivity to negative stimuli (Munafo, Brown, and Hariri, 2008) and elevated hypothalamic-pituitary-adrenal (HPA) activation (Gotlib, Joormann, Minor, and Hallmayer, 2008). This hypersensitivity is postulated to mediate the bottom-up negative information processing bias of schema-congruent information (Dannlowski et al., 2007; Monk et al., 2008). Empirical evidence examining the efficacy of cognitive therapy indicates depressive symptom reduction appears to operate via reduced activation of the amygdala-hippocampal subcortical regions and increased activation of higher-order prefrontal cortex (PFC) regions implicated in control of negative emotion (see Clark and Beck, 2010). In support, pharmacological interventions for depression appear to influence the initial bottom-up deployment of attention via reduction of the amygdala-based stimulus appraisal system, whereas psychological interventions influence top-down processing by altering activity in the lateral PFC (Browning, Holmes, and Harmer, 2010).

In summary, modern cognitive models argue that the ability to control the contents of working memory via efficient cognitive inhibitory functioning differentiates individuals who initiate ruminative responses and negative attention and memory biases that sustain negative affect, from those who do not (Joormann, 2010). This process appears to be dependent on prefrontal top-down control over subcortical bottom-up emotional reactivity (Beck, 2008; Mayberg, 1997). We will now examine if the predictions of these new integrated models are supported by empirical data.

EXPERIMENTAL DATA FOR COGNITIVE MODELS OF DEPRESSION

Depressive Cognition

The meta-analysis of Phillips et al. (2010) found an overall correlation of .23 between depression and self-referential negative biases in attention, memory, interpretation, and self-esteem. This association was found to explain 53% of the variance in depression in the pooled sample of 7032 participants. These results are consistent with predictions of Bower's and Beck's cognitive models. Furthermore, negative information processing biases were found to significantly predict depression in cross-sectional ($r = .21$), remitted ($r = .19$), and prospective ($r = .27$) research designs. This suggests that negative information processing biases in depression are not merely symptoms of depression or temporary consequences of the disorder, but also precede its onset (*vulnerability marker;* Phillips et al., 2010). To complement these quantitative findings, the following section of this chapter will provide a critical review of this research, focusing on ERP data. We first report negative attention and memory biases, and then turn to inhibitory control and efficient emotional regulation deficits.

Emotional Attention Bias

Early behavioural research into negative attention biases[1] in depression typically produced null results (Bradley, Mogg, and Lee, 1997; Mogg et al., 2000; Mogg, Bradley, Williams, and Mathews, 1993; Neshat-Doost, Moradi, Taghavi, Yule, and Dalgleish, 2000). However, more recent studies found evidence that negative attention biases emerge only under conditions of long stimulus exposure (i.e., >1000ms) in both depressed (Gotlib, Krasnoperova, Yue, and Joormann, 2004; Joormann and Gotlib, 2007; Joormann, Talbot, and Gotlib, 2007; Karparova, Kersting, and Suslow, 2007) and dysphoric samples (Caseras, Garner, Bradley, and Mogg, 2007; Koster, Leyman, DeRaedy, and Crombey, 2006; Shane and Peterson, 2007). A similar pattern of results has emerged in the ERP literature. Evidence for negative attention biases in depression manifest more reliably during later sustained attentional processing, indexed by longer latency ERPs (*i.e., P3, SW:* Blackburn, Roxborought, Muir, Glabus, and Blackwood, 1990; Deldin et al., 2001; Deldin, Naidu, Shestyuk, and Casas, 2008; Deveney and Deldin, 2004; Nandrino, Dodin, Martin, and Henniaux, 2004; Shestyuk and Deldin, 2010; Shestyuk et al., 2005), compared to early processing stages (*i.e., P1, N1, P2:* Deldin et al., 2001; Deldin, Keller, Gergen, and Miller, 2000; Dietrich et al., 2000; Serfaty et al., 2002; Shimizu, Saito, and Hoshiyama, 2006). The tendency to observe biases at longer stimulus durations suggest that depression is associated with biases in sustained attention, but not in orienting/shifting attention (Mogg and Bradley, 2005; Wisco, 2009).

Contrary to prevailing consensus, the recent meta-analysis of behavioural measures of negative attention biases in depression by Phillips et al. (2010) unexpectedly found no moderating effect for stimulus duration on negative attention biases in depression. Rather, significant associates between depression and negative attention biases were observed in both early (≤ 400ms, $n = 11$, $r = .19$, $p < .001$) and late (≥ 500ms, $n = 11$, $r = .19$, $p < .001$) stage

---

[1] Recall that the use of the term 'bias' here is not intended to imply either accuracy or inaccuracy, but simply a tendency to process information so as to favour certain types of emotional salience or meaning (Matthews and MacLeod, 2005).

attention processing. It is possible that early attention biases in depression are only observed under conditions of self-referential experimental tasks. For instance, Shestyuk and Deldin (2010) found ERP early attentional processing biases (P2) in depression using personally salient stimuli. It is possible that this facilitation effect is due to the activation of congruent negative self-schemas (Beck, 1967) or associative networks (Bower, 1981). Perhaps the lack of negative early attention biases in depression studies may have been due to the use of experimental stimuli which are not personally salient to the research participants.

Other inconsistencies exist in the ERP attention bias literature for depression. For instance, there are differences in interpretation of a well studied ERP correlate of attention, the P3. For instance, Ilardi, Atchley, Enloe, Kwasny, and Garratt (2007) employed a classic oddball paradigm, in which frequently occurring (80%) neutral words were interposed with rare (20%) negative target words. The researchers found no P3 oddball effects for negative words in their never-depressed or previously depressed (remitted) control samples. However, their dysphoric sample showed the expected *larger* P3 amplitude to negative oddball stimuli compared to neutral stimuli and compared to the two control samples. They argued that this latter effect was indicative of a depressive negative attention bias, which appears a state-like, rather than trait-like, phenomenon of depression. This interpretation is consistent with the theory that enhanced P3 amplitude is an index of greater attentional allocation (Kok, 1997). Kayser, Bruder, Tenke, Stewart, and Quikin (2000) found non-depressed participants showed no early P3 (peak latency 330ms) differences to negative or neutral faces, whereas depressed participants showed enhanced early P3 to negative faces compared to the neural faces and non-depressed participants. Similar to Ilardi et al., Kayser et al. argued that these results suggest depressed individuals show biased attention (discriminative) to negative stimuli. Contrary to these two P3 findings and interpretations, both Blackburn et al. (1990) and Yang, Zhu, Wang, Wu and Yao (2011) found *decreased* P3 amplitude to negative as opposed to positive words in their depressed participants, which they both argued demonstrated a negative attention bias in depression. In contrast the non-depressed participants in Blackburn et al. showed greater P3 to negative versus positive stimuli, whereas, the non-depressed participants in Yang et al. showed no P3 effects. Specifically, these researchers argued that the reduced P3 to negative information in depressed samples might reflect allocation of fewer of resources to negative stimuli due to their increased expectancy of negative material given their negative cognitive schemata (Beck, 1967; Beck et al., 1979), whereas, non-depressed participants show the opposite pattern (Blackburn et al. 1990) or no bias (Yang et al. 2011).

The differences in P3 results in the literature might be the result of differences in sample characteristics, ERP data-analysis techniques, and/or experimental stimulus (words, faces). Future research should make use of data analysis procedures, such as principal components analysis (PCA), to aid in differentiating the independent P3 subcomponents (Bruder et al., in press). Regarding depressive subtype, studies that used standard (non-emotional) oddball paradigms found that depressed patients with melancholic or psychotic depressive features show smaller P3 amplitude. Those with bipolar disorder or melancholic patients also show longer P3 latency (Bruder et al., in press), which suggests slower processing speed.

Nandrino et al. (2004) investigated the role of depressive history on emotional attention biases, comparing ERP results of first-episode and recurrent depressed patients to a non-depressed control group. All participants completed an emotional oddball task twice, once before psychotherapy (therapeutic approach was unspecified) and again after clinical improvement (28 days). The researchers found recurrent depressed participants exhibited larger P3s at frontal and parietal sites to negative stimuli compared to both the first-episode depressed and non-depressed patients. In line with Ilardi et al. (2007), they argued their increased P3 to the negative stimuli represented a negative attention bias in the recurrent depressed group. These results are consistent with the theory that repeated depressive experiences strengthen depressive cognition (Teasdale, 1988), enhancing the individuals' reactivity to negative stimuli. Interestingly, first-episode depressed participants showed significantly *smaller* P3s to positive words compared to both non-depressed and recurrent depressed participants. This possibly indicates attentional avoidance to positive material in first-episode depression. This is consistent with Clark and Watson's (1991) tripartite model which argues that depression is characterised by symptoms of anhedonia and absence of positive affect. After clinical improvement—consistent with predictions of the cognitive models of depression (cf. Beck, 1967; 2008; Joormann, 2010)—the previously observed negative attention bias in the recurrent depressed group disappeared. However, despite similar clinical improvement, first-episode depressed patients continued to exhibit attentional avoidance to positive stimuli (decreased P3 amplitude). Post-treatment, first-episode depressed patients also showed attentional avoidance of negative stimuli (decreased P3 amplitude), which was not present before treatment. This decreased neural reactivity to negative stimuli in both the first-episode and the recurrent patient groups appears to reflect the beneficial impact of psychotherapy in decreasing negative cognitive biases in depression. The absence of improved electrophysiological response to positive stimuli in these first-episode patients possibly reflects the fact that most traditional cognitive interventions do not focus on increasing the processing of positive material. Overall, this ERP study provides important insights into the impact of depressive disorder history on emotional information processing in depression. These results might help explain some of the variance in the P3 results between the ERP studies discussed above. They also suggest important considerations for clinical interventions with the depressed patients, as discussed at the end of this chapter.

In summary, the majority of ERP evidence supports the existence of negative attention bias in depression. The tendency to observe these biases at longer latency ERPs and under conditions of self-referential processing, suggests depressed individuals may suffer an inability to disengage from salient negative information (Gotlib and Joormann, 2010; Wisco, 2009). This difficulty may sustain depressed mood by increasing the availability of negative information in working memory and the likelihood of rumination (Donaldson, Lam, and Mathews, 2007; Joormann, 2010). Further, this facilitated elaborative processing may also result in deeper encoding of negative material into long-term memory, reinforcing the depressed individual's negative core beliefs/self-schemas (Beck, 2008; Joormann, 2010; Williams et al., 1997). The evidence for negative memory biases in depression will now be reviewed.

Emotional Memory Bias

Behavioural investigations consistently show that non-depressed individuals recall significantly more positive than negative stimuli while depressed samples recall more negative than positive stimuli (average 10% more: Matt, Vazquez, and Campbell, 1992). These biases appear dependent on the particular memory process examined, being more reliably found in explicit free-recall or working memory tasks (Deldin et al., 2001; Shestyuk et al., 2005) compared to implicit (Ellwart, Rinck, and Becker, 2003; Watkins, Martin, and Stern, 2000) or effortless recognition memory tasks (Deldin et al., 2000; Deldin et al., 2001;

Dietrich et al., 2000). In addition, emotional memory shows a linear relationship with depressive severity. Memory biases for positive material are more typically observed in non-depressed samples (Deldin et al., 2001; 2008), while dysphoric samples show no memory biases (Jermann, van der Linden, and D'Argembeau, 2008; Ridout, Noreen, and Johal, 2009), and clinically depressed samples more typically show memory biases for negative material (Gilboa-Schnechtman, Erhard-Weiss, and Jeczemien, 2002; Ridout, Astell, Reid, Glen, and O'Carroll, 2003). Unlike attention biases (cf. Nandrino et al., 2004), memory biases appear independent of depressive disorder history, with similar negative memory effects observed in first-episode and recurrent samples (Nandrino, Pezard, Poste, Revillere, and Beaune, 2002; Wessel, Meeren, Peeters, Arntz, and Merckelbach, 2001), and with remitted depressed patients showing similar emotional memory functioning as never-depressed samples (Nandrino et al., 2002; Shestyuk and Deldin, 2010). Negative memory biases in depression have been associated with defective problem solving, increased negative expectation, and delayed recovery from depressive episodes (Peeters, Wessel, Merckelbach, and Boon-Vermeeren, 2002; Raes et al., 2005). Although there is robust support for negative memory biases in depression in the behavioural literature, the ERP evidence for these effects is more equivocal.

Event-related potential investigations of explicit memory performance typically use the Old/New paradigm. In this paradigm, participants' are required to learn a list of stimuli (study phase). They then perform a recognition test, in which they are presented the studied stimuli intermixed with distractor stimuli (test phase). The task requires the participants to identify if they recognise the stimuli as part of the studied list (old stimulus) or not (new stimulus). The ERP *old/new effect* (Table 1) concerns the difference between the ERPs elicited by new and old stimuli. The effect is characterised by enhanced positivity for correctly recognised old stimuli compared to non-recognised new stimuli (Friedman, 1990; Rugg and Nagy, 1987). Dietrich et al. (2000) used the Old/New paradigm to examine recognition memory for positive, negative, and neutral words in depressed and non-depressed participants. Behavioural results found that both non-depressed and depressed participants exhibited enhanced memory for negative words and reduced memory for neutral words, indicating an influence of negative content on recognition in both samples. However, non-depressed participants were found to exhibit much larger Old/New ERPs compared to non-depressed participants, and larger ERP Old/New effect for emotional—positive and negative—stimuli compared to neutral stimuli, suggesting, "intact recognition processes" (Dietrich et al., 2000; p.26). The ERP Old/New effect is hypothesised to reflect neural integration of memory processing of subsystems of the medial temporal lobe system, particularly in the hippocampus and amygdala projections to the prefrontal and parietal cortex (Gordeev, 2007; Rugg, Fletcher, Frith, Frackowiak, and Dolan, 1996). Context integration processes are a major task of the central executive system of working memory (Baddeley, 2000; Baddeley and Hitch, 1974). Therefore, the overall reduction of the ERP Old/New effect in the depressed participants might be the result of general deficits in working memory functioning in the disorder.

In another study, Deldin et al. (2002, as cited in Deldin et al., 2003) presented participants with five lists of 18 self-referent stimuli while ERPs were recorded. Afterwards, participants were required to recall as many words as they could remember. Non-depressed participants exhibited greater recall and increased SW amplitude for processing positive relative to negative stimuli than depressed participants. This is consistent with other ERP studies that find non-depressed participants exhibit greater SW amplitudes in response to positive relative to negative stimuli (Deldin et al., 2001, 2008; Deveney and Deldin, 2004) and demonstrate greater sustained brain activation in response to positive stimuli than depressed participants (Deldin et al., 2001). In contrast, their depressed participants exhibited increased SW amplitude for processing of negative relative to positive stimuli during encoding, which appeared related to their enhanced free recall of negative stimuli. Given that SW is thought to reflect working memory function (Table 1), these observations suggest a failure to initiate or sustain attention to positive information in depressed compared to non-depressed sample. Therefore, depression may be associated with not only preferential processing biases for negative stimuli, but also with the absence of processing biases toward positive stimuli, which would otherwise serve a protective function (Alloy and Abramson, 1988).

Similar to the attention literature discussed above, memory biases in depression also appear to be dependent on stimulus characteristics, such as saliency, with experiments that employ personally salient stimuli (Moritz, Voigt, Arzola, and Otte, 2008) or self-referential encoding procedures (Shestyuk and Deldin, 2010) being more successful in eliciting negative memory biases in depression than in paradigms that do not.

Taken together, research has found depression to be related to biased memory for negative material, whereas euthymia (normal, non-depressed mood) is related to biased memory for positive material. These memory effects are sensitive to stimulus characteristics and task, being amplified for personally salient information and in explicit memory tasks. Recent ERP evidence suggests that these negative memory biases in depression seem to be associated with continued activation and elaboration of this negative information in working memory, which may be the result of a deficit in prefrontal inhibitory control (Joormann, 2010).

Cognitive Deficits in Working Memory Inhibitory Control

This section will review recent empirical evidence for working memory inhibitory control deficits in depression. We will focus first on the evidence for deficits in the ability to keep irrelevant negative material from entering working memory (resistance to distractor interference), and then on the ability to remove negative material from working memory (resistance to proactive interference).

Resistance to Distractor Interference

A number of ERP studies have demonstrated deficits in inhibiting non-emotional distractor stimuli in depressed individuals (Harvey et al., 2004; Kaiser et al., 2003; Linville, 1996; Ruchsow et al., 2008; Zhang, Zhao, and Xu, 2007). Vanderhasselt and DeReadt (2009) provided ERP evidence that distractor interference inhibitory control deficits are moderated by depressive history. During a word-colour Stroop task, larger N450 ERPs were observed for incongruent compared to congruent trials in the sample of never depressed participants, representing normal inhibitory functioning. However, this N450 difference effect was not observed in formally diagnosed depressed participants, which appears to reflect their difficulty inhibiting irrelevant material from entering working memory. This ERP finding significantly correlated with the number of previous depressive episodes ($r = .51$), but was not associated with age of onset or duration of remission. These results suggest that deficits in the ability to keep irrelevant material from entering working memory (the essence of distractor interference) increase with each successive depressive episode. Interestingly, these researchers found no behavioural evidence for this effect, which demonstrates the unique utility of ERP in detecting rapid cognitive control processes that are not always evident in overt behaviour. Overall, these investigations provide modest support for the hypothesis that depressed individuals show distractor interference deficits for non-emotional stimuli. This in turn would deplete their cognitive resources, affecting performance on other tasks (i.e., problem solving). Goeleven, De Readt, Baert, and Koster (2006) used a Negative Affective Priming (NAP) task to examine resistance to distractor interference inhibitory control in a sample of non-depressed, depressed, and remitted-depressed participants. In the NAP task, two consecutive trials are presented to participants; each contains a target and a distracter stimulus (e.g., positive, negative, or neutral facial expressions). For each display, participants were required to indicate the emotion of the target and ignore the distracter. A negative bias is indicated by faster response latencies to negative targets that follow negative distracters on a previous trial. The study found that non-depressed and remitted depressed participants were slower to identify the valence of positive and negative facial expressions following similarly-valanced distracters, whereas depressed participants demonstrated significantly faster responses to negative faces presented after negative distracters (i.e., indicating ineffective inhibition). This effect was not found for positive stimuli (Figure 3). Joormann (2004) found a similar effect in their dysphoric participants and participants with a history of depressive episodes using a NAP task with emotional word stimuli.

These behavioural NAP findings indicate a specific deficit in inhibiting irrelevant negative material from working memory in depression. However, the cross-sectional nature of these investigations makes it difficult to conclude whether these inhibition deficits are a symptom of experiencing depression or whether they actively contribute to perpetuation of the disorder. Addressing this, Zetsche and Joormann (2010) used a prospective design to assess the relation between inhibitory functioning, depressive symptoms, and rumination over a six month interval (time 1: $n = 111$; time 2: $n = 40$ [36%]). They found that depressive symptoms at time 1 were associated with distractor interference inhibitory deficits for negative information in a NAP task, at time 1. Individual differences in this inhibitory performance predicted depressive symptoms and rumination (as measured by the Response Style Scale [RSS]; Nolen-Hoeksema and Morrow, 1991) at time 2. This provides support for the hypothesis that depressive symptoms are preceded and possibly maintained by poor inhibitory control for negative material. There are a number of limitations to this study. First, the results are based on a non-clinical sample of university students, with low overall BDI-II scores. Further, given the high participant attrition rate (64%), the time 2 results are to be interpreted with caution. It may be argued that participants who completed the follow-up assessment were different from those who did not (poor internal validity). Arguably, time 1 BDI-II and RSS scores and performance on the inhibition experimental tasks did not differ between participants who took part in the time 2 follow-up data with those who did not.

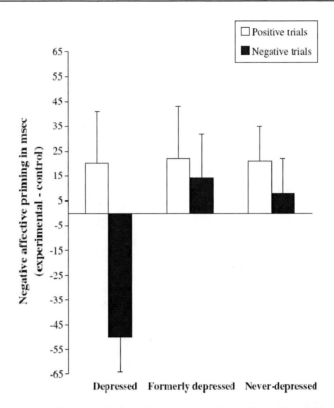

Figure 3. Mean negative affective priming for negative and positive trails in depressed, formerly depressed, and never-depressed participants. Positive values indicate efficient distractor interference inhibitory functioning. Image adapted and reprinted by permission from Goeleven et al. (2006). All rights reserved.

However, it is possible that participants' differed in terms of motivation, which may interact with depression expression and/or individual differences in inhibitory control. Future research should aim to replicate these findings in a large clinical sample using electrocortical dependent measures. Electrophysiological data suggest that the negative priming effect in these behavioural studies is the result of aberrant early frontal inhibition processes, indexed by deviant early fronto-central ERPs during NAP (i.e., reduced frontal amplitude of P2: Gibbons, 2006; increased frontal amplitude of N2: Daurignac, Houde, and Jouvent, 2006). In an ERP investigation using the NAP task, Yao et al. (2010) found non-depressed participants exhibited larger P2 to negative distractor stimuli. Given the relationship between attention allocation and P2 amplitude (Carretié, Mercado, Tapia, and Hinojosa, 2001a; Carretié, Martin-Loeches, Hinojosa, and Mercado, 2001b), this enhanced P2 may reflect increased cognitive effort to overcome inhibition disturbance from the prime distractor in the NAP task. Depressed participants showed abnormally reduced P2 amplitude at central-parietal electrodes for negative, but not for positive distractor stimuli. Therefore, the researchers argued this reflected an inhibition deficit (diminished cognitive control from distractor interference) for negative material in the depressed participants.

As implicated in Beck's (2008) neurobiological model of depression, neuroimaging studies have found a link between inhibitory dysfunction and depression. These studies found that non-depressed individuals engage greater rostral ACC activation to inhibit irrelevant positive information, whereas, depressed individuals engage greater rostral ACC activation to inhibit irrelevant negative information (Eugene, Joormann, Cooney, Atlas, and Gotlib, 2010; Mitterschiffthaler et al., 2008). These results provide further empirical support for the hypothesis that depression is associated with not only deficits in inhibiting attention to negative stimuli but also with deficits in the apparent protective function of the preferential processing of positive stimuli characteristic of healthy individuals.

Taken together, these studies suggest that depression involves deficits in the inhibition of irrelevant information from entering working memory, particularly irrelevant negative material. These distractor interference inhibitory control deficits appear to maintain depressive symptoms. Given that depression is associated with negative rumination and negative memory intrusions, Joormann (2010) argues that the disorder is also associated with deficits in *removing* irrelevant negative material from working memory (resistance to proactive interference inhibitory control).

Resistance to Proactive Interference in Depression

Experimental research on resistance to proactive interference typically uses paradigms that require participants to encode stimuli into memory, which, subsequently they are required to inhibit from working memory. Two promising tasks are the directed-forgetting task and the Sternberg working memory task. In the directed-forgetting task, halfway through an intentional or incidental learning task participants are informed that the trials presented so far are 'to-be-forgotten' (TBF) because they were merely practice. However, at the end of the subsequent list, participants are then asked to recall all of the previous items including those that they were instructed to forget (Bjork, 1972; Epstein, 1972). Efficient proactive inhibitory control is indexed by significantly more 'to-be-remembered' material recalled than TBF material (Friedman and Miyake, 2004; Geiselman, Bjork, and Fishman, 1983). Using a directed-forgetting task, Power, Dalgleish, Claudio, Tata, and Kentish (2000) found that non-depressed students (Experiment 2) recalled more positive TBF items compared to the dysphoric students, and compared to negative TBF items. Dysphoric students (Experiment 2), on the other hand, recalled approximately equal number of TBF positive and negative TBF items, whereas, clinically depressed patients (Experiment 3) exhibited enhanced memory for negative TBF stimuli relative to positive stimuli and to non-depressed participants. These results suggest that similar to memory biases, proactive interference effects for emotional material appears to show a liner relationship with depressive symptoms, with positive proactive inhibition deficits found in non-depressed samples, no deficits observed in dysphoric samples, and negative proactive inhibition deficits found in clinically depressed samples. Consistent with this hypothesis, Hertel and Gerstle (2003) found that impaired ability to successfully inhibit TBF negative words during the directed-forgetting task was significantly correlated with depressive symptoms ($r = .36$, $d = .77$; Hertel and Gerstle, 2003).

Joormann and Gotlib (2008) used a modified Sternberg working memory task to measure resistance to proactive interference deficits in depression. They had participants learn two lists of words, one presented in blue ink and the other in red. Participants were then instructed to remember only one of the word lists (e.g., only blue words), which required participants to inhibit the irrelevant words (e.g., red words) from working memory. A single black word (probe) was subsequently presented to participants, who were required to indicate if the word was presented in the previous relevant memory set (i.e., blue words) by pressing 'yes' or 'no' on the computer keyboard (probes from irrelevant list must be rejected, as must new probes).

In the Sternberg working memory task, it is suggested that differences in reaction times to an intrusion probe (word from irrelevant list) compared to a new probe (a completely new word) indexes the strength of proactive interference inhibitory control (Oberauer, 2005a, 2005b; Ochsner and Gross, 2005). Joormann and Gotlib found that healthy control participants in both neutral and induced sad mood responded faster when presented with negative intrusion material, compared to depressed participants. No differences were found between the two control groups for negative intrusion stimuli or between groups for positive intrusion stimuli. These findings suggest that clinical depression—not just sad mood—is associated with difficulties in removing irrelevant negative information from working memory. Hierarchical regression analysis found that depressive symptoms (measured by the BDI-II; β =.71) and intrusion effects for negative material (step 2; β = .34) together predicted 61% of the variance in individual rumination score (measured by the RSS). No group differences were observed for positive stimuli, supporting the theory that the inhibition deficit is specific to negative information in depression. Further, given that the sad mood-induced participants did not display deficit inhibitory processes, the effect appears specific to depression rather than to general, transient negative mood.

To date, no ERP or neuroimaging studies of resistance to proactive interference inhibitory control for emotional stimuli in depression or dysphoria have been published. Using a similar task to Joormann and Gotlib (2008), unpublished work in our laboratory found that control participants showed no ERP or behavioural differences in their ability to inhibit previously encoded negative or positive word stimuli. However, dysphoric participants showed enhanced frontal Nogo-N2 during inhibition of previously encoded negative stimuli compared to positive stimuli and compared to the non-dysphoric participants (Dati, Cutmore, and Shum, 2011). Like Joormann and Gotlib no group differences existed for the inhibition of previously encoded positive stimuli. These results suggest continual activation of irrelevant negative material in working memory, most likely due to deficits in proactive interference inhibitory control (Joormann, 2010). The validity of these findings, however, requires replication in a clinical sample.

These preliminary results provide support for Joormann's (2010) contention that depression involves deficits in ability to keep irrelevant negative information from entering working memory and in removing this information. To date, only one experiment has examined both resistance to distractor and resistance to proactive interference inhibitory processes together in the same task (Joormann, Nee, Berman, Jonides, and Gotlib, 2010). In this study, non-depressed and depressed participants were required to memorise a set of stimuli while ignoring concurrently presented distractor stimuli. They were then told to remember a subset of the previously memorised material (probe stimuli), and forget the others (suppress stimuli). Inhibition was indexed by longer response latencies on subsequent recognition tasks of the TBF distractor stimuli (indexing distractor interference) and suppress stimuli (indexing proactive interference) compared to new items. Non-depressed and depressed participants showed no deficits in distractor inhibition of negative information. However, compared to non-depressed participants, depressed participants exhibited difficulties keeping TBF negative information from intruding on or remaining active in working memory (effect size: d = 1.17). No group differences were observed for positive information. This is consistent with Joormann and Gotlib's (2008) observation that depression is associated with difficulties in removing irrelevant negative information from working memory. This proactive interference deficit for negative material significantly

correlated with level of depressive symptoms (measured by BDI-II; $r = .50$) and with recurrent negative cognitions (measured by RSS; $r = .41$). These deficits in disengaging from negative material might explain impaired emotional regulation in depression.

This hypothesis is supported by neuroimagining investigations, which find that, unlike non-depressed individuals, depressed individuals do not show the expected engagement of frontal executive control (dorso-lateral and ventro-medial PFC) over subcortical (amygdala) reactivity when asked to regulate negative emotions to picture stimuli (Johnstone, van Reekum, Urry, Kalin, and Davidson, 2007). Consistent with Joormann's model (2010), cognitive inhibitory deficits in depression also appear to reduce the depressed individual's ability to evoke mood-incongruent (positive) memories as an emotional regulation technique (Rusting and DeHart, 2000). Rather, depressed individuals are more likely to respond with maladaptive coping strategies, such as rumination, suppression, or avoidance to repair their negative mood (see Joormann and Gotlib, 2010 for a review).

In summary, depressed individuals have difficulties disengaging from elaborative processing of negative information in working memory. This may involve irrelevant negative memories intruding into working memory or failure to remove once relevant but now irrelevant negative items. This reduced cognitive control appears causally linked to deficits in emotional regulation, resulting in sustained negative mood. This suggests that interventions based on reappraisal mechanisms and cognitive control training have the ability to improve emotional regulation and reduce both the development and maintenance of depression. The last section of this chapter attempts to translate these experimental findings into psychotherapeutic interventions for the depressed patient.

CLINICAL IMPLICATIONS

Research evidence presented throughout this chapter suggests that depressed individuals show processing biases towards negative and away from positive information. Based on this research, we suggest that interventions that strengthen top-down attention control may help the depressed patient to (a) disengage from negative cognitions and (b) enhance attendance to positive stimuli. Together, this may serve to regulate their mood and reduce vulnerability to relapse. This could be achieved through cognitive behavioural therapy (CBT), attention training, and positive psychotherapy interventions. We also argue that incorporating the ERP into clinical interventions with the depressed patient may aid in clinical assessment, diagnosis, and treatment evaluation.

Cognitive Behavioural Therapy

The recommended first-line treatment for depression is CBT (NICE, 2004). It emphasises challenging and restructuring depressed patient' negative cognitions to be more evidence-based and adaptive (see Beck and Dozois, 2011). As argued in recent models of depression (Beck, 2008; Joormann, 2010) this requires substantial top-down control over reflexive bottom-up cognitions (Clark and Beck, 2010). Consistent with these predictions, reviews of fMRI and PET studies that effectiveness of CBT appears to be associated with reduced

activation of the limbic regions implicated in the generation of negative emotion—particularly in the amygdala and hippocampus—and with increased action of anterior regions involved in executive control over negative emotions (see Clark and Beck, 2010 for a review). For instance, a recent study found that effectiveness of CBT in depressed participants was associated with significant increases in ventromedial PFC activation (r = .57; a in Figure 4; Ritchey, Dolcos, Eddington, Strauman, and Cabeza, in press). In regards to emotional information processing, symptom relief with CBT was associated with enhanced discrimination of emotional and neutral items in the right amygdala (b in Figure 4), and greater activity in response to positive versus neutral stimuli in the left anterior temporal lobe and ventrolateral PFC (c in Figure 4). It is important to note, however, that improvements in emotional processing in depression cannot be solely attributed to the effects of CBT with these cognitive alternations also observed in other intervention modalities, such as pharmacotherapy (Harmer et al., 2009). This suggests that symptom relief in depression is associated with decreased emotional information processing biases more generally.

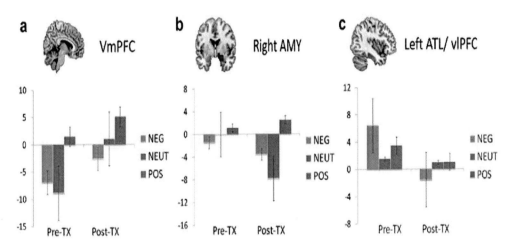

Figure 4. Neural correlates of changes in emotional processing in depression with effective treatment with CBT. Error bars denote SEM. Pre-Tx = pre-treatment, Post-Tx = post-treatment. VmPFC = ventromedial prefrontal cortex, AMY = amygdala, ATL = anterior temporal lobe; vlPFC = ventrolateral prefrontal cortex. Image adapted from Ritchey et al. (in press) with permission. All rights reserved.

Research comparing CBT and antidepressant treatment for depression, show that CBT appears to be unique in its ability to change enduring, core schema structures (Dozois et al., 2009; Quilty, McBride, and Bagby, 2008) and improve top-down cognitive control (Fu et al., 2008; Goldapple et al., 2004; Linden, 2006; Ritchey et al., in press). Note, that deficits in these cognitive factors are argued to characterise depression vulnerability in recent cognitive models of depression (Beck, 2008; Joormann, 2010). Thus, the unique ability of CBT to challenge core negative schemas and improve cognitive inhibitory control might account for observations of reduced depressive relapse following CBT (25%) compared to antidepressant (60%) interventions (Gloaguen, Cottraux, Cucherat, and Blackburn, 1998). Extensive empirical data support the efficaciousness of CBT for depression (mean d = 0.67; Cuijpers, van Straten, Bohlmeijer, Hollon, and Andersson, 2010). However, it remains possible the effect size estimates for CBT are inflated due to publication bias (e.g., mean adjusted d =

0.42; see Cuijpers et al., 2010). Given that improvement of attention control (working memory) appears to have an important role in the origin, maintenance, and recurrence of depressive episodes, adjunctive therapies to CBT aimed at strengthen working memory control processes might aid in treatment.

Attention Training Interventions

Research shows that attention biases to emotional information can be trained and untrained (Derryberry and Reed, 2002; MacLeod, Rutherford, Campbell, Ebsworthy, and Holker, 2002). Depressed individuals have also been shown to successfully learn to inhibit negative information from awareness (*resistance to proactive interference:* Joormann, Hertel, Brozovich, and Gotlib, 2005) and to keep it from entering their working memory (*resistance to distractor interference:* Joormann, Hertel, LeMoult, and Gotlib, 2009), by being provided with simple cognitive control strategies. As with training to divert attention away from negative stimuli, preliminary data show that individuals can be trained to selectively direct attention to positive stimuli (Wadlinger and Isaacowitz, 2008). These results have yet to be replicated in clinically depressed samples. Positive psychotherapy (PPT) interventions provide another promising approach to increase positive cognitions, feelings, and behaviour in depressed patients (Seligman, Rashid, and Parks, 2006). A recent meta-analysis of 51 PPT interventions with 4266 individuals found this approach significantly decreases depressive symptoms (mean $r = -.31$; Sin and Lyubomirsky, 2009).

Mindfulness-based interventions can be conceived as attention control training (Baer, 2003) with an influence on increasing attention control (Jha, Krompinger, and Baime, 2007), reducing ruminative thinking (Ramel, Goldin, Carmona, and McQuaid, 2004), and improving working memory inhibitory control (Jha, Stanley, Kiyongag, Wong, and Geifand, 2010). Random control trail (RCT) studies support the therapeutic utility of mindfulness for the treatment of depression (Kuyken et al., 2010; Ma and Teasdale, 2004; Teasdale et al., 2000) and for decreasing the rates of depressive relapse (Bondfolfi et al., 2010; Teasdale et al., 2000). Meta-analytic review of 727 studies, of which 39 were analysed, found mindfulness interventions were associated with a relatively large effect size (Hedges' $g = 0.95$) for improving depressive symptoms (Hofmann, Sawyer, Witt, and Oh, 2010). Neurobiological data suggest that these effects are mediated via more flexible top-down emotion regulation by engaging frontal cortical structures (particularly the ACC) to dampen bottom-up automatic amygdala activity (see Chiesa, Brambillia, and Serretti, 2010 for a review). However, placebo effects and standard CBT interventions have been shown to activate similar frontal areas to achieve effective emotional regulation (Chiesa et al., 2010). In light of this, further investigation is needed to compare and indentify specific neuro-cognitive modifications induced by mindfulness intervention compared to those induced by standard cognitive therapy components and placebo.

Other, more explicit attention bias training techniques have been developed as interventions for depressed clients. These techniques typically use methodologies where patients are trained to reduce negative attention biases with computer dot-probe tasks. Here, a dot probe is set to appear on 90% of trails on the opposite side of a negative self-referential word stimulus, prompting participants to divert their attention away from negative information (MacLeod, Rutherford, Campbell, Ebsworthy, and Holker, 2002). This training

contrasts to the control condition, which uses the same cues as in the training condition, but the ratio of trials to divert attention away from negative information is 50% (chance). Preliminary studies using this simple attention retraining procedure have been shown to be successful in reducing symptoms of clinical (Papageorgiou and Wells, 2000; Siegle, Ghinassi, and Thase, 2007) and subclinincal depression (Wells and Beevers, 2010), after as little as two weeks of training. Consistent with Joormann (2010) and Beck's models, reductions in negative attention biases using these attention training interventions have been found to be associated with reductions of rumination (RSS, $d = 1.26$; Siegle et al., 2007) and to mediate improvements in depressive symptoms ($r = .52$, $d = 1.04$; Wells and Beevers, 2010). However, these latter results need to be interpreted with caution given the questionable internal validity of Wells and Beevers's study due to high participant attrition rate of 53%. Further, consistent with Beck (2008) neurobiological model, Siegle et al. found that exposure to adjunctive attention training interventions showed normalisation of amygdala activity (reduced over-reactivity to negative personally relevant stimuli and increased reactivity to positive stimuli; $\eta^2 = .05$) and increased left dorsolateral PFC during performance of a cognitive task (digit span; $\eta^2 = .05$).

More recently, Baert, De Raedt, Schacht, and Koster (2010) found that attention training interventions might be dependent on depressive severity. They found that attention bias training procedure did not change negative attention biases in dysphoric or clinically depressed participants compared to the control procedure. They found that dysphoric participants with mild depressive severity (BDI-II: 14 – 18) showed small improvement in depressive symptom severity ($d = 0.73$ to 0.57) with attention bias training, but for dysphoric participants with moderate to severe symptoms severity (BDI-II >19) attention training led to increases in depressive symptoms ($d = 0.76$ to 1.28) and in fatigue ($d = 1.36$). In the clinically depressed sample, there were no beneficial effects to attention bias training on top of therapy and/or medication. These results suggest that it might be beneficial to wait until depressive symptom remission before considering attentional retraining procedures. However, one could argue that Baert et al.'s null findings on improvement of attention biases following intervention may indicate that the training procedure did not work. This would explain the study's inability to replicate previous positive findings with severe depression (cf. Papageorgiou and Wells, 2000; Siegle et al., 2007). Arguing against this, Baret et al. did replicate those of Wells and Beevers (2010) with mild depression, suggesting effective attention retraining.

It has also been argued that dot-probe attention tasks lack sensitivity and reliability in measuring changes in depressive cognition (Schmukle, 2005). For instance, these behavioural reaction times measure the delay between stimulus presentation and behavioural output, which may comprise motor and cognitive components (Mialet, Pope, and Yurgelun-Todd, 1996). This suggests the need to explore other more sensitive markers of cognitive processing in depression that are relatively free from extraneous error variance, such as the ERP (Kok, 1997). Further, there are methodological concerns that limit the validity of attention training interventions. Specifically, current studies have small samples and non-clinical control samples. There also is little evidence that the observed neurobiological effects are acting through the theorised improvements in bottom-up and top-down cognitive control (Siegle et al., 2007). Examination of more direct data relative to disrupted cognitive information processing in depression may allow for more precise identification and characterization of

these aberrant processes to inform diagnosis, and treatment interventions/evaluation. The ERP may provide a useful clinical tool here.

Use of EEG and ERP in Depression Treatment

The high temporal resolution of the ERP allows for more sensitive assessment of the specific cognitive component(s) disrupted in the depressed client (i.e., ERPs can differentiate between orienting, selective, and sustained attention). These benefits might compensate for their low spatial resolution and their limited ability to detect changes occurring in deep sub-cortical structures (e.g., amygdala). Further, compared to neuroimagning techniques, ERPs are not expensive to use and do not require extensive training to administer and interpret. As such, there are opportunities for the clinical utilisation of the ERP as objective marker of cognitive processing in depression treatment (Alhaj, Wisniewski, and McAllister-Williams, in press).

While research has attempted to define objective ERP markers for cognitive bias and deficits in depression, as outlined throughout this chapter, current data is inconsistent and may be due to heterogeneity in relatively small samples. However, clinical research is starting to address this issue in hope it will increase clinical utility of the ERP. A recent large study by Kemp et al. (2009) found preliminary evidence for two particular ERP biomarkers in depression diagnosis and cognitive conceptualisation. Using a neural oddball task, the researchers found the P2 amplitude showed a negative linear relationship with depressive severity, with it being smallest in healthy controls (n =116), medium in participants with dysphoric mood (n =127), and largest in patients with clinical depression (n = 78). Consistent with previous research (see Bruder et al., in press for a review) they also observed the expected reduction in P3 amplitude in the clinically depressed sample, however these effects were not found for the healthy control or dysphoric samples. This research suggests that the P2 ERP has promise as a possible biomarker of risk for depression—that is it could predict who might become depressed. The P3 on the other hand, may be used to differentiate clinical from subclinical depression, and provide information on impaired selective attention/stimulus discrimination in depression. Further, given that previous work indicates that the P2 and P3 are under partial genetic control (Katsanis, Iacono, McGue, and Carlson, 1997), these electrophysiological markers might also have potential as pertinent endophenotypic indicators for depression vulnerability (Kemp et al., 2009).

Enhanced amplitude of the P2 also shows promise as a predictor of non-response to antidepressant treatment in depressed clients relative to treatment responders and healthy control participants (Vandoolaeghe, van Hunsel, Nuyten, and Maes, 1998). Early data also show promise in the ERPs ability to predict and evaluate treatment response. For instance, decreased P3 amplitude has been found to be able to predict poor response to electroconvulsive therapy (ECT) in melancholic depression (Ancy, Gangadhar, and Janakiramaiah, 1996). Other research shows that delayed latency of the P300 normalises after four weeks selective serotonin reuptake inhibitor (SSRI) treatment in depression (Hetzel et al., 2005), suggesting potential of the ERP for use in treatment evaluation. The EEG has also shown promise as a potential biomarker to increase prediction of antidepressant response (see Alhaj et al., in press for a review).

The translation of the utility of the ERP into clinical interventions with the depressed client has not yet been fully realised. Advances in understanding the association between the electrophysiology and improvement in depressive cognition could lead to better individualized treatment selection. Future research should aim to establish the psychometrics of these potential electrophysiological markers (i.e., test-retest reliability, sensitivity, specificity, discriminative ability), and provide further data on their incremental validity (ERP modulations at different levels of depressive severity, sensitivity to depressive symptom change). This represents a promising direction for future treatment research, which might provide the foundation for more efficacious assessment for depressive disorders.

CONCLUSION

The ability to control the contents of working memory is likely to be critical in differentiating people who recover easily from negative affect from those who initiate a cycle of recurrent negative cognitive and worsening mood. ERPs have been found to be an important index of information processing biases and deficits in depression and their neurophysiologic underpinnings. The clinical implications of the material presented throughout this chapter suggest that psychotherapy could achieve symptom reduction by helping the depressed patient to strengthen top-down cognitive control over sustained processing of bottom-up cognitions (Clark and Beck, 2010).

To date, few investigations have experimentally integrated study of affect, working memory and brain potential. Current evidence for the recent cognitive models for depression (cf. Beck, 2008; Joormann, 2010) has been largely indirect, using correlational and cross-sectional designs. Therefore, this literature is limited in its ability to specify how these processes are related to each other in depressive experiences. Longitudinal investigations are needed to examine individual differences in these cognitive profiles prior to the onset of depression, during a depressive episode, and in symptom remission. This future work will promote development for more precise neuro-cognitive models of depression, which will support improvements in how we can treat this recurrent disorder.

ACRONYMS

Affective Norms for English Words	ANEW
American Psychiatric Association	APA
Anterior cingulate cortex	ACC
Beck Depression Inventory-Second Edition	BDI-II
Blood level deoxygenation	BOLD
Cognitive Behaviour Therapy	CBT
Current source density	CSD
Diagnostic and Statistical Manual, fourth edition, text-revised	DSM-IV-TR
Electroconvulsive therapy	ECT
Electroencephalography	EEG
Error Related Negativity	ERN

Event-related Potential	ERP
Hypothalamic-pituitary-adrenal	HPA
International Classification of Disease-10th edition	ICD-10
Late Positive Potential	LPP
Long-term memory	LTM
Medial Frontal Negativity	MFN
Mindfulness-Based Stress Reduction	MBSR
Negative Affective Priming	NAP
Positive psychotherapy	PPT
Prefrontal cortex	PFC
Principle components analysis	PCA
Randomised Control Trial	RCT
Response Style Scale	RSS
Selective Serotonin Reuptake Inhibitor	SSRI
Short allele serotonin transporter gene	5-HTTLPR
Short-term memory	STM
Slow Wave	SW
To-be-forgotten	TBF

REFERENCES

Alexopoulos, G. S., Murphy, C. F., Gunning-Dixon, F. M., Kalayam, B., and Katz, R., Kanellopoulos, D., et al. (2007). Event-related potentials in an emotional go/no-go task and remission of geriatric depression. *NeuroReport: Cognitive Neuroscience and Neuropsychology, 18*(3), 217-221.

Alhaj, H., Wisniewski, G., and McAllister-Williams, R. H. (in press). The use of the EEG in measuring therapeutic drug action: Focus on depression and antidepressants. *Journal of Psychopharmacology.*

Alloy, L. B., and Abramson, L. Y. (1988). Depressive realism: Four theoretical perspectives. In L. B. Alloy (Ed.), *Cognitive process in depression* (pp. 223-265). New York: Guilford Press.

Alloy, L. B., Abramson, L. Y., Hogan, M. E., Whitehouse, W. G., Rose, D. T., and Robinson, M. S., et al. (2000). The Temple-Wisconsin cognitive vulnerability to depression project: Lifetime history of axis I psychopathology in individuals at high and low cognitive risk for depression. *Journal of Abnormal Psychology, 109*(3), 403-418.

Ancy, J., Gangadhar, B. N., and Janakiramaiah, N. (1996). 'Normal' P300 amplitude predicts rapid response to ECT in melancholia. *Journal of Affective Disorders, 41*(3), 211-215.

Anderer, P., Saletu, B., Semlitsch, H. V., and Pascual-Marqui, R. D. (2002). Structural and energetic processes related to P300: LORETA findings in depression and effects of antidepressant drugs. *Methods and Findings in Experimental and Clinical Pharmacology, 24*, 200-206.

Baddeley, A. D. (2000). The episodic buffer: A new component of working memory? *Trends in Cognitive Sciences, 4*(11), 417-423.

Baddeley, A. D., and Hitch, G. J. (1974). Working memory. In G. H. Bower (Ed.), *The psychology of learning and motivation* (Vol. 8, pp. 47-89). New York: Academic Press.

Baer, R. A. (2003). Mindfulness training as a clinical intervention: A conceptual and empirical review. *Clinical Psychology: Science and Practice, 10*, 125-143.

Baert, S., De Raedt, R., Schacht, R., and Koster, E. H. W. (2010). Attentional bias training in depression: Therapeutic effects depend on depression severity. *Journal of Behavior Therapy and Experimental Psychiatry, 41*, 265-274.

Beck, A. T. (1967). *Depression: Clinical, experimental and theoretical aspects.* New York: Harper and Row.

Beck, A. T. (1996). Beyond belief: A theory of modes, personality, and psychopathology. In P. Salkovski (Ed.), *Frontiers of Cognitive Therapy* (pp. 1-25). New York: Guilford.

Beck, A. T. (2008). The evolution of the cognitive model of depression and its neurobiological correlates. *The American Journal of Psychiatry, 165*(8), 969-977.

Beck, A. T., and Dozois, D. J. A. (2011). Cognitive therapy: Current status and future directions. *Annual Review of Medicine, 62*, 397-409.

Beck, A. T., Rush, A. J., Shaw, B. F., and Emery, G. (1976). *Cognitive therapy of depression.* New York: Guilford.

Beste, C., Willemssen, R., Saft, C., and Falkenstein, M. (2010). Response inhibition subporcesses and dopaminergic pathways: Basal ganglia disease effects. *Neuropscyhologia, 48*(2), 366-373.

Bjork, R. A. (1972). Theoretical implications of directed forgetting. In A. W. Melton and E. Martin (Eds.), *Coding processes in human memory* (pp. 1-32). Washington, DC: Winsten.

Blackburn, I. M., Roxborought, H. M., Muir, W. J., Glabus, M., and Blackwood, D. H. (1990). Perceptual and physiological dysfunction in depression. *Psychological Medicine, 20*, 95-103.

Blackwood, D. H. R., Whalley, L. J., Christie, J. E., Blackburn, I. M., St. Clair, D. M., and McInnes, A. (1987). Changes in auditory P3 event-related potential in schizophrenia and depression. *British Journal of Psychiatry, 150*, 154-160.

Bondfolfi, G., Jermann, F., Van der Linden, M., Gex-Fabry, M., Bizzini, L., and Rouget, B. W., et al. (2010). Depression relapse prophylaxis with mindfulness-based cognitive therapy: Replication and extension in the Swiss health care system. *Journal of Affective Disorders, 122*(3), 224-231.

Bower, G. H. (1981). Mood and memory. *American Psychologist, 36*, 129-148.

Bower, G. H., Monteiro, K. P., and Gilligan, S. G. (1978). Emotional mood as context for learning and recall. *Journal of Verbal Learning and Verbal Behavior, 17*, 573-585.

Bradley, B. P., Mogg, K., and Lee, S. C. (1997). Attentional biases for negative information in induced and naturally occurring dysphoria. *Behaviour Research and Therapy, 35*, 911-927.

Browning, M., Holmes, E. A., and Harmer, C. J. (2010). The modification of attentional bias to emotional information: A review of techniques, mechanisms, and relevance to emotional disorders. *Cognitive, Affective, and Behavioural Neuroscience, 10*(1), 8-20.

Bruder, G. E., Kayser, J., and Tenke, C. E. (in press). Event-related brain potentials in depression: Clinical, cognitive and neurophysiologic implications. In S. J. Luck and E. S. Kappenman (Eds.), *Event-related potential components: the ups and downs of brainwave recordings*. New York: Oxford University Press.

Bruder, G. E., Tenke, C. E., Stewart, J. E., Towey, J. P., Leite, P., and Voflmaier, M., et al. (1995). Brain event-related potentials to complex tones in depressed patients: Relations to perceptual asymmetry and clinical features. *Psychophysiology, 32*, 373-381.

Bruder, G. E., Tenke, C. E., Towey, J. P., Leitw, P., Fong, R., and Stewart, J. E., et al. (1998). Brain ERPs of depressed patients to complex tones in an oddball task: Relation of reduced P3 asymmetry to physical anhedonia. *Psychophysiology, 35*, 54-63.

Burkhart, M. A., and Thomas, D. G. (1993). Event-related potential measures of attention in moderately depressed subjects. *Electroencephalography and Clinical Neurophysiology/Evoked Potentials Section, 88*(1), 42-50.

Carretié, L., Mercado, F., Tapia, M., and Hinojosa, J.A. (2001a). Emotion, attention, and the 'negativity bias', studied through event-related potentials. *International Journal of Psychophysiology, 41*, 75–85.

Carretié, L., Martin-Loeches, M., Hinojosa, J.A., and Mercado, F. (2001b). Emotion and attention interaction studied through event-related potentials. *Journal of Cognitive Neuroscience, 8*, 1109–1128.

Caseras, X., Garner, M., Bradley, B. P., and Mogg, K. (2007). Biases in visual orienting to negative and positive scenes in dysphoria: An eye movement study. *Journal of Abnormal Psychology, 116*(3), 491-497.

Chiesa, A., Brambillia, P., and Serretti, A. (2010). Functional neural correlates of mindfulness meditations in comparison with psychotherapy, pharmacotherapy and placebo effect. Is there a link? *Acta Neuropsychiatrica, 22*, 104-117.

Chiu, P. H., and Deldin, P. J. (2007). Neural evidence for enhanced error detection in major depressive disorder. *American Journal of Psychiatry, 164*, 608-616.

Chiu, P. H., Holmes, A. J., and Pizzagalli, D. A. (2008). Dissociable recruitment of rostral anterior cingulate and inferior frontal cortex in emotional response inhibition. *NeuroImage, 42*, 988-997.

Ciesla, J. A., and Roberts, J. E. (2007). Rumination, negative cognition, and their interactive effects on depressed mood. *Emotion, 7*(3), 555-565.

Clark, D. A., and Beck, A. T. (1999). *Scientific foundations of cognitive theory and therapy of depression*. New York: John Wiley and Sons.

Clark, D. A., and Beck, A. T. (2010). Cognitive theory and therapy of anxiety and depression: Convergence with neurobiological findings. *Trends in Cognitive Sciences, 14*(9), 418-424.

Clark, L. A., and Watson, D. (1991). Tripartite model of anxiety and depression: Psyhometric evidence and taxonomic implications. *Journal of Abnormal Psychology, 100*(3), 316-336.

Coolidge, F. L., and Wynn, T. (2009). *The rise of homo sapiens: The evolution of mordern thinking*. Chichester, West Sussex: Wiley-Blackwell.

Cuijpers, P., van Straten, A., Bohlmeijer, E., Hollon, S. D., and Andersson, G. (2010). The effects of psychotherapy for adult depression are overestimated: A meta-analysis of study quality and effect size. *Psychological Medicine, 40*, 211-223.

Curran, T., and Friedman, W. J. (2004). ERP old/new effects at different retention intervals in recency discrimination tasks. *Cognitive Brain Research, 18*(2), 107-120.

Dannlowski, U., Ohrmann, P., Bauer, J., JKugel, H., Arolt, V., and Heindel, W. (2007). Amygdala reactivity to masked negative faces is associated with automatic judgemental biases in major depression: A 3T fMRI study. *Psychiatry Neuroscience, 32*, 423-429.

Dati, R. A., Cutmore, T. R. H., and Shum, D. H. K. (2011). Proactive interference inhibitory control of emotional stimuli in dysphoria: An electrophysiological study. *Manuscript in preparation.*

Daurignac, E., Houde, O., and Jouvent, R. (2006). Negative priming in a numerical Piaget-like task as evidenced by ERP. *Journal of Cognitive Neuroscience, 18*, 730-736.

Deldin, P. J., Deveney, C. M., Kim, A. S., Casas, B. R., and Best, J. L. (2001). A slow wave investigation of working memory bias in mood disorders. *Journal of Abnormal Psychology, 110*, 267-281.

Deldin, P. J., Keller, J., Gergen, J. A., and Miller, G. A. (2000). Right-posterior face processing anomaly in depression. *Journal of Abnormal Psychology, 109*, 113-121.

Deldin, P. J., Naidu, S. K., Shestyuk, A. Y., and Casas, B. R. (2008). Neurophysiological indices of free recall memory biases in major depression: The impact of stimulus arousal and valence. *Cognition and Emotion, 23*(5), 1002.

Deldin, P. J., Shestyuk, A. Y., and Chiu, P. H. (2003). Event-related brain potential indices of memory biases in major depression. In M. F. Lenzenweger and J. M. Hooley (Eds.), *Principles of experimental psychopathology: Essays in honor of Brendan A. Maher* (pp. 195-209). Washington, DC: American Psychological Association.

Derryberry, D., and Reed, M. A. (2002). Anxiety-related attentional biases and their regulation by attentional control. *Journal of Abnormal Psychology, 111*, 225-236.

Deveney, C. M., and Deldin, P. J. (2004). Memory of faces: A slow wave ERP study of major depression. *Emotion, 4*(3), 295-304.

Dietrich, D. E., Emrich, H. M., Waller, C., Wieringa, B. M., Johannes, S., and Munte, T. F. (2000). Emotion/cognition-coupling in word recognition memory of depressive patients: An event-related potential study. *Psychiatry Research, 96*, 15-29.

Donaldson, C., Lam, D., and Mathews, A. (2007). Rumination and attention in major depression. *Behavior Research and Therapy, 45*, 2664-2678.

Dozois, D. J. A., Bieling, P. J., Patelis-Siotis, I., BHoar, L., Chudzik, S., and McCabe, K., et al. (2009). Changes in self-schema structure in cognitive therapy for major depressive disorder: A randomised clinical trial. *Journal of Consulting and Clinical Psychology, 77*, 1078-1088.

Ellwart, T., Rinck, M., and Becker, E. S. (2003). Selective memory and memory deficits in depressed inpatients. *Depression and Anxiety, 17*(4), 197-206.

Epstein, W. (1972). Mechanisms in directed forgetting. In G. H. Bower (Ed.), *The psychology of learning and motivation* (Vol. 6, pp. 52-72). New York: Academic Press.

Engle, R. W., and Kane, M. J. (2004). Executive attention, working memory capacity, and a two-factor theory of cognitive control. In B. Ross (Ed.), *The psychology of learning and motivation* (Vol. 44, pp. 145-199). New York: Academic Press.

Eugene, F., Joormann, J., Cooney, R. E., Atlas, L. Y., and Gotlib, I. H. (2010). Neural correlates of inhibitory deficits in depression. *Psychiatry Research: Neuroimaging, 181*(1), 30-35.

Folstein, J. R., and van Petten, C. (2008). Influence of cognitive control and mismatch on the N2 component of the ERP: A review. *Psychophysiology, 45*(1), 152-170.

Friedman, D. (1990). ERPs during continuous recognition memory for words. *Biological Pscyhiatry, 30*(1), 61-87.

Friedman, D., Cycowicz, Y. M., and Gaeta, H. (2001). The novelty P3: An event-related brain potential (ERP) sign of the brain's evaluation of novelty. *Neuroscience and Biobehavioural Reviews, 25*, 355-373.

Friedman, N. P., and Miyake, A. (2004). The relations among inhibition and interference control functions: A latent-variable analysis. *Journal of Experimental Psychology: General, 133*(1), 101-135.

Fu, C. H. Y., Williams, S. C. R., Cleare, A. J., Scott, J., Mitterschiffthaler, M. T., Walsh, N. D., et al. (2008). Neural responses to sad facial expressions in major depression following cognitive behavioral therapy. *Biological Pscyhiatry, 64*(6), 505-512.

Geiselman, R. E., Bjork, R. A., and Fishman, D. L. (1983). Disrupted retrieval in directed forgetting: A link with post-hypnotic amnesia. *Journal of Experimental Psychology: General, 112*(58-72).

Gilboa-Schnechtman, E., Erhard-Weiss, D., and Jeczemien, P. (2002). Interpersonal deficits meet cognitive biases: Memory for facial expressions in depressed and anxious men and women. *Psychiatry Research, 113*(3), 279-293.

Gloaguen, V., Cottraux, J., Cucherat, M., and Blackburn, I. M. (1998). A meta-analysis of the effects of cognitive therapy in depressed patients. *Journal of Affective Disorders, 49*, 59-72.

Goeleven, E., De Raedt, R., Baert, S., and Koster, E. H. W. (2006). Deficient inhibition of emotional information in depression. *Journal of Affective Disorders, 93*, 149-157.

Goldapple, K., Segal, Z. V., Garson, C., Lau, M. A., Bieling, P. J., and Kennedy, S., et al. (2004). Modulation of cortical-limbic pathways in major depression: treatment-specific effects of cognitive behavior therapy. *Archives of General Psychiatry, 61*(1), 34-41.

Gordeev, S. A. (2007). The use of endogenous P300 event-related potentials of the brain for assessing cognitive functions in healthy subjects and clinical practice. *Human Physiology, 33*(2), 236-246.

Gotlib, I. H., and Joormann, J. (2010). Cognition and depression: current status and future directions. *Annual Review of Clinical Psychology, 6*(11), 11.11-11.28.

Gotlib, I. H., Joormann, J., Minor, K., and Hallmayer, J. (2008). HPA axis reactivity: A mechanism underlying the associations among 5-HTTLPR, stress, and depression. *Biological Psychiatry, 63*, 847-851.

Gotlib, I. H., Krasnoperova, E., Yue, D. L., and Joormann, J. (2004). Attentional biases for negative interpersonal stimuli in clinical depression. *Journal of Abnormal Psychology, 113*, 127-135.

Hajcak, G., MacNamara, A., and Olvet, D. M. (2010). Event-related potentials, emotion, and emotion regulation: An integrative review. *Developmental Neuropsychology, 35*(2), 129-155.

Hansell, N. K., Wright, M. J., Geffen, G. M., Geffen, L. B., Smith, G., A,, and Martin, N. G. (2001). Genetic influence on ERP slow wave measures of working memory. *Behavior Genetics, 31*(6), 603-614.

Harmer, C. J., O'Sullivan, U., Facaron, E., Massey-Chase, R., Ayres, R., and Reinecke, A., et al. (2009). Effect of antidepressant administration on negative affective bias in depressed patients. *Journal of Abnormal Psychology, 166*, 1178-1184.

Harvey, P. O., Bastard, G. L., Pochon, J. B., Levy, R., Allilaire, J. F., and Dubois, B., et al. (2004). Executive functions and updating of the contents of working memory in unipolar depression. *Journal of Psychiatric Research, 38*(6), 567-576.

Hasher, L., and Zacks, R. T. (1988). Working memory, comprehension, and aging: A review and a new view. In G. H. Bower (Ed.), *The psychology of learning and motivation* (pp. 193-225). San Diego, CA: Academic Press.

Hasher, L., Zacks, R. T., and May, C. P. (1999). Inhibitory control, circadian arousal, and age. In D. Gopher and A. Koriat (Eds.), *Attention and performance* (pp. 653-675). Cambrige, MA: MIT Press.

Hertel, P. T. (1997). On the contribution of deficient cognitive control to memory impairments in depression. *Cognition and Emotion, 11*, 569-583.

Hertel, P. T., and Gerstle, M. (2003). Depressive deficits in forgetting. *Psychological Science, 14*(6), 573-578.

Hetzel, G., Moeller, O., Evers, S., Erfurth, A., Ponath, G., and Arolt, V., et al. (2005). The astroglial protein S100B and visually evoked event-related potential before and after antidepressant treatment. *Psychopharmacology, 178*(2-3), 161-166.

Hofmann, S. G., Sawyer, A. T., Witt, A. A., and Oh, D. (2010). The effects of mindfulness-based therapy on anxiety and depression: A meta-analytic review. *Journal of Consulting and Clinical Psychology, 78*, 169-183.

Ilardi, S. S., Atchley, R. A., Enloe, A., Kwasny, K, Garratt, G. (2007). Disentangling attentional biases and attentional deficits in depression: An event-related potential P300 analysis.*Cognitive Theory Research, 31*, 175-187.

Ingram, R. E. (1984). Toward an information-processing analysis of depression. *Cognitive Therapy and Research, 8*(5), 443-477.

Ingram, R. E., and Siegle, G. J. (2009). Methodological issues in the study of depression. In I. H. Gotlib and C. L. Hammen (Eds.), *Handbook of depression* (Vol. 2, pp. 69-92). New York: The Guilford Press.

Jermann, F., van der Linden, M., and D'Argembeau, A. (2008). Identity recognition and happy and sad facial expression recall: Influence of depressive symptoms. *Memory, 16*(4), 364-373.

Jha, A. P., Krompinger, J. W., and Baime, M. J. (2007). Mindfulness meditation modifies subsystems of attention. *Cognitive Affective Behavioral Neuroscience, 7*(2), 109-119.

Jha, A. P., Stanley, E. A., Kiyongag, A., Wong, L., and Geifand, L. (2010). Examining the protective effects of mindfulness training on working memory capacity and affective experience in a military cohort. *Emotion, 10*, 54-64.

Johnson, M. K., Nolen-Hoeksema, S., Mitchell, K. J., and Levin, Y. (2009). Medial cortex activity, self-reflection and depression. *Social Cognitive and Affective Neuroscienc, 4*(4), 313-327.

Johnstone, T., van Reekum, C., Urry, H., Kalin, N., and Davidson, R. J. (2007). Failure to regulate: Counterproductive recruitment of top-down prefrontal-subcortical circuitry in major depression. *Journal of Neuroscience, 27*, 8877-8884.

Joormann, J. (2004). Attentional bias in dysphoria: The role of inhibitory processes. *Cognition and Emotion, 18*, 125-147.

Joormann, J. (2005). Inhibition, rumination, and mood regulation in depression. In R. W. Engle, G. Sedek, U. von Hecker and D. N. McIntosh (Eds.), *Cognitive limitations in aging and psychopathology: Attention, working memory, and executive functions* (pp. 275-312). New York: Cambridge University Press.

Joormann, J. (2009). Cognitive aspects of depression. In I. H. Gotlib and C. L. Hammen (Eds.), *Handbook of depression* (Vol. 2, pp. 298-321). New York The Guilford Press.

Joormann, J. (2010). Cognitive inhibition and emotion regulation in depression. *Current Directions in Psychological Science, 19*(3), 161-166.

Joormann, J., Eugene, F., and Gotlib, I. H. (2008). Parental depression: Impact on offspring and mechanisms underlying transmission of risk. In S. Nolen-Hoeksema (Ed.), *Handbook of adolescent depression* (pp. 441-471). New York: Guilford.

Joormann, J., and Gotlib, I. H. (2007). Selective attention to emotional faces following recovery from depression. *Journal of Abnormal Psychology, 116*, 80-85.

Joormann, J., and Gotlib, I. H. (2008). Updating the contents of working memory in depression: Interference from irrelevant negative material. *Journal of Abnormal Psychology, 117*(1), 182-192.

Joormann, J., Hertel, P. T., Brozovich, F., and Gotlib, I. H. (2005). Remembering the good, forgetting the bad: Intentional forgetting of emotional material in depression. *Journal of Abnormal Psychology, 114*, 640-648.

Joormann, J., Hertel, P. T., LeMoult, J., and Gotlib, I. H. (2009). Training forgetting of negative material in depression. *Journal of Abnormal Psychology, 118*, 34-43.

Joormann, J., Nee, D. E., Berman, M. G., Jonides, J., and Gotlib, I. H. (2010). Interference resolution in major depression. *Cognitive, Affective, and Behavioural Neuroscience, 10*, 21-33.

Joormann, J., Talbot, L., and Gotlib, I. H. (2007). Biased processing of emotional information in girls at risk for depression. *Journal of Abnormal Psychology, 116*, 135-143.

Joormann, J., Yoon, K. L., and Zetsche, U. (2007). Cognitive inhibition in depression. *Applied and Preventitive Psychology, 12*, 128-139.

Kaiser, S., Unger, J., Kiefer, M., Markela, J., Mundt, C., and Weisbrod, M. (2003). Executive control deficit in depression: Event-related potentials in a go/nogo task. *Psychiatry Research: Neuroimaging, 122*, 169-184.

Karparova, S. P., Kersting, A., and Suslow, T. (2007). Deployment of attention in clinical depression during symptom remission. *Scandinavian Journal of Psychology, 48*(1), 1-5.

Katsanis, J., Iacono, W. G., McGue, M. K., and Carlson, S. R. (1997). P300 event-related potential heritability in monozygotic and dizygotic twins. *Psychophysiology, 34*, 47-58.

Kawasaki, T., Tanaka, S., Wang, J., Hokama, H., and Hiramatsu, K. (2004). Abnormalities of P300 cortical current density in unmedicated depressed patients revealed by LORETA analysis of event-related potentials. *Psychiatry and Clinical Neurosciences*(58), 68-75.

Kayser, J., Bruder, G. E., Tenke, C. E., Stewart, J. W., and Quitkin, F. M. (2000). Event-related potentials (ERPs) to hemifield presentations of emotional stimuli: Differences between depressed patients and healthy adults in P3 amplitude and asymmetry. *International Journal of Psychophysiology, 36*, 211-236.

Kayser, J., Tenke, C. E., Kroppmann, C. J., Fekri, S., Alschuler, D. M., and Gates, N. A., et al. (2010). Current source density (CSD) old/new effects during recognition memory for words and faces in schizophrenia and health adults. *International Journal of Psychophysiology, 75*(2), 194-210.

Kemp, A. H., Hopkinson, P. J., Hermens, D. F., Rowe, D. L., Sumich, A. L., and Clark, R., et al. (2009). Fronto-temporal alterations within the first 200ms during an attentional task distinguish major depressed mood and healthy controls: A potential biomarker? *Human Brain Mapping, 30*, 602-614.

Khateb, A., Pegna, A. J., Landis, T., Mouthon, M. S., and Annoni, J.-M. (2010). On the origin of the N400 effects: An ERP waveform and source localization analysis in three matching tasks. *Brain Topography, 23*(3), 311-320.

Kok, A. (1997). Event-related-potential (ERP) reflections of mental resources: A review and synthesis. *Biological Psychology, 45*, 19-56.

Koster, E. H. W., Leyman, L., DeRaedy, R., and Crombey, G. (2006). Cueing of visual attention by emotional facial expressions: The influence of individual differences in anxiety and depression. *Personality and Individual Differences, 41*, 329-339.

Kutas, M., and Hillyard, S. A. (1980). Reading senseless sentences: Brain potentials reflect semantic incongruity. *Science, 207*, 203-205.

Kutas, M., and Hillyard, S. A. (1982). The lateral distribution of event-related potentials during sentence processing. *Neuropscyhologia, 20*, 579-590.

Kuyken, W., Byford, S., Byng, R., Dalgleish, T., Lewis, G., and Taylor, R., et al. (2010). Study protocol for a randomized controlled trial comparing mindfulness-based cognitive therapy with maintenance anti-depressant treatment in the prevention of depressive relapse/recurrence: The PREVENT trial. *Trials, 11*(99), 1-10.

Lau, E. F., Phillips, C., and Poeppel, D. (2008). A cortical network for semantics: (De)Constructing the N400. *Nature Reviews Neuroscience, 9*, 920-933.

Lim, C. L., Gordon, E., Rennie, C., Wright, J. J., Bahramali, H., and Li, W. M., et al. (1999). Dynamics of SCR, EEG, and ERP activity in an oddball paradigm with short interstimulus intervals. *Psychophysiology, 36*, 543-551.

Linden, D. E. J. (2006). How psychotherapy changes the brain - the contribution of functional neuroimaging. *Molecular Psychiatry, 11*, 528-538.

Linville, P. (1996). Attention inhibition: Does it underlie ruminative thought? In R. S. Wyer Jr (Ed.), *Ruminative thoughts: Advances in social cognition* (Vol. 9, pp. 121-133). Mahwah, NJ: Lawrence Erlbaum Associates Inc.

Luck, S. J. (2005). *An introduction to the event-related potential technique.* London: Massachusetts Institute of Technology.

Ma, S. H., and Teasdale, J. D. (2004). Mindfulness-based cognitive therapy for depression: Replication and exploration of differential relapse prevention effects. *Journal of Consulting and Clinical Psychology, 72*, 31-40.

MacLeod, C., Rutherford, E., Campbell, L., Ebsworthy, G., and Holker, L. (2002). Selective attention and emotion vulnerability: Assessing the casual basis of their association through experimental manipulation of attentional bias. *Journal of Abnormal Psychology, 111*, 107-123.

Matt, G. E., Vazquez, C., and Campbell, W. K. (1992). Mood-congruent recall of affectively toned stimuli: A meta-analytic review. *Clinical Psychology Review, 12*, 227-255.

Matthews, A., and MacLeod, C. (2005). Cognitive vulnerability to emotional disorders. *Annual Review of Clinical Psychology, 1*, 167-195.

Mayberg, H. S. (1997). Limbic-cortical dysregulation: A proposed model of depression. *Journal of Neuropsychiatry and Clinical Neurosciences, 9*, 471-481.

McNeely, H. E., Christensen, B. K., West, R., and Alain, C. (2003). Changes in neurophysiological correlates of conflict processing precede behavioural disturbance in patients with schizophrenia. *Journal of Abnormal Psychology, 112*, 678-688.

McNeely, H. E., Lau, M. A., Christensen, B. K., and Alain, C. (2008). Neurophysiological evidence of cognitive inhibition anomalies in persons with major depressive disorder. *Clinical Neurophysiology, 119*(7), 1578-1589.

Mialet, J. P., Pope, H. G., and Yurgelun-Todd, D. (1996). Impaired attention in depressive states: a non-specific deficit? *Psychological Medicine, 26*, 1009-1020.

Mitterschiffthaler, M. T., Williams, S. C. R., Walsh, N. D., Cleare, A. J., Donaldson, C., and Scott, J., et al. (2008). Neural basis of the emotional Stroop interference effect in major depression. *Psychological Medicine, 38*, 247-256.

Mogg, K., and Bradley, B. P. (2005). Attentional bias in generalized anxiety disorder versus depressive disorder. *Cognitive Therapy and Research, 29*, 29-45.

Mogg, K., Bradley, B. P., Dixon, C., Fisher, S., Twelftree, H., and McWilliams, A. (2000). Trait anxiety, defensiveness and selective processing of threat: An investigation using two measures of attentional bias. *Personality and Individual Differences, 28*, 1063-1077.

Mogg, K., Bradley, B. P., Williams, R., and Mathews, A. (1993). Subliminal processing of emotional information in anxiety and depression. *Journal of Abnormal Psychology, 102*, 304-311.

Monk, C. S., Klein, R. G., Telzer, E. H., Schroth, E. A., Mannuzza, S., and Moulton, J. L. I., et al. (2008). Amygdala and nucleus accumbens activation to emotional facial expressions in children and adolescents at risk for major depression. *American Journal of Psychiatry, 165*, 90-98.

Moritz, S., Voigt, K., Arzola, M., and Otte, C. (2008). When the half-full glass is appraised as half empty and memorised as completely empty: Mood-congruent true and false recognition in depression is modulated by salience. *Memory, 16*(8), 810-820.

Munafo, M., Brown, S., and Hariri, A. (2008). Serotonin transporter (5-HTTLPR) genotype and amygdala activation: A meta-analysis. *Biological Psychiatry, 63*, 852-857.

Nandrino, J.-L., Dodin, V., Martin, P., and Henniaux, M. (2004). Emotional information processing in first and recurrent major depression episodes. *Journal of Psychiatric Research, 38*, 475-484.

Nandrino, J., Pezard, L., Poste, A., Revillere, C., and Beaune, D. (2002). Autobiographical memory in major depression: A comparison between first and recurrent patients. *psychopathology, 35*, 335-340.

Neshat-Doost, H. T., Moradi, A. R., Taghavi, M. R., Yule, W., and Dalgleish, T. (2000). Lack of attentional bias for emotional information in clinically depressed children and adolescents on the dot probe task. *Journal of Child Psychology and Psychiatry and Allied Disciplines, 41*, 363-368.

NICE (2004). *Depression: management of depression in primary and secondary care.* London: Author.

Nieuwenhuis, S., and Yeung, N. (2003). Electrophysiological correlates of anterior cingulate function in a go/no-go task: Effects of response conflict and trial type frequency. *Cognitive, Affective, and Behavioural Neuroscience, 3*, 17-26.

Nolen-Hoeksema, S. (1991). Responses to depression and their effects on the duration of depressive episodes. *Journal of Abnormal Psychology, 100*, 569-511.

Nolen-Hoeksema, S., and Morrow, J. (1991). A prospective study of depression and post-traumatic stress symptoms following a natural disaster: The 1989 Loma Prieta Earthquake. *Journal of Personality and Social Psychology, 61*, 115-121.

Nolen-Hoeksema, S., Wisco, B. E., and Lyubomirsky, S. (2008). Rethinking rumination. *Perspectives on Psychological Science, 3*(5), 400-424.

Norman, D. A., and Shallice, T. (1986). Attention to action: willed and automatic control of behavior. In R. J. Davidson, G. E. Schwarts and D. Shapiro (Eds.), *Consciousness and self-regulation: Advances in research and theory* (pp. 1-18). New York: Plenum Press.

Oberauer, K. (2005a). Binding and inhibition in working memory: individual and age differences in short-term recognition. *Journal of Experimental Psychology: General, 134*, 368-387.

Oberauer, K. (2005b). Control of the contents of working memory-a comparison of two paradigms and two age groups. *Journal of Experimental Psychology: Learning, Memory, and Cognition, 31*, 714-728.

Ochsner, K. N., and Gross, J. J. (2005). The cognitive control of emotion. *Trends in Cognitive Sciences, 9*(5), 242-249.

Ogura, C., Nageishi, Y., Omura, F., Fukao, K., Ohta, H., and Kishimoto, A., et al. (1993). N200 component of event-related potentials in depression. *Biological Pscyhiatry, 33*, 720-726.

Papageorgiou, C., and Wells, A. (2000). Treatment of recurrent major depression with attention training. *Cognitive and Behavioral Practice, 7*(4), 407-413.

Pause, B. M., Raack, N., Sojka, B., Goder, R., Aldenhoff, J. B., and Ferstl, R. (2003). Convergent and divergent effects of odours and emotions in depression. *Psychophysiology, 40*, 209-225.

Peeters, F., Wessel, I., Merckelbach, H., and Boon-Vermeeren, M. (2002). Autobiographical memory specificity and the course of major depressive disorder. *Comprehensive Psychiatry, 43*(5), 344-350.

Phillips, W. J., Hine, D. W., and Thorsteinsson, E. B. (2010). Implicit cognition and depression: a meta-analysis. *Clinical Psychology Review, 30*, 691-709.

Pierson, A., Ragot, R., van Hoof, J., Partiot, A., Tenault, B., and Jouvent, R. (1996). Heterogeneity of information-processing alterations according to dimensions of depression: An event-related potentials study. *Biological Psychiatry, 40*, 98-115.

Polich, J. (2003). Overview of P3a and P3b. In J. Polich (Ed.), *Detection of change: Event-related potential and fMRI findings* (pp. 83-98). Boston, MA: Kluwer.

Polich, J. (2007). Updating P300: An integrative theory of P3a and P3b. *Clinical Neurophysiology, 118*, 2128-2148.

Power, M. J., Dalgleish, T., Claudio, V., Tata, P., and Kentish, J. (2000). The directed forgetting task: Application to emotionally valent material. *Journal of Affective Disorders, 57*, 147-157.

Quilty, L. C., McBride, C., and Bagby, R. M. (2008). Evidence for the cognitive mediational model of cognitive behavioral therapy for depression. *Psychological Medicine, 38*, 1531-1541.

Raes, F., Hermans, D., Williams, J. M. G., Demyttenaere, K., Sabbe, B., and Pieters, G., et al. (2005). Reduced specificity of autobiographical memory: A mediator between rumination and ineffective problem-solving in major depression? *Journal of Affective Disorders, 87*(2-3), 331-335.

Ramel, W., Goldin, P. R., Carmona, P. E., and McQuaid, J. R. (2004). The effects of mindfulness meditation on cognitive process and affect in patients with past depression. *Cognitive Therapy and Research, 28*(4), 433-455.

Ridout, N., Astell, A. J., Reid, I. C., Glen, T., and O'Carroll, R. E. (2003). Memory bias for emotional facial expressions in major depression. *Cognition and Emotion, 17*, 101-122.

Ridout, N., Noreen, A., and Johal, J. (2009). Memory for emotional faces in naturally occuring dysphoria and induced sadness. *Behaviour Research and Therapy, 47*(10), 851-860.

Ritchey, M., Dolcos, F., Eddington, K. M., Strauman, T. J., and Cabeza, R. (in press). Neural correlates of emotional processing in depression: Changes with cognitive behavioral therapy and predictors of treatment response. *Journal of Psychiatric Research.*

Robinson, L. A., and Alloy, L. B. (2003). Negative cognitive styles and stress-reactive rumination interact to predict depression: A prospective study. *Cognitive Therapy and Research, 27*, 275-292.

Roschke, J., and Wanger, P. (2003). A confirmatory study on the mechanisms behind reduced P300 waves in depression. *Neuropschopharacology, 28*, S9-S12.

Rossignol, M., Philippot, P., Crommelinck, M., and Campanella, S. (2008). Visual processing of emotional expressions in mixed anxious-depressed subclinical state: An event-related potential study on a female sample. *Clinical Neurophysiology, 38*, 267-275.

Rottenberg, J. (2007). Major depressive disorder: Emerging evidence for emotion context insensitivity. In J. Rottenberg and S. L. Johnson (Eds.), *Emotion and psychopathology: Bridging affective and clinical science* (pp. 1). Washington, DC: American Psychological Association.

Ruchsow, M., Groen, G., Kiefer, M., Beschoner, P., Hermle, L., and Ebert, D., et al. (2008). Electrophysiological evidence for reduced inhibitory control in depressed patients in partial remission: A go/nogo study. *International Journal of Psychophysiology, 68*(3), 209-218.

Rugg, M. D., and Curran, T. (2007). Event-related potentials and recognition memory. *Trends in Cognitive Sciences, 11*(6), 251-257.

Rugg, M. D., Fletcher, C. D., Frith, C. D., Frackowiak, R. S. J., and Dolan, R. J. (1996). Differential activation of the prefrontal cortex in successful and unsuccessful memory retrieval. *Brain, 119*(6), 2073-2083.

Rugg, M. D., and Nagy, M. E. (1987). Lexical contribution to nonword-repetition effects: Evidence from event-related potentials. *Memory and Cognition, 15*, 473-481.

Ruscio, J., Brown, T. A., and Ruscio, A. M. (2009). A taxometric investigation of DSM-IV Major Depression in a large outpatient sample. *Assessment, 16*, 1257-1144.

Ruscio, J., and Ruscio, A. M. (2000). Informing the continuity controversy: a taxometric analysis of depression. *Journal of Abnormal Psychology, 109*, 473-487.

Rusting, C. L., and DeHart, T. (2000). Retrieving positive memories to regulate mood: Consequences for mood-congruent memory. *Journal of Personality and Social Psychology, 78*, 737-752.

Sabatinelli, D., Lang, P. J., Keli, A., and Bradley, M. M. (2007). Emotional perception: Correlation of functional MRI and event-related potentials. *Cerebral Cortex, 17*(5), 1085-1091.

Sara, G., Gordon, E., Kraiuhin, C., Coyle, S., Howson, A., and Meares, R. (1994). The P300 ERP component: An index of cognitive dysfunction in depression. *Journal of Affective Disorders, 31*, 29-38.

Schmukle, S. C. (2005). Unreliability of the dot probe task. *European Journal of Personality, 19*, 595-605.

Seligman, M. E. P., Rashid, T., and Parks, A. C. (2006). Positive psychotherapy. *American Psychologist, 61*, 774-788.

Serfaty, M. A., Bothwell, R., Marsh, R., Ashton, H., Blizard, R., and Scott, J. (2002). Event-related potentials and cognitive processing of affectively toned words in depression. *Journal of Psychophysiology, 16*, 56-66.

Shane, M. S., and Peterson, J. B. (2007). An evaluation of early and late stage attentional processing of positive and negative information in dysphoria. *Cognition and Emotion, 21*(4), 789-815.

Shestyuk, A. Y., and Deldin, P. J. (2010). Automatic and strategic representation of self in major depression: Trait and state abnormalities. *American Journal of Psychiatry, 167*(5), 536-544.

Shestyuk, A. Y., Deldin, P. J., Brand, J. E., and Deveney, C. M. (2005). Reduced sustained brain activity during processing of positive emotional stimuli in major depression. *Biological Psychiatry, 57*, 1089-1096.

Shimizu, H., Saito, H., and Hoshiyama, M. (2006). Cognitive mechanism for meaning of emotive words in depressed personality: An event-related potential study. *Nagoya Journal of Medical Science, 68*, 35-44.

Siegle, G. J., Ghinassi, F., and Thase, M. E. (2007). Neurobehavioural therapies in the 21st century: Summary of an emerging field and an extended example of cognitive control training for depression. *Cognitive Therapy and Research, 31*, 235-262.

Sin, N. L., and Lyubomirsky, S. (2009). Enhancing well-being and alleviating depressive symptoms with positive psychology interventions: A practice-friendly meta-analysis. *Journal of Clinical Psychology: In Session, 65*(5), 467-487.

Smith, J. L., Smith, E. A., Provost, A. L., and Heathcote, A. (2010). Sequence effects support the conflict theory of N2 and P3 in the go/nogo task. *International Journal of Psychophysiology, 75*(3), 217-226.

Tays, W. J., Dywan, J., Mathewson, K. J., and Segalowitz, S. J. (2008). Age differences in target detection and interference resolution in working memory: An event-related potential study. *Journal of Cognitive Neuroscience, 20*, 2250-2262.

Teasdale, J. D. (1983). Negative thinking in depression: Cause, effect, or reciprocal relationship? *Advances in Behaviour Research and Therapy, 5*(1), 3-25.

Teasdale, J. D. (1988). Cognitive vulnerability to persistent depression. *Cognition and Emotion, 2*(3), 247-274.

Teasdale, J. D., Segal, Z. V., Williams, J. M. G., Ridgeway, V. A., Soulsby, J. M., and Lau, M. A. (2000). Prevention of relapse/recurrence in major depression by mindfulness-based cognitive therapy. *Journal of Consulting and Clinical Psychology, 68*, 615-623.

Thompson, R. J., Mata, J., Jaeggi, S. M., Buschkuehl, M., Jonides, J., and Gotlib, I. H. (2010). Maladaptive coping, adaptive coping, and depressive symptoms: Variations across age and depressive state. *Behaviour Research and Therapy, 48*(6), 459-466.

Urretavizcaya, M., Moreno, I., Benlloch, L., Cardoner, N., Serrallonga, J., and Menchon, J. M., et al. (2003). Auditory event-related potentials in 50 melancholic patients: Increased N100, N200 and P300 latencies and diminished P300 amplitude. *Journal of Affective Disorders, 74*, 293-297.

Vanderhasselt, M. A., and De Raedt, R. (2009). Impairments in cognitive control persist during remission from depression and are related to the number of past episodes: An event related potentials study. *Biological Psychology, 81*, 169-176.

Vandoolaeghe, E., van Hunsel, F., Nuyten, D., and Maes, M. (1998). Auditory event related potentials in major depression: Prolonged P300 latency and increased P200 amplitude. *Journal of Affective Disorders, 48*(2-3), 105-113.

Wadlinger, H. A., and Isaacowitz, D. M. (2008). Looking happy: The experimental manipulation of a positive visual attention bias. *Emotion, 8*(1), 121-126.

Watkins, P. C., Martin, C. K., and Stern, L. D. (2000). Unconscious memory bias in depression: Perceptual and conceptual processes. *Journal of Abnormal Psychology, 109*(2), 282-289.

Wells, T. T., and Beevers, C. G. (2010). Biased attention and dysphoria: manipulating selective attention reduces subsequent depressive symptoms. *Cognition and Emotion, 24*(4), 719-728.

Wessel, I., Meeren, M., Peeters, F., Arntz, A., and Merckelbach, H. (2001). Correlates of autobiographical memory specificity: The role of depression, anxiety and childhood trauma. *Behaviour Research and Therapy, 39*(4), 409-421.

Williams, J. M. G., Watts, F. N., MacLeod, C., and Mathews, A. (1997). *Cognitive psychology and emotional disorders*. Chichester, England: Wiley.

Wisco, B. E. (2009). Depressive cognition: Self-reference and depth of processing. *Clinical Psychology Review, 29*, 382-392.

Yamashita, O., Galka, A., Ozaki, T., Discay, R., and Valdes-Sosa, P. (2004). Recursive penalized least squares solution for dynamical inverse problems of EEG generation. *Human Brain Mapping, 21*(4), 221-235.

Yang, W., Zhu, X., Wang, X., Wu, D., and Yao, S. (2011). Time course of affective processing bias in major depression: an ERP study. *Neuroscience Letters, 487*, 372-377.

Yao, S., Liu, M., Liu, J., Hu, Z., Yi, J., and Huang, R. (2010). Inhibition dysfunction in depression: Event-related potentials during negative affective priming. *Psychiatry Research: Neuroimaging, 182*, 172-179.

Zetsche, U., and Joormann, J. (2010). Components of interference control predict depressive symptoms and rumination cross-sectionally and at six months follow-up. *Journal of Behaviour Therapy and Experimental Psychiatry, 42*(1), 65-73.

Zhang, B.-W., Zhao, L., and Xu, J. (2007). Electrophysiological activity underlying inhibitory control processes in late-life depression: A go/nogo study. *Neuroscience Letters, 419*, 225-230.

Chapter 7

MIGRAINE AND VISUAL DISCOMFORT: THE EFFECTS OF PATTERN SENSITIVITY ON PERFORMANCE

Elizabeth Conlon, Leanne Prideaux and Kirsteen Titchener*
School of Psychology, and Behavioural Basis of Health Research Program
Griffith Health Institute
Griffith University, Gold Coast, Queensland. Australia.

ABSTRACT

Exposure to stimuli such as the striped repetitive patterns found on pages of text, glare sources, or flickering light produces unpleasant somatic and perceptual effects in susceptible individuals. These effects, referred to as visual discomfort produce poor efficiency during reading or performance of tasks where relevant information must be extracted from irrelevant visual clutter. The current studies had two aims. First, we determined whether groups with migraine were more likely than other individuals to experience anomalous sensitivity when exposed to repetitive striped patterns or flickering light. The second aim was to determine whether poor efficiency on reading or visual search tasks in groups with visual discomfort could be ameliorated or exacerbated by varying the way that the stimulus patterns were presented. We found that half of the individuals with migraine reported high levels of visual discomfort. This everyday difficulty explained the perceptual and performance difficulties found in these individuals when they were exposed to repetitive striped patterns. Individuals with high visual discomfort had poorer reading comprehension than those with low visual discomfort regardless of the way that the text was presented. In addition, they performed more slowly than individuals with low visual discomfort when reading single words in lines of paragraphs of text, and when searching for specific stimuli in a cluttered visual scene. These effects were found regardless of the way the visual stimuli were presented. We concluded that while increased sensitivity to some stimulus patterns in the environment increases the somatic and perceptual effects reported with pattern viewing, individuals with high levels of visual discomfort have difficulty attending to task relevant stimuli and ignoring irrelevant stimuli in the environment. The implications of these findings for everyday functional performance in individuals with visual discomfort are discussed.

*E-mail: e.conlon@griffith.edu.au

INTRODUCTION

There are many stimuli found in the environment that can induce unpleasant somatic (e.g., sore, tired eyes, dizziness, headache) and perceptual (e.g., illusions of colour, shape and motion) effects in individuals (Conlon, Lovegrove, Barker, and Chekaluk, 2001; Wilkins et al., 1984).

Examples of these stimuli include fluorescent and stroboscopic lights, light flickering through trees and the patterns of stripes found on clothing, picket fences and pages of text. In most individuals, the side-effects induced produce reports of mild discomfort. Two groups who report disabling sensitivity to these stimuli are those with migraine (Cao, Welch, Aurora, and Vikingstad, 1999; Friedman and De Ver Dye, 2009; Hay, Mortimer, Barker, Debney, and Good, 1994) and visual discomfort (Conlon and Hine, 2000; Wilkins, 1995; Wilkins et al., 1984).

Migraine is a severe recurrent form of headache that occurs in about 8% of adults in the population (Bates et al., 1993). The headache is characterized by throbbing pain, often on one side of the head, increased sensitivity to light and sounds and experience of nausea and vomiting. In about 10% of individuals with migraine, the headache is preceded by a visual aura (Cologno, Torelli, and Manzoni, 1998; Lance, 1993). The aura is characterized by visual phenomena such as the appearance of flashes of light, blurred vision or the appearance of complex zigzag patterns that appear to move across the visual field (Lance, 1993). Regardless of the type of migraine experienced, during the headache phase individuals can suffer severe effects, which have a negative impact on their capacity to undertake normal daily activities (Friedman and De Ver Dye, 2009).

During the period between headaches, the interictal phase, some individuals with migraine report persistent unpleasant somatic and perceptual effects when exposed to bright or flickering light (Drummond and Woodhouse, 1993; Hay et al., 1994; Main, Dawson, and Gross, 1997) or to repetitive striped patterns (Cao et al., 1999; Chronicle, Wilkins, and Coleston, 1995; Coleston and Kennard, 1993; Conforto et al., 2010; Harle, Shepherd, and Evans, 2006; Huang, Cooper, Satana, Kaufman, and Cao, 2003; Marcus and Soso, 1989; Wilkins et al., 1984). This sensitivity differs from the photophobia reported during the headache phase of migraine (Evans, Patel, and Wilkins, 2002).

The anomalous sensitivity to light and pattern experienced by migraine sufferers during the interictal phase has been described as a generalized sensory sensitivity produced by a chronic state of central nervous system hyperexcitability (Huang et al., 2003; Welch, 1987; Welch, Barkley, Tepley, and Ramadan, 1993). Up to 50% of individuals with migraine may experience this form of visual difficulty when exposed to light and pattern (Shepherd, 2001).

Visual discomfort is a term used to describe the perceptual and somatic difficulties that can occur following exposure to bright light and repetitive striped patterns like that shown in Figure 1 (Wilkins et al., 1984). Consistent with the explanation of the visual difficulties found in migraine, symptoms of visual discomfort are also thought to occur because of massive excitation in the visual cortex with exposure to visual patterns with specific spatial characteristics (Wilkins, 1995). The activity produced by GABA-ergic inhibitory neurons does not adequately modulate the excitatory activity generated by these stimuli (Chronicle and Mulleners, 1996; Lauritzen, 1994; Meldrum and Wilkins, 1984). The main reason why increased excitation to these stimulus patterns is thought to underpin the effects is that greater difficulties are reported when the pattern presented is large, when the spatial frequency of the pattern is between 1 and 4 c/deg and when the ratio of the size of the black to white stripes in the pattern is 50% (duty cycle, See Wilkins, 1995 for a review). These parameters are consistent with those that produce maximum excitation in the visual system (Wilkins, Binnie, and Darby, 1980).

Figure 1. Square-wave pattern that can induce unpleasant somatic and perceptual effects in individuals with migraine or visual discomfort. The spatial frequency is determined by the number of cycles (one black and one white bar) per degree of visual angle). At a viewing distance of 57 cm, the spatial frequency of this pattern is about 3 c/deg.

Although the somatic and perceptual difficulties induced in observers with visual discomfort have been well established, there has been less research on the functional consequences of this anomalous sensitivity. Somatic and perceptual difficulties that occur during reading have been reported in individuals with visual discomfort (Conlon, Lovegrove, Chekaluk, and Pattison, 1999; Wilkins and Nimmo-Smith, 1984; 1987). These effects are induced because the text page also forms a striped pattern that produces discomfort. Individuals who report severe symptoms of visual discomfort also show evidence of poor reading efficiency (Conlon et al., 1999; Conlon and Sanders, 2011; Evans and Joseph, 2002; Hollis and Allen, 2006; Singleton and Trotter, 2005; Wilkins, Jeanes, Pumfrey, and Laskier, 1996) and have significantly longer visual search times than individuals who report few symptoms of visual discomfort (Allen, Gilchrist, and Hollis, 2008; Conlon et al., 1998).

When individuals have been classified using the criteria for both migraine *and* visual discomfort, poorer performance on visual search tasks (with or without a striped repetitive pattern background) has been found in the group with high visual discomfort, regardless of their migraine status. Groups with migraine (with or without aura) *and* low visual discomfort show no evidence of poor performance (Conlon and Hine, 2000; Conlon and Humphreys, 2001). These results suggest that the presence or absence of co-morbid visual discomfort in individuals with migraine may explain the presence of everyday visual difficulties that occur because of increased pattern sensitivity.

The independent and combined effects of migraine and visual discomfort on reports of perceptual and somatic difficulties induced with pattern viewing have received little research attention. The first two studies reported here, investigated the effects of migraine and visual discomfort on pattern sensitivity. Based on the findings of the first two studies, the final three studies determined whether producing textual formats that either exacerbate or ameliorate the symptoms of visual discomfort can correspondingly decrease or increase reading efficiency in groups with high or low visual discomfort.

STUDY 1: PATTERN SENSITIVITY IN GROUPS WITH MIGRAINE AND VISUAL DISCOMFORT

Study 1 aimed to determine if reports of somatic and perceptual difficulties induced with pattern viewing could be explained independently by migraine with or without aura, visual discomfort of a combination of both. We expected that more reports of anomalous sensitivity to pattern would be found in the groups with migraine than in the headache free control group (Drummond and Woodhouse, 1991). In addition, the severity of reports of perceptual and somatic difficulties induced with pattern viewing was expected to be greatest in individuals with high visual discomfort, regardless of headache classification.

Method

Participants

There were 170 volunteers obtained from the University student population. Observers had normal or corrected to normal visual acuity and were classified into headache groups using the criteria of the International Headache Society (IHS, 1988). There were 68 who were headache free (M_{age} = 23.43, SD = 7.56 years), 50 with migraine without aura (M_{age} = 25.50, SD = 10.57 years), and 53 with migraine and aura (M_{age} = 33, SD = 9.65 years). All participants were headache free at the time of testing, had no medication in the 48 hours prior to testing and had not had a headache within the previous 72 hours.

Visual discomfort was evaluated using the Visual Discomfort Scale (Borsting, Chase, and Ridder, 2007; Conlon et al., 1999) which has an internal consistency of 0.91. The Visual Discomfort Scale (VDS) is a measure used to determine the frequency and severity of reports of everyday visual and perceptual difficulties that occur in individuals with exposure to bright lights and striped repetitive patterns, particularly pages of printed text (Conlon et al., 1999).

There were 78 individuals (M_{age} = 28.44, SD = 10.27 years) classified with high visual discomfort because their scores on the VDS were greater than 40%, (M_{VDS} = 42.5%, SD = 15.7%). There were 92 (M_{age} = 25.78, SD = 9.33 years) with low visual discomfort (M_{VDS} = 13.70%, SD = 6.5%).

In the group with high visual discomfort there were 44 (81.9%) who also had migraine with visual aura, 30 (56.6%) who also had migraine without aura and 6 (8.6%) with non-migraine headache. In the group with low visual discomfort, there were 10 (10.9%) who had migraine with aura, and 23 (25.0%) who had migraine without aura. The remaining 59 (64.1%) reported few headaches. University human research ethics committee approval was obtained for this project, with all participants providing informed consent.

Stimuli

A circular 4 c/deg square wave grating (see Figure 1) with a contrast of .8 was used. When viewed at a distance of 57 cm the pattern subtended a visual angle of 10°. Two rating scales, one for reports of somatic difficulty and one for reports of perceptual difficulty were used. Both scales used a range from 0 to 3 with 0 indicating no induced perceptual or somatic difficulty and 3 indicating somatic or perceptual difficulties so severe that it was impossible to view the stimulus pattern for 10 seconds.

Procedure

After explanation of the pattern sensitivity task, each participant scanned the striped repetitive pattern for 10 seconds and immediately rated the extent of somatic and perceptual difficulty induced by the pattern. No participant ceased viewing during the task because of somatic difficulty. Participants then completed the migraine and visual discomfort questionnaire.

Results and Discussion

The correlation between ratings of perceptual and somatic difficulty from pattern viewing was $r(168)$ = .66, $p < .001$. Using the ratings of somatic and perceptual difficulty as the dependent variables, two one-way ANOVA's for the migraine groups were conducted. The assumptions of the analysis were met. These results are shown in Figure 2. Significant group effects were found for the ratings of somatic difficulty, $F(2, 167)$ = 12.81, $p < .001$, $p\eta^2$ =.13, and perceptual difficulty, $F(2, 167)$ = 12.0, $p < .001$, $p\eta^2$ =.13. The group with migraine and visual aura reported significantly greater perceptual difficulty than the group with migraine without aura, $t(167)$ = 2.33, $p = .021$, Cohen's d = .47 and the control group, $t(167)$ = 4.89, $p < .001$, Cohen's d =.98. In addition, the migraine without aura group reported significantly greater induced perceptual difficulty than the control group, $t(167)$ = 2.35, $p = .020$, Cohen's d = .45. When ratings of somatic difficulty were evaluated, no significant difference was found between the migraine groups, $t(167)$ = 1.45, $p = .147$, Cohen's d = .27. These groups reported significantly greater somatic difficulty than the control group, $t(167)$ =4.82, $p < .001$, Cohen's d = .75. These findings replicate previous reports of increased pattern sensitivity in groups with migraine (Cao et al., 1999; Marcus and Soso, 1989; Shepherd, 2001). Although both groups with migraine reported similar levels of induced somatic difficulty, the migraine with aura group reported significantly greater perceptual difficulty, a result consistent with previous research (Coleston and Kennard, 1993, 1995).

When the same analysis was repeated using the groups with visual discomfort, the group with high visual discomfort rated the striped repetitive pattern as significantly more somatically difficult (M = 1.40, SD = .76), $F(1, 167)$ = 29.86, $p < .001$, Cohen's d = .78 and significantly more perceptually difficult (M = 1.49, SD = .73), $F(1, 167)$ = 25.67, $p < .001$, Cohen's d = .77 to view than the group with low visual discomfort ($M_{somatic}$ = 0.78, SD = .70, $M_{perceptual}$ = 1.40; SD = .61). These results replicate earlier findings (Conlon et al., 1999; Conlon et al., 2001).

The extent that the co-existence of visual discomfort and migraine could explain reports of somatic and perceptual difficulty found was investigated. Individuals in the migraine groups were classified as either high or low in visual discomfort. These groups were compared to the headache free, low visual discomfort control group. These results are shown in Figure 3. When reports of perceptual difficulty were evaluated, a significant groups effect was obtained, $F(2, 162)$ = 20.87, $p < .001$, $p\eta^2$ = .20. The group with migraine and high visual discomfort reported significantly greater perceptual difficulty than either the migraine group with low visual discomfort, $t(162)$ = 4.18, $p < .001$, Cohen's d = .66, or the control group, $t(162)$ = 6.31, $p < .001$, Cohen's d = .95. No significant difference in reports of perceptual difficulty was found between the control and migraine with low visual discomfort groups, $t(162)$ = 1.59, $p = .113$, Cohen's d = .35.

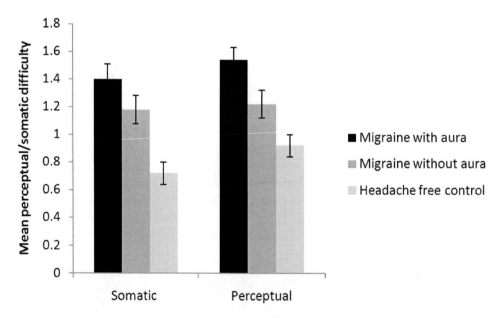

Figure 2. Study 1. Ratings of mean somatic and perceptual difficulty for the migraine with aura (n = 53), migraine without aura (n = 50) and headache free control groups (n = 68). Error bars represent ± 1 standard error.

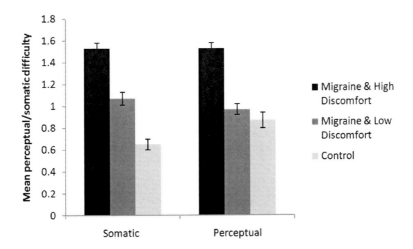

Figure 3. Study 1. Ratings of mean somatic and perceptual difficulty for the group with migraine with high visual discomfort (n = 59), the group with migraine with low visual discomfort (n = 44) and headache free /low visual discomfort control group (n = 62). Error bars represent ± 1 standard error.

There was also a significant groups effect found for reports of somatic difficulty, $F(2,162) = 22.69$, $p < .001$, $p\eta^2 = .22$. The group with migraine and high visual discomfort reported significantly greater somatic difficulty than either the group with migraine and low visual discomfort, $t(162) = 3.89$, $p < .001$, Cohen's $d = .75$, or the control group, $t(162) = 6.68$, $p < .001$, Cohen's $d = 1.21$. The group with migraine and low visual discomfort reported significantly greater somatic difficulty than the control group, $t(162) = 2.23$, $p = .027$, Cohen's $d = .49$.

These results show that the immediate perceptual and somatic effects reported with pattern viewing are most severe in the group with high visual discomfort. When the groups were classified using migraine and visual discomfort criteria, the group with migraine and high visual discomfort reported significantly greater somatic and perceptual difficulties with pattern viewing than other groups. Interestingly, the group with migraine and low visual discomfort reported significantly greater somatic difficulty than the control group with pattern viewing. This finding suggests that the influence of migraine alone on pattern sensitivity may predominantly result in visual fatigue and other types of somatic difficulties. These results are consistent with a lower threshold of sensitivity in migraine and visual discomfort (Huang et al., 2003; Welsh et al., 1993; Wilkins, 1995).

STUDY 2: SPATIAL AND TEMPORAL CONTRAST SENSITIVITY IN GROUPS WITH MIGRAINE AND VISUAL DISCOMFORT

Reports of anomalous somatic and perceptual effects with pattern viewing are based on subjective judgments. A more objective measure of sensitivity to light and pattern is obtained with measurement of the contrast sensitivity function (CSF). The CSF is a measure of the minimum amount of contrast required for observers to reliably detect the presence of a pattern with specific spatial (spatial frequency) or temporal (flicker rate) characteristics. The more contrast needed to reliably detect the presented stimulus, the higher the contrast threshold. This measure is generally reported as contrast sensitivity which is the reciprocal of contrast threshold. The higher the contrast sensitivity, the more sensitive an individual is to the presented stimulus.

When measuring temporal contrast sensitivity in groups with migraine, more contrast is required for these groups to reliably detect the stimuli presented, when these are flickered at different rates (Chronicle and Mulleners, 1996; Coleston, Chronicle, Ruddock, and Kennard, 1994; Conforto et al., 2010; Khahil, 1991; McKendrick, Vingrys, Badcock and Heywood, 2001). That is, individuals with migraine have lower temporal contrast sensitivity than the control group.

Regarding spatial contrast sensitivity in migraine groups, the findings are inconsistent. Reduced spatial contrast sensitivity has been found in a migraine without aura group only (Benedek, Tajti, Janaky, Vicsei, and Benedek, 2002), migraine with aura group only, (Khahil 1991), and in migraine groups with and without aura groups (Coleston et al., 1994). The coexistence of migraine and visual discomfort in some but not all individuals might explain the inconsistent results found in measures of spatial contrast sensitivity.

In one study that investigated spatial and temporal contrast sensitivity in groups with high and low visual discomfort, reduced spatial contrast sensitivity was found in the group with high visual discomfort for spatial frequencies between 1 and 12 c/deg, but there was no evidence of group differences in temporal contrast sensitivity, which was assessed using stimuli that flickered at 6 Hz (Conlon et al., 2001). These findings and those reviewed previously suggest that poor temporal contrast sensitivity may be a specific characteristic of migraine and that poor spatial contrast sensitivity may be a characteristic of high visual discomfort. These hypotheses were tested in Study 2.

Method

Participants

There were 76 volunteers with normal or corrected to normal visual acuity obtained from the University community. Individuals were classified into groups with migraine using the same criteria as those used in Study 1. There were 24 in the migraine free control group (M_{age} = 23.12, SD = 7.03 years), 26 in the migraine with aura group (M_{age} =34.80, SD = 8.90 years) and 15 in the migraine without aura group (M_{age} = 24.6, SD = 10.68 years). Visual discomfort was assessed using a combination of scores on the Visual Discomfort Scale (Conlon et al., 1999) and on a measure of sensitivity to pattern obtained from viewing a 4 c/deg striped pattern for 10 seconds. Individuals with a combined score on these measures of at least 50% were placed in the group with high visual discomfort. There were 34 in the group with high visual discomfort (M_{age} =31.28, SD = 9.55 years) and 42 in the group with low visual discomfort (M_{age} = 25.74, SD = 10.23 years). In the group with high visual discomfort there were 14 with migraine and visual aura and 6 with migraine without aura. In the group with low visual discomfort there were 12 from the migraine with aura group and 9 from the migraine without aura group. The additional 11 participants in the groups with visual discomfort were individuals reporting headache that could not be classified as migraine, so were included in the analysis of the groups with visual discomfort only. All participants were headache free at the time of testing and none had taken headache medication in the 48 hours prior to testing. University Human Research Ethics committee approval was obtained for this project.

Apparatus and Stimuli

Stimuli were generated and responses recorded using the Cambridge Research System hardware and operating system, VSG version 2/4. The task was performed on a Dell Opliplex GX1 computer and displayed on a 21 inch Hitachi HM-4721-D monitor. Responses were made using the Cambridge Research Systems CB3 Response Box. The mean screen luminance was 12 cd/m^2 measured with a Tektronix J18 photometer, fitted was a J1823 narrow-angled head. The refresh rate of the screen used to display the visual stimuli was 100 frames per second. Edges of the screen were masked with dark card, with a central circular portion of screen visible, subtending 18.9° of visual angle, at a viewing distance of 86 cm. Spatial frequencies of 0.3, 1.0, 4.0, and 8.4 c/deg were tested in the stationary CSF condition. Figure 4, shows an example pattern of spatial frequencies that range from low to high and used in the current study. With measurement of the temporal CSF, a spatial frequency of 0.3 c/deg was flickered at temporal frequencies of 2, 8, 20 and 33 Hz.

Procedure

Each participant viewed the stimuli binocularly with natural pupils from a viewing distance of 86 cm, controlled using a chinrest. The duration of each stimulus presentation was one second with an inter-stimulus interval between stimulus presentations of one second. A two- alternative forced choice technique was used (2AFC) to measure sensitivity. The 2AFC task required participants to determine on which side of the computer screen, left or right, the stimulus was presented.

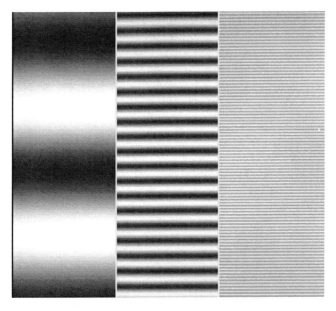

Figure 4. Spatial frequencies ranging from low to high. Stimuli similar to these were used in the Study 2.

Results and Discussion

Threshold estimates were converted to log contrast sensitivities for all spatial and temporal conditions. All assumptions of the mixed repeated analysis of variance were met with the exception of sphericity, which was corrected with the Huynh-Feldt correction.

Migraine Groups

Using log contrast sensitivity as the dependent variable, a 4 (temporal frequency: 2, 8, 20 and 33 Hz) × 3 (group: migraine with and without aura, control) mixed ANOVA which met the assumptions was conducted. These results are shown in Figure 5. Significant main effects were found temporal frequency, $F(3, 163) = 1706.1$, $p < .001$, $p\eta^2 = .965$, and group, $F(2, 63) = 5.92$, $p = .004$, $p\eta^2 = .16$. There was no significant interaction found between migraine group and temporal frequency, $F(6, 163) = 1.78$; $p = .116$, $p\eta^2 = .054$. The significant main effect of temporal frequency was consistent with the characteristic temporal contrast sensitivity function found. Contrast analysis was used to evaluate the sensitivity differences found between migraine groups. There was no significant difference in thresholds found between the headache free control group and migraine without aura group, $t(63) = .91$, $p = .365$. The migraine with aura group had significantly lower temporal contrast sensitivity than the control group, $t(63) = 3.35$, $p = .001$, and the group with migraine without aura, $t(63) = 2.06$, $p = .040$.

Using log contrast sensitivity as the dependent variable, a 4 (spatial frequency: 0.3, 1, 4 and 8 c/deg) × 3 (group: migraine with and without aura, control) mixed ANOVA which met the assumptions was conducted. These results are shown in Figure 5. A significant main effect was found for spatial frequency, $F(4, 248) = 8.40$, $p < .001$, $p\eta^2 = .12$. The significant main effect of spatial frequency was consistent with the characteristic spatial contrast sensitivity function found previously (Conlon et al., 2001). No significant main effect, $F(2, 63) = 1.33$, $p = .273$, $p\eta^2 = .041$, or interaction was found between migraine group and spatial frequency, $F(8, 248) = 0.337$, $p = .95$, $p\eta^2 = .011$ (see Figure 5).

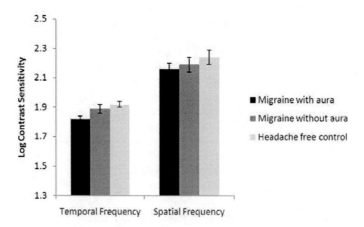

Figure 5. Study 2. Mean log contrast sensitivity for the spatial and temporal stimuli used, for the migraine with aura (n = 26), migraine without aura (n= 15) and headache free control (n = 24) groups. Error bars represent ± 1 standard error. (Please note that the average sensitivity collapsed across spatial and temporal frequency is represented to show the groups effect.)

Visual Discomfort

Using log contrast sensitivity as the dependent variable, a 4 (temporal frequency: 2, 8, 20 and 33 Hz) × 2 (group: high and low visual discomfort) mixed ANOVA which met the assumptions was conducted. These results are shown in Figure 6. Consistent with the characteristic effects produced for temporal contrast sensitivity, significant main effect was found for the temporal frequency, $F(3, 183) = 37.99$, $p < .001$, $p\eta^2 = .38$. There was no significant main effect found for group, $F(1, 61) = 1.12$; $p = .294$, $p\eta^2 = .02$. Unexpectedly a significant interaction was found between temporal frequency and group, $F(3, 183) = 3.62$, $p = .014$, $p\eta^2 = .06$. Contrast analysis on the significant interaction found that the group with high visual discomfort was more sensitive to contrast than the group with low visual discomfort when the stimulus was modulated at 33 Hz, $F(1, 63) = 4.36$, $p = .041$, $p\eta^2 = .06$ only.

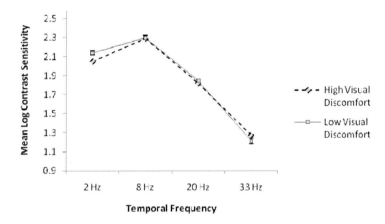

Figure 6. Study 2. Temporal sensitivity of the groups with high (n = 34) and low (n = 42) visual discomfort. Error bars represent ± 1 standard error.

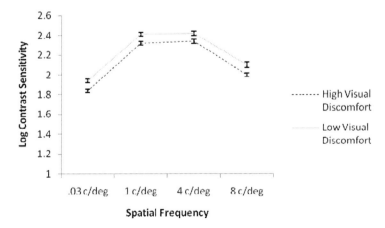

Figure 7. Study 2. Spatial contrast sensitivity for the groups with high (n = 34) and low (n = 42) visual discomfort. Error bars represent ± 1 standard error.

Using log contrast sensitivity as the dependent variable, a 4 (spatial frequency: 0.3, 1, 4 and 8 c/deg) × 2 (group: high and low visual discomfort) mixed ANOVA which met the assumptions was conducted. These results are shown in Figure 7. Significant main effects for spatial frequency, $F(4, 248) = 281.2; p < .001$, $p\eta^2 = .82$, and group, $F(1, 63) = 5.68, p = .020$, $p\eta^2 = .084$ were found.

The significant main effect of spatial frequency was consistent with the characteristic spatial contrast sensitivity function found previously for these groups (Conlon et al., 2001). There was no significant interaction found between spatial frequency and group, $F(4, 248) = 0.305, p = .875$. The group with high visual discomfort was significantly less sensitive across the spatial frequency range than the group with low visual discomfort.

The findings of the study support our hypotheses that the migraine groups would have reduced sensitivity on the measure of temporal contrast sensitivity and the group with high visual discomfort would have reduced spatial contrast sensitivity. Consistent with previous findings, the migraine with aura group had reduced temporal contrast sensitivity only (McKendrick et al., 2001).

Findings of reduced spatial contrast sensitivity in the group with high visual discomfort but neither of the groups with migraine, supports our hypothesis that visual discomfort accounts for the inconsistent results obtained in previous studies that examined spatial contrast sensitivity. In previous studies that have found reduced spatial contrast sensitivity in migraine (Benedek et al., 2002; Coleston et al., 1994; Khahil, 1991), unmeasured co-morbid visual discomfort may provide an explanation. In the current study, half of the migraine with aura group also had high visual discomfort, whereas less than half of the no aura migraine group did. When all participants with high visual discomfort regardless of migraine classification were included in a single group, reduced spatial contrast sensitivity was found, replicating previous findings (Conlon et al., 2001).

In addition to the depressed spatial CSF found in the group with high visual discomfort, increased temporal sensitivity was found at the fastest flicker rate tested (33 Hz). No evidence of increased temporal sensitivity was found in a previous study for the group with high visual discomfort, but stimuli were temporally modulated at a much slower rate (6 Hz, Conlon et al., 2001). In the current study there was no evidence of reduced temporal sensitivity at slower rates, suggesting that the increased sensitivity of the group with high visual discomfort only occurs in their response to fast flicker. This finding is consistent with reports of increased sensitivity to light produced by high flicker, for example fluorescent lighting in the group with high visual discomfort (Wilkins, 1995).

The results of these two studies suggest that reports of visual discomfort principally explain reports of increased perceptual difficulties with *pattern* viewing in individuals with or without migraine. Individuals with migraine and visual discomfort, only have difficulty when exposed to striped repetitive pattern. Co-morbid experience of both difficulties explains the inconsistent reports found in the literature concerning spatial contrast sensitivity in migraine groups (Benedek et al, 2002; Khahil, 1991). The presence of visual discomfort in migraine sufferers fails to explain the reduced temporal contrast sensitivity found in the migraine with aura group. This suggests that there are different underlying neural mechanisms responsible for hyperexcitability to pattern and to flicker. There is considerable evidence that flicker and other forms of temporal information are processed in the magnocellular visual pathway, with pattern processed in the parvocellular visual pathway (McKendrick et al., 2001). Reports of anomalous side-effects with pattern viewing and findings of reduced spatial contrast sensitivity in the group with high visual discomfort suggest that hyperexcitability to pattern in this group may affect the way these individuals process pattern only. This conclusion is consistent with previous findings that also found no evidence of poor temporal processing in a group with visual discomfort (Conlon, Sanders, and Wright, 2009).

The following studies investigated the specific ways that sensitivity to pattern and light influences performance in groups with high and low visual discomfort on reading and visual search tasks. The classification of visual discomfort was used because visual discomfort and not migraine distinguished between individuals showing increased sensitivity to pattern. These studies aimed to determine the impact of the repetitive striped pattern formed by the continuous lines of text on reading performance in groups with visual discomfort. It was expected that the pattern percept most similar to the striped repetitive pattern that induced discomfort would also produce the greatest performance difficulties.

STUDY 3: VISUAL DISCOMFORT AND READING EFFICIENCY

The pattern of lines formed by a single spaced text page forms a global striped pattern with similar spatial characteristics to patterns that induce greatest somatic and perceptual difficulties in susceptible individuals (Conlon et al., 1999; Conlon et al., 2001; Wilkins, 1995; Wilkins and Nimmo-Smith, 1984; 1987). The spatial frequency of a text page is obtained by treating the interline spacing as the bright bar and the lines of text as the dark bar of a cycle in a square-wave (Wilkins and Nimmo-Smith, 1984; 1987). The subjective clarity and visual comfort of the global text format presented in different spatial arrangements has been investigated (Wilkins and Nimmo-Smith, 1987). Observers report that single spaced text produces poorest reading comfort. Increasing interline spacing produces reports of increased clarity and comfort of the text page (Wilkins and Nimmo-Smith, 1987). In addition, it has been argued that ergonomically, the spacing between the letters in words could be condensed slightly and the spacing between the lines increased to improve the clarity and comfort of text (Wilkins and Nimmo-Smith, 1987). Although changing the spatial characteristics of text has produced subjective reports of increased clarity, the impact of these changes on reading efficiency has not been assessed.

Individuals with high visual discomfort have reduced reading efficiency compared to groups with low visual discomfort when text is presented in single spaced format (Conlon and Sanders, 2011). Difficulty ignoring the global pattern formed by the text page, to focus on the words and letters presented is one explanation for poorer reading efficiency (Conlon et al., 1998). This explanation is based on a four level object hierarchy of visual attention when reading (McConkie and Zola, 1979). According to this model a page of text constitutes the global text page. The line, word and letter levels make up the other components of the hierarchy. In skilled reading, the page level is ignored, with the line level the focus when readers move from one line to the next. In skilled reading, the major focus occurs at the word level. In individuals with high visual discomfort, pattern interference induced by the global text page may interfere with the capacity of these individuals to focus on the lines, words and individual letters.

When manipulating the spatial characteristics of the text page, consistent with subjective reports of viewing comfort, we expected that reading efficiency would be significantly poorer for single spaced text than for text with wider interline spacing. In addition, when text was presented with wider inter-line spacing, with or without condensed letters, we expected to find increased reading efficiency. The high visual discomfort group was expected to read single spaced text significantly less efficiently than the groups with lower levels of visual discomfort. In addition, the subjective comfort and readability of text was expected to be poorer for single spaced text, with increased comfort and readability reported when text was presented with a wider interline spacing.

Glare on a text page can be induced because of unwanted light entering the eye (Garcia and Weirville, 1985). Visual fatigue, headache, and eye-strain are frequently reported following text exposure in the presence of glare (Bachner, 1997; Garcia and Weirville, 1985; Springer, 1997). Wilkins (1995) has established that artificial lighting induces glare and increases visual discomfort. Individuals who experience severe difficulties when reading complex information in the presence of light sources trade speed for accuracy as a form of compensation to reduce the anomalous impact of the glare source (Garcia and Weirville, 1985). Fluorescent lighting may increase the effects of glare during reading, particularly if text is presented on glossy text pages.

In the current study the impact of single spaced glossy pages of text was compared with the effects of single spaced matt finish paper. We expected that if unwanted glare induced from the glossy pages increases difficulties for individuals with visual discomfort that poorest reading efficiency, and poorer comfort and readability would be found with presentation of single spaced glossy text pages. The group with high visual discomfort was expected to have the poorest reading efficiency and report reduced comfort and readability when compared to the other groups.

Method

Participants

There were 42 volunteers obtained from the university population. There were 16 with high visual discomfort (>60%), 10 with moderate visual discomfort (35 to 60%) and 16 with low visual discomfort16 (< 35%) all assessed using the VDS (Conlon et al., 1999). All participants had normal or corrected to normal visual acuity and English as a first language. University Human Research Ethics committee approval was obtained for this project.

Apparatus and Materials

Each of the A4 text pages was produced in Times New Roman font. The margins at the top and bottom of each page were 2.45 cm, and on the left and right, 3.54 cm. There were 640 words presented on each page, including the target text paragraph of 200 words, which was demarcated from other text using arrows. There were four conditions, two presented text in a single spaced format in 12 point font.

One of these pages was presented on matt paper, and one on high gloss paper. The second two texts had an interline spacing set at 16 points. In the first, the font was 12 point and the inter-letter density was increased by 20%. In the second, uncondensed letters were presented in a 10 point font. These conditions were generated to maintain an equal number of words on the text pages (see Figure 8 for example text formats).

(a)

> In the language of the ancient Khmer, the Khmer people of contemporary Kampuchea, Angkor means the city or capital. Geographically it denotes some 75 square miles of fertile plain between the Kulen Hills and the lake of Tonle Sap, where between the 9th and 11th centuries AD, a dozen Khmer kings constructed successive capitals. These

(b)

> In the language of the ancient Khmer, the Khmer people of contemporary Kampuchea, Angkor means the
>
> city or capital. Geographically it denotes some 75 square miles of fertile plain between the Kulen Hills and
>
> the lake of Tonle Sap, where between the 9th and 11th centuries AD, a dozen Khmer kings constructed

(c)

> In the language of the ancient Khmer, the Khmer people of contemporary Kampuchea, Angkor means the city or
> capital. Geographically it denotes some 75 square miles of fertile plain between the Kulen Hills and the lake of
> Tonle Sap, where between the 9th and 11th centuries AD, a dozen Khmer kings constructed successive capitals.

Figure 8. Text presentations used in Study 3. (a) Single spaced text in 12 point font used with a matt and gloss background. (b) Ten point font with 16 point spacing between the lines. (c) Twelve point font with 16 point spacing between the lines. The spacing between characters reduced by 20%.

The pages of text were positioned on a reading stand fixed at a 45^0 angle with a 30 by 40 square cm white perspex board placed upon it to ensure a uniform background for all conditions. Reading distance was 30 cm, which was controlled with a chin rest.

Reading Passages

The four reading passages each had Flesh (1948) reading ease scores at Grade 12 level. Each contained 200 words to avoid the confounding effects of memory. In a pilot study which assessed the reading rate and comprehension of normal readers, the textual passages were found to be comparable. No significant differences were found between reading passages on either reading rate or comprehension. For further description of the text passages used see Conlon and Sanders (2011).

Procedure

Following assignment to groups with low, moderate or high visual discomfort, participants undertook the reading task individually. The text passages were positioned under twin 26-watt fluorescent tubes covered by a standard diffuser. When combined with the light emanating from four 120-watt incandescent lamps spaced uniformly in a rectangle in the ceiling, the average luminance of the light projected onto the text pages was 305 cd/m^2. A practice trial was conducted to familiarize participants with the lighting and the arrows indicating the paragraph to be read on each text page. Participants silently read each text page as quickly as possible, consistent with good comprehension. Reading speed for each text passage was timed with a stop watch. After reading was completed, four comprehension questions that addressed factual (or literal) material presented in the text were asked. After this process, the presentation format of the text passage read was rated on two four point scales, for readability and viewing comfort. A score of 0 indicated no difficulties and a score of 4 difficulties so severe that text could not be easily read, or caused somatic and perceptual difficulties so great that efficient reading was impossible.

Results

Readability and Visual Comfort of the Textual Presentations

Significant linear correlations were found between measures of readability and comfort for the textual presentation formats used. These correlations (r) were .68 for the 10 point double spaced text, .82 for the single spaced text, .71 for the single spaced matt text and .77 for the double spaced condensed text. These results showed that regardless of the way the text was presented, there was a strong association between readability and viewing comfort in the sample as a whole. Using the readability and comfort ratings as dependent variables, a 3 (group) × 4 (textual presentation format) mixed MANOVA was conducted. These results are presented in Figure 9. The was a statistically significant multivariate main effect found for group, $F(4, 76) = 12.67, p < .001, p\eta^2 = .40$, with no significant effects found for presentation format, $F(6, 34) = 0.87, p = .56, p\eta^2 = .13$. There were no significant interactions found between presentation format and group, $F(12, 68) = 0.40, p = .96, p\eta^2 = .06$. Statistically significant group effects were found for readability, $F(2, 39) = 25.98, p < .001, p\eta^2 = .57$ and for text comfort, $F(2, 39) = 26.55, p < .001, p\eta^2 = .58$. No significant difference was found between the groups with low versus moderate visual discomfort in the subjective reports of text readability, $t(39) = 0.66, p = .510$, Cohen's $d = .22$.

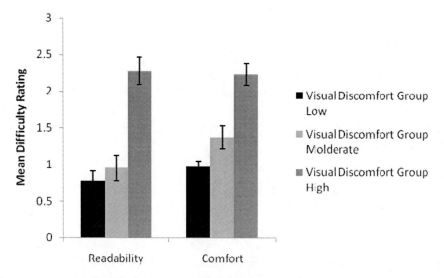

Figure 9. Study 3. Mean readability and comfort ratings for the groups with low (n = 16) moderate (n =16) and high (n = 16) visual discomfort. Standard error bars represent ± 1 standard error.

The group with high visual discomfort reported that all the texts regardless of presentation format were significantly less readable than either of the other groups combined, $t(39) = 7.00$, $p < .001$, Cohen's $d = 2.24$. When viewing comfort was considered, the group with moderate visual discomfort reported significantly less viewing comfort than the group with low visual discomfort, $t(39) = 2.02$, $p = .050$, Cohen's $d = 0.65$. The group with high visual discomfort reported significantly less viewing comfort than the group with moderate visual discomfort, $t(39) = 4.27$, $p < .001$, Cohen's $d = 1.37$.

Reading Efficiency

Reading efficiency was evaluated using the reading rate in words per minute and percentage comprehension scores. Within group correlations were generated to assess the associations between reading speed and reading comprehension. A speed accuracy trade-off was found in the groups with moderate, $r = -.66$, and high, $r = -.50$, visual discomfort with presentation of the double spaced condensed text. The group with high visual discomfort also showed evidence of a speed accuracy trade-off when single spaced text in matt, r = -.48 and gloss, r = -.46, formats was presented. These results suggest that the group with high visual discomfort skim read text that induces discomfort, as a form of compensation (Garcia and Weirville, 1985).

Using mean reading rate in words/minute and mean correct comprehension scores as separate dependent variables, two 4 (textual presentation) × 3 (group) mixed factorial ANOVA's, which met all assumptions were conducted. These results are presented in Table 1. For reading rate, there were no statistically significant main effects, (group, $F(2, 39) = 0.310$, $p = .74$, $p\eta^2 = .02$, textual presentation, $F(6, 34) = 1.06$, $p = .40$, $p\eta^2 = .16$) or interaction found, $F(4, 76) = 3.12$, $p = .20$, $p\eta^2 = .02$. For reading comprehension, there was a significant main effect found for group, $F(2, 39) = 6.02$, $p = .005$, $p\eta^2 = .24$. There was no significant difference in comprehension between the groups with low versus moderate visual discomfort, $t(39) = 1.58$, $p = .123$, Cohen's $d = .51$, but the group with high visual discomfort had significantly poorer reading comprehension than the other groups combined, $t(39) = 3.29$, $p = .002$, Cohen's $d = 1.05$.

These results show that regardless of the global presentation format of the text pages, the group with high visual discomfort reported poorer text readability, poorer comfort and objectively had poorer reading comprehension than the other groups tested. Although these results are consistent with findings of reports of poorer reading efficiency in the group with high visual discomfort, they fail to support our hypothesis that text with wide interline spacing, presented in either normal or condensed letter format would produce increased reading efficiency and single spaced glossy text poorest reading efficiency.

Table 1. Mean reading rate and comprehension for the groups with low (n = 16), moderate (n = 10) and high (n = 16) visual discomfort. Standard deviations are presented in brackets

	Visual Discomfort Group		
	Low	Moderate	High
Reading Rate (words/minute)	167.9 (40.3)	157.5 (26.3)	159.6 (37.7)
Reading Comprehension /4	2.04 (.62)	2.45 (.63)	1.57 (.71)

These results suggest that regardless of the spatial characteristics that form the global page percept, the group with high visual discomfort had difficulty disengaging attention from the global pattern presented to attend to the increasingly more specific line, word and letter levels on the text page. These findings are consistent with pattern interference induced from the global text page, the first level in the object hierarchy used when reading (McConkie and Zola, 1979).

The results for the condensed letter format are consistent with Wilkins and Nimmo-Smith's (1987) report that condensing text would not produce added reading difficulties in normal readers. In the current study when 16 point leading was used, the letter format produced reading efficiency in both groups consistent with that obtained when normal inter-letter spacing was used. However, the finding that regardless of textual presentation format used, the group with high visual discomfort had poorer reading comprehension suggests that the global repetitive pattern in any form produces attentional difficulties for the group with high visual discomfort, with presentation of linguistically difficult text.

The finding of poorer reading comprehension in the group with high visual discomfort is consistent with those found in a previous study that did not manipulate the textual presentation format (Conlon and Sanders, 2011). In that study the linguistic complexity of the text was manipulated. The same four linguistically difficult passages used in the current study and four less linguistically difficult passages were presented. When less linguistically complex text was presented, there were no significant differences found between the groups with high or low visual discomfort on reading comprehension. These findings suggest that the linguistic complexity of the textual presentation may also contribute to the visual processing difficulties found for the group with high visual discomfort.

The Rate of Reading Test was developed to assess difficulties with visual perceptual processing during reading (Wilkins et al., 1996). This test presents high frequency words on lines of closely spaced text. Words are read aloud and poor performance is interpreted as indicating perceptual difficulties during reading (Wilkins et al., 1996). In order to rule out difficulties produced when comprehending linguistically complex text as an explanation for the findings of Study 3, Study 4 presented unrelated high frequency words in either a single line or paragraph format. We expected that if the global percept alone induced difficulties for the group with high visual discomfort then poorer performance would be found on paragraphs but not on single lines.

A study that has investigated the repetitive nature of the letter groupings that constitute individual lines on a text page has suggested that the letters forming the line may also form a repetitive pattern stimulus (Jainta, Jaschiniski, and Wilkins, 2005). This occurs because of the periodicity of the individual letter strokes. To reduce the impact of this periodicity we also manipulated the size of the individual letters within the words on the line by presenting some letters in 12 point font and others in 24 point font. The manipulation aimed to reduce the periodicity produced within words on lines and direct attentional resources required to the individual letters presented in the high frequency words (Bock, Monk, and Hulme, 1993). If the repetitive pattern formed at the line level also causes increased perceptual difficulties for the group with high visual discomfort, we expected that when the font was uniform, poorer performance would be found relative to the group with low visual discomfort. When mixed font text was presented, performance was expected to improve in the group with high visual discomfort because the periodicity of the line was reduced. This was expected to reduce the performance differences between the groups.

STUDY 4: READING DISORDERED TEXT

Method

Participants

There were adult 24 volunteers, 12 with high visual discomfort (VDS score > 70%) and 12 with low visual discomfort (VDS score < 35%). All participants were University students, had English as a first language and normal or corrected to normal visual acuity. University Human Research Ethics committee approval was obtained for this project.

Stimuli and Materials

Stimuli were generated using the V-scope software program (Rensick and Enns, 1992) and presented on a Powermac computer with a high resolution monitor. There were four textual presentation formats, each presented in Times New Roman Font. In two conditions, 11 lines of single spaced text were presented in paragraph form with five lines above and 5 lines below the target text line. The target line was indicated by arrows at the beginning and the end of the line. In two conditions a single line of text was presented. In two of the conditions, the words were presented in 12 point font (see Figure 10a). In the remaining two conditions, the size of the font of the letters within the words was manipulated. Half of the letters were presented in 12 point and half of the letters were presented in 24 point font (see Figure 10b). There were seven words presented on each text line, with the constraint that a total of 35 letters were presented on each line. Words ranged in length from 4 to 7 letters.

Filler text consisted of high frequency words that were not included in the target lines of text. The stimulus words used in each condition were obtained from the 500 most frequently used words in the English language (Kucera and Francis, 1967). Pilot testing demonstrated that there were no significant differences in the time required to orally read the text lines.

(a)

plant numbers each give money start cannot
three summer road true sound where garden
might others face open story short things
catch strong some than young kinds father
** enough care threes done they between every **
each plant give money start numbers cannot
road three true sound where summer garden
face might open story short others things
move names days than young kind strong father

(b)

plaNt nuMbErs EaCh glvE mOnEy start CanNot

Figure 10. Stimuli used in Study 4. (a) Normal text in the paragraph condition. (b) Mixed font text in the single line condition.

Procedure

The study was conducted in a dimly lit room. Following an explanation of the task and practice trials for each of the different stimulus conditions, the 10 experimental trials were conducted. Presentation of each of the conditions was randomized within and between groups to control for learning effects. Reading accuracy was recorded on a response sheet. Timing was computer controlled with timing beginning when the space bar was pressed to begin a trial and stopped when the space bar was pressed when the participant had read the target line of text. The proportion of errors made across conditions was negligible so no formal error analysis was conducted.

Results and Discussion

Using the mean response time as the dependent variable, a 2 (group, high or low visual discomfort) × 2 (presentation: paragraph or single line) × 2 (font size: uniform or mixed) mixed ANOVA which met the assumptions was conducted. These results are presented in Figure 11. There was a statistically significant main effect of group, $F(1, 22) = 11.55$, $p = .003$, $p\eta^2 = .34$, with no significant interactions involving group. Regardless of the condition presented, the group with high visual discomfort was significantly slower when reading different texts than the group with low visual discomfort. There was a significant main effect of presentation, $F(1, 22) = 5.63$, $p = .027$, $p\eta^2 = .20$, and for the font size, $F(1, 22) = 49.02$, $p < .001$, $p\eta^2 = .69$. Regardless of group membership, single lines of text were read significantly more quickly than text lines embedded in paragraphs. Significantly slower performance was also found when reading words in the mixed compared to uniform sized font. Regardless of the condition presented, the group with high visual discomfort read the high frequency words significantly more slowly than the group with low visual discomfort. This occurred even though the linguistic difficulty of the words used was low.

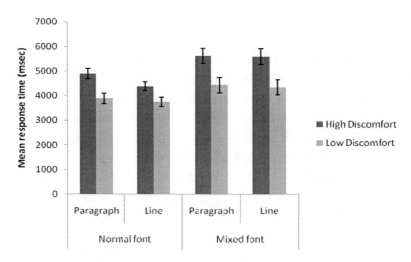

Figure 11. Study 4. Mean response time of the high (n = 12) and low (n = 12) visual discomfort groups. Standard error bars represent ± 1 standard error.

Although both groups read the isolated line level stimuli more quickly than those embedded within paragraphs, performance of the group with high visual discomfort did not normalize in these conditions. In addition, presentation of the words presented in mixed font conditions produced a further reduction in reading speed, an effect that was expected for the group with low visual discomfort, but not high. These results fail to support our hypothesis that the striped repetitive pattern formed by the page of text alone explains poorer reading efficiency for the group with visual discomfort. One explanation for these results concerns the visual clutter produced by the presented stimuli, regardless of whether this occurs at a page, line or word level. In each case the target stimuli are placed in close proximity to one another. The results suggest that even at a single line level when multiple letters are presented in periodic (same font) or a non-periodic (different font) structure, these patterns induce difficulties in individuals with high visual discomfort. One explanation of these findings is that observers with high visual discomfort have difficulty extracting the target stimuli from irrelevant features in a cluttered visual environment. Some studies have shown that the group with high visual discomfort has difficulties extracting relevant target stimuli from a cluttered visual scene, regardless of whether or not a striped repetitive stimulus is used (Conlon et al., 1998; Conlon and Humphreys, 2001). The final experiment conducted examined this possibility by presenting stimuli embedded in a cluttered non-striped visual environment.

STUDY 5: VISUAL CLOSURE TEST

The visual closure subtest of the Illinois Test of Psycholinguistic Abilities (ITPA) is a test that assesses an observer's ability to identify specific details concealed in different ways in a cluttered visual scene (Kirk, McCarthy, and Kirk, 1968; Sattler, 1986). This test relies on identification of specific visual stimuli and, in this respect, is a test of ability to identify local detail from a global visual scene. The stimulus patterns are non-repetitive line drawings in black on a white background. If the striped repetitive nature of either the page or line of printed text induces the visual discomfort that causes inefficient reading performance in the group with high visual discomfort, then there should be no difference between groups with high or low visual discomfort in performance on the visual closure test because repetitive striped patterns are not present. However, if the performance difficulties experienced by the group with high visual discomfort are more generalised than sensitivity to the pattern alone, this groups' performance should be poorer than that of other groups when searching for hidden objects in cluttered visual scenes.

Method

Participants

Forty-two observers with normal or corrected to normal vision volunteered. There were 14 participants in each of the control, moderate and high visual discomfort groups. Participants were classified in the same way as in Experiment 3. Human Research Ethics approval was obtained for this study, with all observers providing informed consent.

Stimuli and Apparatus

The five stimulus sheets (one practice trial; four test trials) from the ITPA test, and a stopwatch were used. In each stimulus pattern fourteen or fifteen target figures were embedded within the cluttered visual scene.

Procedure

Each participant was tested individually following the standardised instructions of the test and administration of one practice trial. Individuals were questioned on experience of unpleasant physical and perceptual effects following the task. There were no reports of experience of any unpleasant perceptual or somatic effects while performing the task. The total number of correct responses on each trial, excluding the practice item was summed for each observer. The maximum possible score was 55.

Results and Discussion

The ANOVA produced a significant main effect for group, $F(2, 39) = 10.14$, $p < .001$, $p\eta^2 = .34$. Comparison analysis revealed that the groups with low ($M = 43.36$, $SD = 4.7$) or moderate ($M = 40.79$, $SD = 5.0$) visual discomfort obtained similar scores on the task, $F(1, 39) = 1.70$, $p > .05$. The group with high visual discomfort ($M = 34.71$, $SD = 5.9$) obtained significantly lower scores than either of the other groups combined, $F(1, 39) = 18.58$, $p < .001$. These findings suggest that the global stimulus, regardless of its repetitive nature can interfere with processing efficiency for the group with high visual discomfort. Although this task does not involve repetitive pattern stimuli, the observers must search the global pattern for specific local details. In this respect the task is similar to those used when extracting letters and words from a text page. Performance on a visually based task in which observers must differentiate between different elements in a scene may simply be poorer for individuals with high visual discomfort. This suggests that difficulty extracting relevant target stimuli from irrelevant clutter or noise is a specific difficulty for the group with high visual discomfort. Although striped repetitive patterns may present particular difficulties for individuals with high visual discomfort, performance difficulties may occur regardless of the presentation format used.

GENERAL DISCUSSION

The first aim of the current research was to determine the extent that visual perceptual difficulties reported in sensitive individuals with exposure to striped repetitive patterns and flickering light are a general characteristic of migraine headache, or occur because of a more specific visual perceptual difficulty, visual discomfort. The first two studies demonstrated that the perceptual and somatic difficulties generated with pattern exposure were mainly explained by visual discomfort. However, there was also evidence of reports of increased somatic difficulty in individuals with migraine and low visual discomfort, relative to a control group who were free of headache and visual discomfort. The second aim of the research was to determine whether poor efficiency on reading and visual search tasks in groups with visual discomfort could be explained by visual system hyperexcitability to striped repetitive patterns, or to a more general difficulty extracting relevant stimuli from irrelevant clutter presented in a visual scene. The findings from these studies suggested that individuals with high visual discomfort had slower more laborious reading, poorer reading comprehension and poorer capacity to search for relevant stimuli in irrelevant clutter than individuals with low visual discomfort. The findings will be discussed in three ways. First, the everyday difficulties that may occur in groups with migraine will be discussed. Second, how visual discomfort influences reading efficiency will be addressed. Finally, the more general functional consequences of visual discomfort will be discussed.

Migraine headache is a recurrent chronic disorder that results in reduced quality of life in sufferers (Friedman and de Ver Dye, 2009; Lance, 1993). The disability costs of migraine in the workplace are also high, with lost work days and reduced productivity incurred during the headache phase (Friedman and de Ver Dye, 2009). The findings of the current research show that although most migraine sufferers report unpleasant somatic effects when exposed to striped repetitive patterns, only some show evidence of perceptual difficulties with pattern exposure. These findings are important for two reasons. First, although a high proportion of individuals with migraine experience visual discomfort, it is only those reporting severe symptoms that also experience functional difficulties when reading or performing other visual tasks. Second, the difficulties experienced by these observers occur on an everyday basis, not just during the headache phase of migraine. These findings suggest that specific assessment of the somatic, perceptual and performance difficulties that can occur because of visual discomfort should be undertaken in individuals reporting everyday performance difficulties, regardless of migraine diagnosis. The capacity to distinguish between individuals with migraine and with visual discomfort will lead to increased awareness in the workplace and in educational institutions of the types of difficulties that produce disabling effects in these individuals. Awareness of these difficulties can lead to adjustments to the work environment of sensitive individuals. For example, these individuals have been found to benefit from working in natural lighting (Wilkins, 1995). In addition, increased time may be allocated to tasks that produce increased difficulties for these individuals. Both awareness, and changes made to the physical environment for sensitive observers will act to improve quality of life and increase individual productivity in individuals with migraine and high visual discomfort.

Previous studies have found that people with high visual discomfort report unpleasant somatic and perceptual effects with exposure to striped repetitive patterns or text pages (Conlon et al., 1999; 2001). Consistent with these findings, in Study 3, when the spatial characteristics of the global pattern were manipulated, poorer readability and poorer viewing comfort was reported by the groups with moderate and high visual discomfort. Importantly, this occurred regardless of the spacing presented between the lines or text, or the spacing used between individual letters. These findings suggest that the visual perceptual difficulties experienced by individuals with severe difficulties occur regardless of the format used to present pages of text. The poorer reading comprehension found in the group with high visual discomfort regardless of the way text was presented is consistent with experience of somatic, perceptual and performance difficulties in this group only. The persistence of performance difficulties found in the group with high visual discomfort when stimuli were presented in a single line or within a non-repetitive pattern is further evidence of poor processing efficiency in this group. These findings suggest that for the group with high visual discomfort, the difficulties extend beyond increased sensitivity to repetitive striped patterns.

One explanation of these difficulties for the group with high visual discomfort is that that for these individuals the visual system contains increased internal noise. This may occur because of increased spontaneous discharge from cells excited by visual stimulation that have not been completely inhibited by the GABA-ergic neurons that in a well functioning system modulate this activity. This would produce a 'noisy system' that would be similar to a noisy TV screen. This would produce poor efficiency for the group with high visual discomfort when extracting complex visual signals from irrelevant stimuli in complex visual scenes. The result of this difficulty would be poor efficiency when reading, or performing other visual tasks that require attention to visual details. If the repetitive striped nature of the pattern alone could explain the performance difficulties found in the group with high visual discomfort, improved performance should have been obtained when the global structure presented was minimized or not presented. Some support for the idea of increased noise in the visual system in observers with high visual discomfort has been obtained. In a recent study, observers with high visual discomfort and dyslexia were found to have increased difficulties compared to a control group when extracting target stimuli from irrelevant clutter (Northway, Manahilov, and Simpson, 2010).

In the group with high visual discomfort, the strategy used when performing the different reading tasks was also dependent on the task instructions. In Study 3, when individuals silently read text for good comprehension, a speed accuracy trade-off was employed by the group with high visual discomfort. The high negative linear correlations found between reading speed and comprehension score for the high visual discomfort group supports this conclusion. A form of skim reading may have been employed with little attention directed to the individual words presented in the 'noisy' and unpleasant visual environment (Garcia and Weirville, 1985). In the final two studies, a speed-accuracy trade-off could not be used as observers were required to read each of the individual words presented in the lines of text or find target stimuli in the disorganized visual scenes. In these cases, slow laborious performances were observed. Due to the visual perceptual and somatic difficulties experienced with exposure to complex visual materials, the group with high visual discomfort appears to develop techniques to minimize text exposure at the expense of skilled performance.

In contrast to the performance difficulties found in the group with high visual discomfort, the group with moderate visual discomfort report poor text comfort and readability when the text is presented in a repetitive pattern arrangement. This does not produce poorer reading efficiency. In addition, this group neither report somatic difficulties nor have reduced accuracy in a visual search task when stimuli are presented in a non-cluttered visual scene. These findings suggest that for individuals with moderate visual discomfort, reducing the impact of the striped repetitive patterns by presenting less text on the page may reduce the somatic types of difficulty reported. In an early study on the difficulties induced by striped repetitive pages of text, Wilkins and Nimmo-Smith (1984) found that individuals reporting principally poor reading comfort found a significant benefit when using a reading mask that reduced the number of lines presented on a page to about three.

CONCLUSIONS

Reducing the available text to a few lines or changing its spatial arrangement in other ways may not improve the reading performance of the group with high visual discomfort. The results of each of the studies conducted suggest that the increased internal noise generated in the group with high visual discomfort produces poor capacity to direct attention to the relevant target stimuli presented in the visual arrays, regardless of the nature of the global pattern formed. Simply changing the way these patterns are presented will not alleviate these difficulties in sensitive observers. There have been some reports that using individually selected coloured filters or glasses can reduce the impact of the somatic and perceptual difficulties induced in individuals with migraine or visual discomfort (Evans and Joseph, 2002; Northway et al., 2010; Wilkins, 1995). Successful use of this simple remedy to alleviate the symptoms will increase the quality of life, well being and performance efficiency in these individuals. This will also act to increase productivity in the workplace or for students when studying. While future research should continue to investigate the neural reasons that individuals experience visual discomfort, research efforts should also be directed to ways to alleviate these symptoms in sensitive individuals.

REFERENCES

Allen, P. M., Gilchrist, J. M., and Hollis, J. (2008). Use of visual search in the assessment of pattern-related visual stress (PRVS) and its alleviation by colored filters. *Investigative Ophthalmology and Visual Science, 49,* 4210-4218.

Bachner, J. P. (1997). Eliminating those glare errors. *Managing Office Technology, 7,* 15-22.

Bates, D., Blau, J. N., Campbell, M. J., Clifford-Rose, F., Cull, R. E., and Cummings, W. J., K., et al. (1993). *Migraine Management Guidelines.* Richmond: Synergy Medical Education.

Benedek, K., Tajti, J., Janaky, M., Vicsei, L., and Benedek, G. (2002). Spatial contrast sensitivity of migraine patients without aura. *Cephalalgia, 22,* 142-145.

Bock, J. M., Monk, A. F., and Hulme, C. (1993). Perceptual grouping in visual word recognition. *Memory and Cognition. 21, 81-*88.

Borsting, E., Chase, C. H., and Ridder, W. H. (2007). Measuring visual discomfort in college students. *Optometry and Visual Science, 84,* 745-751.

Cao, Y., Welch, K. M. A., Aurora, S., and Vikingstad, E. M. (1999). Functional MRI_BOLD of visually triggered headache in patients with migraine. *Archives of Neurology, 56,* 548-554.

Chronicle, E. P., and Mulleners, W. M. (1996). Visual system dysfunction in migraine: A review of clinical and psychophysical findings *Cephalalgia, 16,* 525-535.

Chronicle, E., Wilkins, A., and Coleston, D. M. (1995). Thresholds of detection of a target against a background grating suggest visual dysfunction in migraine with aura but not migraine without aura. *Cephalalgia, 15,* 321-324.

Coleston, D. M., Chronicle, E., Ruddock, K. H., and Kennard, C. (1994). Precortical dysfunction of spatial and temporal visual processing in migraine. *Journal of Neurology, Neurosurgery and Psychiatry, 57,* 1208-1211.

Coleston, D. M. and Kennard, C. (1993). Visual changes in migraine: Indications of cortical dysfunction. *Cephalalgia, 13*, s1311.

Coleston, D. M., and Kennard, C. (1995). Responses to temporal visual stimuli in migraine: The critical flicker fusion test. *Cephalalgia, 15,* 117-122.

Conforto, A. B., Lois, L. A., Amaro, E., Paes, A. T., Ecker, C., and Young, W. B., et al. (2010). Migraine and motion sickness independently contribute to visual discomfort. *Cephalalgia, 30,* 161-169.

Cologno, D., Torelli, P., and Manzoni, G. C. (1998). Migraine with aura: A review of 81 patients at 10-20 years' follow-up. *Cephalalgia, 18,* 690-696.

Conlon, E., and Hine, T. (2000). The influence of pattern interference on performance in migraine and visual discomfort groups. *Cephalalgia, 20,* 708-713.

Conlon, E., and Humphreys, L. (2001). Visual search in migraine and visual discomfort groups. *Vision Research, 41,* 3063-3068.

Conlon, E., Lovegrove, W., Barker, S., and Chekaluk, E. (2001). Visual discomfort: The influence of spatial frequency. *Perception, 30,* 571-581.

Conlon, E., Lovegrove, W., Chekaluk, E., and Pattison, P. (1999). Measuring visual discomfort. *Visual Cognition, 6,* 637-663.

Conlon, E. G., Lovegrove, W. J., Hine, T., Chekaluk, E., Piatek, K. and Hayes-Williams, K. (1998). The effect of visual discomfort and pattern structure on visual search. *Perception, 27,* 21-33.

Conlon, E. G., and Sanders, M. A. (2011). The reading rate and comprehension of adults with impaired reading skills or visual discomfort. *Journal of Research in Reading, 34,* 193-214.

Conlon, E. G., Sanders, M. A., and Wright, C. M. (2009). Relationships between global motion and global form processing, practice, cognitive and visual processing in adults with dyslexia or visual discomfort. *Neuropsychologia, 47,* 907-915.

Drummond, P. D., and Woodhouse, A. (1993). Painful stimulation of the forehead increases photophobia in migraine sufferers. *Cephalalgia, 13,* 321-324.

Evans, B. J., and Joseph, R. (2002). The effect of coloured filters on the rate of reading in an adult student population. *Ophthalmic and Physiological Optics, 22,* 535-545.

Evans, B. J. W., Patel, R., and Wilkins, A. J. (2002). Optometric function in migraine before and after treatment with tinted spectacles. *Opthalmic and Physiological Optics, 22,* 130-142.

Flesh, R. (1948). A new readability yardstick. *Journal of Applied Psychology, 32,* 221-233.

Friedman, D. I., and De Ver Dye, T. (2009). Migraine and the environment. *Headache, June,* 941-952.

Garcia K. D., and Wierville W. W. (1985). Effect of glare on performance in a VDT reading-comprehension task. *Human Factors, 27,* 163-173.

Harle, D. E., Shepherd, A. J., and Evans, B. J. W. (2006). Visual stimuli are common triggers of migraine and are associated with pattern glare. *Headache, 46,* 1431-1440.

Hay, K. H., Mortimer, M. J., Barker, D. C., Debney, L. M. and Good, P. A. (1994). 1044 Women with migraine: The effect of environmental stimuli. *Headache, 34,* 166-168.

Headache Classification Committee of the International Headache Society. (1988). Classification and diagnostic criteria for headache disorders, cranial neuralgias, and facial pain. *Cephalalgia, 8,* suppl, 7, 1-96.

Hollis, J., and Allen, P. M. (2006). Screening for Meares-Irlen sensitivity in adults: Can assessment methods predict changes in reading speed. *Ophthalmic and Physiological Optics, 26,* 566-571.

Huang, J., Cooper, Y. G., Satana, B., Kaufman, D. I., and Cao, Y. (2003). Visual distortion provoked by a stimulus in migraine associated with hyperneuronal activity. *Headache, 43,* 664-671.

Jainta, S., Jaschiniski, W., and Wilkins, A. J. (2005). Periodic letter strokes within a word affect fixation disparity during reading. *Journal of Vision, 5,* 1-11.

Khahil, N. (1991). *Investigations of visual function in migraine by visual evoked potentials and visual psychophysical tests.* Unpublished PhD Thesis. University of London.

Kirk, S. A., McCarthy, J. J., and Kirk, W. D. (1968). *Illinois test of psycholinguistic abilities.* Urbana Illinois: University Press Illinois.

Kucera, H., and Francis, W. N. (1967). *Computation analysis of present-day American English.* Rhode Island: Brown University Press.

Lance, J. W. (1993). *Mechanisms and management of headache.* 5th Ed. Oxford: Butterworth-Heimemann Ltd.

Lauritzen, M. (1994). Pathophysiology of migraine aura. The spreading depression theory. *Brain, 117,* 199-210.

Main, A., Dawson, A., and Gross, M. (1997). Photophobia and phonophobia in migraineurs between attacks. *Headache, 37,* 492-495.

Marcus, D. A., and Soso, M. J. (1989). Migraine and stripe-induced visual discomfort. *Archives in Neurology, 46,* 1129-1132.

McConkie, G. W. and Zola, D. (1987). Visual attention during eye-fixations while reading. In M Coltheart (Ed.), *Attention and Performance XII* (pp 385-401). Hillsdale: Lawrence Earlbaum.

McKendrick, A. M., Vingrys, A. J., Badcock, D. R., and Heywood, J. T. (2001). Visual dysfunction between migraine events. *Investigative Ophthalmology and Visual Science, 42,* 626-632.

Meldrum, B. S., and Wilkins, A. J. (1984). Photosensitive epilepsy in man and the baboon: Integration of pharmacological and psychological evidence (pp 51-77). In P. A. Schwartzkroin and H.V. Wheal (Eds.), *Electrophysiology of epilepsy.* London: Academic Press

Northway, N., Manahilov, V., and Simpson, W. (2010). Coloured filters improve exclusion of perceptual noise in visually symptomatic dyslexics. *Journal of Research in Reading, 33,* 223-230.

Rensick, R. A., and Enns, J. T. (1992), *Reference manual for Vscope and Emaker.* Vancouver: Micropsych Software.

Sattler, J. M. (1986). *Assessment of children* (3rd Ed). San Diego: Jerome Sattler.

Shepherd, A. J. (2001). Increased visual after-effects following pattern adaptation in migraine: A lack of intracortical excitation? *Brain, 124,* 2310-2318.

Singleton, C. and Trotter, S. (2005). Visual stress in adults with and without dyslexia. *Journal of Research in Reading, 28,* 365-378.

Springer, C. J. (1997). Ergonomics at the video display terminal: Problems, solutions and benefits. *Professional Safety, 42,* 30-37.

Welch, K. M. A. (1987). Migraine: A biobehavioral disorder. *Archives of Neurology, 44,* 323-327.

Welch, K. M., Barkley, G. L., Tepley, N., and Ramadan, N. M. (1993). Central neurogenic mechanisms in migraine. *Neurology, 43*, 21-25.

Wilkins, A. J. (1995). *Visual stress.* Oxford: Oxford University Press.

Wilkins, A. J., Binnie, C. D., and Darby, C. E. (1980). Visually induced seizures. *Progress in Neurobiology, 15,* 85-117.

Wilkins, A. J., Jeanes, R. J., Pumfrey, P. D., and Laskier, M. (1996). Rate of reading test: Its reliability, and its validity in the assessment of the effects of coloured overlays. *Ophthalmic and Physiological Opt*ics, *16*, 491-487.

Wilkins, A. J. and Nimmo-Smith, I. (1984). On the reduction of eye-strain when reading. *Ophthalmology and Physiological Optics, 4*, 53-59.

Wilkins, A. J. and Nimmo-Smith, I. (1987). The clarity and comfort of printed text. *Ergonomics, 30,* 1705-1720.

Wilkins, A. J., Nimmo-Smith, I., Tait, A., McManus, C., Sala, S., G., and Tilley, A., et al. (1984). A neurological basis for visual discomfort. *Brain, 107,* 989-1017.

Chapter 8

FROM THRESHOLDS TO COLOUR NAMES: THE APPLICATION OF AN OPPONENT-PROCESS MODEL

Trevor J. Hine[1,], William H. McIlhagga[2] and Graeme R. Cole[3]*

[1] School of Psychology and Applied Cognitive Neuroscience Research Unit, Behavioural Basis of Health, Griffith Health Institute, Griffith University, Queensland, Australia.
[2] School of Optometry and Vision Sciences, University of Bradford, Bradford, West Yorkshire, United Kingdom.
[3] School of Engineering, Murdoch University, Murdoch, Western Australia.

ABSTRACT

The human ability to see colour is not important just from the viewpoint of visual science, but also has a central role in categorisation in cognition and information processing as well as in the development of naming in linguistics. Colour contributes to emotions, and has a role in group identification in social psychology and affects the connection between people, spaces and architecture. This chapter describes a rigorous psychophysical methodology along with resultant data that may further elucidate a solution to this problem: predicting what colours a person sees given a pattern of stimulation at the receptor array. The cone weights into the two chromatic and one luminance detection mechanisms previously obtained for each observer was compared with colour appearance measures after adaptation to an equal energy white. Both light levels and adaptation states were designed to best match a natural environment. Similar to the detection mechanisms, the red/green process of colour appearance opposes L and M cones, with no S cone input and the blue yellow process opposes S cones with a combination of L and M cones. The $L{:}M$ ratio in the latter process varied among observers, but was always similar to the $L{:}M$ ratio in a light/dark (brightness) process. The Opponent Processes themselves were best modelled by nonlinear combinations of cone contrasts. Unlike the concomitant detection mechanisms, the blue/yellow process best fit the data of two observers when a non-linear red-green opponent term was included in its cone weights. Finally, data were collected on which one of 11 basic colour

---

*E-mail: t.hine@griffith.edu.au

terms was used by each observer when presented with the stimuli. 'Red' proved to be the most stable colour both in terms of identification and stability of use both within and between observers. There was more variation in the application of blue/yellow colours. This suggests 'red' be used as the colour on signage for rapid and consistent identification and discrimination, and that blues and yellows be avoided. Through the use of a simple model using a random process of wiring among cells, it was shown how changes in materials can best be detected in the world, independent of both the colour and luminance of the light source. This has application in machine vision.

Keywords: Colour opponency, cone contrasts, colour names, nonlinearity.

INTRODUCTION

How humans perceive colour is important to a broad range of fields: graphic design, art, paint production, photography, television and computer graphics, lighting, architecture, interior decoration and textile and ceramics design and production. Within psychology, colour can elicit emotions: certain colours make the viewer 'feel good' (Suk and Irtel, 2009) and this connection is regularly exploited in advertising. Not being able to see a particular colour (for example, 'reddish' green) is important in philosophical argument (Nida-Rumelin and Suarez, 2009). Colour terms used to partition what is a continuum of sensation are pivotal in cognitive research on categories. In particular, is the usage of these terms due to some innate organisation of the visual system and brain, and hence universal, or are they arbitrarily applied like any other set of names (Agrillo and Roberson, 2009; Berlin and Kay, 1969)? Colour plays an active role in everyday life: not just in signals identifying different social groups (for example, uniforms), but also in the built environment in determining how people experience particular living spaces (Smith, 2008).

It may come as a surprise to those who are not familiar with the research area of colour vision, that laws determining colour appearance for an individual – what colour he or she sees – from the pattern of light impinging upon the eye are yet to be worked out. This is the conclusion of two recent reviews in the area of colour vision mechanisms and colour appearance (Eskew, 2009; Stockman and Brainard, 2009). Clearly, there are spatial and temporal interactions that complicate these laws: for example, colour contrast between abutting regions, interactions between borders and the interior colour, as well as colour constancy effects that influence how the colour of a particular region is seen dependent on the colour of other spatially remote regions (Shevell and Kingdom, 2008). However, even with a simple stimulus: for example, an isolated colour 'blob' on a neutral white background, there is a disconnection between mechanisms detecting the presence of the blob and colour appearance mechanisms.

There are three classes of cones: long-wavelength-sensitive or L cones, medium-wavelength-sensitive or M cones, and short-wavelength-sensitive or S cones, and the cone fundamentals have been psychophysically derived and known for some time now (Smith and Pokorny, 1972, 1975; Stockman and Sharpe, 2000; Vos and Walraven, 1971). Detection of a certain colour is not simply determined by the numbers of cones of each class in photoreceptor mosaic inputting into 'second-site mechanisms'. In fact, in people with otherwise normal colour vision, the ratio of the populations varies considerably: in males, the $L:M$ population ratio may vary from 2:1 to 1:2 (Carroll, McMahon, Neitz and Neitz., 2000).

Rather, it is the neural contribution, or 'weight' of each class of cones into the second-site mechanism that is the determining factor. This constitutes the classical cone opponency of the second-site mechanisms and the neural weights into those detection mechanisms have been determined for the three observers in the present study (Cole, Hine, and McIlhagga, 1993).

It was Hering (trans. 1964) in the nineteenth century who stated that all colour sensations are represented along two dimensions, called Opponent Processes: one of red-to-green appearance, and one of blue-to-yellow appearance; along with a third (non-opponent) dimension of luminance. Hurvich and Jameson (1955) modelled Opponent Processes as linear combinations of Judd's (1951) colour matching functions. As cone fundamentals became known (Dartnall, 1957; Smith and Pokorny, 1972, 1975; Stockman and Sharpe, 2000; Vos and Walraven, 1971), the Hurvich and Jameson model was commonly interpreted as showing that the red/green process results from a difference of L and M cone responses, and the blue/yellow process is a difference of S cone and some average of L and M cone responses (e.g. Boynton, 1979; Hurvich, 1981; Jameson and Hurvich, 1968). The non-opponent luminance mechanism (V_λ) is a sum of L and M cone responses, using the standard Smith and Pokorny cone fundamentals. A spectrally similar luminance response is obtained from magnocellular neurons and should be differentiated from the high-order perception of brightness, lightness, and darkness which involves the parvocellular pathway (Lennie, Pokorny, and Smith, 1993).

If the Opponent Processes are linear combinations of cone fundamentals, then all red/green neutral colours (those appearing neither red nor green) should fall on a straight line in a chromaticity diagram, as should all blue/yellow neutrals. There are many papers showing that this is not the case (Burns, Elsner, Pokorny, and Smith 1984; Larimer, Krantz, and Cicerone, 1974, 1975; Lee, Pizlo and Allenbach, 2007; Stockman and Brainard, 2009 (review); Wuerger, Atkinson, and Cropper, 2005), indicating some form of nonlinearity; minor for red/green (see Ingling, Barley, and Ghani, 1996 for an opposing view), but significant for blue/yellow. This is a problem for the hopes that linear Opponent Processes will explain colour appearance (Valberg, 2001). However, these nonlinearities may not be in the Opponent Processes themselves, since cones have a nonlinear response to light which varies with adaptation (Boynton and Whitten, 1970; Chappell and Naka, 1991; Schnapf, Nunn, Meister, and Baylor 1990). Most light will adapt the L and M cones to a similar degree, because their absorption spectra are so similar, but there can be large differences in the adaptive state of S cones compared to L and M cones. It may be, therefore, that nonlinearities in neutral colour appearance locii are due to nonlinearities in the cone response (Chichilnisky and Wandell, 1999). From these considerations, the hypothesis arises that the non-linearities in colour appearance are actually not due higher-order mechanisms as previously assumed, but are actually due to differences in the adaptive state of the cone classes.

To examine this hypothesis, in the current study the red/green and blue/yellow neutral points were examined when all cones were adapted to a white background and this adaptive state to the neutral white was constantly maintained. The spatial stimulus parameters and the observers themselves were the same as our previous study on detection threshold mechanisms in cone contrast space (Cole et al., 1993). This afforded a comparison: cone inputs to detection mechanisms from the earlier study with inputs to higher level processes derived from the current study.

We were also able to look at the luminance process indirectly by a heterochromatic brightness match in the same experiment. We found minor deviations from linearity in the red/green process, but the blue/yellow process was fundamentally nonlinear, even with stable cone adaptation (cf. Knoblauch and Shevell, 2001) and our data supports a model for the blue/yellow process like that of Burns et al. (1984) which includes an absolute value $|L - M|$ opponent term. We also found that the red/green process is almost identical for all observers, but the blue/yellow and brightness processes are not. For each observer, however, the L to M cone weights in the blue/yellow and brightness processes were very similar. Finally, the opponent processes found were not orthogonal combinations of cone responses. We conclude by suggesting that non-orthogonality has a sound computational foundation, despite the benefits of orthogonal mechanisms (Buchsbaum and Gottschalk, 1983).

Opponent Processes theory evolved from a consideration of colour categories, so we were also interested in how colour names matched the neutral locii. Of seven basic colour names: red, green, blue, yellow, purple, orange, pink (Boynton and Olson, 1990), only the usage of blue and green did not match our expectations.

METHOD

Observers and Apparatus

The authors GRC, TJH, and WHM served as observers in these experiments. All tested colour-normal using the Farnsworth-Munsell 100 hue test, and both GRC and TJH have been tested with a Nagel anomaloscope and found to have normal trichromacy. All are experienced observers and were aware of the purposes of the experiment. Subject TJH wore non-tinted prescription lenses. Stimuli were displayed on a Tektronix 690SR colour monitor controlled by a colour graphics system (PDI-James Sokoll Pty. Ltd, Milton, Queensland) driving red, green and blue guns through 12-bit DACs with a 60 Hz vertical refresh rate. The monitor was free viewed by the observer (whose head was stabilized in a chin and forehead rest) via a front-surfaced aluminium mirror which was used to deflect the viewing path away from the optical setup used in the laboratory for another experiment (Cole et al., 1993). The entire apparatus was contained within a light-tight fabric tunnel, and experiments were conducted in a darkened room. The spectral irradiances of the monitor's phosphors were measured by Bryan Powell at the ABC Laboratories, Sydney, Australia (Powell, 1989). The relationship between frame buffer value (fed into the DAC) and the phosphor radiance, measured with a United Detector Technologies Model 371 radiometer with a Model 260 PIN photodiode, was linearised with an inverse lookup table which achieved excellent gamma-correction ($R^2 = 0.996$ average for each gun).

The stimulus was a 2° diameter circular spot, blurred by convolution with a Gaussian of $\sigma = 0.25°$. This is the same spatial form as the stimulus used in earlier detection studies (Cole et al., 1993) with the same observers, and allowed for direct comparison with those prior results. Stimuli were transiently (between 200 ms and 1000 ms, temporal square wave) superimposed on top of a constant white adapting field of 5.83° diameter with Judd (1951) chromaticity coordinates $x = 0.33$, $y = 0.34$, and a luminance of 147 cdm^{-2}. This is very close to the CIE Standard D65 illuminant (0.31, 0.33) which represents 'white light'. Four small black fixation spots were placed on the adapting field in a diamond arrangement, $2°$ from the stimulus centre.

Representation of Stimuli

In the study of post-receptoral processes, a convenient representation of stimulus colour is in terms of cone responses. The cone response depends on the quantal catch of the cone when exposed to the stimulus, and on the adaptive state of the cone. When a dark-adapted cone is exposed to a steady light of intensity I, it first responds strongly, but the response then drops to around half the initial level and stabilises (Normann, Perlmann and Hallett, 1991). The cone has then become adapted to the light. If the light intensity is changed by a small amount ΔI, the response of the cone changes by an amount proportional to $\Delta I/I$ – Weber's Law. The constant of proportionality is independent of I for high retinal illumination (Schnapf et al., 1990). If the change ΔI is not transient, the cone will adapt to the new light intensity.

If our adapting field produces quantal catches L, M, and S, in the long-wave-length, medium-wave-length and short-wave-length cone classes, respectively, and the stimulus generates quantal catches $L + \Delta L$, $M + \Delta M$, and $S + \Delta S$ (so ΔL, ΔM, and ΔS are the changes in quantal catch due to the stimulus), then the cone contrasts of the stimulus are $\Delta L/L$, $\Delta M/M$, and $\Delta S/S$. These are proportional to the incremental cone responses produced by the stimulus (for small ΔL, ΔM, and ΔS), but the constants of proportionality for each cone are not known. However, our adapting field is 'unique white', so L, M, and S cone quantal catches on the adapting field are not biased as a function of intensity (Walraven and Werner, 1991), and thus the cones should all have similar constants of proportionality. The vector of cone contrasts ($\Delta L/L$, $\Delta M/M$, $\Delta S/S$) will be called the 'stimulus contrast'. This cone contrast space is a three dimensional colour space where the axes are the L, M, and S cone contrasts of the stimulus (Noorlander, Heuts, and Koenderink, 1981). Given that the adaption of the cones were maintained at an equal level for the duration of all experiments, and light levels enabled the cones to respond following Weber's law, other physiologically based colour spaces, like MacLeod and Boynton (1979), were deemed not as suitable as cone contrasts. Cone contrasts were computed by the methods described in Cole and Hine (1992), taking into account the spectral irradiances of monitor's phosphors, reflectance of the mirror and Smith and Pokorny (1975) cone fundamentals. We computed the Judd (1951) chromaticity values of stimuli from the spectral radiances.

Procedure

Colour Neutral Point Estimation. The experimental procedure was designed to precisely locate a number of neutral points for each observer. As noted above, this was done in a Weberian regime of high background illumination where the adaptive state of each cone class was maintained at a constant and equal level (see below). Four neutral points for each chromatic Opponent Process were accurately estimated as this suffices to reject a linear model.

Two of the four neutral points were lighter or darker than the adapting field, and two were approximately equiluminant. Four achromatic light/dark neutral points were also determined using the same method. These were distributed around the hue circle (one yellow, one violet, one red and one green). The following description of the task for blue/yellow mechanism is provided for clarity of specific detail. Procedure for each other mechanism was entirely analogous.

Stimulus presentation began after 90 s of adaptation to the white background. Stimuli were on screen for at least 200 ms up to a maximum of 1 s until the subject responded: 'blue', 'yellow', or 'neither' by pressing one of three coded buttons on a subject response box. The subject then readapted to the white field for at least the same amount of time as the stimulus was present, before the next stimulus was displayed. In a single experiment, stimulus contrasts were selected from a line in cone contrast space as described above (see Figure 1). Contrasts at one end of the chosen line appeared clearly blue, and at the other end appeared clearly yellow. At some intermediate point, stimuli are neither blue nor yellow, though there may been residual red or green. This was a blue/yellow neutral point.

At least seven equally spaced points along the line were selected as the contrasts to be displayed. These points can be numbered 1,2, ...i... n, starting from the blue end of the line. If the current stimulus had contrast index of i, the next stimulus could have contrast index of i, or $i + 1$, or $i + 2$, selected at random. Thus the stimulus contrasts tested in each run tracked along the line. When the end of the line (index n) was reached, the direction of this tracking was reversed.

The tracking was always from blue to yellow then back to blue, and this cycle was repeated six to eight times and all points along the line were displayed a number of times. This tracking was used because the regular repetition of more saturated colours near indices 1 and n made observer responses more consistent near the neutral point. As well, unpredictable jumps between one contrast and the next prevented the observer from counting to a neutral point.

The results from at least four experiments, using the same contrast line, were used to estimate a single neutral point. All four experiments for one neutral point were completed within two days. Most of the neutral points were retested after one month.

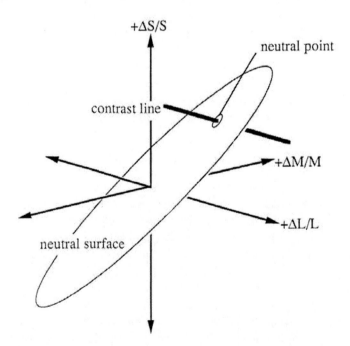

Figure 1. Cone contrast space: the axes of this space plot the L, M, and S cone contrasts. A neutral surface of an opponent process is shown, together with a line of contrasts that crosses it.

Colour Names. In the final experiment, we recorded colour names for stimuli in cone contrast space. In these experiments, the stimulus was displayed for 1 s, and the observer simply said what colour they saw. This was recorded by the experimenter, who was blind to the stimulus and its cone contrasts. Stimuli were always displayed at the maximum contrast of the monitor, and selected at random from 140 predetermined directions in cone contrast space displayed in two sessions of 70 each. After the data was recorded, the colour names were reduced, where necessary, to one of the basic terms red, green, blue, yellow, violet, purple, orange, brown, white, black, or grey (Boynton and Olson, 1990). No brown was found in the sample, but ochre and olive green did appear (reduced when necessary to orange and green hues, respectively).

RESULTS

Data Analysis for Neutral Points

We assumed that the response of each opponent process was linear near the neutral point, that is, it possessed a good first-order Taylor approximation around the neutral point with no assumption as to its linearity anywhere else. Let the linear response of the opponent process be given by

$$\text{response} = n_L \Delta L/L + n_M \Delta ML/M + n_S \Delta S/S + e \qquad (1)$$

where e is a normally-distributed noise term, $(\Delta L/L, \Delta M/M, \Delta S/S)$ is the stimulus contrast, and n_L, n_M, and n_S are the normalised neural weightings applied to each cone class. We also assumed that the observer's perceived colour depended on the response and an internal criterion k, such that the colour was 'blue' if response $> k$, 'yellow' if response $< -k$, and 'neither' otherwise. The neutral point is the contrast that returns a zero average response. If the variance in e is comparable to the criterion k, the same stimulus contrast may elicit different perceptions at different times. Note that this does not violate Opponent Process theory which only says that opponent colours cannot be perceived simultaneously.

As stimulus contrasts fall on a line, they can be written as $(\Delta L/L, \Delta M/M, \Delta S/S) = (l_0, m_0, s_0) + t.(l_d, m_d, s_d)$, for initial point (l_0, m_0, s_0), normalised direction vector (l_d, m_d, s_d), and distance t. Accordingly, the response in (1) may be rewritten as

$$\text{response} = \beta(t - t_n) + e \qquad (2)$$

where $\beta = n_L.l_d + n_M.m_d + n_S.s_d$. This expresses the response in terms of the distance t along the contrast line from the initial point. The average response is zero when $t = t_n$, so the neutral point is $(l_0, m_0, s_0) + t_n.(l_d, m_d, s_d)$. From this equation we can work out likelihoods of observer responses: 'blue', 'yellow' or 'neither' for each value of t, as a function of parameters β and t, and criterion k, and so estimate these parameters from the observer's frequency of the 3AFC responses by maximum likelihood (for example, Bulmer, 1979).

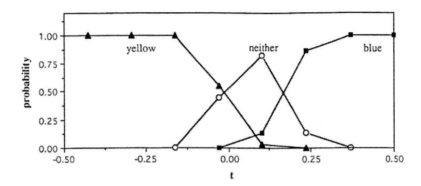

Figure 2. Data from an experiment on the blue/yellow process. The curves give the frequency of observer response as a function of the distance, t, along the line in cone-contrast space (Equation (2)). Some stimuli elicit 'blue' or 'yellow' responses on different presentations.

In every instance, this model fitted the data extremely well, sometimes approaching the best fit possible, and errors for the neutral point parameter were very small. An illustration of the data from track through a line in cone contrast space is shown in Figure 2.

Opponent Process Mechanisms

The left hand column of Figure 3 shows cone contrasts of red/green and blue/yellow neutral points for each of the three observers. The right hand column shows the Judd (1951) chromaticities of these same points, together with the spectral locus and the 690SR monitor gamut. The neutral points of a linear Opponent Process should lie on a plane through the origin of cone contrast space. The normal to this neutral plane is a vector (n_L, n_M, n_S), which is also the relative cone weightings of the Opponent Process, as in Equation (1). We can fit a plane to a set of neutral points (L_i, M_i, S_i), $i = 1...m$, by finding the unit vector (n_L, n_M, n_S) that minimises the sum of squares:

$$\sum_{i=1}^{m}(n_L L_i + n_M M_i + n_S S_i)^2 / \sigma_i^2 \tag{3}$$

where σ_i^2 is the variance of the i–th neutral point estimate. The minimum of this expression is approximately chi-squared with $m - 2$ degrees of freedom, and measures the total squared deviation from a plane. The fit of this model to our data is generally poor; only the red/green neutral points for observer TJH fall on a plane. These poor fits, however, are largely due to the variation in neutral points over one month. Differences between repeated neutral point estimates are significantly larger than the variances of individual estimates σ_i^2, so the latter are poor measures of neutral point variability. To overcome this problem, we compared the residual sum-of-squares from a linear model with the residual sum-of-squares of the best possible fit (which uses the mean of two repeated neutral points as an estimate of them both), using an F ratio. A model which is not significantly worse than the best possible fit is acceptable. These *F* ratios are shown in Table 1. This procedure improves the fit of the linear model, but it is still not statistically acceptable in most cases.

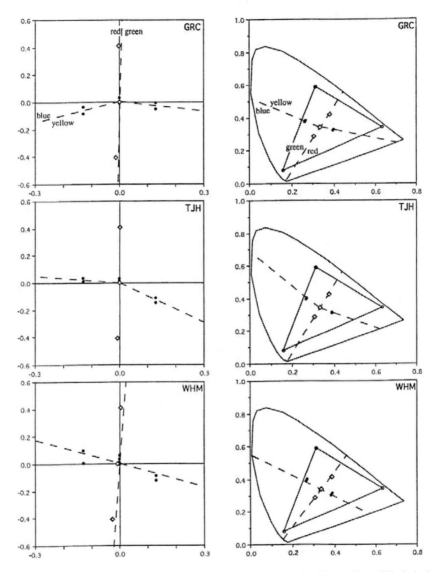

Figure 3. Neutral Points. The left hand column plots neutral points for blue/yellow (filled circles) and red/green (empty diamonds) projected onto the plane defined by $\Delta L/L + \Delta M/M + \Delta S/S = 0$. The x axis is roughly red-to-green; the y axis is roughly yellow-to-blue. A coordinate (x,y) on this plane has cone contrast x(−0.7071, 0.7071, 0) + y(−0.408, −0.408, 0.816). Data near the origin actually lie above or below this plane. The lines give neutral locii. The blue/yellow neutral locii are from a nonlinear model (equation 4) for subjects GRC and TJH, and from a linear model (equation 1) for subject WHM. Red/green neutral locii are all from a linear model (equation 1). SEM bars are about the same size as the plot symbols. The right hand column plots the Judd (1951) chromaticities of neutral points and modelled neutral locii. Also shown is the spectral locus and the 690SR monitor gamut (the large triangle).

Whether or not the red/green process is linear, the best linear fit can be thought of as a first approximation to the Opponent Process (that is, the linear term in a Taylor-series expansion). The best linear fit to the red/green neutral points is shown in Figure 3. It is almost identical for all observers, and implies that the red/green process is a balanced opposition of L and M cone contrasts. The red/green neutral locus lies very close to the S cone contrast axis (that is, the tritanopic confusion line), indicating little S cone influence on red/green perceptions, contrary to other cancellation studies (Burns et al., 1984; Hurvich and Jameson 1955; Knoblauch and Shevell, 2001; Shevell and Humanski, 1988), and cardinal directions (Krauskopf, Williams, and Heeley, 1982), but consistent with Wuerger et al. (2005) as well as our own detection studies using the same observers and same stimulus (Cole et al. 1993).

The blue/yellow neutral points are not planar, except (just) for observer WHM. The blue/yellow neutral points plotted in Figure 3, like those of Burns et al. (1984), can be described by a linear model augmented with a nonlinear opponent term:

$$\text{response} = n_L \Delta L/L + n_M \Delta M/M + n_S \Delta S/S + n_A \bullet \left| \Delta L/L - \Delta M/M \right| \qquad (4)$$

where $\left| ... \right|$ is the absolute value. This model, which has $m - 3$ degrees of freedom, fits the data of both GRC and TJH. The neutral locus predicted from the nonlinear blue/yellow model are plotted in Figure 3, and the F-ratios of this model are also shown in Table 1. with statistical significance.

Heterochromatic Brightness Matching

The technique for finding colour neutrals can be applied to judgements of light/dark. In this case, the subject is asked to say whether the chromatic stimulus is lighter or darker than the white adapting field.

The response may be governed by a heterochromatic brightness mechanism (Wagner and Boynton, 1972), but since the judgements are based on stimuli contiguous with the adapting reference point, there is the possibility that the observer will employ a criterion akin to the minimally-distinct border (Boynton and Kaiser, 1968).

We found that in all cases a linear model (Equation 1) was an acceptable fit to the light/dark neutral points (Table 1). We computed spectral sensitivity curves for our light/dark mechanism, again on the assumption that ratio of quantal catches in each cone class due to the background field was unaltered during the course of the experiment (Figure 4). Above about 470 nm, all curves are close to V_λ, even though there is considerable variation in cone weightings.

Below 470 nm, the curves diverge, showing more S cone input than V_λ, (which has none: Smith and Pokorny, 1975, Stockman and Sharpe, 2000). These differences could be explained by large variations in macular pigment density (Sharpe, Stockman, Knau and Jägle,1998; Wyszecki and Stiles, 1967, p. 218), but it is more likely that the S cone contribution is an intrusion of a brightness judgement.

Table 1. *F*-ratios for model fits

	red/green	blue/yellow	blue/yellow	light/dark
	linear	linear	nonlinear	linear
GRC	126.42[a]	30.99[b]	1.25[c]	2.35[b]
TJH	3.73[a]	7.78[b]	1.23[c]	1.00[b]
WHM	19.57[b]	2.90[b]	11.22[c]	3.34[b]

[a] No repeat measures of red/green neutrals available. This is a chi-squared variate with two degrees of freedom: $\chi^2(2) = 5.99$ for $p = 0.05$. [b] F-ratio with (6, 4) degrees of freedom, comparing model fit with best possible fit. $F(6, 4) = 6.16$ for $p = .05$. [c] F-ratio with (5, 4) degrees of freedom, comparing model fit with best possible fit. $F(5, 4) = 6.26$ for $p = .05$.

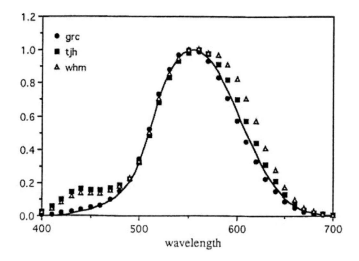

Figure 4. The spectral sensitivity of the light/dark process extrapolated from neutral locii. The continuous curve shows V_λ for comparison.

Individual Results Compared

The linear components (n_L, n_M, n_S) of the red/green, blue/yellow and light/dark processes for each of the three observers are also listed in Table 2. The red/green process is almost the same for all observers and each is within 2% of the same components estimated from the detection data (Cole et al., 1993).

On the other hand, the L to M cone ratios in the blue/yellow and light/dark mechanisms vary. For each observer, however, the L to M ratio for each of the blue/yellow and light/dark mechanisms is very similar. For the light/dark mechanism, these ratios are substantially different from the detection ratios, except that observer WHM in both cases has a n_L of close to 1 (0.94 for detection, 0.997 for the current brightness estimation data). The results are closer when considering blue/yellow: for example, GRC has a small n_L compared to the other observers in both cases (–0.38 for detection, –0.34 for the current chromatic neutralisation data, in both data sets TJH and WHM's components are close to –0.75).

Table 2. Cone Weights for Post-Receptoral Channels

Subject	Channel	nL	nM	nS	nA
GRC	red/green	0.70	-0.71	0.01	-
	blue/yellow	-0.33	-0.53	0.78	-
	blue/yellow nonlinear	-0.34	-0.51	0.79	0.24
	light/dark	0.77	0.64	0.00	-
TJH	red/green	0.70	-0.71	0.01	-
	blue/yellow	-0.73	0.05	0.68	-
	blue/yellow nonlinear	-0.71	0.01	0.71	0.25
	light/dark	0.97	0.24	0.09	-
WHM	red/green	0.69	0.73	-0.03	-
	blue/yellow	-0.75	0.04	0.67	-
	blue/yellow nonlinear	-0.74	0.03	0.67	0.12
	light/dark	0.997	0.03	0.06	-

Note. The linear weights have been normalised to 1: $nL2 + nM2 + nS2 = 1$. The parameters nL, nM, and nS, for the red/green, blue/yellow linear, and light/dark processes are defined in equation (1). The parameters nL, nM, nS and nA for the blue/yellow nonlinear model are defined in equation (4).

This pattern of variation among observers is unlikely to be the result of variations in pre-retinal filtering (by the lens, the macular pigment, or any other source), nor is it likely to be a result of cone pigment polymorphism (Neitz and Jacobs, 1990). Of course, the true cone contrasts for each observer may deviate from our nominal contrasts because of these factors, so the cone contrast axes for an individual observer may not precisely match up with the nominal axes.

A linear transformation, incorporating all the effects listed above, can be applied to each observer's axes to align them with the nominal ones (Smith and Pokorny, 1995). The same transformation must be applied to the entire observer's data and this is also a function of the primaries constituting the stimuli. If the differences between say, TJH and GRC are due to the above factors, a linear transformation of GRC's data will bring it into line with TJH's. Rotating GRC's data by 40 degrees will bring the light/dark and blue/yellow neutrals into register with TJH, but such a major transformation (unless contrived and unrealistic) will almost certainly misalign their red/green neutrals. In any case, the factors listed above, unless taken to extremes, will rotate the L and M coordinates by only a few degrees using our RGB phosphor primaries (cf Cole et al., 1993). Slightly more rotation, around ten degrees, can be obtained in the S cone axis as the macular pigments density spectrum is confined to the shorter wavelengths (Stockman and Sharpe, 2000).

Individual differences in Opponent Processes mean that some colours are seen as, say, blue by one observer, but yellow by another. Although the difference in colour responses between observers is clear, the colours being used are not saturated and, unless forced to, observers would not usually ascribe any particular blue or yellow to them. When observers do, however, they disagree.

Colour Names

The results are shown in Figure 5 on the same axes as the left hand column of Figure 3. Each sector represents a separate colour; white, black, and grey stimuli have been ignored. Two observers, GRC and WHM, have adopted a similar criterion for colour names. The third, TJH, did not use violet and uses colour terms over a wider range than GRC and WHM. In TJH's results, orange (part yellow) and purple (part blue) overlap. This does not contradict opponent process theory, since no stimulus in the overlap was simultaneously described as both orange and purple. Instead, it appears that the terms 'orange' and 'purple' may have been applied randomly to stimuli with very little content of either. This is consistent with TJH's broader use of all colour names.

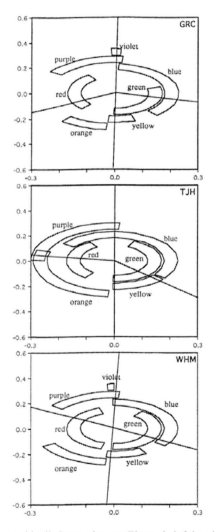

Figure 5. Colour names and neutral locii. Same plane as Figure 3, left hand column. Each colour name applies to a sector depicted by its outer rim. The different distances from the centre are only for clarity. The elliptical shape of the sectors is due to unequal scales on the two axes. Neutral locii are replotted from Figure 3.

The relationship of colour names to the Opponent Processes was as expected, especially in the case of 'red', whose usage seemed to be similar across observers and stable with respect to Opponent processes obtained from both the detection work and in the current study. The terms 'blue' and 'green' did not align with the underlying processes as well as the others. 'Blue' was applied to stimuli which activate both the blue and the green opponent processes. 'Green' was applied to many stimuli which activate both green and yellow opponent processes.

Certainly the boundary between these colour terms were not clear and consistent among our observers and is in line with data by Malkoc, Kay and Webster (2005). In the current study, the observers were free to choose their own colour names. As English lacks specific and widely used terms for blue-green and yellow-green, the names 'blue' and 'green' may be doing double duty. Unique blue, lying on the red/green neutral locus, was generally described as violet.

DISCUSSION

Comparisons with Selected Previous Studies

The red/green process found in these experiments has almost no S cone input and is almost exactly that predicted from detection studies under similar conditions with the same observers (Cole et al. 1993). Results indicating S-cone into the red/green detection mechanisms should be treated with caution (Stockman and Brainard, 2009), however there a number of studies demonstrating S-cone input into red/green appearance (Burns et al., 1984; Ingling et al., 1996; Shevell and Humanski, 1988; Stockman and Brainard, 2009 (review); Wei and Shevell, 1995). There are differences in methodology.

For example, we kept cones adapted to an equal-energy white point within the Weberian regime (about 1000 Td), while Burns et al. (1984) maintained the total luminance at a very low level (20 Td). This can cause large differences in cone adaptation for chromaticities far from white. If two cones have different adaptive states, the same cone contrast may result in different cone responses, depending on retinal illumination (Schnapf et al., 1990). The S cone influence on red/green in Burns et al., near the S cone copunctal point, may be a corollary of this. Overall, the nearly perfect agreement we have between the red/green neutral locus and detection mechanisms is confined to our equal-energy white adapting fields of high luminance.

Our data shows a postreceptoral nonlinearity in the blue/yellow process, in accord with, for example Werner and Wooten (1979), Burns et al. (1984) and Lee et al. (2007), yet detection studies of blue/yellow do not show any large nonlinearity (Cole et al. 1993; Thornton and Pugh, 1983). The reason for this may be simple. In detection studies, most stimuli over a large range of spatio-temporal parameters are detected by the red/green process. To observe detection by blue/yellow, one must use stimuli which are almost neutral for red/green. This reduces the influence of the nonlinear term in the blue/yellow process, making it appear linear.

Neutral colours and neutral surfaces are closely related to cardinal directions (Knoblauch and Shevell, 2001; Krauskopf et al. 1982). A cardinal direction in colour space activates one, and only one, postreceptoral mechanism. If there are three postreceptoral mechanisms, then a cardinal direction must not activate two of them, and so it must lie on both their neutral surfaces. Hence the cardinal direction of one mechanism is the intersection of the neutral surfaces of the other two mechanisms. This means that a cardinal direction is not determined by the mechanism it activates, but by those mechanisms it does not (Stockman and Brainard, 2009).

Our results imply cardinal directions broadly in agreement with other results, but the difference in colour spaces, nonlinearities, and variations in our observers, preclude a detailed comparison. For example, the study of DeValois, DeValois, Switkes and Mahon (1997) used a neutral background upon which hue rating task was conducted. Unlike the current study, they found that the red/green unique hue ratings did not correspond to the standard red/green Opponent Process. However, they assumed that the cone inputs into the first-site mechanisms were fixed for each observer and hence used a MacLeod and Boynton (1979) cone-based space (where the axes are opponent mechanisms) to represent their stimuli. We compared our results to actual estimates of detection mechanism inputs which were different for each observer. DeValois et al. (1997) used a five point rating scale of how 'reddish' or 'greenish', for example, a particular stimulus was. Our response was simply the judgment of the presence or absence of a hue. As far as colour naming was concerned, the red/green naming was again in line with the underling detection mechanisms, especially red. On the other hand, work by Cao, Pokorny, and Smith (2005) on the Boynton and Olson (1990) colour terms suggest that the colour indicated by the term 'red' has some S-cone input.

Explaining Individual Differences in Colour and Luminance

A striking result is the significant difference in the blue/yellow process between observers: two colour-normal people may perceive different colours under exactly the same photometric conditions. It is most unlikely, however, that this has any operational significance. Natural chromaticities cluster around the red/green neutral locus (Burton and Moorhead, 1987), and the differences in blue/yellow are most prominent far from this locus. In real scenes, therefore, there is only a small chance that observers will disagree about what colour an object is. For each observer, the blue/yellow and light/dark processes have similar L to M cone ratios. This is apparent in Table 2, where the plotted weight vectors for these processes are almost diametrically opposite each other. There are no individual variations in the red/green process. This pattern of variation has been observed in other studies: while luminance judgements may vary between observers (due perhaps to varying L and M cone populations) the spectral colour which is equilibrium yellow (i.e. red/green neutral) does not (Pokorny, Smith, and Wesner, 1991). This pattern may be explained by the hit-or-miss hypothesis (Lennie, Haake, and Williams, 1989; Paulus and Kroger-Paulus, 1983). Consider three such receptive fields (Figure 6), which have input into the centre from a single cone and antagonistic surround from a representative sample of cones. If p_L and p_M are the frequencies of L and M cones in the retina, then there are p_L receptive fields with L cone centres, and p_M receptive fields with M cone centres. The response of these idealised receptive fields to uniform fields of colour is: centre cone response – surround (average) cone response = centre cone contrast – ($p_L.\Delta L/L + p_M.\Delta M/M$). When $p_L + p_M = 1$, this simplifies to $p_M.(\Delta L/L -$

$\Delta M/M$) for L-centre cells, and $p_L.(\Delta M/M - \Delta L/L)$ for M centre cells. If the red/green signal arises from an aggregate of these cells, we must weight their influence according to the frequency they occur. Thus the influence from L-centre cells is $p_L.p_M.(\Delta L/L - \Delta M/M)$, and M-centre is $p_M.p_L.(\Delta M/M - \Delta L/L)$. Antagonistic interaction between groups of these cells will produce a red/green signal with evenly weighted L and M cone contributions, regardless of the $L{:}M$ population ratio in the retina. For different reasons, this outcome has also been predicted as the second stage of the DeValois and DeValois (1993) model. Both the DeValois and DeValois model and our current one can be extended to explain recently discovered posterior inferotemporal cortex cells that seem to respond to uniques hues (Neitz and Neitz, 2008; Stoughton and Conway, 2008): here, there must be neural comparison of outputs from each of the red/green and blue/yellow colour appearance mechanisms. If a light/dark process is built from a combination of ON and OFF cells, without regard to their centre cone, the response to coloured gratings and edges will reflect the relative proportions of L and M cones in the retina. For instance, a classic light/dark simple cell consisting of a row of ON-centre cells, and an adjacent row of OFF-cells, will have L centre and M centre cells occurring with frequencies p_L and p_M; the response to coloured borders in its receptive field will be $p_L\Delta L/L + p_M\Delta M/M$. The blue/yellow process may be built from cells with an S cone in the centre, but random antagonistic connections to L and M cones (perhaps in a surround, though not necessarily). In this case, the response to chromatic stimuli will be $\Delta S/S - p_L\Delta L/L - p_M\Delta M/M$, which has the same $L{:}M$ ratio as the light/dark process.

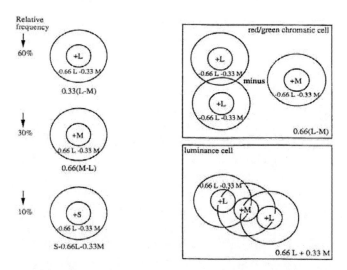

Figure 6. Receptive fields and Opponent Processes. On the left are three kinds of "hit-or-miss" receptive fields, in a retina with L : M : S ratio of 6:3:1. It is assumed that S cones rarely appear in the surround. The relative frequency and chromatic opponency of each receptive field are given. On the right are two channels constructed from these receptive fields. The red/green channel opposes L and M centre cells in their relative frequencies. This yields a balanced opposition of L and M input. The luminance channel sums L and M centre receptive fields without regard to the centre cone. On average, this produces an L:M bias that reflects the ratio of L and M cone populations in the retina. The blue/yellow channel (not shown) is assumed to be very similar to the retinal receptive field, and also reflects this L:M ratio of the retina.

Applications

Wiring up the retina to 'see' surface reflectance. It is often supposed that the colour mechanisms exist to represent changes in reflectance (Rubin and Richards, 1982), that is, a material change in an object. If so, they must be insensitive to changes in illuminant intensity, such as caused by a shadow. This is useful in both artificial and natural vision systems. From the models outlines in the previous section, we can build up a retinal array responsive to surface reflectance.

In cone contrast space, a change in illuminant intensity shifts cone contrasts along a line roughly parallel to the achromatic vector (1,1,1), so the colour mechanisms should be insensitive to such changes. This is the case in our data; the achromatic vector lies on the neutral surfaces of both colour processes (which makes it the cardinal direction for luminance). This achromatic vector is sampled by a light-dark mechanism which is used for acuity judgements. It must sample the retina at the maximum resolution, and so it will receive input from all cones regardless of their type (this is so for L and M cones only; optical aberrations mean that S cones have poor spatial resolution, so they should participate at a rate lower than their population frequency). Thus to achieve optimal acuity, a mechanism will have a cone bias which mirrors the relative cone frequencies in the retina. This will make the light/dark mechanism sensitive to changes in reflectance as well as just changes in luminance, but this need have no effect on computations based on luminance information. This is demonstrated by looking at a black and white photo taken through a coloured filter. Provided there is sufficient contrast, there is no difficulty in interpreting it. The fact that L and M cone quantal catches are highly correlated in natural scenes (Burton and Moorhead, 1987) helps to reduce the effects of cone biases in a light/dark mechanism. With the luminance mechanism constrained to sample all cones, and the colour mechanisms constrained to be insensitive to the achromatic vector, there is no freedom to make them all orthogonal. Within these restrictions, Buchsbaum and Gottschalk's (1983) theory still implies that the two colour mechanisms should be orthogonal to each other, or that one colour mechanism should be orthogonal to the luminance mechanism. As this is not so, perhaps limitations on the retinal receptive fields (the hit/miss hypothesis detailed in the previous section) preclude this ideal.

Colour in everyday life. As opposed to virtually all of the previous studies, our colour appearance and equilibrium data were gathered under luminance levels encountered in normal viewing conditions, rather than taking place under very low light levels in dark laboratories. In the normal environment, the multiplicity of colours in the visual field that are constantly changing on the retinae due to refixations so the cone classes are being adapted to all spectral energies: a neutral white. As well, light levels in most interior settings and certainly outdoors in natural light are powerful enough to maintain these cone classes in the Weberian regime. Each of these naturally occurring circumstances has been reproduced, as best we can, within our methodology. We can then, therefore, apply our data with confidence to everyday life.

When compared with other commonly used colours (Boynton and Olson, 1990), it is clear that 'red' colour appearance and its application in naming is the most stable, least likely to be confused with other colours. This is true for the same normal viewer at different times, and among normal viewers. This colour could be used where its correct identification is paramount: in warning signs at work and in driving environments. Red's stability is due to the fact that its colour appearance is directly related to the red/green chromatic detection mechanism. The latter has fixed cone inputs that were virtually identical for everyone and if the viewer is not red/green colour blind, then the percept of red is the same for everyone. On the other hand, there is considerable intra- and interpersonal variation in the application of colours along the other, blue-yellow chromatic axis. Such colours ought to be avoided when rapid and unambiguous identification is required.

CONCLUSION

This chapter has shown how colour detection data derived from the application of a rigorous methodology can be used to predict colour appearance and colour naming, but only for certain colours. The conditions under which these data were collected were not limited to unnatural, laboratory-only situations. Rather, they involved high levels of illumination encountered in natural settings, ensuring similar levels of functioning of the cone mosaic that occurs in day-to-day viewing. Under these conditions, the appearance of red was the most stable and consistent from all other colours and predicted from a low-level linear detection mechanism identical among observers: a $1: -1$ opponency of the L and M cone responses. On the other hand, blue/yellow judgments showed much more variability among observers and were best modelled by non-linear combination of L, M and S cone responses. Finally, the brightness judgments for each observer involved S cone input (unlike luminance) and a L and M cone input similar to the bue/yellow detection mechanisms. Overall, we concluded that red was the best colour to use to ensure all observers have a similar percept. As well, a model of the colour opponent and brightness mechanisms derived from our data was shown to be useful at discrimination of changes in material independent of colour and brightness of the light source.

REFERENCES

Agrillo, C., and Roberson, D. (2009). Colour language and colour cognition: Brown and Lenneberg revisited. *Visual Cognition, 17,* 412 – 430.

Berlin, B., and Kay, P. (1969). *Basic color terms: Their universality and evolution.* Berkeley, CA: University of California Press.

Boynton, R. (1979). *Human color vision.* New York: Holt Rinehart and Winston.

Boynton, R. M.. and Kaiser, P.K. (1968). Vision: The additivity law made to work for heterochromatic photometry with bipartite fields. *Science, 161,* 366–368.

Boynton, R.M., and Olson, C. X. (1990). Salience of chromatic basic colour terms confirmed by three measures. *Vision Research, 30,* 1311–1317.

Boynton, R. M., and Whitten, D. N. (1970). Visual adaptation in monkey cones: Recordings of late receptor potentials. *Science, 170,* l423–1425.

Buchsbaum, G., and Gottschalk, A. (1983). Trichromacy, opponent colours coding, and optimum colour information transmission in the retina. *Proceedings of the Royal Society of London B, 220,* 89–113

Bulmer, M.G. (1979). *Principles of statistics.* New York: Dover Publications.

Burns, S. A., Elsner, A. E., Pokorny, J., and Smith, V. C. (1984). The Abney effect: Chromaticity coordinates of unique and other constant hues. *Vision Research, 24,* 479–489.

Burton, G. J., and Moorhead, I.R. (1987). Color and spatial structure in natural scenes. *Applied Optics, 26,* 157–170.

Cao, D., Pokorny, J., and Smith, V. C. (2005). Associating color appearance with the cone chromaticity space. *Vision Research, 45,* 1929–1934.

Carroll, C., McMahon, M., Neitz, L. and Neitz, J. (2000). Flicker-photometric electroretinogram estimates of L:M cone photoreceptor ratio in men with photopigment spectra derived from genetics. *Journal of the Optical Society of America A, 17,* 499–509.

Chappell, R. L. and Naka, K–I. (1991). Sensitivity transformation for vertebrate vision. *Visual Neuroscience, 6,* 371–374.

Chichilnisky, E. J. and Wandell, B. A. (1999) Trichromatic opponent color classification. *Vision Research 39,* 3444–3458.

Cole, G. R. and Hine, T. J. (1992). Computation of cone contrasts for color vision research. *Behaviour Research Methods, Instruments, and Computers, 24,* 22–27.

Cole, G. R., Hine, T. J., and McIlhagga, W. (1993). Detection mechanisms in *L, M* and *S* cone contrast space. *Journal of the Optical Society of America A, 10,* 38 – 51.

DeValois, R. L., DeValois, K. K., Switkes, E., and Mahon, L. (1997). Hue scaling of isoluminant and cone-specific lights. *Vision Research, 37,* 885 – 897.

DeValois, R. L., and DeValois, K. K. (1993). A multi-stage color model. *Vision Research, 33,* 1053 – 1065.

Eskew, R. T., Jr. (2009). Higher order color mechanisms: A critical review. *Vision Research, 49,* 2686 – 2704.

Dartnall, H. J. A. (1957). *The visual pigments.* New York: Wiley.

Hering, E. (1964). *Outlines of a theory of the light sense.* (L.M. Hurvich and D. Jameson, Trans.). Cambridge,Mass: Harvard University Press.

Hurvich, L. M. and Jameson, D. (1955). Some quantitative aspects of an opponent–colors theory II: Brightness, saturation, and hue in normal and dichromatic vision. *Journal of the Optical Society of America, 45,* 602–616.

Hurvich, L. M. (1981). *Color vision.* Sunderland, Mass: Sinauer Associates.

Ingling, C. R. Jr., Barley, J. P., and Ghani, N. (1996). Chromatic content of spectral lights. *Vision Research, 36,* 2537–2551.

Jameson, D. and Hurvich, L.M. (1968). Opponent response functions related to measured cone photopigments. *Journal of the Optical Society of America, 58,* 429–430.

Judd, D. E. (1951). Colorimetry and artificial daylight (Tech. Comm. 7). In *Proceedings of the Twelfth Session of the Commission Internationale de l'Eclairage: Vol. 1* Stockholm.

Knoblauch, K. and Shevell, S. K. (2001). Relating cone signals to color appearance: Failure of monotonicity in yellow/blue. *Visual Neuroscience, 18,* 901 – 906.

Krauskopf, J., Williams D. R., and Heeley D. W. (1982). Cardinal directions of color space. *Vision Research, 22,* 1123–1131.

Larimer, J., Krantz, D. H. and Cicerone, C. M. (1974). Opponent-process additivity—I: Red/green equilibria. *Vision Research, 14,* 1127 – 1140.

Larimer, J., Krantz, D. H. and Cicerone, C. M. (1975). Opponent-process additivity—II: Yellow/blue equilibria and nonlinear models. *Vision Research, 15,* 723–731.

Lee, B-S., Pizlo, Z., and Allenbach, J. P. (2007). Characterization of red-green and blue-yellow opponent channels. *Journal of Imaging Science and Technology, 51,* 23 – 33.

Lennie, P., Haake, P. W., and Williams D. R. (1989). The design of chromatically opponent receptive fields. In M.S. Landy and J.A. Movshon (Eds.), *Computational models of visual processing* (pp. 71–82), Cambridge, Mass: MIT Press.

Lennie, P., Pokorny, J., and Smith, V. C. (1993). Luminance. *Journal of the Optical Society of America A, 10,* 1283–1293.

MacLeod, D. I. A., and Boynton, R. M. (1979). Chromaticity diagram showing cone excitation by stimuli of equal luminance. *Journal of the Optical Society of America, 69,* 1183–1185.

Malkoc, G., Kay, P. and Webster, M. A. (2005). Variations in normal colour vision. IV. Binary hues and hue scaling. *Journal of the Optical Society of America A, 22,* 2154 – 2168.

Neitz, J. and Jacobs, G.H. (1990). Polymorphism in normal human color vision and its mechanism. *Vision Research, 30,* 621–636.

Neitz, J, and Neitz, M. (2008). Colour vision: The wonder of hue. *Current Biology, 18,* R700 – R702.

Nida-Rumelin, M. and Suarez, J. (2009) Reddish green: A challenge for modal claims about phenomenal structure. *Philosophy and Phenomenological Research, 78,* 346 – 391.

Noorlander, C., Heuts, M. J. G., and Koenderink, J. J. (1981). Sensitivity to spatiotemporal combined luminance and chromaticity contrast. *Journal of the Optical Society of America, 71,* 453–459.

Normann, R. A., Perlman, I., and Hallett, P. E. (1991). Cone photoreceptor physiology and cone contributions to colour vision. In J.R. Cronly–Dillon (Series Ed) and P. Gouras (Vol. Ed.), *Vision and visual dysfunction: Vol. 6. The perception of colour.* London: MacMillan.

Paulus, W. and Kroger-Paulus, A. (1983). A new concept of retinal colour coding. *Vision Research, 23,* 529–540.

Pokorny, J, Smith, V. C., and Wesner, M. F. (1991). Variability in cone populations and implications. In A. Valberg and B. B. Lee (Eds.), *From pigments to perceptions* (pp. 23–34). New York: Plenum Press.

Powell, B. (1989). *Colorimetric report on the Tektronix 690SR for the Optical Science, A.N.U.* (Report 890001TV). Sydney, Australia: Federal Television Engineering, Australian Broadcasting Corporation.

Rubin, J. M. and Richards, W. A. (1982). Color vision and image intensities: When are changes material? *Biological Cybernetics, 45,* 215–226.

Schnapf, J. L., Nunn, B. J., Meister, M., and Baylor, D.A. (1990). Visual transduction in cones of the monkey *macaca fascicularis. Journal of Physiology, 427,* 681–713.

Sharpe, L. T., Stockman, A., Knau, H., and Jägle, H. (1998). Macular pigment densities derived from central and peripheral spectral sensitivity differences. *Vision Research, 38,* 3233–3239.

Shevell, S. K. and Humanski, R. D. (1988). Color perception under chromatic adaptation: Red/green equlibria with adapted short–wavelength sensitive cones. *Vision Research, 28,* 1345–1356.

Shevell, S. K. and Kingdom, F. A. A. (2008). Color in complex scenes. *Annual Review of Psychology, 59,* 143–166.

Smith, D. (2008). Colour-person-environment relationships. *Color Research and Applications*, *33*, 312 – 319.

Smith, V. C, and Pokorny, J. (1972). Spectral sensitivity of color–blind observers and the cone photopigments. *Vision Research, 12*, 2059–2071.

Smith, V. C., and Pokorny, J. (1975). Spectral sensitivity of the foveal cone photopigments between 400 and 500 nm. *Vision Research, 15*, 161–171.

Smith, V. C., and Pokorny, J. (1995). Chromatic-discrimination axes, CRT phosphor spectra, and individual variation in color vision. *Journal of the Optical Society of America A, 12*, 27 – 35.

Stockman, A., and Brainard, D. H. (2009). Color vision mechanisms. In M. Bass, C. DeCusatis, J. Enoch, V. Lakshminarayanan, G. Li, C. Macdonald, V. Mahajan and E. van Stryland (Eds.), *The Optical Society of America Handbook of Optics, 3rd edition, Volume III: Vision and Vision Optics* (pp. 11.1 – 11.104). New York: McGraw Hill.

Stockman, A. and Sharpe, L. T. (2000). The spectral sensitivities of the middle- and long-wavelength-sensitive cones derived from measurements in observers of known genotype. *Vision Research, 40*, 1711 – 1737.

Stoughton, C. M., and Conway, B. R. (2008) Neural basis for unique hues. *Current Biology, 18*, R698 – R699.

Suk, H-J., and Irtel, H. (2009). Emotional response to color across media. *Color Research and Application, 35*, 64 – 77.

Thornton, J. E. and Pugh, E. N. Jr. (1983) Relationship of opponent-colors cancellation measures to cone antagonistic signals deduced from increment threshold data. In J. D. Mollon and L. T. Sharpe (Eds.). *Colour vision: physiology and psychophysics* (pp. 361–373). London: Academic Press.

Valberg, A. (2001). Unique hues: An old problem for a new generation. *Vision Research, 41*, 1645 – 1657.

Vos, J. J. and Walraven, P. L. (1971). On the derivation of foveal receptor primaries. *Vision Research, 11*, 799–818.

Wagner, G. and Boynton, R.M. (1972). Comparison of four methods of heterochromatic photometry. *Journal of the Optical Society of America, 62*, 1508–1515.

Walraven, J. and Werner, J.S. (1991). The invariance of unique white: a possible implication for normalising cone action spectra. *Vision Research, 31*, 2185–2193.

Wei, J. P. and Shevell, S. K. (1995). Color appearance under chromatic adaptation varied along theoretically significant axes in color space. *Journal of the Optical Society of America A, 12*, 36 – 46.

Werner, J. S. and Wooten, B. R. (1979). Opponent chromatic mechanisms: Relation to photopigments and hue naming. *Journal of the Optical Society of America, 69*, 422–434.

Wuerger, S. M., Atkinson, P. and Cropper, S. (2005). The cone inputs to the unique-hue mechanisms. *Vision Research, 45*, 25–26.

Wyszecki, G. and Stiles, W.S. (1967). *Color science.* New York: John Wiley and Sons.

Chapter 9

MULTISENSORY METHODS FOR EARLY LITERACY LEARNING

Michelle M. Neumann[1,], Merv B. Hyde[2], David L. Neumann[1,3], Michelle Hood[1,3] and Ruth M. Ford[1,3]*

[1] School of Psychology, Griffith University
[2] University of the Sunshine Coast
[3] Behavioural Basis of Health Program,
Griffith Health Institute, Griffith University.

ABSTRACT

The simultaneous stimulation of two or more of the sensory receptors is termed multisensory. Visual, auditory, kinaesthetic and tactile information converges in the brain to be integrated so that an object may be efficiently and accurately perceived. This integration can also play an important role in the learning of new skills. The purpose of this chapter is to review multisensory processing and the use of multisensory methods to enhance early literacy skills in normally developing preschool aged children. Although little empirical research exists on the efficacy of multisensory instruction in early literacy skill acquisition, the few existing studies have been conducted in ecologically valid settings and provide valuable insights into how these strategies may be used to benefit young children's early literacy development. A key component of these strategies may be their incorporation of both a tactile and kinaesthetic component (e.g., tracing and manipulating letters with fingers) in addition to the traditional visual and auditory only methods (e.g., instructor presents a printed letter and says the letter name and/or sound). The application of these multisensory methods in preschool and home settings will be highlighted. The recommendation is made that teachers and parents use multisensory strategies to help scaffold early literacy learning. However, further carefully controlled studies are critical to determine the exact benefits of multisensory processes and instruction in early literacy learning.

---

[*]E-mail: michelle.neumann@griffithuni.edu.au

Keywords: multisensory processing, early literacy, teaching, learning, preschool children.

INTRODUCTION

Our survival in this world is dependent upon the brain's ability to efficiently process and respond to incoming stimuli (Calvert, Spence, and Stein, 2004; Koelewijn, Bronkhorst, and Theeuwes, 2010; Shams and Seitz, 2008). In an artificial setting, like a cognitive research laboratory, stimuli may be unisensory so that they activate only one type of sensory receptor (e.g., the Merkel cells in the skin for touch; Roberts, 2002). However, in real world environments, stimuli generally activate several types of sensory receptors at once. For example, perceiving a fire engine will stimulate visual (seeing the vehicle), auditory (hearing the siren), and tactile (feeling the wind as it rushes by you) sensory receptors. The simultaneous activation of more than one type of receptor is known as multisensory (Spence, 2002). Multisensory input can be bi-modal (e.g., visual-auditory), tri-modal (e.g., visual-auditory-tactile), or involve four or more senses (e.g., visual-auditory-kinaesthetic-tactile-taste; Alias, Newell, and Mamassian, 2010). In the past decade, there has been an increasing interest in the neurological mechanisms underpinning the processing of multisensory stimuli (Calvert et al., 2004) and how multisensory input can be harnessed to optimise teaching approaches and learning in educational settings (Birsh, 2005).

This chapter will review the current knowledge about multisensory processes and the role multisensory teaching methods play in early literacy learning in normally developing children. The review will begin with a discussion of what is currently known about multisensory processing, from the input of information at sensory receptors to the integration of this information in the brain. The critical importance that early experience plays in the development of an efficient multisensory integration system will be addressed. Evidence exists to suggest that the sensory systems, especially in the early years when young children are primed to respond to multisensory experiences to discover their world, may be exploited to enhance acquisition of new knowledge, such as written language. Therefore, studies that have used multisensory learning approaches in teaching early literacy skills in typically developing children will be reviewed. Applications of this research in the preschool and home settings are also discussed. The chapter concludes with suggestions for future research.

THE NEUROPHYSIOLOGICAL BASIS OF MULTISENSORY PROCESSING

Multisensory integration occurs in the brain in less than 100 ms (Koelewijn et al., 2010). This complex neural process plays an important role in determining how efficiently we perceive our world (Spence, 2002). During integration, information from different sensory modalities is synthesised and transformed into a new single output signal (e.g., behavioural response; Calvert and Thesen, 2004). The superior colliculus plays an important role in this process (Calvert et al., 2004; Stein, Stanford, and Rowland, 2009; Wallace and Stein, 2001) and is involved in orienting and attention (Coren, Ward, and Enns, 1996). Electrophysiological studies in cat and monkey brains have located multisensory neurons in the deep layers of the superior colliculus whose primary function is to process input from the multiple senses (Alias et al., 2010; Seitz, Kim, and Shams, 2006; Stein et al., 2009; Wallace, 2004; Wallace and Stein). Evidence for the convergence of multisensory input in the superior colliculus has also been found in humans using neuroimaging studies (Calvert et al.). The superior colliculus does not integrate multisensory information on its own, but is dependent upon inputs from both subcortical and cortical structures (Wallace). For example, tract tracing in monkeys has shown that visual input enters the retina sending this information to the superior colliculus and thalamus simultaneously. These pathways feed back to higher levels of the visual and auditory cortex (Calvert et al.).

Neurophysiological and neuroimaging studies show that multisensory interactions are widespread in the cortex (Bruce, Desimone, and Gross, 1981; Schroeder et al., 2001). Cortical multisensory interactions require multisensory congruence where all stimuli occur close together in time and space (Frassinetti, Bolognini, and Ladavas, 2002; Koelewijn et al., 2010). For example, congruence would mean that a sound should be an ecologically valid match to a given visual object (e.g., a visual percept of dog and an auditory percept of a meowing sound would be incongruent). Furthermore, semantic and object or action related congruence is important in eliciting a strong multisensory response from many cortical areas (Alias et al., 2010).

Cortical areas involved in multisensory convergence include the superior temporal sulcus, temporo-parietal association cortex, parietal cortex, premotor cortex, and prefrontal cortex (Calvert and Thesen, 2004). In addition, at least some of these populations of cortical neurons show integrative features similar to those seen in the superior colliculus (Wallace, Meredith, and Stein, 1992; Wallace and Stein, 2001). Thus, electrophysiological and neuroimaging studies suggests that much of the neocortex is essentially multisensory (Ghazanfar and Schroeder, 2006). Multisensory integration is no longer considered hierarchical but an integration of different sensory systems that could occur at both early and late stages of processing and is mediated via a parallel network of both feed-forward and feed-back connections (Calvert and Thesen, 2004; Koelewijn et al., 2010). For example, functional magnetic resonance imaging (fMRI) studies by Calvert et al. (1997) have shown that slight lip movements directly activate the primary auditory cortex in the absence of any auditory speech sounds presumably via feedback-projections from the visual cortex. Such feedback can improve perception and performance when tasks involve multisensory input. For example, watching a speaker's lips during face-to-face conversation (lip reading) improves speech perception, particularly in noisy conditions (Calvert et al.). Furthermore, the effect of cross-modal integration is demonstrated by the McGurk effect (McGurk and MacDonald, 1976) where vision alters speech perception (e.g., the sound of /ba/ is perceived as /da/ when presented with the lip movement /ga/). The McGurk effect has been found in 5-month-old infants, thus, demonstrating their sensitivity and early ability to integrate multimodal input (Rosenblum, Schmuckler, and Johnson, 1997).

The multisensory pathways outlined so far are well established in adults. Adult humans perform more efficiently and accurately on various attentional, discriminative, and learning tasks when multisensory information is available (Calvert et al., 2004). For example, training adults using multisensory audiovisual tasks (bimodal) resulted in significantly faster learning of image presentations (line drawings) than with unisensory visual training (Lehmann and Murray, 2005). Consistent with this, Seitz et al. (2006) found that a group trained with an audio-visual motion-detection task showed significantly more learning than a group trained solely with a visual motion-detection task over a period of 10 days. They concluded that multisensory training yields more efficient learning and that multisensory interactions should be exploited for the acquisition of new skills. Mousavi, Low, and Sweller (1995) have shown that it is easier to integrate multiple sources of information during learning when the material is physically integrated - aurally and visually - than when information is presented separately, possibly because it reduces the cognitive load by mixing auditory and visual information. Other research has suggested that multimodal processing reduces cognitive load because information from different modalities can be more easily stored in short-term memory and be used to encode long-term representations (Bagui, 1998).

Related research has shown that multisensory stimuli may facilitate the establishment and retrieval of memory (see Shams and Seitz, 2008). For example, recognition memory is better when items are encoded through multisensory experiences (e.g., seeing an image of the item and hearing the sound the item makes) than unisensory experiences (e.g., seeing an image of the item only), even when recognition memory is tested in only one sensory modality (Lehman and Murray, 2005). Research using neuroimaging techniques suggests that in such cases, the presentation of the unisensory test item will activate multiple sensory cortical areas (e.g., visual presentation will activate both visual and auditory cortical areas; Nyberg, Habib, McIntosh, and Tulving, 2000; see also Wheeler, Peterson, and Buckner, 2000). Although such effects may be explained as epiphenomena (Shams and Seitz, 2008), they do suggest that multisensory experiences can enrich memories and result in superior retrieval by recruiting multiple cortical areas (Murray et al., 2004).

In relation to literacy and language skills, Moats and Farrell (2005) describe how active learning, in which students are encouraged to link new literacy and language information (e.g., phonemes, letters, morphemes, words) with established memory through multisensory experiences that gain children's attention, is more effective than rote or passive memorisation. Such findings are explained by Exemplar Theory (Johnson, 2006) in which it is proposed that new objects are evaluated based upon how closely they resemble specific known members (and non-members) of the category. In Exemplar Theory, the strength and storage of a linguistic memory experience is said to be related to the attention given during processing, allowing for production and perception (Johnson).

Knowledge about multisensory integration in the young is not comprehensive (Calvert et al., 2004; Stein et al., 2009). Electrophysiological studies on newborn rhesus monkeys have found that multisensory neurons are present in the deep layers of the superior colliculus and respond to stimuli from different sensory modalities (Wallace and Stein, 2001). These multisensory neurons also show similar convergence patterns to those seen in the adult monkey, although they cannot yet synthesise multisensory input (Wallace and Stein). Human infants are capable within months of birth of integrating multisensory input from arbitrary objects (e.g., the sound a toy produces and its colour or shape) learnt through experience with the simultaneous presentation of two or more modalities (Lickliter and Bahrick, 2004). The McGurk effect noted earlier has been observed in both infants and young children (e.g., Massaro, 1984, 1987). Although this research has shown that auditory-visual perceptual synergy is weaker in the youngest infants, the fact that the McGurk Effect is present shows that hearing and vision interact during speech at an early age. It suggests that speech perception is multimodal, and involves information from more than one sensory modality from the earliest life circumstances (Rosenblum et al., 1997).

THE IMPORTANCE OF EARLY EXPERIENCE IN THE DEVELOPMENT OF MULTISENSORY PROCESSING

Primate studies show that the maturation of multisensory neurons is dependent upon significant postnatal experience with cross-modal (auditory, visual and somatosensory) cues (Wallace and Stein, 2001). Likewise, early experience plays an important role in multisensory development in children (Lehman and Murray, 2005; Wallace, 2004; Stein et al., 2009). Stein et al. argued that it is reasonable to assume that a lack of early cross-modal experience will compromise the future capacity of a child's multisensory integration abilities. Furthermore, it is possible that providing young children with a wider range of multisensory experiences will enhance multisensory integration processes and subsequent encoding, storage, and retrieval of perceptual information (Seitz et al., 2006).

The deprivation of sensory information during early development has neurological and behavioural consequences. For example, the multisensory neurons of animals reared in the dark lack the ability to integrate multiple sensory cues, suggesting that experiential deprivation delays or eliminates the maturation and integrative capacity of these neurons (Stein et al., 2009; Wallace, 2004). Analogous research has been conducted with human subjects whose early vision was obscured by congenital cataracts. When the vision in these individuals was subsequently restored surgically, their visual-perceptual ability appeared normal but their ability to integrate visual and non-visual information was impaired (Putzar, Goerendt, Lange, Rosler, and Roder, 2007). This indicates the importance of early sensory experience in optimising development in multisensory integration. In addition, studies of young children have shown that rich sensory stimulation is critical to brain development. For example, positron emission tomography (PET) scans of 3-year-old Romanian orphans who had been severely deprived of environmental stimulation from birth showed 25% less brain development (size and density) than seen in normally-reared children (Perry, Pollard, Blakley, Baker, and Vigilante, 1995). There are also examples involving congenitally deaf children that demonstrate that their visual perception of speech is restricted and that this impairment is closely related to the amount of residual hearing subsequently available and the nature of the hearing loss in spectral terms (Power and Hyde, 1997). In addition, severely and profoundly deaf students performed better on tasks when auditory and visual (lip reading) input was available than with either auditory or visual input alone (Hyde and Power, 1992; for a review of unisensory versus multisensory communication in the deaf, see Power and Hyde).

Infants respond better in discriminative tasks that use bisensory rather than unisensory stimuli and learn rhythmical events more easily when sensory inputs to more than one modality are used (Lewkowicz and Kraebal, 2004). For example, Bahrick, Flom, and Lickliter (2002) found that 3-month-old infants discriminated a change in the tempo of a toy hammer tapping when audio and visual input were both available but not when presented with unisensory stimuli (i.e., only visual or auditory). Similar results showed that learning was facilitated in 5-month-old infants who discriminated a change in rhythm in bimodal but not unimodal stimulation (Bahrick and Lickliter, 2000). Interestingly, the benefit of using multisensory stimuli in the prenatal period to aid learning has been shown in research with quail embryos. Quails stimulated with a light synchronised with the rate and rhythm of a maternal call learned the call four times faster than counterparts that only received desynchronised stimulation of light and maternal call or maternal call alone (Lickliter, Bahrick, and Honeycutt, 2002).

Whereas brain research has tended to focus on visual and auditory sensory modalities, developing children will also make use of other sensory modalities such as tactile and kinaesthetic to actively explore and learn about their world (Bushnell and Baxt, 1999). Indeed, Katai and Toth (2010) described young children as scientists because they explore their environment using all of their senses. Young children have been shown to be highly skilled at identifying common objects by manipulating them with both hands under a cloth using tactile and kinaesthetic senses (Bushnell and Baxt). Through tactile identification, children as young as 2½ years old could correctly label 80% of miniaturised common objects (e.g., ball, keys, spoon) hidden under a cloth with 5 year olds' performance near 100% (Bigelow, 1981). Tactile stimuli activate the sense of touch and may be active (also called haptic; e.g., tactile input from physically exploring an object) or passive (an object being pressed upon the skin; Stankov, Seizova-Cajic, and Roberts, 2001). Kinaesthetic perception (also known as proprioception) is based on input from receptors in muscles, tendons, joints, and skin, as well as the direct consequence of commands for voluntary movements issued to muscles (Stankov et al., 2001). Developmental studies have shown that tactile and kinaesthetic systems emerge as early as two months after birth in humans (Lhote and Streri, 1998). As such, young children are primed to respond to tactile stimuli. Utilising tactile and kinaesthetic pathways may add to existing visual and auditory information to enhance children's learning about their world (Gallace and Spence, 2009; Katai and Toth). Educators have used multisensory methods that include additional tactile and kinaesthetic components in an effort to enhance children's early literacy learning and memory (e.g., Birsh, 2005; Carreker, 2006; Henry and Hook, 2006; Hodges, 2010; Katai and Toth; Minogue and Jones, 2006; Willis, 2009).

Multisensory approaches to children's learning and education are consistent with Piaget's (1954) theory of cognitive development, which posited that knowledge is constructed through sensori-motor activity. They are also in accord with the broader framework on embodied cognition (Niedenthal, 2007), which rejects the traditional distinction in cognitive psychology between 'higher-level' conceptual processes and 'lower-level' sensorimotor processes in favour of the view that learning and memory are inextricably linked with perceptual and motor pathways. From the perspective of the embodied approach, the modality-specific systems that underlie perception and action are captured during concept formation, meaning that thinking depends fundamentally on mental simulation of prior learning experiences (Bahrick, Lickliter, and Flom, 2007; Barsalou, 1999, 2008; Niedenthal; Rakison and Woodward, 2008).

A HISTORICAL PERSPECTIVE ON MULTISENSORY METHODS

The concept of using methods that simultaneously stimulate auditory, visual, tactile and kinaesthetic inputs in education is not new. Nearly 100 years ago, Marie Montessori pioneered the first multisensory preschool programs for normally developing 3- to 5-year-old children to prepare them for reading and writing (Gettman, 1987; Montessori, 1965;

Richardson, 1997). These pre-reading and writing skills included physical formation of letter shapes, and letter name and sound identification. Montessori's program was designed to "educate the senses" (p. 245; Richardson) by allowing children multisensory experiences via touch boards, tracing wooden plane geometric forms and tracing and colouring-in metal insets. Following these experiences, children were taught to trace sandpaper letters with their fingers and voice the sound of each letter simultaneously using an integrated tactile-kinaesthetic-visual-auditory approach (e.g., the child sees a letter whilst tracing it and saying and hearing its name and/or sound). Other multisensory materials included moveable alphabet and cardboard letters that children could hold and manipulate themselves to help them build words, identify phonemes, and articulate words. Through these experiences, children were learning to develop a conscious attentive process and this was combined with reinforcement and continuous feedback from the teacher. Although arguably overly simplistic, it was Montessori's belief that touching and looking at the letters at the same time fixed the image more quickly through the cooperation of the senses and that looking later becomes reading and touching becomes writing (Gettman).

To further illustrate past use of multisensory strategies, Fernald and Keller (1921) reported case studies on three boys (aged 9 to 10 years) who were of normal intelligence but had failed to learn to read after three or more years in a public school. The multisensory method began by asking the child to say a word he would like to learn. The child watched as the word was written in large script on a blackboard by the researcher. The child looked at the word, pronouncing it to himself whilst tracing it. Tracing was done with the first two fingers over each letter of the word written on the blackboard. The child repeated this until he could write the word correctly from memory. Fernald and Keller suggested that lip and hand kinaesthetic elements were the essential link between the visual cue and the word. They stressed the need for tactile experiences, such as finger tracing, reporting that learning occurred at a faster rate with the tactile component enhancing memory. However, it is acknowledged that children may successfully learn literacy skills through a range of literacy programs (e.g., Adams, 1990; Snow, Burns, and Griffins, 1998) without an explicit tactile and kinaesthetic teaching component (e.g., Justice and Pullen, 2003).

Orton (1957) argued from a similar viewpoint to Fernald and Keller, that the language system and its sensorimotor connections are all interrelated and that language and literacy skills should be taught simultaneously via different sensory modalities (see also Henry, 1998). This approach was based on simultaneously stimulating visual, auditory, kinaesthetic, and tactile modalities (e.g., words were presented visually followed by tracing the letters with the finger whilst the word was said; Gillingham and Stillman, 1997). Following Orton's work, a number of multisensory literacy programs have been created for remedial purposes (e.g., dyslexia) and for normally developing children. These include The Wilson Program (Wilson, 2000); the Lindamood-Bell Program (Birsh, 2005); the Spalding Method (Spalding and Spalding, 1990); the Slingerland Approach (Slingerland, 1977); and the Hickey Multisensory Language Course (Combley, 2001). These programs use various multisensory strategies, including sky writing whilst saying letter names and sounds, sand trays, textured objects, sensory putty and finger paints to encourage children to use a range of tactile and kinaesthetic senses. These programs share the same philosophy and can be grouped together under the umbrella of multisensory instruction in that they are systematic, sequential, explicit, and direct methods of instruction that utilize combined visual, auditory, kinaesthetic and tactile stimulation to foster early literacy skill acquisition. Furthermore, what differentiates these multisensory programs from typical visual and auditory methods (i.e., say a letter sound while looking at the letter shape) is the addition of tactile and/or kinaesthetic components during the literacy activity.

A REVIEW OF MULTISENSORY EARLY LITERACY STUDIES

Early literacy skills impact upon a child's future reading ability and wellbeing in society (Snow et al., 1998). The early literacy skills children need to acquire in the preschool years to become successful readers include print awareness (Clay, 1998; Justice and Ezell, 2001; Lomax and McGee, 1987), alphabet knowledge (letter sound and name knowledge; Bowman and Treiman, 2004; Foulin, 2005; Levin, Shatil-Carmon, and Asif-Rave, 2006), phonological awareness (Byrne and Fielding-Barnsley, 1989; Mann and Foy, 2003) and early writing skills (Aram and Biron, 2004; Welsch, Sullivan, and Justice, 2003). These are foundational skills upon which children build conventional literacy skills (independent and fluent word reading and writing), with alphabet knowledge and phonological awareness being the strongest predictors of future reading ability (Adams, 1990; Blair and Savage, 2006; Bowey, 2005; Castles and Coltheart, 2004; Ehri and Roberts, 2006; Foulin, 2005; Molfese, Beswick, Molnar, and Jacobi-Vessels, 2006; Snow et al., 1998; Stuart and Coltheart, 1988). For example, children's ability to identify letters in kindergarten and delete initial and final phonemes in words (phonological awareness) was found to be the strongest predictor of their reading skills in first grade (Scanlon and Vellutino, 1996). Other important predictors of reading skills at the end of first grade include general cognitive ability and receptive vocabulary in kindergarten (Bowey).

Very few empirical studies have tested the effects of multisensory (use of visual, auditory, kinaesthetic and tactile stimuli) methods on early literacy acquisition in normally developing preschool aged children. An extensive literature search was conducted to identify any published studies that had examined the use of multisensory methods for early literacy skill acquisition in preschool age children. PsycINFO, ERIC, and Google Scholar databases were searched by combining the key terms "multisensory", "multimodality", "perceptual learning" or combinations of "auditory", "visual", "tactile", "haptic", and "kinaesthetic". This search was further narrowed by use of key words "learning", "teaching", "literacy", "education", "school", or "preschool". This resulted in 74 articles that were further screened to exclude studies of participants older than 6 years or non-normally developing children (e.g., hearing impaired). Articles that were reviews or descriptions of multisensory teaching approaches without any assessment of the approach were also excluded. The search yielded four studies that met all criteria of being multisensory methods to teach early literacy skills to normally developing preschool children (Bara, Gentaz, Cole, and Sprenger-Charolles, 2004; Neumann, Hood and Neumann, 2009; Neumann and Neumann, 2010; Zafrana, Nikoltsou, and Daniilidou, 2000) and one that met all criteria but which focussed on literacy in the first year of school (Joshi, Dahlgren, and Boulware-Gooden, 2002). Three studies were conducted in educational settings (Bara et al., 2004; Joshi et al.; Zafrana et al.) and two in the home setting (Neumann et al.; Neumann and Neumann).

Zafrana et al. (2000) conducted a 3-month multisensory literacy program in a preschool setting with 17 Greek children aged 3½ to 5 years old. It was regarded as a pilot study and there was no control group or formal pre- or post- testing. However, observational data were collected on children's literacy behaviours during each session. In the first phase of each session, the teacher presented the literacy material to children during a 10- to 15-minute presentation. The material in each session consisted of two letters of the alphabet and their sounds and these were changed each week. In the second phase of each session, children played with the learning materials (small sandpaper letters stuck on white card and small objects with matching picture and word cards) independently for up to 30 minutes. During this second session, the teacher allowed the children to explore and manipulate the sandpaper letters themselves and play 'tombola', which involved matching pictures and 4-letter words like a game of bingo. Children were also encouraged to simultaneously touch and follow the shape of the letter while pronouncing it. Connecting the letter sound (phoneme) and its shape (grapheme) to the movements of the fingers were considered by the authors to enhance children's memory of letter-sound associations.

Children were also encouraged to trace the sandpaper letters with the forefinger and middle finger whilst closing their eyes in order to focus on using both tactile and kinaesthetic senses to memorise letter shapes. During writing, it was observed that if children had forgotten how to write a letter, they retraced sandpaper letters without prompting before returning to write their letter correctly. Their initial formations of irregularly large letter shapes gradually improved with increased motor control. Zafrana et al. (2000) suggested that this multisensory activity was helpful because it facilitated the letter writing process. Writing was observed to be the most popular activity (93.9%) followed by identifying letters (69.9%) then reading words (14.5%).

Zafrana et al. (2000) concluded that children of preschool age are able to learn letter names, shapes and sounds through multisensory activities and can develop a powerful motivation for this if given the appropriate environment. At the end of the 3-month program, they reported that all children performed basic writing and recognised alphabet letters and some words. However, since the study had no formal assessments of children's literacy gains or a comparison control group, it is not possible to conclude that the children significantly improved across the program or that any of the improvements were due to the multisensory component of the program. It is also not clear to what extent the tactile and kinaesthetic activities made any independent contribution to learning.

Bara et al. (2004) conducted a training study based on the Montessori multisensory program in a French preschool setting to investigate whether visual, auditory, and tactile-kinaesthetic (the authors used the synonymous term 'haptic') exploration of letters increased children's understanding of the alphabetic principle (that letters represent sounds). Sixty pre-reading children (Mean age = 5 years, 7 months) were allocated equally to one of the three training conditions (multisensory, visual whole letters, visual letter formation). Individual training groups consisted of five to six children. Training sessions (25 min duration) occurred once a week for seven weeks and one revision session. Each session was designed to develop phonemic awareness, knowledge of letters and letter/sound correspondences, and use of the alphabetic principle (measured as the ability to decode pseudo words). Children were pre- and post-tested on pseudo word decoding, letter recognition and phonological awareness (rhyme, initial and final phoneme).

Children in the multisensory condition explored 3-dimensional foam letters using visual, auditory, tactile and kinaesthetic senses. They were instructed to visually explore the letters with their fingers and to run their index finger along the letter outline in a fixed exploratory order as if it were being written by hand. The foam letters were then placed under a cover so they could not be seen and children were asked to think of the letter while exploring it using only their tactile and kinaesthetic senses. The aim was to identify (name) the letter. Children in the second group (visual whole letters) viewed letters printed on a piece of paper and glued to a small board and were encouraged to visually attend to the lines and curves in the letter shape. Children in the third group (visual letter formation) viewed letters as they took shape on a computer screen (i.e., they visually followed the sequential formation of the letter shape). In all of the training sessions, children also recited nursery rhymes and played matching word and picture games that emphasised the focal letter. Results showed that the multisensory group had greater understanding of the alphabetic principle and decoding skills than the other two groups. Bara et al. (2004) suggested that engaging these additional visual, auditory, tactile and kinaesthetic modes enhanced perceptual function and efficiency. Adding tactile and kinaesthetic stimulation may make the connections between letters and sounds easier to learn and, thereby, improve decoding skills. They also suggested that using tactile-kinaesthetic exploration activities in early literacy programs may encourage young children to process letters in a more investigative way, something they would probably not do spontaneously if letters were presented only in visual form.

Joshi et al. (2002) compared the literacy skill outcomes of Grade 1 children exposed to the established Orton-Gillingham multisensory program ($n = 24$) to those exposed to a traditional program that used primarily basal reader books ($n = 32$). Both groups received 50 minutes of daily instruction over the academic year. Prior to the study commencing, the teachers of the multisensory group received 42 hours training in the use of the multisensory techniques. Lessons for the multisensory group combined three modalities: auditory, visual, and kinaesthetic (activities involved simultaneously seeing letters, hearing their sounds and writing letters and words in the air). The multisensory program included direct and systematic instruction in phonemic awareness, alphabet activities, oral language, reading, spelling practice, reading comprehension, and vocabulary development. Post-test results showed that the multisensory group made statistically significant gains in phonological awareness, decoding, and reading comprehension whereas the control group only made gains in reading comprehension.

However, it is difficult to conclude that the improvement in the multisensory group was due to the multisensory instruction alone because the control group did not receive the same systematic, explicit, and sequential reading instruction as the multisensory group. Nevertheless, Joshi et al. maintained that their study provided evidence that a multisensory program based on the Orton-Gillingham technique can be successfully implemented at the first grade level. Further work with improved methodology and appropriate research design is required to isolate any effects specifically attributable to multisensory instruction.

In the home setting, Neumann et al. (2009) reported a case study of a mother supporting the development of her preschool child's alphabet knowledge, early writing, and print motivation by using a multisensory approach coupled with environmental print (e.g., labels on cereal boxes; see Neumann, 2007). The multisensory approach aimed to simultaneously stimulate visual, auditory, kinaesthetic, and tactile receptors by interacting with environmental print via four main steps. The mother and child looked at the target print (visual) and pointed to a letter within the print, saying the letter name and sound (e.g., "An M for Milk makes a [mmm] sound"; auditory). They also formed the letter shape in the air with their hands and arms (kinaesthetic) and traced the letter on the product label with their finger (tactile). The tracing of the letter shape on the product label and in the air was accompanied by directional language (e.g., the mother and child moved their hands in the shape of an M saying "up, down, up, down"). Neumann et al. reported that this approach fostered letter name knowledge and also supported the recall of letter shapes and letter formation during the child's early writing attempts. For example, the child asked, "How do I write *monster*?" The mother replied that, "M for monster goes up, down, up, down. Let's write it in the air (they moved their hands in the shape of the letter using the directional language)" (p. 317; Neumann et al.). The child was reported to then confidently write M on paper, self-guiding himself using the mother's directional language.

In another case study, Neumann and Neumann (2010) reported the use of the same multisensory strategy combined with environmental print to scaffold another preschool child's letter shaping, word, and story writing. The child, Roseanna, was observed exploring and interacting with environmental print that she had found in her home, and was observed to copy letters and words on her own (e.g., My Little Pony, Mr Happy, Pop Tops). The mother also scaffolded the child's shaping of environmental print letters and words using the multisensory strategy, for example, as the child traced letters on toy labels and cereal boxes (e.g., Thomas the Tank and Oat Flakes) and in the air (e.g., M for McDonalds). Through Roseanna's own natural multisensory explorations of environmental print and her mother's scaffolding, the child evidenced her intrinsic motivation to learn more about letter names, shapes and sounds. These two case studies suggest that multisensory teaching approaches may be incorporated into the home environment to foster early literacy skills. However, these conclusions are based on case studies that are limited by issues of generalisability and the lack of a comparison group. Further research is required on the efficacy of multisensory strategies in the home setting.

It is clear that empirical research on the use of multisensory methods in early literacy learning is limited. The few studies that exist show that adding simultaneous stimulation of kinaesthetic and tactile receptors to stimulation of the auditory and visual receptors that typically occurs when children are taught to look at a letter and listen to its sound or name may enhance early literacy learning in educational settings (Bara et al., 2004; Joshi et al., 2002; Zafrana et al., 2000) and the home setting (Neumann et al., 2009; Neumann and Neumann, 2010).

It may be useful to view multisensory methods as 'scaffolding' tools that aid in the acquisition of new knowledge either in educational or home settings. Multisensory strategies can be used by teachers and parents to actively engage children. Wood, Bruner, and Ross (1976) used the term scaffolding to describe how tools or techniques can be used to allow a child to achieve a goal that would otherwise be beyond his or her unassisted efforts. The scaffolding becomes unnecessary once the child can achieve unassisted. For example, adding tactile and kinaesthetic stimulation might scaffold early efforts to learn letters but when a child has mastered the name, shape, and sound of a letter this stimulation is no longer needed (Neumann et al., 2009). Within this scaffolding framework, it is useful to consider the applications of multisensory methods separately for the preschool and home settings.

APPLICATIONS

Multisensory Methods in the Preschool Setting

The preschool environment is one in which children are surrounded by objects that are designed to stimulate their sensorimotor development (e.g., jigsaw puzzles, blocks, play dough). Children are also surrounded by printed and writing materials (e.g., story books, alphabet charts, posters, paint brushes, crayons) designed to develop emergent literacy skills acquired prior to conventional word reading (e.g., Otto, 2008). Piaget (1954) emphasised the importance of this sensorimotor period and the need to allow children to learn by exploring their environment. Early literacy skills are often introduced through play-based activities by using environmental print, alphabet books, plastic/magnetic letters and games involving large cards printed with letters or loose letter tiles and making letters from play dough (Otto, Vukelich, Christie and Enz, 2008). Interactions with letters could be further fostered by encouraging children to specifically trace letters with their fingers, move their hands around plastic letters or form letter shapes in the air with large arm movements whilst saying their name or sound (Gettman, 1987; Lesiak, 1997; Richardson, 1997).

A multisensory approach may be used either during informal literacy activities or for more directed learning. Zafrana et al's (2000) multisensory program was open-ended, meaning that children were encouraged to explore letters independently through multisensory activities, for example, self-initiating the tracing of sand paper letters. In contrast, children in Bara et al.'s (2004) study were trained and directly instructed to interact with letters repeatedly in a specific and sequential way (i.e., to follow the letter's shape visually whilst running their index finger along its outline). When participating in multisensory learning activities independently, some children may derive more benefit than others (e.g., more advanced children may engage in more complex activities on their own). For this reason, children at any level of development may benefit most from multisensory activities when they are provided with instruction where teachers intentionally scaffold their learning and encourage them to use multisensory strategies during literacy activities.

For example, we suggest that a teacher could focus on the letters of children's favourite toy or cereal box label (e.g., Weet-Bix). This could be done by simultaneously looking at and pointing to the letter W on the box (visual), saying and hearing its name and sound (auditory), forming the letter shape in the sky (kinaesthetic) then tracing its shape on the box (tactile). In addition, making letters from different materials (e.g., clay or natural materials from the garden or beach) whilst saying the letter's name and sound then tracing the letter may also make letter learning more engaging and stimulating. By encouraging children to trace letters (with their finger) that they find on surrounding signs, posters, and in alphabet and story books during the preschool day or on their favourite food packaging at lunch time, children may become motivated to explore letters in a multisensory way.

Multisensory Methods in the Home Setting

The quality of the home literacy environment (e.g., shared story book reading, letter teaching, access to printed materials) has a significant impact upon the development of a child's emergent literacy skills (e.g., letter identification, phonological awareness) (Britto, Fuligni, and Brooks-Gunn, 2006; Byrne et al., 2006; Hood, Conlon, and Andrews, 2008; Saracho, 1997; Snow et al., 1998; Weigel, Martin, and Bennett, 2006). In the home setting, children are often surrounded by print materials such as books, magazines, posters, newspapers, magnetic letters, and writing materials. Home literacy activities can also include reading of surrounding print (e.g., labels on food and toy packaging; Otto, 2008; Purcell-Gates, 1996). In addition, the close relationship between parent and child provides many opportunities for quality literacy activities to occur when parents are sensitive to their child's interests and are able to appropriately scaffold their learning (Dodici, Draper, and Peterson, 2003).

Incorporating multisensory stimulation into parent-child interactions with print may provide a simple and effective way for young children to learn about print in a fun way (Neumann et al., 2009; Neumann and Neumann, 2010). For example, we suggest that when a parent begins to read a storybook to their child, they could look at and point to a letter on the title page (visual), say its name and sound (auditory), write the letter in the sky (kinaesthetic) then trace the letter with a finger (tactile) whilst saying the letter sound again. These four steps (*point, say, move, and trace*) could be also used to explore letters on a child's favourite food packaging, toy label, or sign. As the child masters each letter, the scaffolding provided via this multisensory method will no longer be needed for that letter. It is also possible that young children will adopt these multisensory strategies themselves to explore and learn about letters, words, and other forms of print such as numerals by a form of self-scaffolding. Furthermore, tracing letters with fingers and forming letter shapes in the air may help children write letters and words on paper during child-initiated writing activities such as labelling drawings or copying printed labels from food or toy packaging (Neumann et al.,; Neumann and Neumann).

SUGGESTIONS FOR FUTURE RESEARCH

Behavioural, neuropsychological and neuroimaging research suggests that multisensory integration occurs at multiple levels in the brain and that the simultaneous processing of more than one type of sensory information is a common experience and may enhance learning and memory (Calvert et al., 2004; Shams and Seitz, 2008). However, many questions remain regarding how multisensory integration develops in young children and what types of multisensory environments and experiences may optimise learning. Although it appears that the visual, auditory, kinaesthetic and tactile sensory systems are closely connected, the exact nature and functioning of this cross-modal association needs further investigation (Bara et al., 2004; Birsh, 2005; 2006). Empirical evidence is also scarce on the efficacy of multisensory methods in educational and home settings. It is also unlikely that all sensory modalities will contribute equally to learning during the process of early brain development. It has been found, for example, that young children often have a preference for auditory over visual stimuli (Robinson and Sloutsky, 2004).

Empirical research is required to investigate and validate multisensory methods for teaching and enrichment in educational and home settings. Furthermore, despite the crucial importance of learning to read, there is limited knowledge as to how audio-visual integration of information about print works and which mechanisms are involved (Blomert and Froyen, 2010), and there is a specific need to clarify the role that tactile and kinaesthetic components of multisensory programs play in the literacy learning process. Methodologically sound interventions that include appropriate control groups and pre- and post- assessments of a range of early literacy measures are needed to determine which modality combinations (visual-auditory-kinaesthetic-tactile) and multisensory activities produce the best learning outcomes for normally developing children in preschool and home settings. This could be tested with a randomised control study in which children are randomly allocated to either an auditory-visual program or a program with the same auditory-visual activities but with an added kinaesthetic-tactile component to the letter learning. Understanding more about the role of multisensory processing and instructional methods will aid in the creation of new ways to enhance young children's early literacy knowledge.

CONCLUSION

Although there is little empirical research investigating multisensory methods in early literacy learning, many educators believe that "hands-on" multisensory experiences that involve the manipulation of objects are powerful teaching tools (e.g., Birsh, 2005; Carreker, 2006; Henry and Hook, 2006; Hodges, 2010; Katai and Toth, 2010; Minogue and Jones, 2006; Willis, 2009). However, to determine the specific benefits of multisensory methods it is important to study multisensory integration in laboratory-based experiments in addition to using ecologically valid real world settings (Alias et al., 2010; Degelder and Bertelson, 2003; Gallace and Spence, 2009; Spence, 2002). Thus, further research is needed into the efficacy of the tactile-kinaesthetic component of multisensory approaches. This work may provide the necessary link between brain research and educational practice and contribute to greater understanding about optimising young children's early literacy development.

AUTHOR NOTE

Thanks to Sharon Dookharam for assistance in conducting the literature search.

REFERENCES

Adams, M. J. (1990). Beginning to read: Thinking and learning about print. Cambridge, MA: MIT Press.

Alias, D., Newell, F. N., and Mamassian, P. (2010). Multisensory processing in review: From physiology to behaviour. *Seeing and Perceiving*, 23, 3-38.

Aram, D., and Biron, S. (2004). Joint storybook reading and joint-writing interventions among low SES preschoolers: Differential contributions to early literacy. *Early Childhood Research Quarterly*, 19, 588-610.

Bagui, S. (1998). Reasons for increased learning using multimedia. *Journal of Education Multimedia Hypermedia*, 7, 3-18.

Bahrick, L. E., and Lickliter, R. (2000). Intersensory redundancy guides attentional selectivity and perceptual learning in infancy. *Developmental Psychology*, 36, 190-201.

Bahrick, L. E., Flom, R., and Lickliter, R. (2002). Intersensory redundancy facilitates discrimination of tempo in 3-month-old infants. *Developmental Psychobiology*, 41, 352-363.

Bahrick, L. E., Lickliter, R., and Flom, R. (2007). Intersensory redundancy guides the development of selective attention, perception, and cognition in infancy. *Current Directions in Psychological Science*, 13, 99-102.

Bara, F., Gentaz, E., Cole, P., and Sprenger-Charolles, L. (2004). The visuo-haptic and haptic exploration of letters increases the kindergarten-children's understanding of the alphabetic principle. *Cognitive Development*, 19, 433-449.

Barsalou, L. W. (1999). Perceptual symbol system. *Behavioral and Brain Sciences*, 22, 577-660.

Barsalou, L. W. (2008). Grounded cognition. *Annual review of Psychology*, 59, 617-645.

Bigelow, A. E. (1981). Children's tactile identification of miniaturized common objects. *Developmental Psychology*, 17, 111-114.

Birsh, J. R. (Ed.) (2005). *Multisensory teaching of basic language skills*. Baltimore, Maryland: Paul H. Brookes.

Birsh, J. R. (2006). What is multisensory structured language? *Perspectives: The International Dyslexia Association*, 32, 15-20.

Blair, R., and Savage, R. (2006). Name writing but not environmental print recognition is related to letter-sound knowledge and phonological awareness in pre-readers. *Reading and Writing*, 19, 991-1016.

Blomert, L., and Froyen, D. (2010). Multi-sensory learning and learning to read. *International Journal of Psychophysiology*, 77, 195-204.

Bowey, J. A. (2005). Predicting individual differences in learning to read. In Margaret J. Snowling, and Charles J. Hulme (Ed.), *The science of reading: A handbook* (pp. 155-172). Oxford, UK: Blackwell.

Bowman, M., and Treiman, R. (2004). Stepping stones to reading. *Theory into Practice*, 43, 295-303.

Britto, P. R., Fuligni, A. S., and Brooks-Gunn, J. (2006). Reading ahead: Effective interventions for young children's early literacy development. In S. B. Neumann, and D. K. Dickinson (Eds.), *Handbook of early literacy research*: Vol. 2. (pp. 311-332). New York, NY: Guildford Press.

Bruce, C., Desimone, R., and Gross, C. G. (1981). Visual properties of neurons in a polysensory area in superior temporal sulcus of the macaque. *Journal of Neurophysiology,* 46, 369-384.

Bushnell, E. W., and Baxt, C. (1999). Children's haptic and cross-modal recognition with familiar and unfamiliar objects. *Journal of Experimental Psychology: Human Perception and Performance.* 25, 1867-1881.

Byrne, B., and Fielding-Barnsley, R. (1989). Phonemic awareness and letter knowledge in the child's acquisition of the alphabetic principle. *Journal of Educational Psychology*, 81, 313-321.

Byrne, B., Olson, R. K , Samuelsson, S., Wadsworth, S, Corley, R., and DeFries, J. C., et al. (2006). Genetic and environmental influences on early literacy. *Journal of Research in Reading*, 29, 33-49.

Calvert, G. A., Bullmore, E. T., Brammer, M. J., Campbell, R., Williams, S. C. R., and Mcguire, P. K., et al. (1997). Activation of auditory cortext during silent lipreading. *Science*, 276, 593-595.

Calvert, G. A., and Thesen, T. (2004). Multisensory integration: Methodological approaches and emerging principles in the human brain. *Journal of Physiology*, 98, 191-205.

Calvert, G., Spence, C., and Stein, B. E. (Eds.) (2004). *The handbook of multisensory processes.* London, UK: MIT Press.

Carreker, S. (2006). Teaching the structure of language through seeing, hearing and doing. *Perspectives: The International Dyslexia Association*, 32, 24-28.

Castles, A., and Coltheart, M. (2004). Is there a causal link from phonological awareness to success in learning to read? *Cognition*, 91, 77-111.

Clay, M. M. (1998). *By different paths to common outcomes.* York, Maine: Stenhouse.

Combley, M. (Ed.) (2001). *The Hickey Multisensory Language Course.* London, UK: Whurr Publishers.

Coren, S., Ward, L. M., and Enns, J. T. (1996). *Sensation and perception.* New York, NY: Harcourt Brace College Publishers.

Degelder, B., and Bertelson, P. (2003). Multisensory integration, perception and ecological validity. *Trends in Cognitive Sciences*, 7, 460-467.

Dodici, B. J., Draper, D. C., and Peterson, C. A. (2003). Early parent-child interactions and early literacy development. *Topics in Early Childhood Special Education*, 23, 124-136.

Ehri, L. C., and Roberts, T. (2006). The roots of learning to read and write: Acquisition of letters and phonemic awareness. In S. B. Neuman and D. K. Dickinson (Eds.), *Handbook of early literacy research*: Vol. 2. (pp. 113-130). New York, NY: Guildford Press.

Fernald, G., and Keller, H. (1921). The effect of kinaesthetic factors in the development of word recognition in the case of non-readers. *The Journal of Educational Research*, 4, 355-377.

Foulin, J. N. (2005). Why is letter-name knowledge such a good predictor of learning to read? *Reading and Writing*, 18, 129-155.

Frassinetti, F., Bolognini, N., and Ladavas, E. (2002). Enhancement of visual perception by crossmodal visuo-auditory interaction. *Experimental Brain Research*, 147, 332-343.

Gallace, A., and Spence, C. (2009). The cognitive and neural correlates of tactile memory. *Psychological Bulletin*, 135, 380-406.

Gettman, D. (1987). *Basic Montessori: Learning activities for under-fives.* London, UK: Christopher Helm.

Ghazanfar, A. A., and Schroeder, C. E. (2006). Is the neocortex essentially multisensory? *Trends in Cognitive Sciences*, 10, 278-285.

Gillingham, A., and Stillman, B. W. (1997). *The Gillingham manual: Remedial training for children with specific disability in reading, spelling, and penmanship* (8th ed.). Cambridge, MA: Educators Publishing Service.

Henry, M. K. (1998). Structured, sequential, multisensory teaching: The Orton legacy. *Annals of Dyslexia*, 48, 3-26.

Henry, M. K., and Hook, P. (2006). Multisensory instruction: Then and now. *Perspectives: The International Dyslexia Association*, 32, 9-11.

Hodges, D. A. (2010). Can neuroscience help us do a better job of teaching music? *General Music Today*, 23, 3-12.

Hood, M., Conlon, E., and Andrews, G. (2008). Preschool home literacy practices and children's literacy development: A longitudinal analysis. *Journal of Educational Psychology*, 100, 252-271.

Hyde, M. B., and Power, D. J. (1992). Receptive communication abilities of hearing impaired students. *American Annals of the Deaf*, 137, 389-398.

Johnson, K. (2006). Resonance in an exemplar-based lexicon: The emergence of social identity and phonology. *Journal of Phonetics*, 34, 485-499.

Joshi, R. M., Dahlgren, M., and Boulware-Gooden, R. (2002). Teaching reading in an inner city school through a multisensory teaching approach. *Annals of Dyslexia*, 52, 229-242.

Justice, L. M., and Ezell, H. K. (2001). Word and print awareness in 4-year-old children. *Child and Language Teaching and Therapy*, 17, 207-225.

Justice, L. M., and Pullen, P. C., (2003). Promising interventions for promoting emergent literacy skills: Three evidence-based approaches. *Topics in Early Childhood Special Education*, 23, 99-113.

Katai, Z., and Toth, L. (2010). Technologically and artistically enhanced multi-sensory computer-programming education. *Teaching and Teacher Education*, 26, 244-251.

Koelewijn, T., Bronkhorst, A., and Theeuwes, J. (2010). Attention and multiple stages of multisensory integration: A review of audiovisual studies. *Acta Psychologica*, 134, 372-384.

Lehman, S., and Murray, M. M. (2005). The role of multisensory memories in unisensory object discrimination. *Cognitive Brain Research*. 24, 326-334.

Lesiak, J. L. (1997). Research based answers to questions about emergent literacy in kindergarten. *Psychology in the Schools*, 34, 143-160.

Levin, I., Shatil-Carmon, S., and Asif-Rave, O. (2006). Learning of letter names and sounds and their contribution to word recognition. *Journal of Experimental Child Psychology*, 93, 139-165.

Lewkowicz, D. J., and Kraebel, K. S. (2004). The value of multisensory redundancy in the development of intersensory perception. In G. Calvert, C. Spence, and B. E. Stein (Eds.), *The handbook of multisensory processes* (pp. 655-678). London, UK: MIT Press.

Lhote, M., and Streri, A. (1998). Haptic memory and handedness in 2-month-old infants. *Laterality*, 3, 173-192.

Lickliter, R., Bahrick, L. E., and Honeycutt, H. (2002). Intersensory redundancy facilitates perceptual learning in bobwhite quail embryos. *Developmental Psychology*, 38, 15-23.

Lickliter, R., and Bahrick, L. E. (2004). Perceptual development and the origins of multisensory responsiveness. In G. Calvert, C. Spence and B. E. Stein (Eds.), *The handbook of multisensory processes* (pp. 643-654). London, UK: MIT Press.

Lomax, R. G., and L. M. McGee. (1987). Young children's concepts about print and reading: Toward a model of word reading acquisition. *Reading Research Quarterly*, 22, 237-256.

Mann, V. A., and Foy, J. G. (2003). Phonological awareness, speech development, and letter knowledge in preschool children. *Annals of Dyslexia*, 53, 149-173.

Massaro, D. W. (1984). Children's perception of visual and auditory speech. *Child Development*, 55, 1777-1788.

Massaro, D. W. (1987). *Speech perception by ear and eye: A paradigm for psychological inquiry*. Hillsdale, NJ: Lawrence Erlbaum Assoc, Inc.

McGurk, H., and MacDonald, J. W. (1976). Hearing lips and seeing voices. *Nature*, 264, 746-748.

Minogue, J., and Jones, M. G. (2006). Haptics in education: Exploring an untapped sensory modality. *Review of Educational Research*, 76, 317-348.

Moats, L. C., and Farrell, M. L. (2005). Multisensory structured language education. In J. R. Birsch (Ed.), *Multisensory teaching of basic language skills* (2nd ed., pp. 23-41). Baltimore, Maryland: Paul H. Brookes.

Molfese, V. J., Beswick, J. L., Molnar, A., and Jacobi-Vessels, J. (2006). Alphabetic skills in preschool: a preliminary study of letter naming and letter writing. *Developmental Neuropsychology*, 29, 5-19.

Montessori, M. (1965). *Dr. Montessori's own handbook*. New York, NY: Schocken Books.

Mousavi, S. Y., Low, R., and Sweller, J. (1995). Reducing cognitive load by mixing auditory and visual presentation modes. *Journal of Educational Psychology*, 87, 319-334.

Murray, M. M., Michel, C. M., Grave de Peralta Menendez, R., Ortigue, S., Brunet, D., and Gonzalez Andino, S. L., et al. (2004). Rapid discrimination of visual and multisensory memories revealed by electrical neuroimaging. *Neuroimage*, 21, 125-135.

Neumann, M. M. (2007). *Up Downs: A fun and practical way to introduce reading and writing to children aged 2-5*. Sydney, Australia: Finch.

Neumann, M. M., Hood, M., and Neumann, D. L. (2009). The scaffolding of emergent literacy skills in the home environment: A case study. *Early Childhood Education Journal*, 36, 313-319.

Neumann, M. M., and Neumann, D. L. (2010). Parental strategies to scaffold emergent writing skills in the pre-school child within the home environment. *Early Years: An International Journal of Research and Development*, 30, 79-94.

Niedenthal, P. (2007). Embodying cognition. *Science*, 316, 1002-1005.

Nyberg, L., Habib, R., McIntosh, A.R., and Tulving, E. (2000). Reactivation of encoding-related brain activity during memory retrieval. *Proceedings of the National Academy of Sciences*, 97, 11120-11124.

Orton, J. L. (1957). The Orton story. *Bulletin of the Orton Society*, 7, 5-8.

Otto, B. (2008). *Literacy development in early childhood: Reflective teaching for birth to age eight*. Upper Saddle River, New Jersey: Pearson.

Perry, B. R., Pollard, R. Blakley, T. Baker., W and Vigilante, D. (1995). Childhood trauma, the neurobiology of adaptation and use dependent development in the brain: How states become traits. *Infant Mental Health Journal*, 16, 271-291.

Piaget, J. (1954). *The construction of reality in the child*. New York, NY: Basic Books.

Power, D. J., and Hyde, M. B. (1997). Multisensory and unisensory approaches to communicating with deaf children. *European Journal of Psychology of Education*, 12, 449-464.

Purcell-Gates, V. (1996). Stories, coupons, and the 'TV Guide': Relationships between home literacy experiences and emergent literacy knowledge. *Reading Research Quarterly*, 31, 406-428.

Putzar, L., Goerendt, I., Lange, K., Rosler, F., and Roder, B. (2007). Early visual deprivation impairs multisensory interactions in humans. *Nature Neuroscience*, 10, 1243-1245.

Rakison, D. H., and Woodward, A. L. (2008). New perspectives on the effects of action on perceptual and cognitive development. *Developmental Psychology*, 44, 1209-1213.

Richardson, S. O. (1997). The Montessori preschool: Preparation for writing and reading. *Annals of Dyslexia*, 47, 241-256.

Roberts, D. (Ed.) (2002). *Signals and Perception: The Fundamentals of Human Sensation.* New York, NY: Palgrave MacMillan.

Robinson, C. W., and Sloutsky, V. M. (2004). Auditory dominance and its change in the course of development. *Child Development,* 75, 1387-1401.

Rosenblum, L.D., Schmuckler, M.A., and Johnson, J.A. (1997). The McGurk effect in infants. *Perception and Psychophysics,* 59, 347-357.

Saracho, O. N. (1997). Using the home environment to support emergent literacy. *Early Child Development and Care,* 127-128, 210-216.

Scanlon, D. M., and Vellutino, F. R. (1996). Prerequisite skills, early instruction, and success in first-grade reading: selected results from a longitudinal study. *Mental Retardation and Developmental Disabilities Research Reviews,* 2, 54-63.

Schroeder, C. E., Lindsley, R. W., Specht, C., Marcovici, A., Smiley, J. F and Javitt, D. C. (2001). Somatosensory input to auditory association cortex in the macaque monkey. *Journal of Neurophysiology,* 85, 1322-1327.

Seitz, A. R., Kim, R., and Shams, L. (2006). Sound facilitates visual learning. *Current Biology,* 16, 1422-1427.

Shams, L., and Seitz, A. R. (2008). The benefits of multisensory learning. *Trends in Cognitive Sciences,* 12, 411-417.

Slingerland, B. (1977). *A multi-sensory approach to language arts for specific language disability children.* Cambridge, MA: Educators Publishing Service.

Snow, C. E., Burns, S., and Griffin, P. (1998). *Preventing reading difficulties in young children.* Washington, DC: National Academy Press.

Spalding, R. B., and Spalding, W. (1990). *The writing road to reading.* New York, NY: William Morrow and Company.

Spence, C. (2002). Multisensory integration, attention and perception. In D. Roberts (Ed.), *Signals and perception* (pp. 346-354). New York, NY: Palgrave Macmillan.

Stankov, L., Seizova-Cajic., and Roberts, R.D. (2001). Tactile and kinaesthetic perceptual processes within the taxonomy of human abilities. *Intelligence,* 29, 1-29.

Stein, B. E., Stanford, T. R., and Rowland, B. A. (2009). The neural basis of multisensory integration in the midbrain: Its organisation and maturation. *Hearing Research,* 258, 4-15.

Stuart, M., and Coltheart, M. (1988) Does reading develop in a sequence of stages? *Cognition,* 30, 139-181.

Vukelich, C., Christie, J., and Enz, B. (2008). *Helping young children learn language and literacy: Birth through kindergarten.* Boston, MA: Pearson.

Wallace, M. T., Meredith, M. A and Stein, B. E. (1992). Integration of multiple sensory modalities in cat cortex. *Experimental Brain Research,* 91, 484-488.

Wallace, M. T., and Stein, B. E. (2001). Sensory and multisensory responses in the newborn monkey superior colliculus. *The Journal of Neuroscience,* 21, 8886-8894.

Wallace, M. T. (2004). The development of multisensory integration. In G. Calvert, C. Spence, and B. E. Stein (Eds.), *The handbook of multisensory processes* (pp. 625-641). London, UK: MIT Press.

Weigel, D. J., Martin, S. S., and Bennett, K. K. (2006). Contributions of the home literacy environment to preschool-aged children's emerging literacy and language skills. *Early Child Development and Care,* 176, 357-378.

Welsch, J. G., Sullivan, A., and Justice, L. M. (2003). That's my letter!: What preschoolers' name writing representations tell us about emergent literacy knowledge. *Journal of Literacy Research*, 35, 757-776.

Wheeler, M. E., Peterson, S. E., and Buckner, R. L. (2000). Memory's echo: Vivid remembering reactivates sensory-specific cortex. *Proceedings of the National Academy of Sciences,* 97, 11125-11129.

Willis, J. (2009). What brain research suggests for teaching reading strategies. *Educational Forum*, 73, 333-346.

Wilson, B. (2000). *Wilson reading system*. Millbury, MA: Wilson Language Training.

Wood, D., Bruner, J. C., and Ross, G. (1976). The role of tutoring in problem solving. *Journal of Child Psychology and Psychiatry*, 17, 89-100.

Zafrana, M., Nikoltsou, K., and Daniilidou, E. (2000). Effective learning of writing and reading at preschool age with a multisensory method: A pilot study. *Perceptual and Motor Skills*, 91, 435-446.

Chapter 10

THE ROLE OF COGNITIVE AND PERCEPTUAL FACTORS IN EMERGENT LITERACY

Michelle Hood[1], Elizabeth Conlon and Glenda Andrews*

Behavioural Basis of Health Program,
Griffith Health Institute and School of Psychology
Griffith University.

ABSTRACT

This chapter reviews the limited existing evidence of the role of auditory and visual temporal processing in predicting the emergent literacy skills of letter-word identification and phonological awareness. It also reports the results of a new study that examined these relationships in 129 pre-school aged Australian children (mean age 5.36 years), after controlling for the contributions of age, nonverbal ability, attention, and memory. Both auditory and visual temporal processing were significantly related to letter-word identification, and this held even when the contribution of phonological awareness to letter-word identification was considered. However, contrary to expectations we did not find that visual temporal processing was more strongly associated with letter-word identification than auditory temporal processing. Temporal processing and phonological awareness each accounted for independent variance in letter-word identification. This has practical implications for early identification of children who might be at risk of later reading difficulties. Inclusion of both temporal and phonological processing predictors is likely to improve accuracy of prediction. The importance of controlling age, nonverbal ability, attention and both visuospatial and auditory-verbal memory skills in studies of temporal processing and reading is emphasised.

Keywords: Auditory Temporal Processing, Visual Temporal Processing, Phonological Processing, Letter Identification, Reading Development.

---

[1] * Email: michelle.hood@griffith.edu.au

INTRODUCTION

Perceptual factors, in particular, auditory and visual temporal processing ability, are related to reading ability (see Farmer and Klein, 1995, for review). The relationship between auditory and visual temporal processing and reading ability has been demonstrated in school-aged children, adolescents, and adults using psychophysical (Cacace, McFarland, Ouimet, Schreiber, and Marro, 2000; Chung et al., 2008; de Martino, Espesser, Rey, and Habib, 2001; Eden, Stein, Wood, and Wood, 1995; Habib et al., 2002; Landerl and Willburger, 2010; Reed, 1989; Richardson, Thomson, Scott, and Goswami, 2004; Talcott et al., 2000, 2002; Tallal, 1980), anatomical (Galaburda, Menard, and Rosen, 1994), electrophysiological (Lehmkuhle, Garzia, Turner, Hash, and Baro, 1993), and neuroimaging (Demb, Boynton, and Heeger, 1998) paradigms. Longitudinal studies have also demonstrated a significant relationship between pre-school psychophysical measures of auditory and visual temporal processing and subsequent reading ability (Hood and Conlon, 2004; Kevan and Pammer, 2009; Lovegrove, Slaghuis, Bowling, Nelson, and Geeves, 1986; Share, Jorm, MacLean, and Matthews, 2002). However, very little work to date has examined the relationships between auditory and visual temporal processing and emergent literacy skills prior to formal reading (Boets, Wouters, van Wieringen, and Ghesquière, 2006a, b). Establishing that individual differences in temporal processing are related to emergent literacy in a similar manner to the relationships already established with later reading ability strengthens support for a causal role for temporal processing in the development of reading ability and disability.

Emergent literacy skills are the foundation upon which young children build subsequent reading and other literacy skills. The two emergent literacy skills that are the strongest predictors of future reading ability are letter knowledge (letter naming and sound knowledge) and phonological awareness (Adams, 1990; Bowman and Treiman, 2004; Ehri and Roberts, 2006; Foulin, 2005; Levin, Shatil-Carmon, and Asif-Rave, 2006; Molfese, Beswick, Molnar, and Jacobi-Vessels, 2006; Muter and Diethelm, 2001). These two skills make independent contributions to early reading (Bradley and Bryant, 1991; Share, Jorm, MacLean, and Matthews, 1984) and differ between older groups with reading disability versus normal reading (Brady and Shankweiler, 1991; Catts, Fey, Zhang, and Tomblin, 2001; Swan and Goswami, 1997).

This chapter reviews the existing evidence of a relationship between temporal processing and literacy skills, including emergent literacy, and reports results of a new study on the relationships between auditory and visual temporal processing and letter-word identification and phonological awareness. It also highlights the importance of taking into account other cognitive and perceptual factors such as attention, memory, and general cognitive ability when examining these relationships. The chapter begins with a review of the role of the phonological awareness and letter knowledge in reading development and disability.

Phonological Awareness and Reading

Phonological awareness refers to the conscious ability to use and manipulate the sounds of the language to process written and oral language (Wagner and Torgesen, 1987). Common phonological awareness tasks are ones that require detection of phonological units at the syllable (e.g., rhyme detection) or phoneme level (e.g., initial sound or alliteration detection) and those that require segmentation and deletion of these phonological units. Syllables correspond to identifiable articulatory bursts, so they are the smallest independently articulated segments of speech (Wagner and Torgesen, 1987). They are the easiest and earliest phonological units for which children develop conscious awareness (Treiman and Zukowski, 1991). Rhyming words involve units that are usually between syllables and phonemes in size (Treiman, 1985). From 3 years of age, children can isolate and detect syllables and recognise rhymes (MacLean, Bryant, and Bradley, 1987). Phonemes are single meaningful units of speech sound (Rack, 1994). Phonemes are more difficult to separate from the acoustic stream of speech because, unlike syllables, they have no distinct boundaries. Thus, phoneme awareness generally develops later, around 5 to 6 years of age (Treiman and Zukowski, 1991). Phoneme awareness tasks include phoneme counting, phoneme deletion, and segmenting words into phonemes.

Longitudinal studies have demonstrated that phonological awareness measured before school entry predicts subsequent reading ability (Boets et al., 2010; Bowey, 1994; 1995; Bradley and Bryant, 1983; Bryant, MacLean, Bradley, and Crossland, 1990; Lundberg, Olofsson, and Wall, 1980; Puolakanaho et al., 2007). Cross-sectional studies with older English- or French- speaking children showed similar relationships between phonological awareness and reading to those found in the longitudinal studies (Betourne and Friel-Patti, 2003; Plaza and Cohen, 2003).

In their classic longitudinal study, Bradley and Bryant (1983) found that rhyme and alliteration detection abilities at 4 to 5 years accounted for significant variance (47.98% for 4-year-olds and 29.88% for 5-year-olds) in single word reading scores measured 3 years later. However, when IQ, verbal ability, age, and memory were controlled, smaller, albeit still significant, percentages of variance were explained (10% and 4%, respectively). Other longitudinal studies confirmed that rhyme detection at 4 to 5 years was the most important predictor of single word reading ability or discriminator between good and poor reading ability groups 2 to 3 years later (Bryant et al., 1990; Ellis and Large, 1987). However, others failed to find significant relationships with rhyme tasks (Lundberg, Frost, and Peterson, 1988; Muter and Diethelm, 2001; Muter, Hulme, Snowling, and Taylor, 1997).

Phoneme sensitivity may be a more important predictor of subsequent word reading than rhyme sensitivity (Bowey, 2002). For example, Lundberg et al. (1980) found that performance on kindergarten measures that required analysis of phonemes was more strongly predictive of Grade 1 reading achievement in Scandinavian children than those that required analysis of syllables, like rhyme tasks. Muter and Diethelm (2001) obtained similar results with English speaking and multilingual children.

Poor readers or those with dyslexia perform more poorly than do average or good readers on measures of rhyme detection and phonological segmentation (Brady and Shankweiler, 1991; Swan and Goswami, 1997). Thus, better reading development is associated with greater phonological awareness and when this is impaired, reading difficulties result. This is referred to as the phonological processing deficit hypothesis (Wagner and Torgesen, 1987).

Phonological awareness also predicts letter knowledge (Bradley and Bryant, 1983; Ellis and Large, 1987; Fritjers, Barron, and Brunello, 2000; Lundberg et al., 1980). For example, Fritjers et al. (2000) found 45% common variance between phonological sensitivity and letter knowledge. This is at least partially due to shared variance with letter-sound knowledge. However, Adams (1990) argued that the names of many letters also contain information about the sound of that letter (e.g., *b, d, j;* although letters such as *m, c, s* do not), so provide a link to phonology.

Letter Knowledge and Reading

Children learning to read an alphabetic language such as English must learn letter–sound (grapheme-phoneme) pairs. While typically developing beginner readers acquire this knowledge very quickly, certainly within the first year of beginning to read, automaticity in terms of auditory-visual integration occurs over an extended period (Blomert, in press). Blomert and Willems (2010) showed that many pre-readers at familial risk for dyslexia failed to acquire this letter-sound knowledge after training, although they did not show phonological awareness deficits.

Letter name and sound knowledge predict early word and non-word reading, reading comprehension, and spelling (Badian, 1993, 1995; Bond and Dykstra, 1967; Bowey, 1995; Gallagher, Frith, and Snowling, 2000; McBride-Change, 1999; Muter and Diethelm, 2001; Muter et al., 1997; Puolakanaho et al., 2007; Scarborough, 1998). Letter name knowledge measured before or at the start of first grade predicted around one third of the variance in word and non-word identification and reading comprehension at the end of first grade (Bond and Dykstra, 1967; Bowey, 1995). Leppänen, Aunola, Niemi, and Nurmi (2008) found that kindergarten letter knowledge was the strongest predictor of reading skills (reading comprehension, text reading and word chain reading) in Grade 4, indicating long-term predictive utility. Not only the accuracy but also the speed of naming letters strongly predicts reading acquisition (Badian, 1993). Adams (1990) argued that letter naming is related to early reading because greater fluency in letter identification frees conscious resources to manipulate phonological segments in order to decode the word.

Letter knowledge also differentiates between groups with reading disability or familial risk for disability and those with normally developing reading (Boets et al., 2006b; Catts et al., 2001; Puolakanaho et al., 2007; Torppa, Poikkeus, Laakso, Eklund, and Lyytinen, 2006). Torppa et al. (2006) found that children with delayed letter knowledge development were more likely to have a family history of dyslexia, whereas those with precocious letter knowledge development were not, and that delayed letter knowledge prior to school predicted Grade 1 reading ability. They also found that phonological skill predicted delayed letter knowledge. Boets et al. (2006b) found that an at-risk group of kindergarten-aged children (parent with dyslexia) differed significantly from a control group (no parent with dyslexia) on letter knowledge. In a follow-up study when these children were in Grade 3, Boets et al. (2010) reported that those who were formally diagnosed with dyslexia had significantly poorer letter knowledge when in kindergarten. Those not diagnosed by Grade 3 did not differ on kindergarten letter knowledge regardless of whether there was familial risk or not.

The Temporal Processing Hypothesis

Temporal processing is the ability to process very brief, rapidly presented or changing (temporal) stimuli. It is related to normally developing reading (Hood and Conlon, 2004; Kevan and Pammer, 2009; Lovegrove et al., 1986; Share et al., 2002) as well as reading disability (Chung et al., 2008; de Martino et al., 2001; Eden et al., 1995; Farmer and Klein, 1993; Habib et al., 2002; Kevan and Pammer, 2009; Landerl and Willburger, 2010; Reed, 1989; Richardson et al., 2004; Talcott et al., 2000; 2002; Tallal, 1980). Thus, better reading development is associated with greater temporal processing skills and when these are impaired, reading difficulties result. This is referred to as the temporal processing deficit hypothesis (Farmer and Klein, 1995; Habib, 2000).

Various psychophysical tasks have been used to measure auditory and visual temporal processing in children. The study reported in this chapter used temporal order judgment (TOJ) tasks. TOJ tasks involve reporting the correct order or the first stimulus in a sequence of two or more rapidly presented stimuli to either the visual or the auditory modalities. Auditory TOJ tasks can use non-verbal tones (e.g., low, 100 Hz, and high, 305 Hz, tones) or speech sounds (e.g., /ba/ and /da/; Heath, Hogben, and Clark, 1999; Reed, 1989). Normally, listeners can correctly judge auditory temporal order when interstimulus intervals (ISIs; the interval between the two stimuli) are around 17 to 40 ms or longer (Hirsch, 1959; Kanabus, Szelag, Rojek, and Pöppel, 2002). However, groups with aphasia, lesions of the posterior left hemisphere, or reading difficulties show much longer thresholds; that is, need longer ISIs to report order accurately (Kanabus et al., 2002; Wittman, Burtsher, Fries, and von Steinbuchel, 2004). In her classic study, Tallal (1980) found that 8- to 12-year-olds with dyslexia were significantly less accurate than a control group at judging auditory temporal order at ISIs up to 305 ms. Many studies have subsequently replicated these findings with children and adolescents with various languages (Chung et al., 2008; de Martino et al., 2001; Farmer and Klein, 1993; Goswami et al., 2002; Habib et al., 2002; Landerl and Willburger, 2010; Reed, 1989; Richardson et al., 2004; Stark, Tallal, and McCauley, 1988). Other studies failed to find significant between-group differences on auditory TOJ (Marshall, Snowling, and Bailey, 2001; Nittrouer, 1999). Chung et al. (2008) found that in Chinese children the group differences only occurred with chronological age-matched controls and not with reading age-matched controls. Other studies have also found significant between-group differences at longer ISIs, up to 428 ms (Cestnick and Jerger, 2000; Waber et al., 2001), suggesting a more generalized impairment than for just very rapidly presented stimuli (Klein, 2002).

To date, only two studies (Hood and Conlon, 2004; Share et al., 2002) have shown that pre-reading non-verbal auditory TOJ predicts subsequent reading development. Hood and Conlon (2004) found that auditory TOJ at short ISIs (up to 300 ms) explained significant variance in Grade 1 word identification and reading rate, after controlling for age, memory, attention, general cognitive ability, the quality of the home literacy environment, and visual temporal processing. Share et al. (2002) found auditory TOJ at both short and long ISIs predicted word reading accuracy and rate and non-word reading accuracy in second and third grades, after controlling for attention and the number of trials taken to learn the TOJ task.

Some (Brady, 1997; Studdert-Kennedy and Mody, 1995) have questioned whether TOJ deficits in those with reading difficulties are due to a deficit in auditory temporal processing or to difficulties in identification or discrimination. For example, Mody, Studdert-Kennedy, and Brady (1997) found the typical TOJ deficit of poor readers ($n = 20$ Grade 2 children) only occurred with phonetically similar pairs of syllables like /ba/ and /da/ but not with dissimilar pairs like /ba/ and /sa/. However, Denenberg (1999) identified several methodological and statistical flaws in Mody et al.'s study, which might explain these contradictory results. Other evidence also counters an interpretation in terms of faulty discriminative capacity. de Martino et al. (2001) obtained significant between-group differences using quite distinct consonants,

/p/ and /s/. Furthermore, the lack of significant between-group differences on simple stimulus identification tasks, which involve only discriminative capacity, also argues against this interpretation (Farmer and Klein, 1995; Wright, Bowen, and Zecker, 2000).

Visual TOJ tasks are sensitive measures of information transmission speed (Ulrich, 1987). According to the general threshold model of temporal order judgement, there must be a minimal difference between the arrival times at a temporal comparator of responses to the two visual stimuli for order to be perceived correctly. If the two visual responses arrive too closely together, the comparator cannot distinguish the order and perceives them as simultaneous. Thus, the ISI between the stimuli and the transmission latencies of the visual signals from the retina to the comparator determine whether the order is correctly perceived (Stelmach and Herdman, 1991). Ulrich (1987) presents a different explanation that focuses on attention switching, attentional dwell time, and the time taken to detect the first stimulus before switching attention to the other stimulus. As soon as the presence of the first stimulus is registered, attention switches to the other stimulus. If attentional dwell time is prolonged or attentional shifting is sluggish, longer ISIs would be required between the two stimuli to allow time for the switch. At short ISIs, the second stimulus would have occurred before attention switched, resulting in the incorrect decision that the second stimulus arrived simultaneously with or before the first one.

In the earliest reported study of visual TOJ and reading, Muller and Bakker (1968, cited in Bakker and Satz, 1970) found that accuracy of judging the order of two-stimulus sequences of red and yellow light flashes presented with 75 ms ISIs to 12-year-old reading-delayed boys was related to the extent of the reading delay. In other studies with 8- to 12-year-old children with various languages, groups of poor or disabled readers had significantly higher thresholds or were significantly less accurate than age-matched controls when judging the order of verbal (e.g., *BOX* and *FOX*) or non-verbal (e.g., # and *and*) stimuli (Brannan and Williams, 1988; Bretherton and Holmes, 2003; Cacace et al., 2000; Chung et al., 2008; Landerl and Willburger, 2010; May, Williams, and Dunlap, 1988). However, a few studies failed to find significant between-group differences on visual TOJ, despite finding significant differences on auditory TOJ tasks in the same sample (Heim, Freeman, Eulitz, and Elbert, 2001; Farmer and Klein, 1993; Reed, 1989). The type of control group (chronological age or reading age matched) might explain differences as Chung et al. (2008) found.

Brannan and Williams (1988) found that the minimum ISI required to judge order correctly accounted for 44% of the variance in reading level when stimuli were non-verbal and 30% of the variance when stimuli were verbal. Other studies found that visual TOJ performance accounted for around 10% of the variance in word and non-word identification (Farmer and Klein, 1993; Landerl and Willburger, 2010). A couple of studies found that visual TOJ explained independent variance in reading to that explained by auditory TOJ, after controlling for factors such as age, IQ, and attention (Chung et al., 2008; Hood and Conlon, 2004; Landerl and Willburger, 2010).

Results with longitudinal predictive studies of the relationship between pre-school visual temporal processing and subsequent reading have been mixed. Using an unselected sample, Hood and Conlon (2004) found that visual TOJ measured prior to school entry did not predict Grade 1 reading but when measured concurrently was related to Grade 1 reading rate. Kevan and Pammer (2009) found that pre-school frequency doubling sensitivity was predictive of Grade 1 letter-word identification and word attack skills, after controlling for age, IQ, and prior letter knowledge, but that coherent motion detection was not. Boets et al. (2008) found that coherent motion detection was only indirectly related to Grade 1 reading and spelling via its relationship with kindergarten letter identification. Thus, controlling prior letter knowledge in Kevan and Pammer's study would explain their null result. More work examining the relationship of preschool visual temporal processing and this emergent literacy skill is needed to understand fully the relationship with subsequent reading.

Auditory and visual temporal processing are believed to be related to reading development via different mechanisms. Tallal (2003; 2004) argued that impairments in auditory temporal processing interfere with early speech perception. Individual differences in the degree to which the brain responds to differences in speech sounds and the speed with which it does so appear to be present from birth (Benasich and Tallal, 2002; Lyytinen et al., 2005; Molfese, 2000). Interference with speech perception in the first year of life is hypothesised to result in the formation of unstable phonemic representations (Tallal, 2003; 2004). The formation of stable phonemic representations requires the ability to segment the steady acoustic stream into chunks of time in the order of tens of milliseconds and to form neural representations based on the consistency and frequency of the particular neural firing patterns generated. In contrast, the formation of stable syllabic representations only requires chunking over durations in the order of hundreds of milliseconds due to syllables representing independent articulatory bursts (Tallal, 2003). Unstable phonemic representations impair subsequent phonological processing, which, in turn, interferes with normal reading development.

Consistent with this hypothesis, Galaburda et al. (1994) found more small and fewer large neurons in the Medial Geniculate Nucleus (MGN) in the left hemisphere in the brains of five dyslexic adults at post-mortem. This was not observed in the brains of controls and no differences between controls and dyslexic brains were observed in the right hemisphere or in mean neuronal area. Large neurons are important for processing the frequency and amplitude changes that signal phonetic contrasts (Rauschecker, 1998). Galaburda et al. concluded that the reduced number of large neurons in the left hemisphere could result in impaired processing of rapid temporal auditory transitions, and that this could underlie the phonological deficits found in dyslexia.

Visual temporal processing is a function of the magnocellular visual pathway (M pathway; Lennie, Trevarthen, van Essen, and Wässle, 1990). The M pathway provides the major input to the posterior parietal cortex (Lehmkuhle, 1993; Lennie et al., 1990), which is involved in various functions relevant to reading, such as eye-movement control, visuospatial attention, and peripheral vision (Corbetta et al., 1998; Marois, Chun, and Gore, 2000; see also Stein and Walsh, 1997). Physical or chemically induced lesions of the posterior parietal cortex can produce acquired dyslexia with characteristic reading errors, including letter omissions and letter naming errors (Brunn and Farah, 1991).

These different mechanisms have given rise to modality-specific hypotheses regarding these relationships. Auditory temporal processing is hypothesised to be associated with phonological processes in reading due to its interference the development of stable phonemic representations (Tallal, 2003; 2004). Visual temporal processing has been associated with orthographic processes, via which readers recognize symbols (including letters), words, or spelling sequences as visual wholes (Boets, Wouters, van Wieringen, De Smedt, and Ghesquiere, 2008; Sperling, Lu, Manis, and Seidenberg, 2003; Talcott et al., 2000).

While there is evidence that temporal processing is related to reading, very little work to date has examined the relationships between auditory and visual temporal processing and the important emergent literacy skills of phonological processing and letter identification. Establishing that temporal processing is related to emergent literacy as well as reading strengthens support for a causal role in the development of reading ability and disability by establishing temporal precedence. We are aware of only a few studies (Boets et al., 2006a; b; Share et al., 2002) that have examined these relationships. The following sections review this evidence and evidence of relationships between temporal processing and phonological processing and letter knowledge in older samples.

Relationship of Temporal Processing and Phonological Processing

Auditory temporal processing measured using TOJ tasks (Chiappe, Stringer, Siegel, and Stanovich, 2002; Farmer and Klein, 1993; Marshall et al., 2001; Share et al., 2002) as well as gap detection (Chiappe et al., 2002) and frequency modulation (FM) detection tasks (Cornelissen, Hansen, Hutton, Evangelinou, and Stein, 1998; Talcott et al., 2000) was significantly related to phonological processing in school-aged children, adolescents, and adults. However, two studies with school-aged or older participants failed to find significant relationships between auditory temporal processing and phonological processing in children (Bretherton and Holmes, 2003; Watson and Miller, 1993). Using a sample of Dutch pre-school aged children ($N = 62$), half of whom were at familial risk of dyslexia, Boets et al. (2006a; b; see also Boets et al., 2008; 2010) found that 2 Hz FM-detection was related to a range of phonological awareness skills, including rhyme identity and initial and end sound identities. This was independent of differences in age and nonverbal ability. However, gap detection was not. Using an unselected sample of English-speaking children, Share et al. (2002) found relationships between auditory TOJ accuracy at school entry and phoneme segmentation at school entry and at Grade 2. However, as already discussed, these results were found at both long and short ISIs.

Significant relationships were found between phonological awareness and visual temporal processing measured using visual TOJ (Farmer and Klein, 1993; Kinsbourne, Rufo, Gamzu, Palmer, and Berliner, 1991), rapid visual sequencing (the temporal dot task; Eden et al., 1995), coherent motion detection (Talcott et al., 2002), gap detection (Chiappe et al., 2002), and contrast sensitivity (Olson and Datta, 2002) in school-aged children, adolescents, and adults. Boets et al. (2006a; 2008) failed to find a significant correlation between coherent motion and phonological processing in their preschool sample, despite finding a significant correlation between auditory temporal processing and phonological processing. However, based on the specific hypothesis that auditory, and not visual, temporal processing is related to reading via phonological processing, we would expect auditory temporal processing to show stronger relationships with phonological processing and visual temporal processing to show stronger relationships with the orthographic task of letter identification.

Temporal Processing and Letter Knowledge

Fewer studies have examined temporal processing and letter processing. In 9- to 11-year olds, Cornelissen et al. (1998) found there was a significant positive, but non-linear, relationship between coherent motion detection and the number of letter errors made in reading. This relationship was independent of phonological awareness, IQ, age, and reading ability. Boets et al. (2006a; b) found that both coherent motion detection and 2-Hz FM-detection were significantly correlated with letter knowledge in preschoolers, after age and general cognitive ability were partialled out. In their control group, visual temporal processing accounted for more variance in letter knowledge than did auditory temporal processing, but in their at-risk group, only auditory temporal processing was independently related to letter knowledge. Boets et al. (2008) showed further that the relationship between coherent motion detection and letter knowledge was independent of any variance associated with phonological processing. More research examining these relationships in a larger unselected sample of English speaking pre-readers is required.

The Current Study

The current study examined the relationships between auditory and visual temporal processing, measured using TOJ tasks, and the emergent literacy skills of phonological awareness (rhyme detection and phonological deletion) and letter-word identification or naming (Letter-word Identification subtest of the Woodcock Diagnostic Reading Battery; Woodcock, 1997). We chose letter-word identification or naming alone rather than including letter sound knowledge to try to get as clean a measure of early orthographic skill as possible without inclusion of phonological skill associated with letter sound knowledge.

We controlled for general cognitive ability, short-term memory, attention, and speech and language difficulties. Consistent with previous studies (e.g., Boets et al., 2006a; b; Share et al., 2002), nonverbal reasoning was used as a measure of general cognitive ability. Rosen (2003) provided evidence that the relationship between reading and auditory temporal processing may be at least partially explained by overlapping variance with nonverbal ability. Wagner and Torgesen (1987) criticised many existing studies for not controlling nonverbal ability and short-term memory. Auditory-verbal short-term memory predicts early reading (Mann and Liberman, 1984) and is involved in performance on auditory (McArthur and Bishop, 2001) and visual (Booth, Perfetti, MacWhinney, and Hunt, 2000) temporal processing tasks. Nazir and Huckauf (2008) argued that skilled reading relies on pattern memories that develop through training with print in early levels of visual processing. On this basis, we also controlled visuospatial memory, which is likely to play a role in storage of these abstract visual letter symbols.

Differences in attention might also influence temporal processing accuracy (Davis, Castles, McAnally, and Gray, 2001; Landerl and Willburger, 2010; Stuart, McAnally, and Castles, 2001). Temporal processing tasks require sustained vigilance because they involve many trials (McArthur and Bishop, 2001). Poor visual (Eden et al., 1995; Stuart et al., 2001) and auditory (Breier, Fletcher, Foorman, Klaas, and Gray, 2003) temporal processing has been associated with the presence of Attention Deficit Disorders; although Waber et al. (2001) found the difference between learning impaired and non-learning impaired groups on an auditory TOJ task remained when participants with these disorders were excluded. There is also a high co-morbidity between Attention Deficit Disorders and reading disability (Dykman and Ackerman, 1991; Semrud-Clikeman et al., 1992). Landerl and Willburger (2010) found that alertness, flexibility of attention and sustained attention accounted for 27% of the variance in visual and 20% in auditory TOJ in German schoolchildren, although even with this accounted for visual TOJ still was significantly related to reading. Therefore, we included catch trials on all temporal processing tasks to measure poor attending (based on Stein's, 2003, argument) and assessed general inattentiveness during all testing.

There is also some evidence that the relationship between auditory TOJ performance and reading difficulty is related to comorbid language difficulty (Heath et al., 1999; Stark et al., 1988; Tallal, 1980; Tallal and Stark, 1982). We excluded any children identified as having speech and language problems.

We hypothesised auditory temporal processing would be more strongly correlated with phonological awareness and visual temporal processing with letter-word identification. We also examined whether temporal processing accounted for independent variance in letter-word identification to that explained by phonological processing.

METHOD

Participants

We excluded potential participants if they were reported by parents and/or teachers to have intellectual, neurological, or developmental disorders that might constitute biological risk factors for learning problems (Fletcher et al., 2002). They were also excluded if English was not their main language, resulting in a predominantly Caucasian sample, with 6.98% who had Asian or Indigenous heritage. We also excluded children who were reported to have speech and language problems and/or hearing difficulties or a history of ear infections as well as those who had a standardised score below 80 on nonverbal (Raven's Coloured Progressive Matrices; Raven, Court, and Raven, 1986) or verbal ability (Peabody Picture Vocabulary Test-III; Dunn and Dunn, 1981). Finally, we excluded children who were already able to read (defined as being able to identify more than the first few words on the Woodcock Letter-Word Identification subtest, Woodcock, 1997) as the study was focused on letter not word identification. In total, 30 children for whom consent to participate was obtained were excluded based on these criteria.

The final sample comprised 129 children (45.7% girls; mean age 5 years, 4 months, $SD =$ 3 months, range = 4 years, 10 months to 5 years, 11 months). All were reported to have normal or corrected to normal vision. They were enrolled in government Preschools on the Gold Coast, Australia. The Preschools consisted mainly of low to middle class families. Preschool was a non-compulsory year prior to school entry, which was attended by 92.6% of eligible children during the period of this study (Education Queensland, 2006). Children attended Preschool for 12.5 hours over 2.5 days each week. There was a play-based curriculum but children were encouraged to write their names on art works, were regularly read to, and engaged in games to promote phonological awareness, such as singing nursery rhymes. Formal instruction in reading and writing did not begin until the following year (Grade 1).

Materials

Temporal Processing Tasks

Auditory Temporal Order Judgement (Auditory TOJ). The Sound Order sub-test of the Dyslexia Early Screening Test (DEST; Nicolson and Fawcett, 1996) assesses auditory temporal order judgement in children aged 4.50 to 6.42 years. Nicholson and Fawcett reported one-week test-retest reliability for children aged 5.50 to 6.50 years of .64. Sound stimuli (155ms duration) consisted of low (duck quack, 166 Hz) and high (mouse squeak, 1430 Hz) tones presented in random order on an audiotape played on a Sony TCM 939 portable tape player. Short inter-stimulus intervals (ISIs) of varying length (8, 15, 30, 60, 150, and 300 ms) separated the two stimuli. There were 4 identification (single sound), 4 practice, and 14 experimental trials (2 or 3 trials at each ISI). Two trials with 947 ms ISIs were used as catch trials to detect inattention during this task. Participants reported the sound that occurred first, giving their best guess if they were not sure (a two alternate forced-choice, 2AFC, response format). The dependent measure was overall accuracy, collapsed across all ISIs (max = 14). Overall accuracy scores have been used previously with children and adolescents in both between-groups and normative designs (Farmer and Klein, 1993; Marshall et al., 2001; Share et al., 2002).

Visual Temporal Order Judgement (Visual TOJ). This was based on Reed's (1989) task and used nonverbal stimuli, which are considered purer tests of visual processing than verbal stimuli as the latter involve greater phonological processing (Vellutino, 1979). Stimuli were presented on an IBM compatible PC with a 17-inch monitor at a screen refresh rate of 18 ms. Viewing was binocular, under natural light conditions, and at a distance of 57cm. A 500 ms high frequency auditory cue preceded each trial. A central white fixation cross appeared 500 ms prior to stimulus onset and remained visible throughout each trial. Participants were trained to fixate on this throughout. Stimuli were white circles, subtending 1° of visual angle, presented on a grey background (space average luminance 15 cd/m^2). The first stimulus appeared randomly to either the left or right of fixation, followed by the second stimulus on the opposite side. Stimulus duration was 83 ms. ISIs of 11, 22, 33, 44, 55, 75, 100, 150, and 200 ms separated presentation of the first and second stimuli. The proximal distance of each stimulus to central fixation subtended 2° of visual angle. Figure 1 illustrates the task.

There were 4 identification (single stimulus only), 4 practice (2 each at 44 and 200 ms ISIs), and 72 experimental (8 at each ISI, half with initial right and half with initial left presentation) trials. Eight catch trials, involving only a single stimulus, were interspersed randomly among the experimental trials to detect poor attentional vigilance (Stein, 2003). Trials were presented in blocks of 10, with rest breaks between blocks. Participants indicated the side on which the stimulus first appeared (a 2AFC response format) either verbally or by pointing. The dependent measure was overall accuracy, collapsed across ISI (max = 72). An overall accuracy measure was used in previous studies with a visual TOJ task (Farmer and Klein, 1993).

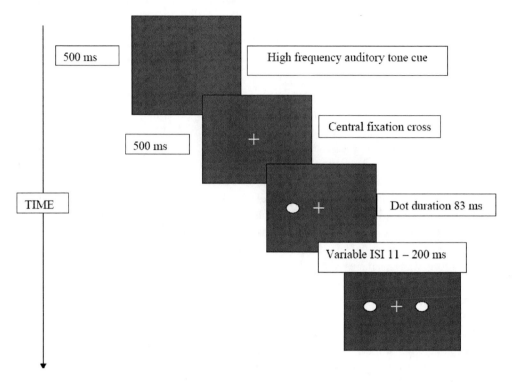

Figure 1. Visual temporal order judgement task.

Phonological Awareness

There were two measures of phonological awareness: the Rhymes subtest from the Cognitive Profiling System (CoPS; Singleton, Thomas, and Leedale, 1997) and the Phonemic Segmentation subtest from the Dyslexia Screening Test (DST; Fawcett and Nicolson, 1996). CoPS is a computerized early screening test for children aged 4.5 years and over. In validation studies, the CoPS' prediction rate for reading risk was over 90%, with acceptable false negative (12.0% to 16.7%) and false positive (around 2 %) rates (Fawcett, Singleton, and Peer, 1998). On each Rhymes trial, the child saw four stimulus pictures on the computer screen and heard their names, followed by a target picture and its name. All pictures remained visible throughout the trial to reduce memory demands. Participants chose the stimulus picture/word that rhymed with the target picture/word. There were 2 practice and 8 rhyme trials. The dependent measure was the number of correct trials (max = 8).

The test-retest reliability of the DST in a sample of 6.5- to 12-year-olds was .88 (Fawcett and Nicolson, 1996). On the Phonemic Segmentation subtest, the experimenter read a word, which the participant repeated with a specified phonological segment deleted (e.g., say *train* without *t*-results in *rain*). The segments to be deleted ranged from single words within compound words (2 trials), syllables within multisyllabic words (1 trial) and phonemes (9 trials). The location of the deleted segment varied across initial, medial, and final positions within the word. Two practice trails preceded 12 experimental trials. The dependent measure was the number of correct deletions (max = 12). Scores on the Rhymes and Phonemic

Segmentation tasks were summed to form a composite phonological awareness measure (max = 20).

Letter-Word Identification

This was the Letter Word Identification subtest of the Woodcock Diagnostic Reading Battery (WDRB; Woodcock, 1997). It involves retrieval of letters and words from the mental lexicon. As the participants were pre-readers, the task mostly focused on letter identification. Reported internal consistency was .94 for 5- to 18-year-olds (Woodcock, 1997).

Control Measures

Auditory-verbal memory. This was the Digit Span Forward subtest from the DEST (Nicolson and Fawcett, 1996). Reported 1-week test-retest reliability for 5.42- to 6.42- year-olds was .63 (Nicolson and Fawcett, 1996). There were two trials per span length from 2 to 9 digits. Digits were read out at 1-second intervals. Children immediately recalled the sequence of digits. Testing ceased when both trials at a given span length were recalled incorrectly. The score was the number of correctly recalled trials (max = 16).

Visuospatial memory. The Rabbits subtest of CoPS was used (Singleton et al., 1997). A rabbit appears in a random sequence of rabbit holes at different spatial locations on the computer screen. The sequence of holes ranges from two (initial level) to four (final level) out of 10 possible holes. The child indicated the correct sequence of holes the rabbit appeared in by pointing to them after the sequence finished. There were two to three trials at each number of holes. The dependent measure was the total number of holes recalled in correct order (max = 32).

Attention. There were three measures of attention; scores on catch trials for the two TOJ measures and the total score on Inattentiveness items from the Guide to Assessment of Test Session Behavior (GATSB; Glutting and Oakland, 1993) completed during sessions by the experimenter. Stein (2003) argued that using the proportion of catch trials missed on psychophysical tasks as a covariate allows the effects of inattention or lack of motivation to be partialled out. The GATSB includes 9 items regarding concentration and attention to task during testing (e.g., *Is sensitive to minor disturbances of competing stimuli such as noises, lights, visual phenomena*) rated on a 3-point Likert scale (1 = *Usually applies* to 3 = *Doesn't apply*, some items reverse scored), yielding a total score out of 27. There were 8 catch trials on the visual TOJ on which only a single stimulus appeared. These were interspersed randomly among the experimental trials to detect poor attention or random responding. There were two catch trials on the auditory TOJ task where stimuli were presented at extremely long ISIs (947ms), which should be detectable by all children unless not attending well. Scores on each measure were standardised (due to differences in the measurement scales) and summed to form a composite attention measure. Higher scores indicated greater attention.

Nonverbal Cognitive Ability. We used Raven's Coloured Progressive Matrices (Raven et al., 1986), with reported Cronbach's alpha for an Australian sample (mean age 5.5 years) of 0.80.

Procedure

This research had ethical clearance and schools and parents provided written consent. Testing occurred in the final term (Term 4) of the Preschool year. Testing was individual, in a quiet room at the school, conducted over several sessions of 5 to 15 minutes each to minimise fatigue and boredom.

Testing ceased if a child was inattentive, uncooperative, or fatigued. Standardised testing procedures were used for the commercial tests. Administration procedures for other tests are described under Materials. Measures were administered in random order. The GATSB was completed at each testing sessions and scores averaged.

RESULTS

There was 1.9% missing data. Little's Missing Completely at Random Test (conducted via SPSS version 17 Missing Values Analysis) indicated that these were missing completely at random, $\chi^2(43, N = 129) = 51.15$, $p = .18$. Multiple imputation was used to replace the missing data and the pooled estimate (based on five imputations) was used in subsequent analyses.

Table 1 shows the descriptive statistics for the control measures, the temporal and phonological processing measures, and letter-word identification. Attention and visuospatial memory were negatively skewed. Scores were first reflected and then inverse or square root transformed, respectively, to normalise the distribution. Results are reported with these transformed variables but there was little difference between transformed and untransformed results. All other variables were normally distributed. Gender was a dummy coded categorical variable (*Female* = 0, *Male* = 1).

The descriptive statistics (Table 1) indicate that letter-word identification was, on average, a measure of letter identification (scores up to 14 consisted of letter identification), with only a few children able to identify some of the initial words (e.g., *to*).

Zero-order Correlations

Table 2 presents the zero-order correlations between all measures. Note the negative correlations with visuospatial memory are a result of the reflected transformation. Of the potential control measures (age, gender, attention, auditory-verbal memory, visuospatial memory, and nonverbal ability), only gender was not associated with letter-word identification or phonological awareness. Thus, gender was not controlled in subsequent analyses.

Being older, paying better attention on tasks, exhibiting better memory and having greater nonverbal ability were all associated with greater letter-word identification skills. The variance that these variables accounted for in letter-word identification was controlled for in subsequent analyses. Both temporal processing measures showed significant moderate correlations with letter-word identification, indicating that better auditory and visual temporal processing were associated with better identification skills. Phonological awareness showed a significant strong positive correlation with letter-word identification. Of the control measures, nonverbal reasoning was not significantly correlated with phonological awareness so was not included in those analyses. Both temporal processing measures showed weak positive correlations with phonological awareness.

Table 1. Descriptive Statistics

Measures	Mean (Standard Error of the Mean)	Range	Maximum Scores
Age (years)	5.35 (0.02)	4.83 – 5.92	
Nonverbal Ability (CPM) [a]	108.15 (0.90)	81 – 135	
Attention [b]	0.00 (0.17)	-6.81 – 1.53	
Digit Span	5.31(0.12)	2 – 9	16
Visuospatial Memory	20.30 (0.51)	2 – 31	32
Auditory TOJ	10.76 (0.22)	4 – 14	14
Visual TOJ	43.92 (0.63)	22 – 60	72
Phonological Awareness	7.73 (3.70)	0 – 14	20
Letter-Word Identification	10.36 (0.26)	4 – 17	

[a] Standardised scores with M of 100 and SD of 15; [b] Standardised scores with M of 0 and SD of 1.

Table 2. Correlations between Control Measures, Temporal Processing, Phonological Awareness and Letter-Word Identification

	1	2 [a]	3	4 [b]	5	6 [c]	7	8	9	10
1 Age	1.00									
2 Gender [a]	-.10	1.00								
3 Nonverbal	.24**	.19*	1.00							
4 Attention [b]	.29**	.02	.18	1.00						
5 Auditory Verbal Memory	.15	.13	.20*	.15	1.00					
6 Visuospatial Memory [c]	-.33**	-.22*	-.39**	-.28**	-.31**	1.00				
7 ATOJ	.35**	.23**	.32**	.18*	.31**	-.39**	1.00			
8 VTOJ	.21*	.14	.33**	.41**	.22*	-.33**	.32**	1.00		
9 Phonological Awareness	.30**	.07	.18	.28**	.28**	-.19*	.29**	.18*	1.00	
10 Letter-Word Identification	.36**	-.00	.33**	.22*	.16*	-.26**	.38*	.32**	.51**	1.00

[a] Female = 0, Male = 1. [b] Reflected inverse transformation, [c] Reflected square root transformation.
*$p < .05$, ** $p < .01$.

Prediction of Phonological Awareness by Temporal Processing

In order to address the first question of whether pre-reading measures of temporal processing were significantly related to phonological awareness and to test the hypothesis that auditory temporal processing would be more strongly related to this skill, phonological awareness was regressed on the temporal processing measures. Table 3 summarises the results.

The relevant control measures (age, attention, auditory verbal memory, and visuospatial memory) identified via the zero order correlations were entered at Step 1 to account for the variance they explained. They accounted for 19.14% of the variance in phonological awareness. Age, attention, and auditory verbal memory each made significant independent contributions, explaining 4.05%, 4.52%, and 4.65%, respectively, of the variance. At Step 2, neither the addition of visual or auditory temporal processing explained significant additional variance, although auditory TOJ approached significance.

Table 3. Regression of Phonological Awareness on Control and Temporal Processing Measures

	Variable	B (SE B)	sr	p
Step 1.	1. Age	2.82 (1.14)	.20	.013*
	2. Attention[a]	2.04 (0.22)	.21	.008**
	3. Auditory verbal Memory	0.60 (0.22)	.22	.008**
	4. Visuospatial Memory[b]	-0.11 (0.38)	-.02	.781
	$R^2 = .19$ (Adj. $R^2 = .17$), $F(4, 124) = 7.32$, $p < .001$			
Step 2.	5. Visual TOJ	0.03 (0.05)		.492
	$\Delta R^2 = .00$, $F(1, 123) = 0.47$, $p = .492$			
Step 2.	5. Auditory TOJ	0.25 (0.14)	.14	.07
	$\Delta R^2 = .02$, $F(1, 123) = 3.28$, $p = .072$			

$*p < .05$, $** p < .01$.
[a] Reflected and inverse transformed;
[b] Reflected and square root transformed.

Prediction of Letter-Word Identification by Temporal Processing

Table 4 summarises the regression of the temporal processing measures on letter-word identification. At Step 1, age, attention, nonverbal ability, auditory verbal memory, and visuospatial memory explained 20.24% of the variance in letter-word identification. Age and nonverbal ability independently accounted for 6.51% and 4.49% of the variance, respectively. At Step 2, auditory temporal processing explained an additional 4.06% of the variance. When visual temporal processing was entered at Step 2, it explained 2.76% more variance than the control measures. When auditory and temporal processing measures were entered together at Step 2, they explained 5.92% of the variance. Only auditory temporal processing made a significant independent contribution, explaining 3.19% of that variance.

**Table 4. Regression of Letter-Word Identification on Control
Measures and Temporal Processing Measures**

	Variable	B (SE B)	sr	p
Step 1.	1. Age	2.85 (0.90)	.26	.002**
	2. Attention[a]	0.09 (0.63)	.02	.889
	3. Nonverbal	0.16 (0.07)	.21	.018*
	4. Auditory verbal Memory	0.10 (0.18)	.05	.577
	5. Visuospatial Memory[b]	-0.21 (0.33)	-.05	.519
	$R^2 = .20$ (Adj. $R^2 = .17$), $F(5,123) = 6.25$, $p < .001$			
Step 2.	6. Visual TOJ	0.07 (0.04)	.17	.039*
	$\Delta R^2 = .03$, $F(1,122) = 4.34$, $p = .039$			
Step 2.	6. Auditory TOJ	0.28 (0.11)	.20	.011*
	$\Delta R^2 = .04$, $F(1,122) = 6.54$, $p = .012$			
Step 2.	6. Visual TOJ	0.06 (0.04)	.14	.083
	7. Auditory TOJ	0.25 (0.11)	.18	.023*
	$\Delta R^2 = .069$, $F(2,121) = 4.86$, $p = .01$			

*$p < .05$, ** $p < .01$. [a]Reflected and inverse transformed; [b]Reflected and square root transformed.

Prediction of Letter-Word Identification by Phonological Awareness and Temporal Processing

Finally, both temporal processing and phonological awareness predictors were included in the same hierarchical analysis predicting letter-word identification (see Table 5).

**Table 5. Regression of Letter-Word Identification on Control, Temporal Processing,
and Phonological Processing Measures**

	Variable	B (SE B)	sr	p
Step 1.	1. Age	2.70 (0.91)	.24	.003**
	2. Attention[a]	0.27 (0.30)	.07	.361
	3. Nonverbal	0.16 (0.07)	.21	.02*
	4. Auditory verbal Memory	0.09 (0.18)	.04	.608
	5. Visuospatial Memory[b]	-0.17 (0.33)	-.04	.614
	$R^2 = .21$ (Adj. $R^2 = .17$), $F(5,123) = 6.44$, $p < .001$			
Step 2.	6. Phonological Awareness	0.34 (0.06)	.39	<.001**
	$\Delta R^2 = .15$, $F(1,122) = 28.37$, $p < .001$			
Step 3.	7. Visual TOJ	0.06 (0.03)	.13	.072
	8. Auditory TOJ	0.18 (0.10)	.13	.075
	$\Delta R^2 = .04$, $F(2,120) = 3.84$, $p = .024$			

*$p < .05$, ** $p < .01$. [a]Reflected and inverse transformed; [b]Reflected and square root transformed.

At Step 1, the five control measures explained 20.74% of the variance in letter-word identification, with age and nonverbal ability making significant independent contributions. At Step 2, the addition of phonological awareness explained a further 14.96% of the variance in letter word identification. At Step 3, the addition of visual and auditory temporal processing explained another 3.88% of the variance; however, neither temporal processing predictor made a significant independent contribution. Overall, the control measures and the phonological and temporal processing predictors explained 39.56% of the variance in letter-word identification. With all variables entered, only phonological awareness independently explained a significant 13.35% of variance.

DISCUSSION

These results show that, prior to the emergence of word reading, auditory and visual temporal processing measures account for a significant percentage of the variance in letter-word identification but not in phonological awareness. This significant relationship with letter-word identification is independent of the effects of age, attention, nonverbal ability, and auditory verbal and visuospatial memory, as well as phonological awareness. This study adds to the limited evidence of a relationship between temporal processing skills and this important pre-reading skill, extending Boets et al.'s (2006a; b; 2008) finding to a larger unselected sample of English-speaking children. It confirms that relationships between temporal order judgement and word identification previously found in older samples and longitudinal studies (Brannan and Williams, 1988; Chung et al., 2008; Hood and Conlon, 2004; Farmer and Klein, 1993; Landerl and Willburger, 2010; Share et al., 2002) are preceded by an earlier relationship with pre-reading letter-word identification. This provides important support for a causal role of temporal processing in reading development as it establishes that the relationship is present with emergent literacy before reading has emerged. A major strength of this study is that it provides evidence of covariation between these perceptual abilities and pre-reading skills before any effects of reading failure or reading remediation have occurred. It is possible that the temporal processing deficits found in older children and adults with dyslexia could be a result of, rather than a cause of, reading failure (Ramus, 2004). Establishing pre-existing relationships in pre-readers rules out this possibility and begins to establish temporal precedence for temporal processing difficulties. However, we acknowledge that the design, as with all of the studies in this area, is correlational and, as such, cause-and-effect conclusions cannot be drawn. It remains possible that even at this early stage, some aspect of poor letter identification leads to poor temporal processing or that both of these are due to some as yet unidentified third variable, rather than that pre-existing temporal processing difficulties lead to poor letter-word identification.

Our results were only partially consistent with our hypotheses and with the findings of Boets et al. (2006a; b; 2008). We did not find that visual temporal processing was more strongly related to the orthographic task, letter-word identification. With both temporal processing measures entered in the regression equation, only auditory temporal processing made a significant independent contribution. Boets et al. (2010) only found a specific relationship between visual temporal processing and letter knowledge after removing variance shared with phonological skill from letter knowledge. As we did not partial out this variance, that might explain our conflicting findings. While we attempted to ensure our letter knowledge task was an orthographic task by focussing only on letter-word identification (naming) rather than including letter sound knowledge, we acknowledge that Adams (1990) argument that letter name knowledge is strongly linked to letter sound knowledge might explain also our results. Auditory temporal processing might have been more strongly related to our measure because of the strong phonological element in letter names.

We controlled for memory and attention, known correlates of temporal processing, and ensured that children with speech and language problems were excluded based on criticisms that this might explain the relationship between temporal processing and reading skills (Heath et al., 1999; Stark et al., 1988; Tallal and Stark, 1982). Boets et al. (2006 a; b; 2008) did not control these factors. Our more stringent test of the temporal processing hypothesis might also explain the inconsistent results.

In contrast to the results with letter-word identification, neither temporal processing measure accounted for significant variance in phonological awareness, after controlling for age, nonverbal ability, attention, and memory. This was despite significant zero-order correlations between the temporal and phonological measures. As expected, auditory TOJ showed stronger zero-order correlations with phonological awareness than visual TOJ. However, this shared variance was fully explained by the control measures. Auditory temporal processing did still show a marginal trend toward explaining independent variance in phonological awareness ($p = .07$), but this failed to reach significance.

Our findings are consistent with previous studies that also failed to find significant relationships between auditory temporal order judgement and phonological processing (Bretherton and Holmes, 2003; Richardson et al., 2004; Watson and Miller, 1993). However, they are inconsistent with the temporal processing hypothesis that auditory temporal processing underlies phonological processing, and that this relationship explains the relationship between auditory temporal processing and reading (Tallal, 1980; 2003). They are also inconsistent with previous findings at this emergent literacy stage (Boets et al., 2006a; b; Share et al., 2002). Share et al. found a significant relationship between phonological segmentation and auditory TOJ but at both long and short ISIs, suggesting a more generalized impairment than for just rapid temporal processing (Klein, 2002). Boets et al. only found a relationship between phonological awareness and auditory temporal processing when the latter was assessed using 2-Hz FM detection, not when measured using a gap detection task. Ahissar, Protopapas, Reid, and Merzenich (2000) found around 45% of the variance shared between FM detection and auditory TOJ in adults, suggesting that these tasks measure the same construct. However, gap detection and auditory TOJ appear to measure different constructs, with gap detection possibly measuring some more general aspect on cognitive ability (Au and Lovegrove, 2001). Thus, it seems unlikely that our null relationship with phonological awareness is due to some artefact of the task employed in our study. We chose this auditory TOJ task because it was part of a commercially available dyslexia screening battery designed for this pre-school age range. However, it did have limitations. For example, there was a 50% chance of guessing correctly and few trials, making it somewhat insensitive. More work at this emergent literacy stage with different auditory temporal processing measures, particularly those that are more closely aligned with the temporal processing hypothesis (e.g., the ability to discriminate between speech stimuli that rely specifically on rapid auditory spectro-temporal processing) is needed for clarification.

In addition, as already discussed briefly, our study represents a more stringent test of the hypothesis than the previous studies that found significant relationships due to our controlling for a wider range of potentially confounding factors; in particular, attention and memory. Attention and memory were significantly correlated with temporal processing, phonological awareness, and letter-word identification. Thus, attention and memory affect not only temporal processing performance. Although Boets et al. (2006b) did not control for attention or memory, they conceded that central non-auditory attention factors might explain their finding of high levels of intra-individual variability. Share et al. (2002) found that when they controlled for attention and the number of trials taken to learn the task, the correlation between auditory TOJ and phonological segmentation at school entry was greatly reduced, although it remained significant ($r = .25$). However, they did not also control for memory. Like attention, auditory verbal memory is associated with both temporal processing and reading skills (Booth et al., 2000; Mann and Liberman, 1984; McArthur and Bishop, 2001).

While we did attempt to adequately control for attention and memory, the control tasks had some limitations. Attention was likely better controlled for on the visual temporal processing task by the use of the fixation cross and catch trials that largely ensured children sustained attention (incorrect responses on the catch trials were very low). The measure of attention to the auditory temporal processing task was not as adequate with the use of very long ISI trials. Replication is needed with an auditory task that incorporates catch trials of one sound only throughout. Another solution is to incorporate a battery of attention measures such as that used by Landerl and Willburger (2010), although they found that even with their range of measures of attention controlled for, visual temporal processing remained significantly related to reading. One of the problems with our measure of visuospatial memory was that it is likely to have had a strong temporal component because children had to watch a rabbit pop up in a rapid sequence of holes and remember the order of the holes. Thus, it is likely that it partialled out some aspects of temporal processing and not just visuospatial memory. Replication with a measure of visuospatial memory that does not have a temporal component (e.g., memory for static visuospatial arrays) is needed. We argue that future studies of temporal processing and reading must adequately control for attention and memory as well as nonverbal reasoning.

In light of the inconsistent findings in the literature, several authors have proposed alternative explanations to those put forward by the temporal processing hypothesis for the relationship between temporal processing and reading. These explanations do not involve a co-relationship with phonological processing, something we failed to find, but focus on a co-relationship with more general language skills. Marshall et al. (2001) argued that a general language skill, such as verbal labelling, might better explain why auditory temporal processing sometimes shows a relationship with phonological skill and, thereby, a relationship with reading. Wagner and Torgesen (1987) argued that the ease of using verbal labels is associated with phonological ability. Bretherton and Holmes (2003) argued that a verbal labelling weakness might also explain the relationship between visual temporal processing and reading, because children first need to utilise verbal labels (the left one came first) even when a manual response (pointing) is used as in the current study. This requires further exploration.

Our null results for the relationship between auditory temporal processing and phonological awareness meant that any variance temporal processing explained in letter-word identification was not due to shared variance with phonological awareness. The final question examined whether temporal processing could add anything to the explanation of letter-word identification over the control measures and phonological awareness. Results showed that temporal processing explained a small but significant amount of additional variance in letter-word identification. Although only around 4% additional variance was explained, this is consistent with the amount of variance explained in other studies, when less controls were included (e.g., in Boets et al., 2008, visual temporal processing explained 6.76% of the variance in orthographic processing, with only nonverbal ability controlled). That additional variance was shared between the auditory and visual measures, with neither making a significant independent contribution. Before phonological awareness was added to the regression equation, auditory temporal processing did explain unique variance in letter-word identification. With phonological awareness added, it no longer did. This suggests that a very small amount of variance in letter-word identification is common to phonological awareness and auditory temporal processing.

Implications and Applications

The results reported here and evidence reviewed from previous studies show that temporal processing measures are related to letter-word identification before formal reading emerges. This provides important support for a potentially causal pathway from pre-existing temporal processing to emergent literacy, and, as Boets et al. (2008) showed, from there to formal literacy skills. However, as noted earlier in the discussion, these studies are all correlational so cannot establish causality. Notwithstanding that, there are implications for using these measures in early screening batteries designed to identify children who are at risk of reading difficulties before they begin school. With regard to the role of temporal processing in predicting early phonological awareness, and thereby, being related to reading, our results and the evidence reviewed are mixed. We failed to find a specific relationship between auditory temporal processing and phonological processing. This has theoretical implications for understanding the mechanism by which auditory temporal processing is related to reading. The results of the current study and previous studies reviewed here also have implications for what other perceptual and cognitive factors need to be controlled when examining the relationship between temporal processing and reading skills in order to rule out alternative explanations. Each of these implications and associated applications will be discussed here.

A lot of research effort over the last few decades has gone into the development of early detection tests to identify children at risk for reading difficulties once they begin school. Most existing approaches focus on inclusion of phonological awareness and an associated phonological skill, rapid automatised naming (RAN, Wagner and Torgesen, 1987) as well as letter knowledge. These are traditionally the strongest emergent literacy predictors of subsequent reading (e.g., Adams, 1990). The Jyväskylä Longitudinal Study of Dyslexia (e.g., Puolakanaho et al., 2007) showed that pre-school measures of letter knowledge, phonological awareness, and RAN plus an index of familial risk give a prediction probability for differentiating those with dyslexia from normally developing readers in 2nd grade of at least .80. Our results suggest that preschool auditory temporal processing is independently related to letter-word identification and, thus, offers a potentially useful addition to this early screening battery. Auditory temporal processing has the potential to be measured well before traditional predictors like phonological processing and letter knowledge. Individual differences in brain responses to differences in speech sounds appear to be present from birth and are predictive of dyslexia status at approximately 8 years of age (Benasich and Tallal, 2002; Lyytinen et al., 2005; Molfese, 2000).

There has been less work on developing and assessing early measures of visual temporal processing. We used visual TOJ, which was previously used in Hood and Conlon (2004). The parameters were based on the task used by Reed (1989) with a much older sample so some of our failure to find significant results might have been due to task insensitivity with this younger sample. Boets et al. (2006a) used coherent motion detection, while Kevan and Pammer (2009) used coherent motion and frequency doubling sensitivity, but only achieved results with the latter measure. Global motion detection improves after 4 years (Braddick, Atkinson, and Wattam-Bell, 2003), but does not reach maturity until between 7 to 12 years of age (Raymond and Sorensen, 1998). Thus, coherent motion detection tasks might not be suitable for use too early and might be only ideal after about 7 years of age. More work is needed to develop effective pre-school measures of visual temporal processing.

Early identification is important because it means that intervention can begin early. Earlier intervention produces better results than intervention delayed until after reading failure has occurred. Strag (1972) noted that 82% of children who were identified with dyslexia in the first two grades of school achieve normal reading scores with remediation compared with only 46% of those diagnosed at Grade 3. Traditional diagnosis of dyslexia, which is reliant on a general ability: reading ability discrepancy (Lyon, 1995) does not generally occur until about Grade 3. The Committee on the Prevention of Reading Difficulties in Young Children recommended avoiding deferring intervention until third or fourth grade (Snow, Burns, and Griffin, 1998). Improved early screening would allow earlier intervention.

There are a couple of current problems, however, with arguing for the inclusion of temporal processing measures in screening or diagnostic batteries. One is that the contribution of temporal processing to prediction is small and the costs of incorporating these measures into screening batteries needs to be weighed up against the gains. The second is that the mechanism via which temporal processing is related to reading is unclear. Our results, as well as those of several studies reviewed here, fail to support key predictions of the temporal processing hypothesis. We like others (Bretherton and Holmes, 2003; Richardson et al., 2004; Watson and Miller, 1993) did not find, as expected, a relationship between phonological awareness and auditory temporal processing. This contradicts the temporal processing hypothesis. However, some studies do find this relationship at the emergent literacy stage (Boets et al., 2006b; Share et al., 2002). These inconsistencies have lead some to postulate about other mechanisms that explain the relationship between auditory temporal processing and reading skills and that do not involve an indirect path via phonological processing. Shared demands on verbal labelling are one alternative explanation (Bretherton and Holmes, 2003; Marshall et al., 2001; Wagner and Torgesen, 1987). Multifactor hypotheses propose that these perceptual deficits are markers of dysfunctional neural systems related to other mechanisms, like attention (e.g., Hari, Renvall, and Tanskanen, 2001), which have direct effects on orthographic and phonological processing and, subsequently, on reading. Therefore, controlling for attention might result in the relationship between auditory temporal processing and reading skills becoming much reduced or non-significant as we found (see Davis et al., 2001; Landerl and Willburger, 2010; Stuart et al., 2001). More work exploring the role of these other cognitive and perceptual factors in explaining the relationship between temporal processing and reading is needed before the value of temporal processing measures to early screening batteries can be fully determined. If they are simply markers of some other underlying dysfunction, inclusion of measures of those underlying dysfunctions are likely to provide better prediction of reading ability and disability.

CONCLUSION

There is growing, albeit mixed, evidence of relationships between auditory and visual temporal processing and emergent literacy skills to complement the evidence of relationships with reading in older samples. However, the traditional explanation put forward by the temporal processing hypothesis of a specific path from auditory temporal processing to reading via phonological processing is doubtful. The current study did not find a significant relationship between auditory temporal processing and pre-school phonological awareness that was independent of age, attention, and memory. It is vital that future studies control for both attention and memory in order to isolate the specific contribution of temporal processing without these confounding factors playing a role. Also contrary to expectations derived from the temporal processing hypothesis of a specific relationship between visual temporal processing and orthographic skill, visual temporal processing did not account for significant unique variance in letter-word identification once the contribution of auditory temporal processing was taken into account.

Despite the explanations derived from the temporal processing hypothesis not being specifically supported, auditory and visual temporal processing did explain significant additional variance in letter-word identification to that explained by age, attention, nonverbal ability, memory, and phonological awareness. This suggests that their inclusion in early literacy assessment batteries would improve prediction. However, until doubts over the theoretical explanation for their relationship with early literacy are clarified, it remains unclear why that relationship exists and whether it is simply a marker for other correlated impairments or represents a true causal association.

REFERENCES

Adams, M. (1990). *Beginning to read: Thinking and learning about print.* Cambridge, MA: MIT Press.

Ahissar, M., Protopapas, A., Reid, M., and Merzenich, M. (2000). Auditory processing parallels reading abilities in adults. *Proceedings of the National Academy of Sciences*, 97, 6832-6837.

Au, A., and Lovegrove, B. (2001). The role of visual and auditory temporal processing in reading irregular and nonsense words. *Perception*, 30, 1127 – 1142.

Badian, N. A. (1993). Phonemic awareness, naming, visual symbol processing, and reading.*Reading and Writing: An Interdisciplinary Journal*, 5, 87 – 100.

Badian, N. A. (1995). Predicting reading ability over the long term: Changing roles of letter naming, phonological awareness and orthographic processing. *Annals of Dyslexia*, 45, 79- 96.

Bakker, D. J., and Satz, P. (1970). *Specific reading disability: Advances in theory and method.* Rotterdam, Netherlands: Rotterdam University Press.

Benasich, A. A., and Tallal, P. (2002). Infant discrimination of rapid auditory cues predicts later language impairment. *Behavioural Brain Research,* 136, 31-49.

Betourne, L. S. and Friel-Patti, S. (2003). Phonological processing and oral language abilities in fourth-grade poor readers. *Journal of Communication Disorders*, 36, 507-527.

Blomert, L. (in press). The neural signature of orthographic–phonological binding in successful and failing reading development. *NeuroImage.* doi:10.1016/j.neuroimage. 2010.11.003

Blomert, L., and Willems, G. (2010). Is there a causal link from a phonological awareness deficit to reading failure in children at familial risk for dyslexia? *Dyslexia*, 16, 300–317.

Boets, B., De Smedt, B., Cleuren, L., Vandewalle, E., Wouters, J., and Ghesquiere, P. (2010). Towards a further characterization of phonological and literacy problems in Dutch-speaking children with dyslexia. *British Journal of Developmental Psychology*, 28, 5-31.

Boets, B., Wouters, J., van Wieringen, A., De Smedt, B., and Ghesquière, P. (2008). Modelling relations between sensory processing, speech perception, orthographic and phonological ability, and literacy achievement. *Brain and Language*, 106, 29–40.

Boets, B., Wouters, J., van Wieringen, A., and Ghesquière, P. (2006a). Coherent motion detection in preschool children at family risk for dyslexia. *Vision Research*, 46, 527 – 535.

Boets, B., Wouters, J., van Wieringen, A., and Ghesquière, P. (2006b). Auditory temporal information processing in preschool children at family risk for dyslexia: Relations with phonological abilities and developing literacy skills. *Brain and Language*, 97 (1), 64 – 79.

Bond, G. L., and Dykstra, R. (1967). The cooperative research program in first-grade reading Instruction. *Reading Research Quarterly*, 2, 5-142.

Booth, J. R., Perfetti, C. A., MacWhinney, B., and Hunt, S. B. (2000). The association of rapid temporal perception with orthographic and phonological processing in children and adults with reading impairment. *Scientific Studies of Reading*, 4, 101-132.

Bowey, J. A. (1994). Phonological sensitivity in novice readers and nonreaders. *Journal of Experimental Child Psychology*, 58, 134-159.

Bowey, J. A. (1995). Socioeconomic status differences in preschool phonological sensitivity and first-grade reading achievement. *Journal of Educational Psychology*, 87, 476-487.

Bowey, J. A. (2002). Reflections on onset-rime and phoneme sensitivity as predictors of beginning word reading. *Journal of Experimental Child Psychology*, 82, 29-40.

Bowman, M. and Treiman, R. (2004). Stepping stones to reading. *Theory into Practice*, 43, 295-303.

Braddick, O., Atkinson, J., and Wattam-Bell, J. (2003). Normal and anomalous development of visual motion processing: motion coherence and 'dorsal- stream vulnerability'. *Neuropsychologia*, 41, 1769-1784.

Brady, S. A. (1997). Ability to encode phonological representations: An underlying difficulty of poor readers. In B. Blachman (Ed.), *Foundations of reading acquisition and dyslexia: Implications for early intervention* (pp. 21-47). London, UK: Erlbaum Associates.

Brady, S. A., and Shankweiler, D. P. (1991) *Phonological processes in literacy- A tribute to Isabelle Y Liberman.* Hillsdale, NJ: Lawrence Erlbaum Associates.

Bradley, L., and Bryant, P. E. (1983). Categorizing sounds and learning to read- a causal connection. *Nature*, 301, 419-421.

Bradley, L., and Bryant, P. E. (1991). Phonological skills before and after learning to read. In S. A. Brady and D. P. Shankweiler (Eds.), *Phonological processes in literacy- A tribute to Isabelle Y Liberman* (pp. 37-45). Hillsdale, NJ: Lawrence Erlbaum Associates.

Brannan, J. R., and Williams, M. C. (1988). Developmental versus sensory processing deficit effects on perceptual processing in the reading disabled. *Perception and Psychophysics*, 44 , 437-444.

Breier, J. I., Fletcher, J. M., Foorman, B. R., Klaas, P., and Gray, L. C. (2003). Auditory temporal processing in children with specific reading disability with and without Attention Deficit/Hyperactivity Disorder. *Journal of Speech, Language, and Hearing Research*, 46, 31-42.

Bretherton, L., and Holmes, V. M. (2003). The relationship between auditory temporal processing, phonemic awareness, and reading disability. *Journal of Experimental Child Psychology*, 84, 218–243.

Brunn, J., and Farah, M. (1991). The relation between spatial attention and reading: Evidence from the neglect syndrome. *Cognitive Neuropsychology*, 8, 59-75.

Bryant, P. E., MacLean, M., Bradley, L. L., and Crossland, J. (1990). Rhyme and alliteration, phoneme detection, and learning to read. *Developmental Psychology*, 26, 429-438.

Cacace, A. T., McFarland, D. J., Ouimet, J. R., Schreiber, E. J., and Marro, P. (2000). Temporal processing deficits in remediation-resistant reading-impaired children. *Audiology and Neuro-Otology*, 5, 83-97.

Catts, H. W., Fey, M. E., Zhang, X., and Tomblin, J. B. (2001). Estimating the risk of future reading difficulties in kindergarten children: A research-based model and its clinical implementation. *Language, Speech, and Hearing Services in Schools*, 32 38-50.

Cestnick, L., and Jerger, J. (2000). Auditory temporal processing and lexical/nonlexical reading in developmental dyslexics. *Journal of the North American Academy of Audiology*, 11, 501-517.

Chiappe, P., Stringer, R., Siegel, L. S., Stanovich, K. E. (2002). Why the timing deficit hypothesis does not explain reading disability in adults. *Reading and Writing*, 15, 73–107.

Chung, K. K. H., McBride-Chang, C., Wong, S. W. L., Cheung, H., Penney, T. B., Ho, C. S. H. (2008). The role of visual and auditory temporal processing for Chinese children with developmental dyslexia. *Annals of Dyslexia*, 58, 15-35. doi: 10.1007/s11881-008-0015-4.

Corbetta, M., Akbudak, E., Conturo, T. E., Snyder, A. Z., Ollinger, J. M., Drury, H. A.,Linenweber, M. R., et al. (1998). A common network of functional areas for attention and eye movements. *Neuron*, 21, 761-773.

Cornelissen, P. L., Hansen, P. C., Hutton, J. L., Evangelinou, V., and Stein, J. F. (1998). Magnocellular visual function and children's single word reading. *Vision Research*, 38, 471-482.

Davis, C., Castles, A., McAnally, K., and Gray, J. (2001). Lapses of concentration and dyslexic performance on the Ternus task. *Cognition*, 81, B21-B31.

de Martino, S., Espesser, R., Rey, V., and Habib, M. (2001). The "Temporal Processing Deficit" hypothesis in Dyslexia: New experimental evidence. *Brain and Cognition*, 46, 104-108.

Demb, J. B., Boynton, G. M., and Heeger, D. J. (1998). Functional magnetic resonance imaging of early visual pathways in dyslexia. *Journal of Neuroscience*, 18, 6939-6951.

Denenberg, V. H. (1999). A critique of Mody, Studdert-Kennedy, and Brady's "Speech perception deficits in poor readers: Auditory processing or phonological coding". *Journal of Learning Disabilities*, 32, 379-383.

Dunn, L. M., and Dunn, L. M. (1981). *Peabody Picture Vocabulary Test- Revised.* Circle Pines, MN: American Guidance Service.

Dykman, R. A., and Ackerman, P. T. (1991). Attention deficit disorder and specific reading disability: Separate but often overlapping disorders. *Journal of Learning Disabilities*, 24, 96-103.

Eden, G. F., Stein, J. F., Wood, M. H., and Wood, F. B. (1995). Temporal and spatial processing in reading disabled and normal children. *Cortex,* 31, 451-468.

Education Queensland. (2006). *Enrolment statistics.* Retrieved 31st October, 2006 from http://education.qld.gov.au/schools/statistics/pdfs/2004sec1tbl1-3.pdf

Ehri, L. C., and Roberts, T. (2006). The roots of learning to read and write: Acquisition of letters and phonemic awareness. In S. B. Neuman and D. K. Dickinson (Eds.), *Handbook of early literacy research*: Vol. 2. (pp. 113-130). New York, NY: Guildford Press.

Ellis, N. C., and Large, B. (1987). The development of reading: As you seek, so shall you find. *British Journal of Psychology*, 78, 1-128.

Farmer, M. E., and Klein, R. M. (1993). Auditory and visual temporal processing in dyslexic and normal readers. In P. Tallal, A. M. Galaburda, R. R. Llinas, and C. von Euler (Eds.), *Annals of the New York Academy of Sciences*, Vol. 682: Temporal information processing in the nervous system- Special reference to dyslexia and dysphasia (pp. 339-341). New York, NY: New York Academy of Sciences.

Farmer, M. E., and Klein, R. M. (1995). The Evidence for a Temporal Processing deficit linked to dyslexia: A review. *Psychonomic Bulletin*, 2, 460-493.

Fawcett, A. J., and Nicolson, R. I. (1996). *The Dyslexia Screening Test.* London, UK: Psychological Corporation.

Fawcett, A. J., Singleton, C. H., and Peer, L. (1998). Advances in early years screening for dyslexia in the United Kingdom, *Annals of Dyslexia*, 48, 57-88.

Fletcher, J. M., Foorman, B. R., Boudousquie, A., Barnes, M. A., Schatschneider, C., and Francis, D. J. (2002). Assessment of reading and learning disabilities: A research-based intervention-oriented approach. *Journal of School Psychology*, 40, 27-63.

Foulin, J. N. (2005). Why is letter-name knowledge such a good predictor of learning to read? *Reading and Writing*, 18, 129-155.

Fritjers, J. C., Barron, R. W., and Brunello, M. (2000). Direct and mediated effects of home literacy and literacy interest on prereaders oral vocabulary and early written language skill. *Journal of Educational Psychology*, 92, 466-477.

Galaburda, A. M., Menard, M. T., and Rosen, G. D. (1994). Evidence for aberrant auditory anatomy in developmental dyslexia. *Proceedings of the National Academy of Science*, 91, 8010-8013.

Gallagher, A., Frith, U., and Snowling, M. J. (2000). Precursors of literacy delay among children at genetic risk of dyslexia. *Journal of Child Psychology and Psychiatry*, 41, 203-213.

Goswami, U., Thomson, J., Richardson, U., Stainthorp, R., Hughes, D., Rosen, S., and Scott, S. K. (2002). Amplitude envelope onsets and developmental dyslexia: A new hypothesis. *Proceedings of the National Academy of Sciences*, 99, 10911-10916.

Glutting, J. J., and Oakland, T. (1993). *Guide to the assessment of test-session behaviour for WISC-III and WIAT*. San Antonio, TX: Psychological Corporation.

Habib, M. (2000). The neurological basis of developmental dyslexia: An overview and working hypothesis. *Brain*, 123, 2373-2399.

Habib, M., Rey, V., Daffaure, V., Camps, R., Espesser, R., Joly-Pottuz, B., and Demonet, J. (2002). Phonological training in children with dyslexia using temporally modified speech: A three-step pilot investigation. *Journal of Language and Communicative Disorders*, 37, 289-308.

Hari, R., Renvall, H., and Tanskanen, T. (2001). Left minineglect in dyslexic adults. *Brain*, 124, 1373–1380.

Heath, S. M., Hogben, J. H., and Clark, C. D. (1999). Auditory temporal processing in disabled readers with and without oral language delay. *Journal of Child Psychology and Psychiatry*, 40, 637-647.

Heim, S., Freeman, R. B., Eulitz, C., and Elbert, T. (2001). Auditory temporal processing deficit is associated with enhanced sensitivity in the visual modality. *Cognitive Neuroscience*, 12, 507-510.

Hirsch, I. (1959). Auditory perception of temporal order. *Journal of Acoustic Society of America*, 31, 759-767.

Hood, M., and Conlon, E. (2004). Visual and auditory temporal processing and early reading development. *Dyslexia*, 10, 234-252.

Kanabus, M., Szelag E., Rojek E., and Pöppel E. (2002). Temporal order judgement for auditory and visual stimuli. *Acta Neurobiologiae Experimentalis*, 62, 263-270.

Kevan, A., and Pammer, K. (2009). Predicting early reading skills from pre-reading measures of dorsal stream function. *Neuropsychologia*, 47, 3174-3181. doi:10.1016/j.neuropsychologia.2009.07.016.

Kinsbourne, M., Rufo, D. T., Gamzu, E., Palmer, R. L., and Berliner, A. K. (1991). Neuropsychological deficits in adults with dyslexia. *Developmental Medicine and Child Neurology*, 33, 763-775.

Klein, R. M. (2002). Observations on the temporal correlates of reading failure. *Reading and Writing: An Interdisciplinary Journal*, 15, 207-232.

Landerl, K., and Willburger, E. (2010). Temporal processing, attention, and learning disorders. *Learning and Individual Differences*. doi: 10.1016/j.lindif.2010.03.008.

Lehmkuhle, S. (1993). Neurological basis of visual processes in reading. In D. M. Willows, Kruk, R. S., and Corcos, E. (Eds.), *Visual processes in reading and reading disability* (pp. 74-94). Hillsdale, NJ: Erlbaum Associates.

Lehmkuhle, S., Garzia, R. P., Turner, L., Hash, T., and Baro, J. A. (1993). A defective visual pathway in children with reading disability. *The New England Journal of Medicine*, 328, 989-996.

Lennie, P., Trevarthen, C., van Essen, D., and Wässle, H. (1990). Parallel processing of visual information. In L. Spillman and J. S. Werner (Eds.), *Visual perception: The neurophysiological foundations* (pp. 103-128). San Diego, CA: Academic Press, Inc.

Leppanen, U., Aunola, K., Niemi, P., and Nurmi, J. (2008). Letter knowledge predicts grade 4 reading fluency and reading comprehension. *Learning and Instruction*, 18, 548-564.

Levin, I., Shatil-Carmon, S., and Asif-Rave, O. (2006). Learning of letter names and sounds and their contribution to word recognition. *Journal of Experimental Child Psychology*, 93, 139-165.

Lovegrove, W., Slaghuis, W., Bowling, A., Nelson, P., and Geeves, E. (1986). Spatial frequency processing and the prediction of reading ability: A preliminary investigation. *Perception and Psychophysics*, 40, 440-444.

Lundberg, I., Frost, J., and Peterson, O. (1988). Effects of an extensive program for stimulating phonological awareness in preschool children. *Reading Research Quarterly*, 23, 263-284.

Lundberg, I., Olofsson, A., and Wall, S. (1980). Reading and spelling skills in the first school years, predicted from phoneme awareness skills in kindergarten. *Scandinavian Journal of Psychology*, 21, 159-173.

Lyon, G. R. (1995). Toward a definition of dyslexia. *Annals of Dyslexia*, 45, 3-27.

Lyytinen, H., Guttorm, T.K., Huttenen, T., Hämäläinen, J., Leppänen, P. H. T., and Vesterinen, M. (2005). Psychophysiology of developmental dyslexia: A review of findings including studies of children at risk of dyslexia. *Journal of Neurolinguistics*, 18, 167-195.

MacLean, M., Bryant, P. E., and Bradley, L. (1987). *Rhymes*, nursery rhymes, and reading in early childhood. *Merrill-Palmer Quarterly*, 33, 255-282.

Mann, V., and Liberman, I. Y. (1984). Phonological awareness and verbal short-term memory: Can they presage early reading success? *Journal of Learning Disabilities*, 17, 592-599.

Marois, R., Chun, M. M., and Gore, J. C. (2000). Neural correlates of the attentional blink. *Neuron*, 28, 299-308.

Marshall, C. M., Snowling, M. J., and Bailey, P. J. (2001). Rapid auditory processing and phonological ability in normal readers and readers with dyslexia. *Journal of Speech, Language, and Hearing*, 44, 925–940.

May, J. G., Williams, M. C., and Dunlap, W. P. (1988). Temporal order judgements in good and poor readers. *Neuropsychologia*, 26, 917-924.

McArthur, G. M., and Bishop, D. V. M. (2001). Auditory perceptual processing in people with reading and oral language impairments: Current issues and recommendations. *Dyslexia*, 7, 150-170.

McBride-Chang, C. (1999). The ABCs of the ABCs: The development of letter-name and letter-sound knowledge. *Merrill-Palmer Quarterly*, 45, 285-308.

Mody, M., Studdert-Kennedy, M., and Brady, S. (1997). Speech perception deficits in poor readers: Auditory processing or phonological coding? *Journal of Experimental Child Psychology*, 64, 199-231.

Molfese, D. L. (2000). Predicting dyslexia at 8 years of age using neonatal brain responses. *Brain and Language, 72, 238-245.*

Molfese, V. J., Beswick, J. L., Molnar, A., and Jacobi-Vessels, J. (2006). Alphabetic skills in preschool: A preliminary study of letter naming and letter writing. *Developmental Neuropsychology*, 29, 5-19.

Muter, V., and Diethelm, K. (2001). The contribution of phonological skills and letter knowledge to early reading development in a multilingual population. *Language Learning*, 51, 187-219.

Muter, V., Hulme, C., Snowling, M., and Taylor, S. (1997). Segmentation, not rhyming, predicts early progress in learning to read. *Journal of Experimental Child Psychology*, 65, 370-396.

Nazir, T. A., and Huckauf, A. (2008). The visual skill in "reading". In E. L, Grigorenko and A. Naples (eds.), *Single-word reading: Behavioral and biological perspectives*. (pp. 25-42). Mahwah, NJ: Lawrence Erlbaum Associates Publishers.

Nicolson, R. I., and Fawcett, A. J. (1996). *The Dyslexia Early Screening Test*. London, UK: Psychological Corporation.

Nittrouer, S. (1999). Do temporal processing deficits cause phonological processing problems? *Journal of Speech, Language, and Hearing Research*, 42, 925-942.

Olson, R., and Datta, H. (2002). Visual-temporal processing in reading-disabled and normal twins. *Reading and Writing*, 15, 127-149.

Plaza, M., and Cohen, H. (2003). The interaction between phonological processing, syntactic awareness, and naming speed in the reading and spelling performance of first-grade children. *Brain and Cognition*, 53, 287-292.

Puolakanaho, A., Ahonen, T., Aro, M., Eklund, K., Leppanen, P. H. T., Poikkeus, A., Tolvanen, A., et al. (2007). Very early phonological and language skills: Estimating individual risk of reading disability. *Journal of Child Psychology and Psychiatry, 48*, 923-931.

Rack, J. P. (1994). Dyslexia: The phonological deficit hypothesis. In A. J. Fawcett and R. I. Nicolson (Eds.), *Dyslexia in children* (pp. 3-37). Hertfordshire, UK: Harvester Wheatsheaf.

Ramus, F. (2004). Should neuroconstructivism guide developmental research? *Trends in Cognitive Sciences*, 8, 100-101.

Rauschecker, J. P. (1998). Cortical processing of complex sounds. *Current Opinion in Neurobiology*, 8, 516-521.

Raven, J. C., Court, J. H., and Raven, J. (1986). *Raven's Colored Matrices*. London, UK: H. K. Lewis.

Raymond, J. E., and Sorensen, R. E. (1998). Visual motion perception in children with dyslexia: Normal detection but abnormal integration. *Visual Cognition*, 5, 389-404.

Reed, M. A. (1989). Speech perception and the discrimination of brief auditory cues in reading disabled children. *Journal of Experimental Child Psychology*, 48, 70-92.

Richardson, U., Thomson, J. M., Scott, S. K., and Goswami, U. (2004). Auditory processing skills and phonological representation in dyslexic children. *Dyslexia*, 10, 215-233.

Rosen, S. (2003). Auditory processing in dyslexia and specific language impairment: Is there a deficit? What is its nature? Does it explain anything? *Journal of Phonetics*, 31, 509-527.

Scarborough, H. S. (1998). Early identification of children at risk for reading disabilities: Phonological awareness and some other promising predictors. In B. K. Shapiro, P. J. Accardo, and A. J. Capute (Eds.), *Specific reading disability: A view of the spectrum* (pp. 75-119). Timonium, MD: York Press, Incorporated.

Semrud-Clikeman, M., Biederman, J., Sprich-Buckminster, S., Krifcher Lehman, B., Faroane, S. V., and Norman, D. (1992). Comorbidity between ADDH and learning disability: A review and report in a clinically referred sample. *Journal of the American Academy of Child and Adolescent Psychiatry*, 31, 439-448.

Share, D., Jorm, A., MacLean, R., and Matthews, R. (1984). Sources of individual differences in reading acquisition. *Journal of Educational Psychology*, 76, 1309-1324.

Share, D., Jorm, A., MacLean, R., and Matthews, R. (2002). Temporal processing and reading disability. *Reading and Writing: An Interdisciplinary Journal*, 15, 151-178.

Singleton, C. H., Thomas, K. V., and Leedale, R. C. (1997). *CoPS 1 Cognitive Profiling System: Windows Edition*. Beverley, East Yorks, UK: Lucid Research Limited.

Snow, C. E., Burns, M. S., and Griffin, P. (1998). *Prevention of reading difficulties in young children*. Washington, DC: National Academy Press.

Sperling, A. J., Lu, Z., Manis, F. R., and Seidenberg, M. S. (2003). Selective magnocellular deficits in dyslexia: A "phantom contour" study. *Neuropsychologia*, 41, 1422-1429. doi: 10.1016/S0028-3932(03)00044-7.

Stark, R. E., Tallal, P., and McCauley, R. J. (Eds.). (1988). *Language, speech, and reading disorders in children: Neuropsychological studies*. Boston, MA: College-Hill Press.

Stein, J. (2003). Visual motion sensitivity and reading. *Neuropsychologia*, 41, 1785-1793.

Stein, J., and Walsh, V. (1997). To see but not to read. *Trends in Neuroscience*, 20, 147-152.

Stelmach, L. B., and Herdman, C. M. (1991). Directed attention and perception of temporal order. *Journal of Experimental Psychology*, 17, 539-550.

Strag, G. (1972). Comparative behavioural ratings of parents with severe mentally retarded, special learning disability, and normal children. *Journal of Learning Disabilities,* 5, 631-635.

Stuart, G. W., McAnally, K. I., and Castles, A. (2001). Can contrast sensitivity functions in dyslexia be explained by inattention rather than a magnocellular deficit? *Vision Research*, 41, 3205–3211.

Studdert-Kennedy, M., and Mody, M. (1995). Auditory temporal perception deficits in the reading impaired: A critical review of the evidence. *Psychonomic Bulletin and Review,* 2, 508-514.

Swan, D., and Goswami, U. (1997). Phonological awareness deficits in developmental dyslexia and the phonological representations hypothesis. *Journal of Experimental Child Psychology*, 60, 334-353.

Talcott, J. B., Witton, C., McLean, M., Hansen, P., Rees, A., Green, G. G. R., and Stein, J. F. (2000). Dynamic sensory sensitivity and children's word decoding skills. *Proceedings of the National Academy of Sciences,* 97, 2952-2957.

Talcott, J. B., Witton, C., Hebb, G. S., Stoodley, C. J., Westwood, E. A., France, S. J., Hansen, P., et al. (2002). On the relationship between dynamic auditory processing and literacy skills; Results from a large primary-school study. *Dyslexia*, 8, 204-225.

Tallal, P. (1980). Auditory temporal perception, phonics, and reading disabilities in children. *Brain and Language*, 9, 182-198.

Tallal, P. (2003). Language learning disabilities: Integrating research approaches. *Current Directions in Psychological Science*, 12, 206-211.

Tallal, P. (2004). Improving language and literacy is a matter of time. *Nature Reviews. Neuroscience*, 5, 721-728.

Tallal, P., and Stark, R. E. (1982). Perceptual/motor profiles of reading impaired children with or without concomitant oral language deficits. *Annals of Dyslexia*, 32, 163-176.

Torppa, M., Poikkeus, A. M., Laakso, M. L., Eklund, K., and Lyytinen, H. (2006). Predicting delayed letter knowledge development and its relation to Grade 1 reading achievement among children with and without familial risk for dyslexia. *Developmental Psychology*, 42, 1128-1142.

Treiman, R. (1985). Onsets and rimes as units of spoken syllables: Evidence from children. *Journal of Experimental Child Psychology*, 39, 161-181.

Treiman, R., and Zukowski, A. (1991). Levels of phonological awareness. In S. A. Brady and D. P. Shankweiler (Eds), *Phonological processes in literacy- A tribute to Isabelle Y Liberman* (pp. 67-83). Hillsdale, NJ: Lawrence Erlbaum Associates.

Ulrich, R. (1987). Threshold models of temporal-order judgements evaluated by a ternary response task. *Perception and Psychophysics*, 42, 224-239.

Vellutino, F. R. (1979). *Dyslexia: Theory and research.* London, UK: MIT press.

Waber, D. P., Weiler, M. D., Wolff, P. H., Bellinger, D., Marcus, D. J., Ariel, R., Forbes, P., et al. (2001). Processing of rapid auditory stimuli in school-aged children referred for evaluation of learning disorders. *Child Development*, 72, 37-49.

Wagner, R. K., and Torgesen, J. K. (1987). The nature of phonological processing and its causal role in the acquisition of reading skills. *Psychological Bulletin*, 101, 192-212.

Watson, B. U., and Miller, T. K. (1993). Auditory perception, phonological processing, and reading ability/disability. *Journal of Speech and Hearing Research*, 36, 850-863.

Wittman, M., Burtscher, A., Fries, W., and Von Steinbuchel, N. (2004). Effects of brain lesion size and location on temporal-order judgment. *NeuroReport: Clinical Neuroscience and Neuropathology*, 15, 2401-2405.

Woodcock, R. W. (1997). *Woodcock Diagnostic Reading Battery.* Itasca, IL: Riverside Publishing.

Wright, B. A., Bowen, R. W., and Zecker, S. G. (2000). Nonlinguistic perceptual deficits associated with reading and language disorders. *Current Opinion in Neurobiology*, 10, 482-486.

Chapter 11

THE EFFECTIVENESS OF SCHOOL-BASED LEARNING SUPPORT SERVICES FOR CHILDREN WITH WORD-LEVEL READING DISABILITY

Craig Wright[1,2,*] and Elizabeth Conlon[2,3]
[1] Understanding Minds
[2] School of Psychology, Griffith University
[3] Behavoural Basis of Health Program,
Griffith Health Institute, Griffith University.

ABSTRACT

A number of reviews and meta-analyses have identified the variables associated with effective reading interventions for children with word-level reading disability (WLRD). However, it is not clear how effectively these methods are being employed at the school-level. This chapter investigated the effectiveness of learning support services designed to target word-level reading skills in eight Australian primary schools. Student growth in word identification, phonological decoding, prose reading accuracy, and reading subskills was measured over a nine-month period (one school year). Students with WLRD made significant improvements in phonological awareness. There was however no significant improvement in word identification, phonological decoding, prose reading accuracy, and pseudohomophone recognition. Individual analyses showed that 16% of the WLRD sample made ≥10 standard score point improvement on a word-level measure and 46% made ≥9 standard score point improvement on a prose reading accuracy measure. However, only 4% and 11% of the WLRD sample met criteria for clinical significance (post-treatment standard score of ≥92) on word-level and prose reading measures respectively. These findings are contrasted with other findings from the literature, and with an earlier study that involved a more structured and intensive reading intervention program, and recommendations are made which emphasise the need for an explicit, systematic phonics program as the core of reading intervention for students with WLRD. It is suggested that direct instruction programs that provide explicit teacher scripts may

---

[*] E-mail: craig@understandingminds.com.au. Telephone: +61 7 55262516. Fax: +61 7 55751069

provide the best method for ensuring that teachers and para-professionals faithfully translate research results into practice.

INTRODUCTION

The ultimate goal of reading is comprehension. However, to achieve this end children must first learn how to decode print. The majority of children acquire word-level decoding skills regardless of the type of instruction they receive. However, a substantial minority has great difficulty learning word-level skills, such as recognition of irregular words and phonological decoding, despite having adequate general ability and linguistic comprehension. This difficulty occurs in 5-15% of the population (Shaywitz, 1998) and is referred to variously as developmental dyslexia, specific reading disability, and word-level reading disability (hereafter WLRD; Vellutino, Fletcher, Snowling, and Scanlon, 2004).

While reading researchers are a long way from understanding the process of comprehension (Coltheart and Prior, 2007), four decades of research has provided evidence that allows good understanding of typical word-reading development and what goes wrong when children with WLRD fail (Bowey, 2002; 2005; Bradley and Bryant, 1983; Byrne and Fielding-Barnsley, 1989; Chall, 1967; Ehri, 1987; Frith, 1986; Gough and Hillinger, 1980; Goswami, 1986; 1993; Hulme, Muter, Snowling, and Taylor, 1998; Share, 1995; Vellutino et al., 1996; see Castles and Coltheart, 2004; Snowling, 2000; Vellutino et al., 2004 for reviews). There is also a solid body of knowledge showing what children need in early reading instruction and effective methods for teaching children who fail to develop adequate word-level skills (Coltheart and Prior, 2007; Duff and Clarke, 2010). Despite the evidence-based knowledge about reading development, reading difficulties, and treatment for reading difficulties many observers claim that this knowledge is not being taught sufficiently in teacher training programs (Coltheart and Prior, 2007) or applied effectively in schools (Coltheart and Prior, 2007; Pressley, 2002; Torgesen, Wagner, Rashotte, Herron, and Lindamood, 2010). This chapter reports on a study conducted in eight Australian primary (elementary) schools. The purpose of the study was to evaluate the statistical and clinical significance of change made in response to reading intervention in children identified by the school as having WLRD and who were receiving learning support intervention. The chapter begins by reviewing what is known about typical reading development, why some children have difficulty learning how to read words, and what is known about effective treatment techniques for WLRD.

HOW CHILDREN LEARN TO READ

Through the interaction of oral language and visual coding processes, most beginning readers are able to establish a small bank of written words that they recognise by sight (Frith, 1986; Ehri, 1991). In this early stage of reading, children typically use logographic cues for word recognition. For example, they may recognise the word 'school' because it has "two circles in the middle and a stick on the end". However, due to the large visual memory load imposed by the number of words in the English language and the similarity that exists between many words (*dog/god, mess/mass, then/than*), beginning readers must develop more efficient strategies for word recognition. They must develop knowledge of the alphabetic principle; knowledge that there is a systematic relationship between graphemes (letters/letter groups) and phonemes (speech sounds; Byrne and Fielding-Barnsley, 1989; Snowling, 1996). It is generally believed that becoming aware of the alphabetic principle, in turn, is facilitated by the development of phonological awareness (Byrne and Fielding-Barnsley, 1989).

Phonological awareness is the ability to perceive and manipulate the sounds in spoken words (Goswami and Bryant, 1990; Mattingly, 1972). It is not a natural function of the language system; rather it involves explicit and deliberate processing and manipulation of speech sounds (Castles and Coltheart, 2004). It develops from the global to the specific with children first becoming aware of the syllabic structure of speech (Liberman, Shankweiler, Fischer, and Carter, 1974) and then of onset-rime units (Treiman, 1992; Kirtley, Bryant, Maclean, and Bradley, 1989). Finally, children acquire awareness of individual speech sounds or *phonemes*. It is generally accepted that it is the latter, phonemic awareness, which is most important for development of alphabetic knowledge (Snowling, 2000).

Children who are aware that the spoken words *pet, pop* and *pen* all begin with the speech sound /p/ find it much easier to map the phoneme [p] onto the grapheme 'p'. Knowledge of grapheme-phoneme conversion rules (GPCs) provides the beginning reader with an independent device to decode novel words. For example, the child who understands the GPCs for the letters 'a', 'i', 't', 's', and 'p' can not only decode the words *sit* and *pat*, but also the words *sat, pit, tap, tip, sip, spat, spit* and so on. Phonological decoding not only allows the reader to independently identify novel words, but also affords the opportunity to develop word-specific orthographic information; knowledge which is the foundation of efficient and skilled word recognition (Shahar-Yames and Share, 2008).

WORD-LEVEL READING DISABILITY

Four decades of research has shown that the core problem for children defined here as having WLRD consists of deficits in word identification, knowledge of GPCs and phonological decoding skills (Castles and Coltheart, 2004; Snowling, 2000; Vellutino et al., 2004; Vellutino et al., 1996). These word-level weaknesses may be accompanied by broader linguistic weaknesses but are not caused by them (Nation, 2005; Vellutino et al., 2004).

It is likely that there are multiple pathways to WLRD (e.g., Pennington, 2009; Pennington, Wilcutt, and Rhee, 2005) and there may be variations in presentation at different stages of development (Castles and Coltheart, 1993). However, it is generally agreed that limitations in letter knowledge and phonological awareness represent core weaknesses in WLRD (Bowey, 2005; 2006; Castles and Coltheart, 2004; Duff and Clarke, 2010; Hulme et al., 2002; Scarborough, 1990; 2005; Stanovich, 1988; Vellutino et al., 2004). The child who finds it difficult to recognise that the spoken word *pit* comprises three separate phonemes, /p/ /i/ /t/, finds it difficult to understand the GPCs for the letters 'p', 'i' and 't'. Therefore, when they see the novel words *tip* and *it*, they do not have the strategy that allows them to independently decode each of the words. Instead, they must rely on an adult or on inefficient text-based cues such as pictures, salient letters within the word, or sentence context. These strategies lead to high error rates in the range of 75-95% and draw the child's attention away from the data which help form a visual memory for the word; that is, the letter sequence and the logic of the spelling-sound mappings (Dehaene, 2009; Shahar-Yames and Share, 2008). Hence, the word remains novel and it has to be read (or 'guessed') in as effortful a fashion the next time it appears in text.

DEVELOPMENTAL COURSE OF WLRD

There is a pervasive belief within the education community that reading difficulties in young children are part of a developmental lag that is eventually outgrown. This belief has important consequences for students, for if reading difficulties are simply a temporary snag, one need not be concerned and need only wait the problem out. One of the first studies to investigate the developmental course of reading difficulties was the Connecticut Longitudinal Study (Shaywitz, Escobar, Shaywitz, Fletcher, and Makuch, 1992). This large study of 445 children produced important data on a number of topics. Relevant to this chapter, Shaywitz et al. (1999) examined reading progress over a 12-year period in three sub-groups from within the larger sample: superior readers; average readers; and a group referred to as 'persistently poor readers'.

The data on a broad measure of reading skill demonstrated that all three groups improved their skills over time. However, the most important finding was that the gap between superior, average, and poor readers did not close over time. These data suggested that poor readers never catch up to their classmates and that WLRD is not developmental. Rather, it represents a chronic delay in reading ability and the problems persist unless additional teaching is provided.

Not only is poor reading a chronic condition in itself, but poor reading also has deleterious effects on wider development. In a series of papers, Stanovich and his colleagues (e.g. Stanovich, 1986) have used the term *Matthew Effect* to describe how reading difficulties can create larger and wider deficits over time. The Matthew Effect is a biblical reference to the 'rich getting richer and the poor getting poorer'.

Stanovich (1986) argued that good reading not only perpetuates good reading, but that it has a positive affect on the development of oral vocabulary, general knowledge, and other cognitive abilities. There is evidence that the amount children read, rather than oral language and communication is the major contributor to individual differences in children's vocabularies (e.g., Nagy and Anderson, 1984). Research has demonstrated that written text contains far greater complexity of language than normal adult speech or the speech in television programs. In fact, even children's books contain more complex vocabulary than adult prime-time television. Thus, the more one reads, the greater the breadth and sophistication of one's vocabulary development. Given that better readers tend to read more widely than poor readers, they are exposed to a greater volume of words, general knowledge, and other learning experiences. It has been estimated that children at the 10th percentile of word-reading ability (i.e., those with WLRD) are exposed to about 50 000 words per year, while those at the 90th percentile are exposed to about 4 500 000 words per year (Anderson,Wilson, and Fielding, 1988).

The Matthew Effect in WLRD is supported by empirical data. For example, the amount one reads can explain much of the individual variation in vocabulary and general knowledge even after word-reading ability and intelligence are controlled (Cunningham and Stanovich,

1992; 1997). Longitudinal data has shown that poor readers develop poorer vocabulary, listening comprehension, and general language skills than good readers, even when the two groups are matched on these skills at a young age (Share, McGee, and Silva, 1989). The Matthew Effect may also apply to psychosocial factors, with some authors suggesting that WLRD can lead to low self-confidence and self-esteem, social, emotional and behavioural problems, vulnerability to delinquency and crime, early drop out from education, and under- or un-employment (Coltheart and Prior, 2007).

READING INTERVENTIONS FOR WLRD

There have been limited studies of how best to teach lexical (whole word) knowledge to children with specific word-reading disorders (Broom and Doctor, 1995; Brunsdon, Hannan, Coltheart, and Nickels, 2002; Rowse and Wilshire, 2007). However, most broadband treatments take a systematic phonics approach. Experimental data (e.g., deGraff, Bosman, Hasselman, and Verhoeven, 2009; Hatcher, Hulme, and Ellis, 1994; Johnson and Watson, 2006; Torgesen et al., 2001) and a number of reviews (Bowey, 2006; Bus and Van IJzendoorn, 1999; Castles and Coltheart, 2004; Ehri et al., 2001; NICHHD, 2000; Swanson, 1999; Torgerson, Brooks, and Hall, 2006) have consistently found treatments that emphasise systematic teaching of synthetic phonics are the most efficacious for WLRD.

Synthetic phonics explicitly teaches GPCs and encourages the child to use that knowledge to identify novel words by 'decoding' the sounds made by each letter and thereafter blending the sounds into the whole word. For example, a beginning reader who already knows the GPCs for 't' and 'a' is taught that the letter 's' makes the phoneme /s/ and then shown the word 'sat' to decode. The act of decoding 'sat' achieves at least three things: first, accessing the GPCs for 's', 'a' and 't' consolidates the memories and makes it more likely that accurate and fluent recall will occur on subsequent exposures; second, it consolidates the use of phonological decoding as an efficient method for word identification; and third, it provides the child with an opportunity to form a memory of the spelling of 'sat' – doing so obviates the need for decoding and allows the child to simply recognise and name the whole word on subsequent exposures.

Synthetic phonics teaching works best when the instruction is both systematic and cumulative. *Systematic* refers to approaches where GPCs are taught in a pre-specified sequence. *Cumulative* implies that new knowledge in the teaching sequence builds on the previous and that practicing new skills includes review of previous knowledge (Torgerson, et al., 2006). Understanding Words (Wright, n.d.) is a good example of how systematic and cumulative phonics instruction works. Beginning readers are taught single letter-sounds, consonant digraphs (th, ch, sh, ng, qu), graphemes representing 'long' vowel sounds (e.g., ee, oa, oo), r-controlled vowels (e.g., or, ar, ur), and dipthongs (e.g., oi, oy, i-e, ou, er) in a strict sequence. In the initial lessons, children are taught that the letters 't' and 'a' represent the phonemes /t/ and /a/. They are taught that this knowledge will help them identify novel words because they will recognize the word name if they say the sounds the letters make. The word 'at' is then presented and the children are asked to decode it. The act of decoding 'at' helps consolidate the GPC memories for 't' and 'a' and to establish decoding as an effective behaviour. The teaching sequence then introduces the letter 's' representing the phoneme /s/

and the child is confronted with the words 'sat' and 'at'. Introducing letters 'p' and 'i' representing the phonemes /p/ and /i/ allows the child to read *tap, tip, pit, pat, sap, spat* and so on. Systematic and cumulative phonics approaches contrast with whole language programs, ad hoc teaching where there is no logical sequence to the phonics instruction and knowledge is not obtained in a cumulative manner, and approaches where only passing reference is made to GPCs as children read text (Bowey, 2005). A number of reviews (Adams, 1990; Chall, 1967; Ehri, et al., 2001; Torgerson et al., 2006) have found clear advantages for systematic phonics instruction over these other approaches to teaching reading. For example, the National Reading Panel (NICHHD, 2000) conducted a meta-analysis of the efficacy of various instructional approaches. The mean overall effect size produced by synthetic programs was $d = 0.45$, with the strongest effects for improving children's ability to decode regularly spelled words ($d = 0.67$) and nonsense words ($d = 0.60$). Effect sizes for systematic phonics, and indeed for all instructional approaches, decreased as a function of age at which instruction began. Mean effect sizes for systematic phonics in kindergarten was $d = 0.56$; $d = 0.54$ for first grade; and $d = 0.27$ for grades 2-6. This evidence suggests that systematic phonics is always a more effective approach, but that the effects are stronger when provided earlier in the child's education.

The review (NICHHD, 2000) also found that systematic phonics has substantial effects relative to other methods among young children at risk of developing future reading problems. Effect sizes were $d = 0.58$ for kindergartners at risk and $d = 0.74$ for at risk children in grade 1. Phonics instruction also significantly improved the reading of children referred to in this chapter as having WLRD (i.e., children with average IQs but poor reading) for whom the effect size was $d = 0.32$. This effect held regardless of whether instruction was delivered one on one ($d = 0.57$) or in small groups ($d = 0.43$). Furthermore, systematic phonics instruction also led to greater growth in reading comprehension in younger children relative to non-phonics approaches ($d = 0.51$) and made a significant impact on comprehension in children with WLRD ($d = 0.32$).

These data show that systematic phonics approaches are significantly more effective than non-phonics approaches in promoting growth in word-reading in the wider school population. They also show that phonics is a relatively better treatment for WLRD than other methods. Finally, they show that instruction does not have to be delivered one on one and that word-level training can transfer to gains in reading comprehension; presumably by allowing children to access more text.

These conclusions have led to recommendations for inclusion of a systematic phonics program as a key component of all early reading instruction. Furthermore, a systematic phonics program has been identified as being an essential component of intervention for students with WLRD (Department of Education, Skills and Training, 2005; NICHHD, 2000; Rose, 2005; Torgerson et al., 2006). While implementation of these guidelines would arguably provide most children with the best chance of acquiring reading and spelling skills, it is as yet unclear whether these data have managed to bridge the research-practice divide. Most tertiary courses in education provide teachers with barely cursory training in linguistics, cognitive development, and evidence-based methods for teaching of reading (Coltheart and Prior, 2007) and each year a significant number of students transit into high school with poor reading skills (Chall, 2000; Foorman, Francis, Fletcher, Schatschneider, and Mehta, 1998; Snow, Burns, and Griffin, 1998; Torgesen et al., 2001). Furthermore, up to this point there has been little evidence to indicate that the treatments used in controlled trials are effective when implemented in real-world settings.

This chapter aimed to investigate how effective school-based learning support services were for a group of students with WLRD over a 12-month period. The purpose was not to evaluate the type of instruction or to compare school instruction to an evidence-based benchmark. Rather, we were concerned with whether the services typically provided to students in Australian schools made a meaningful difference to growth in reading skills. All schools in the study used an eclectic approach to the teaching of reading. None reported used a specific teaching program. The most common approach was for students to read leveled-reading books with teachers or teacher assistants. Ad hoc prompting or teaching of phonic rules often accompanied this instruction. For example, if the student could not read 'brain' they might be explicitly taught that 'ai' make /ae/ or helped to draw the analogy from the known word 'rain'.

METHOD

Participants

One hundred and thirty participants with English as a first language were recruited from eight Australian primary schools. Children were included in the sample if they had a standardised score of 90 or above on the Colored Progressive Matrices (CPM; Raven, Court, and Raven, 1995), a standardised non-verbal measure of intellectual ability. No child had a history of (a) recurrent ear infections, (b) severe hearing problems and uncorrected vision problems, (c) severe emotional problems, (d) diagnosis of attention deficit hyperactivity disorder (ADHD), or (e) diagnosed developmental disorder (e.g., Autism Spectrum Disorder). Evidence of the presence of each of these disorders was obtained from the students' school records. Reading skills were assessed using the Basic Reading Cluster (BRC) of the Woodcock Diagnostic Reading Battery (WDRB; Woodcock, 1997). The BRC is derived from scores on the Word Identification and Word Attack subtests. The rationale behind using single word-reading and -decoding measures rather than text reading accuracy was that these measures provided a context-free measure of the word-level skills that are accepted to be the most basic and ubiquitous cause of WLRD (Vellutino et al., 2004). Given that the word-reading deficits in WLRD are dimensional rather than categorical (Shaywitz et al., 1992) it was necessary to adopt an arbitrary criterion to define dyslexia. Where to place the cutoff point is a methodological problem for all studies. In the current study, a participant scoring at or below the 15th percentile (more than 1 standard deviation below the population mean) on the BRC was considered to have WLRD. Participants included in the control group had to score at or above the 40th percentile on the BRC. The use of these criteria has been suggested by Snowling (2000) who regards word-level skills at or below the 15th percentile on the BRC in otherwise typical children as a good indicator of the anomalous deficits in word-decoding that are the hallmark of WLRD. These criteria have also been adopted in a number of studies (e.g., Vellutino et al., 1996; Wright and Conlon, 2009a). The participants in the WLRD group were also required to be involved in learning support activities twice weekly where the goal of the activities was to improve reading skills.

Table 1. Selection measures including means and 95%
confidence intervals for WLRD and control groups

	Control (N = 52)	WLRD (N = 61)
Age (years)	8.58 (8.2-8.9)	8.68 (8.27-9.08)
YOS	3.78 (3.32-4.25)	3.87 (3.45-4.28)
IQ	109.26 (106.17-112.36)	102.37 (100.09-104.7)
BRC	111.25 (106.9-115.5)	75.6 (73.7-77.4)

Note. Abbreviations: IQ = standard score on Colored Progressive Matrices; YOS = year of school; BRC = WDRB Basic Reading Cluster standard score.

The final sample consisted of 113 children. There were 61 children with WLRD (42 male; M = 8.58 years; SD = 1.3 years) and 52 children who were typical readers (33 male; M = 8.58 years; SD = 1.57 years). A description of the sample characteristics is presented in Table 1. The study had approval from the University Human Ethics Committee which adheres to the guidelines of the National Health and Medical Research Council of Australia. The parents of all selected children provided written permission for their child to participate in the study.

Measures

Cognitive ability. The Colored Progressive Matrices (CPM; Raven et al., 1995) measures fluid reasoning in primarily non-verbal format. It is a strong measure of g (Kaufman and Kaufman, 1990; r = 0.85 to 0.90 for test-retest reliability).

Receptive vocabulary. The third edition of the Peabody Picture Vocabulary Test (PPVT; Dunn and Dunn, 1997) was used to assess vocabulary. Words of increasing difficulty are read aloud to the student who has to choose which of four pictures best tells the meaning of the word (r = 0.93 for test-retest reliability; r = .94 for internal consistency; all internal consistency statistics are those reported by the test manual).

Verbal short-term and working memory. The digits forward component of the Digit Span Subtest from the WISC-III (Wechsler, 1997) was used as a measure of phonological short-term memory. Participants were required to repeat sequences of orally presented digits. This task was included as a measure of phonological processing and because individuals with WLRD often show substantial difficulty with these tasks (Snowling, 2000). The digits backward component of the same subtest was used as a measure of verbal working memory. Verbal working memory is often a weakness in children with WLRD and has been implicated in reading acquisition (de Jong and Leij, 1999).

Reading Ability Measures

Word identification. The Word Identification subtest from the WDRB (Woodcock, 1997) was used to assess single word identification ability. The task required participants to name single letters and words (r = .94 for internal consistency).

Nonword reading. The ability to use phonological information to decode novel words was assessed with the Word Attack subtest from the WDRB (Woodcock, 1997). The test required the participant to name a series of nonsense words. As the nonsense words are not in the participant's lexicon, they have to be decoded, which relies upon knowledge of grapheme-phoneme conversion rules ($r = .92$ for internal consistency).

Basic reading skills cluster (BRC). Scores on the Word identification and Word Attack subtests of the WDRB (Woodcock, 1997) were transformed into Rasch ability ("W") scores to obtain a composite score representing general reading ability that was used to evaluate growth in reading skills over the school year ($r = .96$ for internal consistency).

Prose reading accuracy. The Neale Analysis of Reading Ability (3rd Edition; Neale, 1999) was used to assess passage reading accuracy. The participants read a series of up to six graded passages. Word-reading errors are subtracted from a total possible passage score of 16. The stopping rule applies when the participant makes 12 or more errors in a single passage. Parallel forms are available for repeat testing. Form A was used at the initial assessment and Form B at post-test ($r_{xx} = .95$ for internal consistency for both forms; parallel form reliability $r = 0.98$; maximum raw score = 100).

Orthographic processing. The Word-Pseudohomophone task (Olson, Forsberg, Wise, and Rack, 1994) was used to measure orthographic skill. Stimuli were generated by the V-Scope software package (Enns and Rensinck, 1992) on a Power Macintosh with a standard monitor. Two words were presented side by side in 28-point Arial font. One was a high frequency word (e.g., take) and the other was a nonsense word with identical phonological output (e.g., taik). On each trial participants were instructed to point to the word from each pair that was correctly spelled. This task is considered a measure of orthographic coding because identification of the correctly spelled word requires the child to have an intact memory for the orthographic form of the word because no phonological cues are available for discrimination. A series of 10 practice trials were conducted prior to presentation of 80 test items that were presented in 4 blocks of 20 trials. Feedback was given after each trial. Split-half reliability for this task is .93 (Olson et al., 1994).

Phonological processing. The Phoneme Segmentation subtest from the Dyslexia Screening Test (DST; Fawcett and Nicholson, 1996) was used as a measure of phoneme elision ability. The first part of the task requires deletion of syllables (say rainbow without the /bow/), blends (say stake without the /st/), and phonemes (say igloo without the /l/) from orally presented words. The second part of the task required the participant to transpose the initial phoneme in two orally presented words (spoonerisms). For example, Shirley Bassey becomes Birley Shassey. Each correct response received 1 point (maximum score = 15; $r = .88$ for test–retest). The Sound Linkage Test of Phonological Awareness (Hatcher, 2000) measures syllable blending, phoneme blending, rhyme oddity awareness, and phoneme segmentation. On the syllable blending subtest participants had to blend orally presented syllables to form a word (win – dow becomes window). The phoneme blending test required participants to blend a string of orally presented phonemes to form aword (d-i-s-c becomes disc). The rhyme oddity test required participants to select the word that did not rhyme from a group of three orally presented words (dog pot log). The phoneme segmentation test required participants to segment orally presented words into their constituent phonemes (cost becomes c-o-s-t). Each correct response received 1 point (maximum = 24; $r = .94$ for internal consistency). The Rapid Automized Naming (RAN) subtest from the DST (Fawcett and Nicholson, 1996) required participants to produce the name of 20 familiar words. Participants were asked to name the test stimuli as quickly as possible following presentation without making mistakes. Performance was taken as the time to correctly name all the test stimuli and was measured with a digital stopwatch ($r = .85$ for test–retest).

Procedure

The initial test battery was administered during the first month of the school year (Phase 1). Administration was conducted in a quiet room at the participants' schools, free from visual and acoustic distractions. Phase 1 testing took approximately 2 hours to complete and was typically conducted in two sessions. Three more phases of reading data were obtained at approximately 10 week intervals throughout the school year.

RESULTS

Table 2 presents results for the additional measures of cognitive ability, phonological processing, orthographic coding and oral reading accuracy at Phase 1. The group with WLRD had significantly lower scores than the control group on measures of IQ, $t(111) = 3.65$, $p <$ .001, $d = .68$, receptive vocabulary $t(111) = 3.0$, $p = .003$, $d = .56$, processing speed, $t(111) =$ 2.3, $p = .02$, $d = .44$, phonological awareness, $t(111) = 7.5$, $p < .001$, $d = 1.45$, basic word-reading skills, $t(111) = 16.1$, $p < .001$, $d = 2.97$, prose reading accuracy, $t(111) = 8.69$, $p <$ .001, $d = 2.6$, orthographic processing, $t(111) = 5.45$, p $< .001$, $d = 1.02$, and phonological short-term memory, $t(111) = 4.5$, $p < .001$, $d = 1.8$, verbal working memory, $t(111) = 3.63$, p $< .001$, $d = .69$, and RAN, $t(111) = -5.5$, $p < .001$, $d = 1.07$. These data are summarised in Table 2. Abbreviations: IQ = standard score on CPM, VOC = standard score on PPVT-III, PA = total raw score on DST Phoneme Segmentation subtest and Sound Linkage Test of Phonological Awareness, RAN = rapid automized naming, STM = short-term memory (Digits Forward from WISC-III), WM = working memory (Digits Backward from WISC-III), OP = orthographic processing (pseudohomophone task), PRA = prose reading accuracy (NARA-III), BRC = WDRB Basic Reading Cluster.

**Table 2. Control and WLRD group differences on measures of
cognitive and reading skills and reading subskills**

	Control (n = 52)	WLRD (n = 61)	p	d
IQ	109.26 (11.1)	102.37 (8.9)	<.001	.68
VOC	103.7 (12.9)	96.26 (13.2)	.003	.56
PA	31.5 (4.1)	25.1 (4.8)	<.001	1.45
RAN	28.1 (9.1)	43.6 (18.4)	<.001	1.07
STM	8.1 (1.8)	6.6 (1.6)	<.001	1.8
WM	4.3 (1.3)	3.4 (1.3)	<.001	.69
OP	60.5 (10.9)	50.4 (8.6)	<.001	1.02
PRA	98.4 (11.5)	75.1 (5.4)	<.001	2.6
BRC	111.25 (15.4)	75.6 (7.1)	<.001	2.97

Analyses of Change in Reading Skills and Reading Subskills

A 4 (testing time) × 2 (reader group) mixed repeated measures ANOVA was performed on the BRC measure. Three separate 2 (testing time) × 2 (reader group) mixed repeated measures ANOVAs were performed on the phonological awareness, orthographic processing and prose reading measures.

The study design in which one group consisted of children with typically developing reading skills and the other group consisted of children with reading difficulties meant that the effects for time and group were expected to be significant at all test times. The primary results of interest from the ANOVAs were the interaction effects. If the learning support intervention offered to participants (with the intent of improving reading skills) was effective, greater improvements in reading skills should be seen over time in the WLRD group relative to the control group.

Basic Reading Skills Cluster

Significant main effects were found for time, $F(3, 109) = 7.5$, $p < .001$, $\eta_p^2 = .17$, and reader group, $F(1, 111) = 213.8$, $p < .001$, $\eta_p^2 = .66$. The WLRD group were poorer readers than controls at all testing phases; however, this effect was modified by a significant interaction between time by group, $F(3, 109) = 5.3$, $p = .02$, $\eta_p^2 = .13$.

A simple effects analysis (see Figure 1) that compared the changes over time in both groups found little change in scores for the control group over the four testing phases. The WLRD group made significant improvement from Phase 1 to Phase 2, $t(109) = 4.67$, $p < .001$, $d = .67$. This improvement was maintained at Phase 3 and 4 testing.

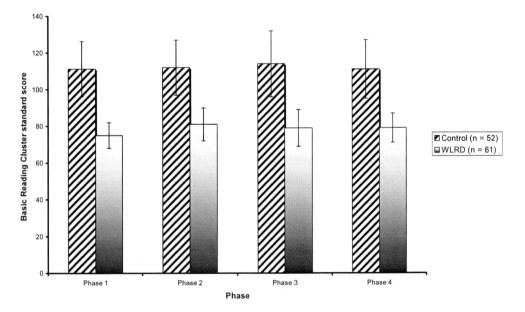

Figure 1. WLRD and control group means and standard deviations (standard scores with mean of 100 and SD of 15) on the Basic Reading Cluster at all testing phases.

Orthographic Processing (Pseudohomophones)

There was no significant main effect of time, $F(1, 111) = 0.09$, $p = .76$, $\eta_p^2 = .001$, but there was a significant main effect of reader group, $F(1, 111) = 50.6$, $p < .001$, $\eta_p^2 = .31$, and a significant interaction between time by group, $F(1, 111) = 8.99$, $p = .003$, $\eta_p^2 = .08$. The interaction is shown in Figure 2. Simple effects analysis that evaluated the change in scores on the orthographic processing measure between Phase 1 and Phase 4 for each group found no significant change across time for the control group, $F(1, 111) = 3.36$, $p = .069$, $\eta_p^2 = .03$. Scores in the WLRD group actually decreased from Phase 1 to Phase 4, $F(1, 111) = 5.91$, $p = .017$, $\eta_p^2 = .05$.

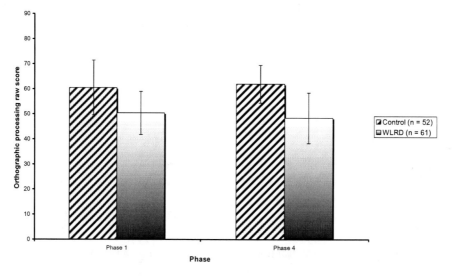

Figure 2. WLRD and control group means and standard deviations (raw scores) on the orthographic processing task at Phases 1 and Phase 4.

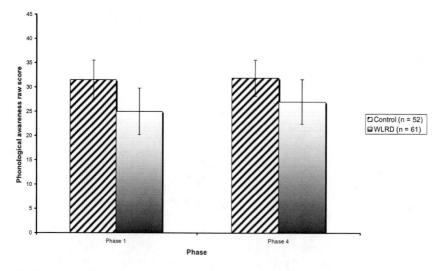

Figure 3. WLRD and control group means and standard deviations (raw scores) on the phonological awareness measure at Phase 1 and Phase 4.

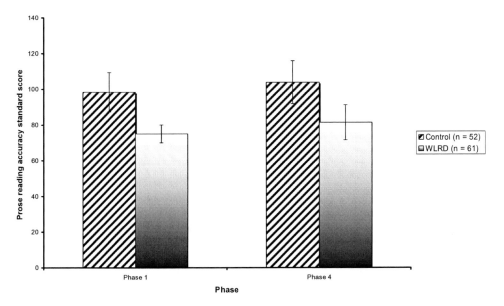

Figure 4. WLRD and control group means and standard deviations (standard scores) on the prose reading accuracy measure at Phases 1 and Phase 4.

Phonological Awareness

Significant main effects were found for time, $F(1, 111) = 17.6, p < .001, \eta_p^2 = .14$ and for reader group, $F(1, 111) = 52.1, p < .001, \eta_p^2 = .32$. These were modified by a significant interaction found between time and reader group, $F(1, 111) = 8.8, p = .004, \eta_p^2 = .07$.

Simple effects analysis on the interaction (see Figure 3) showed that there was no significant change in phonological awareness scores in the control group between Phase 1 and Phase 4, $F(1, 111) = 0.71, p = .40, \eta_p^2 = .01$. In contrast, there was a significant increase in scores on the measure of phonological awareness for the WLRD group from Phase 1 and Phase 4, $F(1, 111) = 27.87, p < .001, \eta_p^2 = .20$.

Prose Reading Accuracy

There were significant main effects found for time, $F(1, 111) = 48.8, p < .001, \eta_p^2 = .3$ and reader group, $F(1, 111) = 186.2, p < .001, \eta_p^2 = .63$. The time by group interaction was not significant, $F(1, 111) = .31, p = .58, \eta_p^2 = .003$. Figure 4 shows that the WLRD group were poorer readers than controls at both Phase 1 and 2.

Individual Response

Analyses of group data arguably obscure significant effects in individual participants (Campbell, 2005; Jacobson and Truax, 1991; Kazdin, 1999; Seligman, 1995). To avoid this problem the data from all 61 children in the WLRD group were evaluated individually.

The effectiveness of a treatment for individuals can be assessed by determining whether any changes are reliable and clinically significant (Jacobson and Truax, 1991; Kazdin, 1999). The reliable change index (RCI; Jacobson and Truax) specifies how great a change is required from pre- to post-test for that change to be considered statistically reliable. The RCI takes into account measurement error (reliability of the test) and sample variability (pre-test standard deviation).

The clinical significance of change has been defined as the practical importance or value of the effect of an intervention. Clinically significant change is that which makes a real and practical difference to everyday life (Kazdin, 1999). Although some quantitative measures have been used (Kendall, Marrs-Garcia, Nath, and Sheldrick, 1999), preset criteria that are acceptable to client, therapist, researcher, or society are frequently used as benchmarks of successful treatment (Campbell, 2005).

For this chapter, treatment effects were considered to be clinically significant when they met two criteria. First, the change made from pre- to post-test in an individual had to be reliable. Second, the individual's score on the reading outcome measures (BRC and prose reading accuracy from NARA-III) at post-test had to meet a preset benchmark of a standard score of ≥ 92. This criterion suggests a return to a functional reading level. Scores below this point, even if they were reliable, represent a level of reading where the child was probably still struggling with classroom work and thus was not considered *clinically significant*.

Reliable Change

The RCI for each individual was calculated using the following formula.

$$RCI = \frac{X_{pre-test} - X_{post-test}}{\text{standard error of measurement } (S_{diff})}$$

$X_{pre-test}$ = individual pre test score
$X_{post-test}$ = individual post test score

The index score for each individual is the difference between the pre- and post-test scores divided by the standard error of measurement. The standard error of measurement is calculated in the following way:

$$S_{diff} = \sqrt{2(SE_{pre})^2}$$

$$SE_{pre} = SD_{pre}\sqrt{1 - r_{xx}}$$

where SD_{pre} = standard deviation of the group at pre-test and r_{xx} = reliability of the measurement instrument.

To determine whether a significant change has occurred, a cut-off score is produced at the .05 level of statistical significance, which corresponds to change of 1.96 standard deviations multiplied by the S_{diff} score. Individuals with an RCI score greater than this value are considered to have made a reliable change due to the treatment (Christensen and Mendoza, 1986):

$$RCI_{critical\ value} = 1.96 \times S_{diff}$$

Participants had to make a 10-standard score-point change from Phase 1 to Phase 4 to meet the RCI criterion for the BRC measure. Ten of 61 children in the WLRD group met this criterion for reliable change. Participants had to make a 9-standard score-point change from Phase 1 to Phase 4 to meet the RCI criterion for the NARA-III prose reading accuracy measure. Twenty-eight of 61 children in the WLRD group met this criterion. These data show that the school-based interventions provoked word-level reading growth above expectations based on test measurement error and normal development in 16% of the WLRD sample. The interventions produced prose-reading growth above expectations in 46% of the WLRD sample.

Clinical Significance

Based on the criteria for clinical significance (reliable change and a minimum standard score of 92), the school-based intervention achieved clinically significant changes in basic word-level reading skills for just 3/61 students (4% of the WLRD sample). Seven of 61 students (11% of the WLRD sample) made clinically significant change in prose reading accuracy. These seven students included two of the three students who made reliable and significant change on the BRC measure. These data showed that, while statistically reliable reading growth was observed in 16-46% of the sample depending upon the measure, very few students returned to average levels of reading ability.

DISCUSSION

A considerable amount is known about how to best teach children who struggle to acquire word-level reading skills. However, there is limited evidence that evidence-based methods are being taught to teachers at a pre-service level or that evidence-based methods are being used in real-world settings. Furthermore, it is unclear how effective the methods currently being employed in Australian schools are at promoting growth in reading skills and alleviating WLRD (Chall, 2000; Coltheart and Prior, 2007; Foorman, et al., 1998; Snow, et al., 1998; Torgesen et al., 2001). This chapter aimed to evaluate the effectiveness of learning support interventions designed to target reading difficulties for a group of primary school aged children in 8 Australian schools.

Results showed that the WLRD group improved relative to the control group in one important reading sub-skill: phonological awareness. The effect size was moderate ($\eta_p^2 = 0.08$). It is possible that these data reflect an improvement as a result of the various interventions delivered by schools. However, there are alternative explanations. First, the relative improvement in the WLRD group may be explained by regression to the mean, which refers to a statistical phenomenon in which scores are likely to regress towards the mean on repeat testing (Campbell and Kenny, 1999). Because of regression to the mean effects, the average score in a group of participants with low scores at pre-test is likely to improve on repeat testing for statistical reasons. One way to control for regression to the mean is to use outcome measures that have high test-retest reliability. In this study all measures had test-retest statistics in the high range; however, due to the lack of a control group with comparable initial severity of reading problem it remains possible that the interaction effects occurred purely for statistical reasons. Future effectiveness studies will need to include an untreated or alternatively treated control group of children with WLRD to control for regression to the mean effects. Second, the WLRD group received extra attention relative to controls and the data may therefore reflect a Hawthorn Effect.

It is also unclear how important these gains are as phonological awareness is a distal cause of WLRD (Castles and Coltheart, 2004) and therefore has, at best, an indirect effect on reading performance. Given the role that phonological awareness is posited to play in word-reading development (Byrne and Fielding-Barnsley, 1989) one might expect an improvement in phonological skills to transfer to improvements in word recognition and decoding. However, there was little evidence that this occurred.

There was a significant group by time interaction for the basic reading skills (BRC) measure ($\eta_p^2 = 0.08$). This interaction reflected a relative improvement in the WLRD group between Phases 1 and 2. However, basic reading skills in the WLRD group did not improve further between Phases 2, 3 and 4 and they remained significantly poorer readers at all phases relative to the control group. Furthermore, the WLRD group had lower scores on a pseudohomophone test at Phase 4 compared to Phase 1 scores. The pseudohomophone task reflects acquired knowledge of the unique spellings of words and one can reasonably expect this orthographic knowledge to increase over time as a result of intervention. These data therefore show that the intervention strategies had little impact on orthographic skills.

It has been argued previously that analyses at the group level can obscure important effects in individuals (Wright and Conlon, 2009b). The current data show some support for this argument as we found that 16% of the WLRD group made statistically reliable gains in word-reading skills equivalent to standard score gains of ≥10. Furthermore, 46% of the WLRD group made statistically reliable gains in prose-reading accuracy equivalent to standard score gains of ≥9. However, only 4% and 11% of the WLRD sample met the combined criteria for clinical significance for word-level reading and prose-reading accuracy respectively. Put another way, 89-96% of the WLRD group remained at a reading level that put them at serious risk for failure in the classroom despite the learning support services provided to them throughout the year.

While this may seem disappointing, several factors have to be taken into account when interpreting these data. First, many of the children in this chapter were in Grade 2 and above and reviews have shown that the effects of most reading interventions approximately halve after Grade 1 (NICHHD, 2000). Second, while only a few children managed to return to normal functioning, 16% and 46% of the sample made standard score growth of ≥9 points on the word-reading and prose reading measures. The response seen in these children compares favourably to many published studies. For example, Hatcher et al. (2006) reported a successful randomised trial of a reading intervention where the average standard score gain on a word-reading measure was 7 points over a twenty-week study. Another recent randomised trial reported an average 5.5 standard score point gain over the course of a twenty-week intervention (Clarke, Snowling, Truelove, and Hulme, 2010). When considered in this context, the effects of the school-based interventions are not as limited as face value suggests.

Applications: Can School-Based Reading Interventions Produce Clinically Significant Benefits?

A number of recent studies suggest that the answer to this key educational question is yes; if the intervention begins early in school. For example, Torgesen et al. (2010) reported that ~80 hours of phonics-based instruction resulted in at least 92% of a group with WLRD improving reading skills to a clinically significant level (based on similar criteria to those used in this chapter). In another study, Mathes et al. (2005) showed that a year-long reading intervention for at-risk children in grade 1 resulted in significantly faster rates of learning for these children compared to their normally developing peers. Only 1-7% of students who received intervention failed to meet the criteria for clinical significance set in the current chapter (reading scores >30th percentile; standard score = 92).

In an Australian context, Wright and Conlon (2009b) have reported the results of a study (n = 13) in which teacher assistants were trained to administer a systematic phonics based program (Understanding Words; Wright, n.d.) to thirteen children. All children had WLRD and many had comorbid developmental weaknesses; including ADHD (n = 4), mild intellectual impairment (n = 1), and semantic-grammatical language deficits (n = 2). Reading intervention was conducted by two novice teacher assistants (TAs) who received approximately four hours of instruction in how to administer Understanding Words, including observation of practice and feedback.

In addition to providing the systematic synthetic phonics instruction reported previously to be most effective for WLRD (e.g., DEST, 2005; NICHHD, 2000), Understanding Words uses direct instruction methodology (see Engelmann and Carnine, 1991 for more). Programs guided by the theory of direct instruction have several important characteristics that make them extremely useful for delivering reading instruction in schools. First, they use clear and concise instructions which script everything the teacher must say and do to introduce the various rules in the program. The scripts are standardised so that teachers rapidly automate the process of delivering a new rule and, because they are so explicit, this task can be easily accomplished by a teacher assistant thus saving teaching costs. Second, each new rule assumes only knowledge or skill implied by what the student has done before. Third, rules are introduced in a clear sequence and only about 10% of a lesson involves new information. That is, they are *systematic*. Fourth, sufficient practice is provided to allow students the opportunity to master the rule within several minutes. However, nothing is taught in only one lesson and cumulative practice occurs over subsequent lessons. Fifth, programs that use direct instruction methodology are scripted to allow for unison responding from students and can therefore be run in groups rather than one on one thus further saving teaching costs. Finally, Understanding Words uses principles of behaviour theory, including positive reinforcement, extinction, and shaping to increase correct responding and to develop efficient reading behaviours.

In contrast to the students in the current chapter, 30-minute sessions were conducted four times weekly over 30 weeks. Three groups had a student to teacher ratio of 3:1 and one group a ratio of 4:1. Reading growth in the WLRD group was compared to that in an untreated control group of average readers. All thirteen students in the WLRD group made clinically significant change in word identification skills ($\eta_p^2 = .32$) and 12/13 made clinically significant change in phonological decoding skills ($\eta_p^2 = .21$). Clinically significant change in word reading fluency was seen in 12/13 participants ($\eta_p^2 = .3$). The criteria for reliable and clinical change were the same as for the current study. Wright and Conlon (2009b) concluded that intensive word-level intervention for 6-9 months has the potential to produce statistically significant and clinically meaningful change in word-level reading skills (even in complex cases).

Future Directions

The evidence is now irrefutable that students who have WLRD need a core reading program that explicitly teaches phonics. For some children, such instruction may not be sufficient, but it is absolutely necessary. The National Inquiry into the Teaching of Literacy (DEST, 2005) made recommendations for the inclusion of phonics teaching in the curriculum and other national reading inquiries have made even stronger demands on teachers to deliver phonics instruction for children with WLRD (e.g., NICHHD, 2000; Rose, 2005). The current data indicate an urgent need for these recommendations to be acted upon at a school-level. There is also an urgent need for professional development for in-service teachers regarding evidence-based reading practices. This training must include significant demonstration of appropriate practice and ongoing professional support within schools to ensure treatment fidelity over time as has been suggested by the leading teacher educator Lorraine Hammond (2010). The project reported on by Wright and Conlon (2009b) in which teacher assistants were provided with training in a direct instruction program (Understanding Words; Wright, n.d.) and then received ongoing professional support from within the school may provide a model of practice which delivers both effective and cost-effective reading intervention for students with WLRD. Perhaps even more importantly, there is a need for early identification and intervention in children at-risk of reading problems as the current data show the difficulty teachers have in remediating chronic deficits in older children.

Just as important as quality is the intensity of an intervention. To draw an analogy to medicine, there is no point having the correct antibiotic if one only takes it once or twice a week. Students in this study were only receiving services twice weekly. Contrast, this with the four-times weekly instruction delivered by the study reported by Wright and Conlon (2009) and it is possible that lack of intensity was a factor in reducing the effectiveness of the school-based instruction. It would be inaccurate to suggest that there is a lack of will on the part of teachers to deliver sufficient instruction to students. The most serious barrier teachers face, and therefore faced by students with WLRD, is a lack of institutional support. The Wright and Conlon (2009b) study showed that all but one student, who had mild intellectual impairment, could learn to read at average levels after 9-months of instruction. When one considers the potential personal and social costs of chronic reading failure, the approximate cost of $1000 per student seems minor. We therefore urge principals and educational authorities to provide learning support teachers with the funding they require to deliver instruction of sufficient quality and intensity to make a meaningful difference to students' lives.

CONCLUSION

Several high-profile reviews have questioned whether the data from research on the teaching of reading is crossing the research-practice divide (e.g., Bowey, 2006; Coltheart and Prior, 2007). Furthermore, while there is a significant amount of controlled-trial data on *efficacious* approaches to the teaching of reading, there is very limited information on how *effectively* reading is taught in real-world settings. This chapter aimed to investigate how effective school-based learning support services were for a group of students with word-level reading disability over a 12-month period.

The data showed that a large majority of students who began the year with poor reading skills remained poor readers at the end of the year. The developmental course of reading skills in the WLRD group is consistent with that reported previously in at-risk children who have not received intervention (Juel, 1988; Shaywitz et al., 1999). For example, Shaywitz et al. (1999) showed that the growth curves of superior, average and poor readers were similar but that the poor readers never closed the gap on the other two groups and Juel (1988) reported that the probability of a child who was a poor reader in first grade remaining a poor reader in fourth grade was .88. The current data therefore add to the body of evidence showing that early reading weaknesses represent a clear developmental difference, not a developmental lag.

The main finding from this chapter was that, at the end of 12-months of learning support services, the WLRD group remained at a reading level that put them at serious risk for failure in the classroom. The inevitable conclusion is that reading teaching in real-world settings, or at least those studied in this chapter, was not effective in altering the developmental course of children with WLRD. Further research is needed into effective methods of delivering professional development to teachers on the teaching of reading and methods by which both effective and cost-effective instruction can be delivered in school settings.

REFERENCES

Adams, M. J. (1990). Beginning to Read: Thinking and Learning About Print. Cambridge, MA: MIT Press.

Anderson, R.C., Wilson, P.T., and Fielding, L.G. (1988). Growth in reading and how children spend their time outside of school. *Reading Research Quarterly*, 23(3), 285–303.

Bowey, J. (2002). Reflections on Onset-Rime and Phoneme Sensitivity as Predictors of Beginning Word Reading. *Journal of Experimental Child Psychology*, 82, 29-40.

Bowey, J. A. (2005). Predicting individual differences in learning to read. In Margaret J. Snowling and Charles Hulme (Ed.), *The science of reading: A handbook* (pp. 155-172) Oxford, UK: Blackwell.

Bowey, J. A. (2006). Need for systematic synthetic phonics teaching within early reading curriculum. *Australian Psychologist*, 41, 120-129.

Bradley, L., and Bryant, P. E. (1983). Categorizing sounds and learning to read: A Causal connection. *Nature*, 30, 419-421.

Broom, Y., and Doctor, E. (1995). Developmental surface dyslexia: A case study of the efficacy of a remediation program. *Cognitive Neuropsychology*, 12, 69-110.

Brunsdon, R. K., Hannan, T. J., Coltheart, M., and Nickels, L. (2002). Treatment of lexical processing in mixed dyslexia: A case study. *Neuropsychological Rehabilitation*, 12, 385-418.

Bus, A. G., and Van IJzendoorn, M. H. (1999). Phonological Awareness and Early Reading: A Meta-Analysis of Experimental Training Studies. *Journal of Educational Psychology*, 91, 403-414.

Byrne, B., and Fielding-Barnsley, R. (1989). Phonemic awareness and letter knowledge in the child's acquisition of the alphabetic principle. *Journal of Educational Psychology*, 81, 805-812.

Campbell, T. C. (2005). An introduction to clinical significance: An alternative index of intervention effect for group experimental design. *Journal of Early Intervention*, 27, 210-227.

Campbell, D., and Kenny, D. (1999). A Primer on Regression Artifacts. New York: Guilford.

Castles, A., and Coltheart, M. (2004). Is there a causal link from phonological awareness to learning to read? *Cognition*, 91, 77-111.

Chall, J. S. (1967). *Learning to read: The great debate*. New York: McGraw-Hill.

Chall, J. S. (2000). The Academic Achievement Challenge: What Really Works in the Classroom. New York: Guilford.

Christensen, L. and Mendoza, J. L. (1986). A method of assessing change in a single subject: an alteration of the RC index. *Behavior Therapy*, 17, 305-308.

Clarke, P., Snowling, M.J., Truelove, E. M., and Hulme, C. (2010). Ameliorating children's reading comprehension difficulties: A randomised controlled trial. *Psychological Science*, 21, 1106-1116.

Coltheart, M., and Prior, M. (2007). Learning to Read in Australia. *Occasional Paper Series - Academy of the Social Science*s (Policy Paper 6), 1, 1-11.

Cunningham, A. E., and Stanovich, K. E. (1992). Tracking the unique effects of print exposure: Associations with vocabulary, general knowledge, and spelling. *Journal of Educational Psychology*, 83, 264-274.

Cunningham, A. E., and Stanovich, K. E. (1997). Early reading acquisition and its relation to reading experience and ability 10 years later. *Journal of Educational Psychology*, 33, 934-945.

deGraff, S., Bosman, A. M. T., Hasselman, F., and Verhoeven, L. (2009). Benefits of systematic phonics instruction. *Scientific Studies of Reading*, 13, 318-333.

Dehaene, S. (2009). *Reading in the brain*. New York: Penguin.

de Jong, P. J., and Leij, A. (1999). Specific contributions of phonological abilities to early reading acquisition: Results from a Dutch latent variable longitudinal study. *Educational Psychology*, 91(3), 450-476.

Department of Education, Science and Training. (2005). Teaching Reading: Report and Recommendations. Canberra: Department of Education, Science and Training..

Duff, F. J., and Clarke, P. J. (2010). Practitioner review: Reading disorders: What are the effective interventions and how should they be implemented and evaluated? *Journal of Child Psychology and Psychiatry*, 52(1), 3-12.,

Dunn, L. M., and Dunn, L. M. (1997). Peabody Picture Vocabulary Test-Third Edition: Manual. Circle Pines, MN: American Guidance Services.

Ehri, L. C. (1987). Learning to read and spell words. Journal of Reading Behavior, 19, 5-31.

Ehri, L. C. (1991). Learning to read and spell words. In L. Rieben and C. Perfetti (Eds.), Learning to Read: Basic Research and its Implications (pp. 57-73). Hillsdale, NJ: Erlbaum.

Ehri, L. C., Nunes, S. R., Willows, D. M., Schuster, B.V., Yaghoub-Zadeh, Z. and Shanahan, T. (2001). Phonemic awareness instruction helps children learn to read: Evidence from the National Reading Panel's meta-analysis. *Reading Research Quarterly*, 36, 250-287.

Engelmann, S., and Carnine, D. (1991). *Theory of instruction: Principles and applications. Eugene*, OR: ADI Press.

Enns, J. T., and Rensinck, R. A. (1992). *V Scope: General purpose tachistoscope for Macintosh*. Vancouver, CA: Micropsych Software.

Fawcett, A. J., and Nicholson, R. I. (1996). *The Dyslexia Screening Test*. London: The Psychological Corporation.

Foorman, B. R., Francis, D. J., Fletcher, J. M., Schatschneider, C. and Mehta, P. (1998). The role of instruction in learning to read: Preventing reading failure in at-risk children. *Journal of Educational Psychology,* 90(1), 37-55.

Frith, U. (1986). A developmental framework for developmental dyslexia. Annals of *Dyslexia*, 36, 69-81.

Gough, P. B., and Hillinger, M. L. (1980). Learning to read: An unnatural act. *Bulletin of the Orton Society*, 30, 179-196.

Goswami, U. (1993). Phonological skills and learning to read. *Annals of the American Academy of Sciences*, 682, 296-311.

Goswami, U. (1986). Children's use of analogy in learning to read: A developmental study. *Journal of Experimental Child Psychology*, 42, 73-83.

Goswami, U., and Bryant, P. (1990). *Phonological skills and learning to read*. Hove: Lawrence Erlbaum Associates.

Hammond, L. (2010). Telling versus showing: What teachers don't learn at PD about teaching reading. Paper presented at Learning Difficulties Australia Annual General Meeeting.

Hatcher, P. (2000). Sound linkage: An integrated program for overcoming reading difficulties. London: Whurr.

Hatcher, P. J., Hulme, C., and Ellis, A. W. (1994). Ameliorating early reading failure by integrating the teaching of reading and phonological skills: The phonological linkage hypothesis. *Child Development*, 65, 41-57.

Hatcher, P., Hulme, C., Miles, J. M. V., Carroll, J. M., Hatcher, J., and Gibbs, S., et al. (2006). Efficacy of small group reading intervention for beginning readers with reading-delay: A randomised controlled trial. *Journal of Child Psychology and Psychiatry* 47, 820-827

Hulme, C., Hatcher, P. J., Nation, K. Brown, A. Adams, J. and Stuart,G. (2002). Phoneme awareness is a better predictor of early reading skill than onset-rime awareness. *Journal of Experimental Child Psychology*, 82, 2-28.

Hulme, C., Muter, V., Snowling, M., and Taylor, S., (1998). Segmentation, not rhyming, predicts early progress in learning to read. *Journal of Experimental Child Psychology*, 71, 3-27.

Jacobson, N. S., and Truax, P. (1991). Clinical significance: A statistical approach to defining meaningful change in psychotherapy research. *Journal of Consulting and Clinical Psychology*, 59, 12-19.

Johnson, R. S., and Watson, J. E. (2006). A seven-year study of the effects of synthetic phonics teaching on reading and spelling attainment. Insight 17. Edinburgh, UK: Scottish Education Executive. Available at http://www.scotland.gov.uk/Resource/Doc/933/ 0044071.pdf.

Juel, C. (1988). Learning to read and write: A longitudinal study of 54 children from first to fourth grades. *Journal of Educational Psychology*, 80(4), 437-447.

Kazdin, A. E. (1999). The meanings and measurement of clinical significance. *Journal of Consulting and Clinical Psychology*, 67, 332-339.

Kendall, P. C. (1999). Clinical significance. *Journal of Consulting and Clinical Psychology*, 67, 283-284.

Kendall, P. C., Marrs-Garcia, A., Nath, S. R., and Sheldrick, R. C. (1999). Normative comparisons for the evaluation of clinical significance. *Journal of Consulting and Clinical Psychology*, 67, 285-299.

Kirtley, C., Bryant, P., MacLean, M., and Bradley, L. (1989). Rhyme, rime and the onset of reading. *Journal of Experimental Child Psychology*, 48, 224-245.

Liberman, I. Y., Shankweiler, D., Fischer, F. W., and Carter, B. (1974). Explicit syllable and phoneme segmentation in young children. *Journal of Experimental Child Psychology*, 18, 201-212.

Mathes, P. G., Denton, C. A., Fletcher, J. M., Anthony, J. L., Francis, D. J., and Schatschneider, C. (2005). The effects of theoretically different instruction and student characteristics on the skills of struggling readers. *Reading Research Quarterly*, 40, 148-182.

Mattingly, I. G. (1972). Reading, the linguistic process and linguistic awareness. In J. Kavanagh and I. Mattingly (Eds.). Language by ear and by eye (pp. 133-147). Cambridge, MA: MIT Press.

Nagy, W. E., and Anderson, R. C. (1984). How many words are there in printed English? *Reading Research Quarterly*, 19, 304-330.

Nation, K. (2005). Connections between reading and language in children with poor reading comprehension. In H. Catts and A. Kamhi (Eds.). Connections between language and reading disabilities (pp. 41-54). Mahwah, NJ: Lawrence Erlbaum.

National Institute of Child Health and Human Development. (2000). Report of the National Reading Panel. Teaching children to read: an evidence-based assessment of the scientific research literature on reading and its implications for reading instruction: Reports of the subgroups (NIH Publication No. 00-4754). Washington, DC: U.S. Government Printing Office.

Ncale, M. D. (1999). Neale Analysis of Reading Ability (3rd Ed.). Melbourne, Vic: ACER Press.

Olson, R., Forsberg, H., Wise, B., and Rack, J. (1994). Measurement of word recognition, orthographic and phonological skills. In G. Reid Lyon (ed.), *Frames of reference for the assessment of learning disabilities: New views on measurement issues* (pp. 243–278). Baltimore, MD: Brookes.

Pennington, B. F. (2009). *Diagnosing learning disorders: A Neuropsychological framework* (2nd ed.). New York: Guildford.

Pennington, B. F., Willcutt, E. G., and Rhee, S. H. (2005). Analyzing comorbidity. In R. V. Kail (Ed.). *Advances in Child Development and Behavior*, vol. 33 (pp. 263-304). Oxford: Elsevier.

Pressley, M. (2002). *Reading instruction that works: The case for balanced teaching* (2nd ed.). New York: Guildford.

Raven, J. C., Court, J. H., and Raven, J. (1995). Colored progressive matrices. Oxford, UK: Oxford Psychologists Press.

Rose, J. (2005). Independent review of the teaching of early reading. Department of Education and Skills: United Kingdom. Available at http://www.standards.dcsf. gov.uk/phonics/report.pdf.

Rowse, H. J. and Wilshire, C. E. (2007). Comparison of phonological and whole-word treatments for two contrasting cases of developmental dyslexia. *Cognitive Neuropsychology*, 24, 817-842.

Scarborough, H. S. (1990). Very early language deficits in dyslexic children. *Child Development*, 61, 1728-1734.

Scarborough, H. S. (2005). The connections between language and reading disability: Reconciling a beautiful hypothesiss with some ugly facts. In H. W. Catts and A.G. Kamhi (Eds.). The connections between language and reading disability (pp. 3-22). Mahwah, NJ: Erlbaum.

Seligman, M. E. P. (1995). *The effectiveness of psychotherapy: The Consumer Reports study. American Psychologist*, 50, 965-974.

Share, D. L. (1995). Phonological recoding and self-teaching: The sin qua non of reading acquisition. Cognition, 55, 151-218.

Share D. L., McGee R., and Silva P. A. (1989). IQ and reading progress: A test of the capacity notion of IQ. *Journal of the American Academy of Child and Adolescent Psychiatry*, 28, 97-100.

Shahar-Yames, D., and Share, D. L. (2008). Spelling as a self-teaching mechanism in orthographic learning. *Journal of Research in Reading*, 31, 22-39.

Shaywitz, S. E. (1998). Dyslexia. *New England Journal of Medicine, 338*, 307-12.

Shaywitz S. E., Escobar, M. D., Shaywitz B. A., Fletcher J. M., and Makuch R. (1992). Evidence that dyslexia may represent the lower tail of a normal distribution of reading ability. *New England Journal of Medicine*, 326, 145-150.

Shaywitz, S. E., Fletcher, J. M., Holahan, J. M., Shneider, A. E., Marchione, K. E, and Stuebing, K. K., et al. (1999). Persistence of dyslexia: The Connecticut Longitudinal Study at adolescence. *Pediatrics*, 104, 1351-1359.

Snow, C. E., Burns, S. M., and Griffin, P. (Eds.). (1998). Preventing reading difficulties in young children. Washington, DC: National Academy Press.

Snowling, M. J. (1996). Contemporary approaches to the teaching of reading. *Journal of Child Psychology and Psychiatry*, 37, 139-148.

Snowling, M. J. (2000). *Dyslexia*. Oxford, UK: Blackwell.

Stanovich, K. E. (1986). Matthew effects in reading: Some consequences of individual differences in the acquisition of literacy. *Reading Research Quarterly*, 21, 360- 407.

Stanovich, K. E. (1988). Explaining the differences between the dyslexic and the Garden-variety poor reader: The phonological-core variable difference modes. *Journal of Learning Disabilities*, 21, 590-612.

Swanson, H. L. (1999). Reading research for students with LD: A Meta-Analysis of Intervention Outcomes. *Journal of Learning Disabilities*, 32, 504-532.

Torgesen, J. K., Alexander, A. W., Wagner, R. K., Rashotte, C.A., Voeller, K., and Conway, T., et al. (2001). Intensive remedial instruction for children with severe reading disabilities: Immediate and long-term outcomes from two instructional approaches. *Journal of Learning Disabilities*, 34, 33-58.

Torgerson, C. J., Brooks, G., and Hall, G. (2006). A systematic review of the research literature on the use of systematic phonics in the teaching of reading and spelling. Department for Education and Skills. London: DfES Research Report 711. Avaailable from http://www.dcsf.gov.uk/research/data/uploadfiles/RR711_.pdf

Torgesen, J. K., Wagner, R.K., Rashotte, C.A., Herron, J., and Lindamood, P. (2010). Computer-assisted instruction to prevent early reading difficulties in students at risk of dyslexia: Outcomes from two instructional approaches. *Annals of Dyslexia*, 60, 40-56.

Treiman, R. (1992). The role of intrasyllabic units in learning to read and spell. In P. Gough, L.C. Ehri, and R. Treiman (Eds.). Reading acquisition (pp. 65-106). Hillsdale, NJ: Lawrence Erlbaum Associates.

Vellutino, F. R., Fletcher, J. M., Snowling, M. J. and Scanlon, D. M. (2004). Specific reading disability (Dyslexia): What have we learned in the past four decades? *Journal of Child Psychology and Psychiatry*, 45, 2-40.

Vellutino, F. R., Scanlon, D. M., Sipay, E. R., Small, S. G., Pratt, A., and Chen, R., et al., (1996). Cognitive profiles of difficult-to-remediate and readily remediated poor readers: Early intervention as a vehicle for distinguishing between cognitive and experiential deficits as basic causes of specific reading disability. *Journal of Educational Psychology*, 88, 601-638.

Wechsler, D. (1997). Wechsler Intelligence Scale for Children (3rd Ed). San Antonio, TX: The Psychological Corporation.

Woodcock, R. W. (1997). Woodcock Diagnostic Reading Battery. Itasca, IL: Riverside Publishing.

Wright, C. (n.d.). Understanding Words: A Complete Reading Program. Retrieved from http://www.understandingwords.com.au.

Wright, C. and Conlon, E. (2009a). Auditory and visual processing in children with dyslexia. *Developmental Neuropsychology, 34*, 330-355.

Wright, C., and Conlon, E. (2009b). Individual response to reading intervention. Combined Abstracts of 2009 Australian Psychology Conferences [CDROM].

INDEX

autobiographical memory, 109, 142, 145
automate, 265
automaticity, 220
avoidance, 69, 77, 120, 127

B

Bandarian Balooch, vii, xi, 57, 65, 70, 71, 72, 73, 74, 75, 78, 86, 104
base, 27, 76, 99, 104
batteries, 237, 238, 239
Beck Depression Inventory, 111, 132
behavior therapy, 137
benchmarks, 262
beneficial effect, 8, 20, 130
benefits, 2, 3, 4, 18, 73, 131, 173, 178, 197, 210, 215
bias, 13, 89, 110, 114, 115, 117, 118, 119, 120, 123, 128, 129, 130, 131, 134, 135, 136, 137, 138, 141, 143, 145, 190, 191
biases, xi, 55, 89, 109, 110, 111, 113, 114, 115, 117, 118, 119, 120, 122, 125, 127, 128, 129, 130, 132, 134, 135, 136, 137, 138, 191
biomarkers, 131
bipolar disorder, 119
blends, 257
blindness, 24
blood, 110
blue/yellow, xii, 175, 177, 178, 179, 180, 182, 183, 184, 185, 186, 188, 189, 190, 192
boredom, 230
brain, 19, 23, 26, 44, 47, 52, 53, 54, 122, 132, 134, 136, 137, 140, 144, 176, 197, 198, 201, 202, 209, 210, 212, 214, 216, 223, 238, 244, 247, 255, 268
brain activity, 144, 214
brass, 30
brightness, 175, 177, 178, 184, 185, 192
buttons, 180

C

caffeine, 68, 81
carbon, 67, 80
carbon dioxide, 67, 80
cartoon, 20
case studies, 203, 207
case study, 206, 207, 214, 267, 268
category a, 26, 38
causal interpretation, ix
causality, 108, 237
central executive, 115, 116, 121
central nervous system, 148
cerebral cortex, 111

challenges, 3, 104
cheese, 28, 30
childhood, 145, 214, 244
chunking, 223
city streets, 67
clarity, 159, 174, 179, 187
classes, 31, 176, 177, 179, 191
classification, 28, 41, 150, 158, 159, 193
classroom, 262, 264, 267
clients, 76, 77, 78, 129, 131
clinical application, 64, 85, 103
clinical assessment, xi, 109, 127
clinical depression, 111, 126, 131, 137, 139
clinical interventions, 109, 120, 127, 132
clinical significance, 249, 250, 262, 263, 264, 265, 268, 270
clinical symptoms, 67
closure, 167
clothing, 148
clustering, 26, 45
cluttered visual scenes, 167
CO_2, 80
coding, 47, 48, 52, 192, 194, 242, 244, 250, 257, 258
coffee, 76
cognition, ix, 21, 22, 79, 105, 111, 117, 120, 130, 132, 135, 136, 142, 145, 175, 192, 202, 211, 214
cognitive abilities, 252
cognitive ability, 204, 218, 221, 225, 235, 258
cognitive biases, 109, 120, 137
cognitive development, 28, 41, 202, 214, 254
cognitive dysfunction, 143
cognitive effort, 124
cognitive flexibility, 22
cognitive function, ix, 18, 19, 21, 22, 137
cognitive level, 102
cognitive load, 200, 214
cognitive models, 110, 114, 117, 118, 120, 128, 132
cognitive process, x, 4, 19, 101, 110, 111, 130, 131, 142, 144
cognitive processing, 110, 130, 131, 144
cognitive profile, 132
cognitive psychology, 41, 202
cognitive research, 176, 198
cognitive skills, 2, 3, 13, 18, 19
cognitive style, 143
cognitive tasks, 3, 114
cognitive theory, 135
cognitive therapy, 117, 129, 134, 136, 137, 140, 144
coherence, 240
college students, 171
color, 192, 193, 194, 195
colour names, 176, 178, 181, 187, 188
combined effect, 150

D

E

F

J

K

L

O

P

Q

R

0 1341 1432402 0

RECEIVED

AUG 0 2 2012

GUELPH HUMBER LIBRARY
205 Humber College Blvd
Toronto, ON   M9W 5L7